THE ATTACK

UPON THE

NORTHEAST KINGDOM

Lies, Lies, and More Damn Lies

D1547674

A BANKER'S STORY

Roger Lussier   8/21/04

ROGER LUSSIER

AUTHOR:	Roger R. Lussier
EDITOR:	Charles Gill
DESIGN & LAYOUT :	Donald Kroitzsh

Printed in the United States of America

Published by:
Northeast Kingdom Publications
PO Box 192
Lyndonville, Vermont 05851 USA
(802) 626-9541

Prepared by:
Five Corners Press
Plymouth, Vermont 05056 USA

THE ATTACK UPON THE NORTHEAST KINGDOM
ISBN: 0-9759048-0-9   US$14.95

Acknowledgments

As most of my readers know I have been self-employed in the Northeast Kingdom for my entire working career. I bought and sold cattle, raised animals, built a very large dairy herd, invested in land, became an auctioneer throughout New England, and cruised timber with my airplane. I became a bank director after successfully developing my own enterprises and eventually became chairman of the Board of one of the most profitable banks in its class in the United States. We made loans, earned a fair profit and the bank and community prospered. But I was always a working businessman.

I learned business from my father. When I was a freshman in High School he became seriously ill. My sister Lucille was at college, and she came home to help us. I was in school at the time but also needed to drop out to help keep the family farm going. I simply began to practice what he had taught us, earning a living, then marrying the nicest girl in high school. We began having a family and making my contribution to the well being of Vermont. It was only years later after my enforced enrollment at "Pen State" that I completed my education and took their graduate training in surviving in the "criminal justice system."

When I decided to write this book I asked several of my trusted friends and associates to assist me doing the research and converting the texts of my account into perhaps a more general narrative for your present reading. Canon Charles Gill has provided that service for me, and I am grateful. He also provided me invaluable assistance with my legal work.

I also have to thank Greg Walker, Ed.D. who also provided me with much assistance with my legal work and not charging me anything while I was in prison.

Additionally I have available to anyone who wishes to review the documentation that supports every conclusion reached in every instance in this narrative. I have paid for and preserved the transcripts of all the trials, the depositions and the records of hearings in all instances. And if you take time to read through the thousands and thousands of pages I believe you will conclude as I have. ***There never was a defense presented.*** This was a "show trial" to demonstrate the use of a process to frighten and harm and remove businesspersons who did not see the need to change their successful way of living. This trial and its consequences for the banks we relied upon for our credit and business loans was simply an attack upon the culture of the Northeast Kingdom. It was in no way a verdict based upon the evidence that was available to the court.

One of the most important lessons I have learned during my lifetime is that there is no cure for jealousy or discrimination.

I want to thank David Turner, a former Vice-President and Manager of the Newport Branch of the Lyndonville Saving Bank, for his invaluable assistance over several years in indexing and organizing and transferring and collecting all of the primary documents referred to in this narrative. He remains now one of my most trusted friends and a man whose own work made this book possible.

And certainly the previous Directors of the Lyndonville Saving Bank that I served with honorably for years, and their Executive Secretary Wendy Davenport, and former Senior Loan Officer Lee Cleveland, should be acknowledged before this community for their service and their honesty and many contributions to our well being.

My son David Lussier earlier collected, organized, and mastered the information and documentation from all of the trials and hearings and reports that made this book verifiable; diverting thousands of hours from himself to this effort, for others.

Mark Whitney came up after my sentencing and told me the restitution was absolutely illegal, and he started working with me. He worked with me and worked hard on several of the suits that I was involved in. Mark is President and CEO of TheLaw.net, a legal research reference firm used by many of the nation's leading legal scholars to conduct documentation and trial-based research. He helped me when I needed it the most. He is also the one who notified the Bailey firm about the Birbal and restitution issues, mentioned later in the book.

Marilyn Hughes was my secretary for many years and even stayed, after her retirement, to help my wife while I was in prison. My wife and I both owe her thanks for her assistance. As a former Executive Secretary of the Lyndonville Savings Bank she is both informed about this story of events and honest in her memory of them.

A special thanks is due to Andy Field, a lawyer and very good friend. Both he and his attorney-daughter did many things for me above and beyond their professional representation. They were there for me and my family when their assistance was truly needed, and it is appreciated.

Several people called me when the Wall St. Journal article came out on 11/29/93. One of them was Bert Lance, who was former Director of the Office of Management and Budget under President Carter. He was upset the way the government was after me and said he had had a similar experience. He advised me to take the stand in my defense. He said that was the only way he won his case, by testifying himself. I wanted to take his advice and told Langrock I wanted to testify; but as my attorney, he did not want me to. He said the government had not proved anything, and he thought we had them beat. I now know that I should have taken Bert Lance's suggestion, and I appreciate the time he took to offer me encouragement and advice, especially at a time when I really needed it.

I would also like to thank John McClaughry for the many letters he wrote on my behalf to Judge Billings and also to the FDIC and the public at large. He has been a staunch and unwavering supporter, and his support is greatly appreciated.

Of course I acknowledge the support of my family, and my wife who suffered more then I did in many ways. My sons Reg, Steve, Richard, David and daughter Kathy were themselves affected by all of the circumstances and publicity and misrepresentations of my character and my intentions. They did their own inquiries, reached their own conclusions and have convinced me that Love indeed is the gift and the purpose of the life we hold so precious daily in our brief years. They kept the home fires burning and helped their mother financially and emotionally.

Last but not least, I would like to thank my son Reg for getting the 2000 people who signed a petition for me after I had been convicted and was in jail. To me that was true friendship and I am eternally grateful.

I have written about the suffering of families; my belief that they suffered more actual pain and discrimination than I did while I was in prison. I have mentioned that my sons offered to "go in my place" and how my wife Evelyn had her property and income seized without any regard for her survival or her own innocence. I noted how Charlie Bucknam, profiting from and living from her investments in the bank, testified that it never occurred to him how she might survive. And I believe him: truth and compassion are qualities he has avoided!

But even in prison there are some conditions that can mitigate the circumstances of your sentence. One is serious family illness of a spouse and another is pre-existing alcoholism and drug dependency. These didn't help either.[1]

As to the first of these: while I was in prison, and for much of the time prior to my admission, my wife suffered from serious medical problems made much worse by the strain of the trial, the publicity, and the illegal seizure of her resources by the bank (later demonstrated to the Court and ordered to be returned to her). Other family stress and the Bank's fraudulent lawsuit took their toll on her, and she suffered greatly. Two of her physicians, Dr. John Elliott and Dr. Michael Billig, wrote letters outlining the seriousness of her condition and requested compassion. I had entered prison at 65 years of age, and was 67 at that time. So on July 1st (Independence weekend) of 1998, with only nine month yet to serve on my sentence, I applied for compassionate release.

I had the encouragement of many petitioners and prominent persons who wrote on my behalf. I wrote to five politicians myself. To my surprise the Senator that showed the most interest and compassion and urged those from Vermont to take a look at all of this was Senator Joseph Biden of Delaware. Perhaps, as a Senator from a wealthy business state with knowledge and experience in banking, he saw some merit in my claims. In any case he recommended consideration be given me in an extended letter[2] to Patrick Leahy. That Senator, from my State of Vermont, didn't get involved. My request, on Evelyn's behalf, was declined. But my admiration and appreciation of Senator Biden is remembered and acknowledged.

The other possible condition for release was to participate in the "alcohol and drug rehabilitation" program which would have given me six months or more off of my sentence. It was recommended that I ask some of my friends to write on my behalf and identify me as a problem closet drinker and try to get into that program. That suggestion came from a lawyer serving time for some other crime. I couldn't, wouldn't and didn't! This was no time to begin a fraud, having suffered from one.

Alas, I failed the drinking test as well. It just goes to show that doing the "right" thing sometimes harms you. Seems that I could offer no evidence or testimony or no police and driving record that I had a problem with alcohol. Seems like in all of my sixty some years of living in Vermont I had not earned a public distinction as a "drunk" and, as a consequence, for what would have normally been admirable behavior, I was turned down for the drinking rehabilitation program. In all my years, I had not drunk enough to qualify.

Now isn't that something – if I had paid more attention to my drinking I could have gotten out of prison sooner.

Most of the attorneys that I had engaged during this odyssey were primarily interested in their own concerns and represented me with some measure of effort and enthusiasm as long as it did not jeopardize their continuing interests or their business with other attorneys. There were several exceptions: Andrew Field, F. Lee Bailey, and Peter DeTroy served their professions honorably.

But it was to another attorney that I owe the necessity of this book. When he asked me what I wanted to accomplish in retaining his representation I told him, "I want the truth to come out." He looked at me skeptically and said that trials were not about the truth, and if I ever wanted anyone to know my side to the story I would have to write a book. And so I have!

The audiences I have in mind as I put this text together are of two different types.

The first is the honest working man of the Northeast Kingdom.

The others that I am writing this for are the great-grandchildren of the Roger Lussier family.

Things being like they are they will eventually hear that their great-grandfather was an outlaw, and that he went to prison. And if the intrusion of government continues as it has and if the Constitution is ignored by the courts and politicians as it is now, then going to prison will no longer be seen as a rare event. (Even now it is not, except for the rich and politically connected).

But I wanted my grandchildren to have an account that for *the first time* presents the defense that should have been presented in 1993.

I will not be able to speak for myself then so I should do it now.

Roger Lussier

Roger Lussier,
Lyndonville, Vermont,
May 8, 2004

[1]See Exhibits page 215 for answer from the Warden
[2]See Exhibits page 216 for letter to Sen. Biden

Preface

Most of us respond to the heroic, to the noble, and we celebrate occasions of triumph and heroism. I have! We read our history and find examples of courage and sometimes find ourselves musing over our own choices. We read the accounts of heroic lives and we reflect upon the opportunities of other citizens who have been called in occasions of suffering to greatness. Sometimes we meet a person present at a significant event and found an opportunity to serve a greater good. We wonder at what our own responses might be if we were challenged by a good or by evil to duel in our own existence. We think of Star Wars, of "Luke Skywalker" and ponder the force that is in us, so to speak. Revealed by him as in us also. "May the force be with us."

None of those heroic goals were apparent to me when I met Roger Lussier for the first time. I quickly realized he was a man of intelligence and ability, but it took a long time for me to realize what a gracious and compassionate person he was in the presence of the harm and betrayal that he had experienced.

When he accounted for me this story of his being an auctioneer, businessman, pilot, dairy farmer, land developer, timber cruiser, bank president and family man it just seemed to be too much for one person. And then when I heard his account of his trial and his conviction for lack of a defense and his imprisonment during his 60's and his losses in earnings and property and reputation and credibility, it seemed to be a tale invented.

Like so many of the others who brought disaster upon themselves and are seeking a more comfortable explanation it seemed imaginary comfort. In Roger's case it was simply as he stated it; his account is true.

I have been a clergyman in the Episcopal Church for over 40 years. I have been told "many a tale" and have seen harm and evil up close. It has also been a privilege of my ministry to travel widely and to hold academic positions of some responsibility at several of our leading universities. I am professionally trained in research methodology and used that skill to reach my conclusions about Roger's conviction.

I have had available to me every document that was used at all of the trials and all of the supporting documents that would have been used in his defense if one had been presented. I have spent five years researching the documents that are gathered in the federal court records and in the depository of documents in Lyndonville. I've interviewed witnesses to the trial and I've talked with court personnel and others who were present while the story was being told in its original form.

And in the process of reading everything that was said and traveling to the sites referred to in the trial and talking with persons who have known Roger and these events I have concluded as you might, that it was a willful, unnecessary and tragic drama acted out posing as Justice, but was in fact Evil seeking to destroy.

Roger had a trial but he never had a defense offered. So it became necessary for him to have what he would have said examined, and since he had been convicted in public opinion as well as in court, it was absolutely necessary that his story not only be announced as true of that presented but also in a way that will allow you to examine the trial documents and reach your own conclusions. This book has an unusual format. He tells his story as a narrative of characters and trials and strategies by agencies of the government to convict him. And he presents for your reading the documents that he would have used and that others used to establish the position they claimed Roger deserved.

When Roger calls someone a liar it is because they lied. And being a direct man himself he will be able to show you the testimony page where they did so in their own words and swore to it. When he says they changed their story he gives you the page, the name, the date of the testimony and the seal of the court saying that it is so. When he says that the current board of the Lyndonville Savings Bank acted in a systematic and willful attempt to misrepresent their standing before the federal court he shows you the page where having posed as one thing they are found out to be another — that they had committed perjury and deceit and then try again.

He tells the story his way and then he gives you all of the information supporting his conclusions but does not make you dependent upon his say so.

Over these years while I have been listening to the story and reading the documents to establish a view of the truth I have come to regard Roger as one of those "heroes" of our hopes and dreams and as an "everyman" who in his own suffering and disgrace and harm served us all well. A native son of his beloved Vermont he walks among us now as an ordinary "Ethan Allen" but the issues of his love of Justice and Vermont and of the Constitution radiates from him like a warrior possessed. Listening to him one evening I was startled with his question, "Why does the government hate the people so much?" I certainly could agree to the asking but shuddered at the implications in the answer.

And this man Roger, this current hero of Vermont if you will (and some will not), emerges from all of the chains and imprisonment and harm to himself as one who is still generous in spirit and loves the community where he lives, and together with his family continues to work for a better time and for the betterment of all. He has a love for the land and the earth that he walks over similar to that attributed to the Native Americans who lived here before him, and I believe he is very much like them. He is of their same spirit. He is a man of his own faith, yet a respecter of the faith of others, a man of his place but allied in interest and respect with those from elsewhere. He has refused to become cynical as he ages and meeting him now is to find a man curious and sincerely interested in the well being of others.

When I lived in Switzerland I came to understand the well-known Swiss story of William Tell. He is not presented in the Olympic stature of the heroic, above us in ability or person, or like our familiar war heroes. William Tell was a private citizen who simply believed it his duty to live within the framework of his Constitution. And when betrayed by the tyrant and asking to "bow" to an unjust authority, William said no. He is forced into a contest that might cost his son his life. William simply engaged that evil with integrity and using his skill and love and ability lived out his destiny. He might have died. He could not bow. And so I think Roger is more like a Vermont "William Tell." And if you think that a stretch, to take an ordinary citizen of this State and compare him with that hero William, then you should know that others have reached this conclusion. Hanging in his office in Lyndonville are the photos (complete with flag and uniforms and signatures) of the "PRO PATRIA" award, given by the National Chairman on behalf of the Army Reserve and the Vermont National Guard for Roger's contributions to the civic betterment of his community and nation.[1]

Successful by every commercial standard, he is a man who is known everywhere. I have accompanied him all over the state, in elevators and courtrooms and banks and business meetings and among friends and barbecues and car dealer lots and cattle pens. Everyone knows Roger and they all know him as he truly is. And everyone is glad to see him and is pleased to have talked with him, to be known by him.

As the President of a leading Bank in its class, Roger was accused of misusing his position for his personal gain at the Bank's and its customer's expense. Hardly. Roger used his compassion and his character and decency to make profitable investments for the Bank and the support of his community and the benefit of the customers in the Northeast Kingdom. As it turned out at great danger to himself. But the documents in this book and all those additional thousands of pages of documents available to you in the federal warehouse and in Lyndonville are there for the reading. And when you contemplate the tragedy that was unnecessarily deposited upon him and his eventual and successful ability to reply to his accusers and to show the orchestrated deception and arrogance that they relied upon to convict him, I believe you will agree that he has finally defended himself, very successfully.

The great-grandchildren of the Roger Lussier family have inherited a wonderful history springing from an incredibly honorable man in the face of odds and evil that sought to destroy him. And like most all oppressors they intended it to his harm, and the larger spirit of our lives converted it to our good. So in this citizen Roger Lussier, man of Vermont, of the Northeast Kingdom, we also have our heroic person. Not the phony patriotic speech of some fast talking defender of the national interest, those persons pretending to be "the whole of the United States" or the greed of self-serving bank directors. This man joins William Tell, and others, as the citizen free beyond his own conflict and issue; a beacon for others.

I am honored to have lived long enough to have such a friend.

The Reverend Canon Charles Gill
Gambier, Ohio
Spring, 2004

[1] see Exhibits page 214 for letter from Office of the Assistant Secretary of Defense.

The Story

Introduction

I want to introduce you, the reader, to some of the most painful and personal episodes in my lifetime. I want to tell you the story of the events that led to my imprisonment and give an account of them so that I may finally be heard for the first time in my defense. I write so that my fellow citizens may be warned of the character of the government that is being imposed upon the free citizens envisioned by our founding fathers and described in the Constitution of the United States.

This narrative begins with a surprise indictment of myself in 1993, with the trial, appeals, imprisonment, and the eventual favorable verdict of "attorney liability." It takes you through the convoluted logic of the "criminal justice system," the sordid pleadings of 28 lawyers, and the conscious, willful and persistent misrepresentation by the directors and legal counselors of the Lyndonville Savings Bank in their pleadings. Pleadings misrepresented in both federal and state courts, and issues of consequence and a summary of the costs to myself and to my family. It ends with the conclusion that the important things in life are to be found among our families and our community. I try to indicate why our positive visions of a country pursuing life and liberty without fear from an intruding and self-serving pretense of "protection" are under threat. I deplore the disregard for its citizens by an immoral agency of government.

Ten years ago the events described herein were probably seen or could be seen as the occasional mistakes necessary to the risks of a democracy. The costs required for the management of our national civil affairs. We did not see clearly that it could be the character and intention of government. We are taught one thing, but we experience something quite different.

We do need sound banks, and we need money and credit, and the use should always be in safe and trustworthy hands. But in this case, while pretending to be diligent and a faithful steward of the public trust, agencies of the government presided over the willful dismantling of a profitable business enterprise. Then they allowed their appointed representatives to hold fire sales and dispose of valuable assets for pennies on the dollar, and to profit for their own personal benefit...the very things they accuse me of.

They create false documents, hide evidence of their inside self-dealing in stocks, and misrepresent their legal basis for fraudulent claims, and get paid for doing it. They claim public benefit despite a contrary conclusion easily reached in an examination of the public records of those proceedings. This is like "pushing the lady in the river, running down stream and pulling her out and then asking the public to regard you as a hero for saving her life."

And finally when they are exposed, they pretend that it was all "an innocent mistake." Well Charlie Bucknam's claims turned out to hardly be innocent, or mistakes! Intentional misrepresentation and fraud is the correct translation.

The government and its sponsored clients can steal and be rewarded. I claim innocence and am punished simply for the claim. The discrepancy between what happened to me, and all of those others who "admitted their guilt" and were guilty is outrageous. It simply defies gravity. Niagara Falls must run upside down. Light must be darkness. Feet must be hands, and hands must be feet, the world indeed must be upside down. Vermont must be flat and a part of Kansas.

Another surprise for me was that the obvious mistakes were repeatedly identified and repeatedly documented and presented to the courts as undeniable. Those courts did everything they could to avoid the obvious. No "Officer of the Court" demonstrated any interest in adjusting the obvious flaws in the process that are documented in these narratives. Rather every attempt was made to hold onto the illusion that reality, or error, was not affecting the courts — or that highly paid lawyers made misrepresenting sworn statements and created false documents on behalf of their clients. And in rare moments when small mistakes were corrected, the mistakes were minimized and the obvious conclusion was avoided. They would not attach "therefore" as a conclusion to the continued and obviously emerging miscarriage of justice in its entirety.

Finally it is a terribly unfair consequence that for the defendant in the "criminal justice system" the costs of all of the proceedings involving him are paid for and suffered by the defendant. And the consequences of prosecution are borne by the defendant, his business community and family. But the consequences of error on behalf of the government or its agents are also paid for by the defendant's resources and by the taxpayer. But there are no consequences to an over zealous prosecutor or a self-serving lawyer, or a Judge's reversed "error" (ignorance?). My mistake is "prison for me." Their conscious deception and fraud is "a simple misunderstanding."

And that is regarded as fair.

The Beginning of an Outrage!

This story takes place in two acts:

ACT ONE is a Federal Criminal Trial: a 20-count indictment of supposed crimes involving the banking system in the United States. That is the Federal criminal trial; an accounting of what the prosecutor for the United States of America said I did wrong, the imagined crimes against the United States. It has a cast of characters, informers, "cooperating witnesses, criminals admitting to that status and getting a good deal for the admission, prosecutors, resting attorneys, witnesses ignored while waiting to testify, witnesses to facts not being brought to the Court by the government, jurors uninformed by facts and kept that way, and even a sitting Judge who repeated a previously overturned (Birble) case and gave written instructions to the jury that disappeared. And then awarded illegal restitution to the F.D.I.C., and upon correction of his error he gave it to the bank as a claim for non-existent losses.

And, ACT TWO is the Federal Civil Trial and later a State Case: a claim by the Lyndonville Saving Bank that they were owed money for alleged losses and the using of what came to be seen as an illegal restitution order. They brought a "civil" claim against me while pretending to be a federally chartered institution themselves. Their actions and attempts to collect $426,000 dollars cost millions of dollars. What was their motive? They also made insurance claims, attached my wife's property, and diverted millions of dollars into unexplained legal fees chasing what they ended up admitting was "a mistake."

All of those responsible for attempting this fraud upon the courts and against me retained their jobs, increased their personal holdings in stock value, and escaped any explanation for their actions. In every sense of the word, that bank "robbed its former President."

Most community bankers were well liked and respected by their community, but can you imagine a bank president getting over two thousand signatures for his release and retrial while he was already in jail and after his trial? Do you think it stretching the truth to say that people this bank had sued for collection of debts would be willing to sign a petition for the President's benefit? Also signing, among the 2000 persons, were 6 local attorneys, doctors, and a priest! And when the prison heard about the petition they wondered if they needed the National Guard. Sounds like the stuff they do movies with.

So you charge him with 20 counts of inside dealing, then you take him to trial, find him guilty, after the defense rests from doing nothing, and sentence him to prison, and announce to the papers you caught the biggest crook living.

Well, what happened really?

"THE FEDERAL CASE"

How do you make a "Federal Case" out of something? We often use that phrase, "don't make a Federal case out of it." It implies Federal is more than some other; not State, not Town, but "Federal." But what is one? How do you get one or find it?

It begins somewhere out of sight, based on some perception of concerns, the phrase or a notation in a report, an overheard opinion, or perhaps even the invented memories of someone wired for betrayal (as a price for their reduced sentence and leniency) set loose upon us. It wanders slowly, gathering some additional weight from others, finds its usefulness in someone's plans, and is given direction and shoved downhill. That is all there is to it. Simply a rumor, a notion or a wish is converted into an investigation, which justifies itself by elaborate procedures of inquiry and record building, and then is attached to a selected victim like a leech to your bloodstream.

Only then as you look down at your attacked arm or leg do you sense the danger, and see your blood being taken. And so it was with me:

A phone call to meet, sitting in a car with a man in Wells River at 6 am in the morning, a man owing our bank money, saying that "I" did something that I did not do and being told again when I disagreed with him that I did. Sounds simple doesn't it, to begin a day with an ordinary breakfast, a business meeting with a bank customer, and not realizing until later that I had been targeted. So that day ended normally, or so I believed. In fact it was my first day on the road to hell! To make a "Federal case" can begin with the high drama of a kidnapping, the armed robbery of an insured financial institution, the removal of the manufacturer's tag from a mattress, or simply serving my community and helping my friends and neighbors in business, and making a reasonable profit doing so. It can be meeting with a man at his request and then going about my work for the day; he leaving to drive to the branch office of the FBI (I have learned it sometimes spells fib) and give an unwitnessed, unverified and entirely self-serving account of the "meeting." This is then turned into a "cooperating witness report," regarded as factual, and typed and signed by the Agent who was not there and then used in every possible location and file as an account of what happened.

Does the Agent believe what is reported? He signs that he was told this. Does the man making the report wish to be believed? Well, he has already agreed to plead guilty to something and is assured that if he "cooperates" his own sentencing will be more lenient. So does he have an interest in cooperating? You bet! The better he reports the better it is for him. But does he have any obligation in unwitnessed and unverified reporting of conversations to speak fairly, to tell the truth? Not necessarily, in fact not at all. It can make him seem less cooperative if his reports look more like dry wells than crime scenes. So he speaks to the choir, so to speak, the already believing and the record keepers. When this meeting was over I went to work. This man, leaving Wells River, goes to the local FBI office where agent Hersh is waiting to get his reports. This "cooperating witness" says I said things I never said, reports I called him not he called me, indicates he tried to get me to see I was wrong and offered to help me also become a "cooperating witness" myself.

The job description of a "cooperating witness" is to provide contact, conversations and opinions, even carry a wire or tape recorder to those meetings sought by the anonymous authority holding his own plea in their hands. To get someone whose true purpose you do not know, usually a friend you trust, to be found in conversations that will appear to incriminate you. So when I ask later, "What have I done wrong?" The reply from this same "cooperating witness" is simply, "It doesn't matter. You need to plead guilty to something and then all of the (unknown) stuff will go away." That is what a "cooperating witness" is, an assassin of facts, reputation, reality, and lifetimes of trust and achievement. He is a Trojan horse, a betrayer often, a liar if necessary and someone who has already demonstrated they will deal...regardless of truth, even about themselves.

The government says this type of thing is necessary to get the evidence to bring the indictment, to take you to trial, to send you to prison and to stop the crime. But where is the safeguard in the bought and often perjured evidence? Where is the crime of false statements or of entrapment? They say the end justifies the means. Yet often the crime of the pursuit of the believed misdeed is greater and less justified than the imagined action itself. Committing crimes in the pursuit of a believed crime is the greater fraud upon our Constitution, the peace of the State, or the oath of office sworn by these upholders of our trust. Yet, and knowingly, this is what they do. From the position of an anonymous person with a typewriter, making signed statements, they emerge in the shadows posing as helpful and pretending to assist your best interest. But you may find such is not the case. If you can manage a man already sworn to guilt to work for you with his pay being a change in his own plight, you will never be able to rely upon this process to reduce the claim of fighting crime. It is the crime! The authority that can order this process and make the deals is the ignored criminal. But does this continue, does it work, can it produce business for the legal system? Absolutely!

Usually the next step in this process is to "spread the risk" of seeming to be charging someone with a crime all by yourself, because you believed or wished to believe it happened. Instead you gather up all of those collected reports (called 302's in the legal inventory) and all of the persons who have participated in the different information gathering events and you go to a Grand Jury. **(Some of those 302's, which might have helped me, were not turned over to the defense attorney.)** This is a gathering of persons who are asked to listen to what is presented to them by persons who are represented to have knowledge of whatever is being proposed as a crime. Their only obligation is to decide if the information is extensive enough for them to conclude that what is said to have happened may have happened. They are not bound to believe it beyond a reasonable doubt, indeed doubt is encouraged. They are doing their job if they have "questions" about the information. But is it possible, could it maybe be seen as a crime if true? And the witnesses, often the makers of the "302's" themselves, already promised to a guilty plea, present this to a Grand Jury. The government's attorney, usually referred to as "The United States," (all of them again, including the individual's wife and children I assume) alleges or interprets this information to show his belief of what happened.

The Grand Jury considers the information presented, not the explanations possible against it, not proved, just stated as so, and answers that it is possible, probable, or maybe possible that what was alleged could have happened. If they say this, if most of them are willing to say this, you are indicted. And of course you are not there to question the information, or its reliability or the person's creditability in their statements. It questions you. And from this "sausage machine" starts all of the continuing orderly processing of indictments, of charges, of procedures, of that giving and swearing to tell "the truth, the whole truth, and nothing but the truth." From this assembled gathering of claims comes the power of the prosecutor to bargain with you or with your lawyer behind your back. From this pile of indictments, gathered like the cargo of a dump truck, all of the eventual disputes and appeals and counterclaims descend. But the power to force and determine the "fair trial" issues is contained in the process of indictment.

The prosecutor *then* says "the Grand Jury" found this to be so and indicted me. The standard in fact is; what is the tolerance of the presenting prosecutor for reality, facts, and integrity. He is, in this process, those 280 million United States persons (including my wife, children and grandchildren) and if he is willing to say to the Grand Jury, "Now this might, or could or possibly does mean this or such," you will most normally be indicted. And from numerous counts in the indictment, 20 or so, you get those claims about if convicted he could get hundreds of years in prison and millions of dollars in fines. Those numerous counts are to impress the public with the assumption *that the word numbers means larger and that numerous means most probably did it.* Those numerous counts are to give the prosecutor many chances to prove you guilty of something, to use as resources for bargains, or to cover mistakes or errors, or lessening the chance of the accused winning at trial. Those counts provide the unlimited power to the manipulation of charges, of offers to reduce in exchange for services, or to dismiss by your attorney negotiating with the prosecutor, or to be tried on some then seeing how you do, and maybe adding more later. There are unlimited combinations of alternatives. But all of it becomes the resources for your later "fair trial."

By the time the trial is to start, that place where everyone is sworn to tell the truth, the whole truth and nothing but the truth, all of these concerns have been processed, and it is only the outcome of all of these negotiations that is set for trial. And in my case, even after conviction, an FBI agent told me that if I would agree to work for them, they could reduce the sentence to home confinement, rather than jail. Could he really do that? How was I to know? How are you to know? There he stood, with badge and "picture ID" saying he could. But as I knew I was innocent of the charges and, in spite of the conviction, I was going to resist and fight. His deal, real or not, was of no interest to me. But he seemed to believe he could, and if he could for me how many others may have received this benefit?

So you can assume that most of the information that brought you into court is out of sight when the trial happens. The pleadings and deals and exchanging of interests, favors, the negotiation of friendships among counsel, all work themselves out. And almost as a secondary concern, when all of this is completed then you go to trial. And those conclusions and agreements are never visible, known only to the Conductor of this arrangement. The defendant does not know what the grand jury did not get to see. It can be national security concerns, protection of sources concerns, contradictory information excluded or denied, but you will never know. The space between the indictments and the trial is like a huge warehouse full of choices, and it is where the results of the trial are usually determined. The rest of it is a choreographed story about the selected information.

Having a lifetime of achievement in business, social and family success I was indicted on 20 counts of crimes against the United States of America, all of it, not just Vermont, or New England, but all 50 States of it, its overseas possessions, territories, and those under current development. It was the whole of the United States of America against Roger Lussier. The resources of 280 plus millions arrayed against me.

Now that is what a "Federal Case" looks like.

What did the whole of the United States of America say I did wrong?

I pose that question simply. In actual fact that question has consumed over:

- 10 years of time,
- 28 different lawyers on all sides,
- 47,000 pages of materials in my possession alone (how many are in the FBI, the US Attorney General, insurance and bank records is unknown)
- Over 55 legal boxes of documents and pages,
- Thousands of phone calls,
- 50 loose leaf folders, and
- A pile of computer disks,
- Cost me over $205,000 in fines, and over $767,592.96 in legal fees,
- Deprived me of my auction business and license,
- Forced me to sell property for taxes,
- Embarrassed and harmed my children's personal and professional lives,
- Threatened my wife's health and well-being,
- Deprived me of any way to earn a living,
- Deprived me of three years of social security, and Medicare insurance,
- Subjected me to physical danger, and by a Judge's error extended my incarceration.
- Deprived me of attending my own civil trial where I was assessed an additional $8,700,000 in restitution, only to have that lawfully overturned.
- Had my bank stock attached and converted to treasury notes with the loss of interest, by the Bank.
- Had my corporation confiscated, including $500,000 in bank stock, and land and equipment valued at $376,603 for a total of $876,603.

The charges are listed in the following pages under the main headings of "The Check Kite," "Colonnade Transaction," "Rowell Transaction," the "Provost Transaction" and the "ARDI Transaction."

Now I have said, and say again 10 years later, after fines and prison and many trials that I did not do this. So how can I in the face of so much material, with so much paper stacked against me, with a jury having convicted me say such a thing? How dare I ask my reader to believe it?

Overall, the answer is equally simple; my case against the whole of the United States of America was never presented. ***There was never a defense presented!*** That simple! Now there will be more about trials later, but for now that is and will be the answer.

I never got to defend myself. Nor was I defended!

When it came time for me to defend myself, as I could have done, wanted to do and had many others with me waiting to do, my attorney simply put on a few character witnesses and then rested the case, and I was abandoned to having a jury decide solely upon the information presented by the prosecutor. (Even then they refused to convict me on three of the 20 counts) It is like a Vermont cow asking the slaughterhouse for a different outcome. Given what the jury was given, with no defense offered, how did they avoid the other three counts? In any case, that is the answer to how I was convicted. My attorney rested...when he should have demolished the case against me, as he would have been able to do. And what were that case and those charges?

The charges were that I helped Charlie Kelton "kite" checks in our bank, that the Lyndonville Savings Bank loaned him money and concealed all of this from the Federal Deposit Insurance Corporation (FDIC) in 1988.

The Check Kiting Transaction

For years the LSB always had substantial amounts of Federal Funds that they sold. During this time period I started to notice that they did not have much in the way of Fed Funds sold and asked the CEO, Tom Thompson, why this was. Tom said he didn't know but would have Marguerite Beane, the Treasurer, at the next Director's meeting to explain it. At the next meeting, Marguerite explained that the Bank gave instant credit to depositors and that a large depositor was Kelton's. The Bank gave instant credit but did not receive credit from the Federal Reserve until the checks cleared, which might be 24 to 36 hours later.

Phil Bovee and I went and met with Kelton and explained this to him and said that the bank couldn't afford to keep his account as it was costing the bank money. Kelton said he was getting a large Line of Credit from the Bank of Boston[1] and would be willing to pay interest on his uncollected funds until the Line of Credit came through and then he would be OK. The letter from the Bank of Boston for the Line of Credit was issued in March 1988 and we started charging Kelton interest in April 1988.

Another point is to understand "float" and the deposit of all checks. Everyone at Lyndonville had his or her checks processed the same way. The problem with any check is there is a delay between the time the "Teller" receives the check from you and the time the bank gets the money. Prior to current regulations and electronic clearing, this period of time could be 24-36 hours, often 1 to five days. Now my grocery check for $34 is not going to affect the bank much. But Charlie, running nine dealerships and selling daily among them was depositing and spending up to a million daily. Interest on that amount, on a daily basis, charging from the time it left our bank until the funds were confirmed, could be about a $1000 per day. So we charged him for our cost. If he had carried, if you carried a large balance that earned us money and reduced our cost, it would have been fine. As it was we charged for our cost. We also charged a bank director in the same way, and for the same reason. The FDIC said they were glad we charged for this. That is not a kite. That is uncollected funds. A kite is in fact a complicated financial maneuver. At the trial were the documents and testimony of experts from the FDIC saying they weren't sure it was a kite. But all of the other experts and investigators, not sure themselves, said I should have known. A kite requires at least two bank accounts for the same party, and the putting of a "deposit" in one of them creating a false balance, then moving that balance to another account at another bank and using the delay in bookkeeping and transit of the check to provide the kite with access to funds that are in fact non-existent.

Charlie said under oath that Bill Murray, the manager of the City Bank, of Claremont, NH, who later went to work for the government, told him "If that is what you have to do to keep your business going, go ahead and do it." Do what? That bank seemed to have started giving Charlie a check-kiting position that he passed on to at least ten other banks beyond Lyndonville. Tom Thompson, the Lyndonville "CEO" reports in his testimony under oath that he never showed me a "kiting suspect report." Only later did he report to me the possibility. Bill Rockford said it was not a kite if the presented checks were good, not returned. And they were always good. Bill Rockford was a Deputy Commissioner of Banking for the State of Vermont, and later became CEO of Lyndonville Savings Bank after I resigned. He presented that conclusion under oath.

As to concealment from them, we had examinations and audits; then we had a special audit from the State of Vermont, and there was no presented evidence from them to us. They did not know, and we did not know.

Lyndonville Saving Bank called City Bank in New Hampshire[2] and the Bank of Vermont in Burlington, Vt. and both banks told the Lyndonville Saving Bank that Kelton was a very good customer and that his checks were good and would be honored.

On June 8, 1988 Tom Thompson, the Executive Vice-President, was ordered by the Directors to return Kelton's overdrawn checks. One of the Directors said that Kelton should be called before the checks were returned. After the meeting I went to New York on business and when I returned that Friday, I went to see Tom and asked him what Charlie had said when the checks were returned. He said he called Charlie and Charlie brought up certified checks to cover his overdraft, so Tom didn't return his checks. Tom said that he had a good understanding with Kelton and that he would monitor Kelton's account on a daily basis.

The amount of his uncollected funds kept growing and on July 13, 1988 the Directors told Tom to stop paying on his uncollected funds immediately but it took Tom another 4 or 5 days to do this.

The FDIC was happy that we were charging Kelton interest for his uncollected funds. Charlie is still in business and never entered personal bankruptcy though his fraud cost everyone millions. He is the forgiven "sinner."

The Bank of Vermont was left with a possible loss of $3,000,000 when the checks were returned on Kelton. The original amount they were owed was a little over $4 million, but Kelton had paid them down to approximately $3 million. Lyndonville loaned $1,500,000 to Raymond Jasmin and $1,500,000 for Kelton's benefit to pay the Bank of Vermont. This loan was well secured by real estate. When the Dartmouth Bank started making threats of involuntary bankruptcy for Kelton, the Bank of Vermont got nervous. If the bankruptcy went through before 90 days had expired from the time they had received the $3 million from Kelton they might have to return that amount because of preferential payment. I called the Bank of Vermont 3 days before the 90 days was up for the preferential payment, and wanted to know if the Bank of Vermont was going to close on the Roundhouse that Lyndonville Savings Bank had taken back in lieu of foreclosure from Kelton. We had agreed to sell the Roundhouse for $1.2 million and the Bank of Vermont thought they could sell it for $2 million. William McMeekin, Senior VP for Bank of Vermont said the deal wasn't going through because the Dartmouth bank wasn't going to accept the money from Bank of Vermont and Kelton. The Bank of Vermont had intended to pay Dartmouth $400,000 up front and the balance on the day of closing. Dartmouth decided they wanted everything up front or not at all. I asked McMeekin if that was going to stop the sale of their bank to Bank of Boston and he said no, it wouldn't stop it. The Bank of Vermont attorneys had issued a legal opinion that they wouldn't have to give back the $3 million. Kelton, when one of his corporations was put in bankruptcy, asked Dartmouth what they were doing. He told them they had a deal worked out and they said they could stop it anytime, but they didn't. Dartmouth Bank told the Bank of Vermont that they thought Kelton had hurt too many people and that he should be put out of business.

The government used the total amount of interest, $103,177.03, that the LSB had charged Kelton for his uncollected funds, as profit to me when I was sentenced. I received none of that money, only the bank did, but it was charged to me. The Lyndonville Bank never lost any money on the check kiting.

After trying to help BOV they turned and sued LSB to try and get the $3 million back if they had to return it.

The Bank of Vermont was sold to the Bank of Boston and disappeared as a corporation. Dartmouth National Bank, which promised to put Kelton in bankruptcy, by such skillful losing of $900,000, which was available and guaranteed, is now out of business. And, of course, Charlie Kelton is doing big business in Bellows Falls, his court-testified cancer and pending death not withstanding. Wonderful, a Lourdes right here in Vermont.

---

[1] see Exhibits pages 1-3 for Letter of Credit
[2] See Exhibits page 4 for list of calls from and to City Bank

Colonnade Story

The Colonnade transaction covers four counts of the indictment against me. The Government said I had entered into the partnership and that I had approved the loan to the partnership. They also claimed that I hid Arthur Elliott's and my interest in the partnership, that I had received $16,000.00 from the partnership and deposited that amount in an insured bank, which is considered money laundering.

On August 11, 1988, I signed a contract with David Archambeau to have an auction on Arthur's Place, Inc. on September 7, 1988. This was a local restaurant, located near the intersection of Route 5 and I-91 in Lyndonville, Vermont. In his trial testimony, Mr. Archambeau said he had been losing money and wanted to stop the bleeding, and that was why he decided to have an auction. This was not a forced auction on Mr. Archambeau's part, as he always had the funds on hand to pay off the note.

We put the real estate and personal property (equipment) up as one unit and it brought $385,000. I talked to Mr. Archambeau and told him that I thought it would bring more if we sold it separately, and we had the choice of doing it either way. The crowd did not want to wait until the end of the day, to see if their bids would be accepted, so in order to keep them there I guaranteed Mr. Archambeau that a split sale would bring him as much if not more than what had been bid as one unit. We announced that we rejected the bid of $385,000 and were going to have an absolute sale with no holdback, splitting up the real estate and personal property. This split sale totaled only $346,778.53.

When I settled with Mr. Archambeau, I used the figure of $385,000, minus the 3% commission of $11,500 and advertising expenses of $5,842.95. I used the $385,000 figure, as that is what I had guaranteed it would bring. This left a net figure to Mr. Archambeau of $367,607, which he was paid. I was left with a loss of $20,828.52 plus the advertising expenses of $5,842.95.

Bill Hill, who was a real estate dealer and good customer of the bank, bought the property and took Arthur Elliott in as a partner. Bill had a buyer for the property that wanted to use the property as an office and manufactured home lot, but was not able to get the zoning changed and so the sale fell through. A few weeks went by. Arthur stopped in my office and told me that the sale did not go through. He was a little nervous about it, and he invited me to become a third partner. I hesitated but told Arthur I would become a partner if I could be reimbursed for all my losses, which amounted to over $26,000 before we split the profit. He said that if I would come in, and if the sale made a profit, there was a chance I could recoup my $20,828.52 but he did not agree to deduct the advertising expense as he said I got the publicity from the advertising. Shortly after this the heat went off in the building and the pipes froze and did a lot of damage. Arthur came in and asked if I could have my boys fix it up, as he did not have the manpower or the time. This we did.

They sold the real estate and after taking out Arthur's expenses we made $58,637. Taking out my loss of $20,828.52 left $37,809.48 as profit. I received a check for $18,905. This is all the money I received. Out of the $18,905, I paid the advertising expenses for the auction, leaving me $13,062. This was just a little more than my commission of 3% would have been if I had sold the business as one unit for $385,000.

I spent approximately $3,000 giving a big New Year's party at the site for a lot of business people. We had decorated the building, hired a band and had a full meal and open bar. I did this mainly for promotional reasons and I believe it is one of the reasons it later sold. After spending approximately $3,000 for the party, the whole transaction did not net me more that $10,000 instead of the $11,500 commission I should have received. This, however, is no one's fault but my own. None of the government's witnesses testified differently from what I have said above. Again, the bank was paid in full and all parties to this transaction were satisfied. Now for that I go to prison?

Now the Prosecutor will say I was in from the beginning in 1988, that by witnessing the document between David Archambeau and Ashley Gray I knew what would eventually happen when Hill and Elliott sold it. Did I know that Hill intended to sell it? That is what he does, did! It was about a poor auction sale in conditions that did not bring about the market price. It was not an inside deal of any kind. Where is "inside" to an auction? Everyone who could read the documents understood that Gray and Archambeau wanted out, and the bank had the loan. I did not process the loan. I joined the eventual partnership on my oral oath to share in the liability in hopes and belief I could recover my expenses. This is what happened, and I recovered what had been spent. Now for that I go to prison? There was no "1988 deal "to do anything but sell the property at auction at the owner's request.

And when it is looked at now you see also that the day Hill sold this investment, the bank was paid off in full, he paid off his note, and I got my expenses and commission. At trial, when the previous owner, Archambeau, was asked if he was happy, he said he was glad to end his losses, that Roger had worked hard to bring the sale up. And even when Gray was asked if he liked losing $100,000, he said "no", but he was satisfied.

The Rowells

A nd the charge regarding the Rowells was that when they were facing foreclosure from the Chittenden Bank, I "stepped in with my brother" and offered to pay off the debt, if the Rowells would auction off their assets to pay off the debt and pay a 15 percent commission plus expenses. It said we split $200,000 as a result. (Four of the indictments involved this deal; I was acquitted on three. It could have been four.)

Now in this charge and in the one to follow both are facing foreclosure *and both parties in these foreclosures sought me out.*

Stop for a moment and think about what is entailed in a foreclosure; you are having your use and ownership of something, usually your home, farm or business, extinguished and returned or transferred to someone else. That is a trauma in feelings and a crisis in events. Time and money become critical and sometimes when facing foreclosure you do end up "a day late and a dollar short." Deadlines are real, and amounts of money are necessary and usually missing. Think about it, if you had the money it would not be happening in the first place. If you could wait a bit until you had more money the time or day of the week would not matter. But they do! And if you cannot find a way to acquire more time or produce more money you will lose whatever is at stake. And with that loss of home or farm you lose the ability to earn more, to protect yourself and family, and to continue the life you know. Foreclosure is usually a reluctant event sought by the party you had promised to pay to reduce their own losses or to recover money already advanced. No party in foreclosure is happy or having good time. And one way or another someone's advantage in that setting is going to be increased, and someone is losing things of great value.

The foreclosing party is usually your lender who had expected its investment to be repaid, and is often quite regretful that the losses have occurred and that you could not complete the mutually agreed upon transaction. Usually the bank that loaned you the money has tried to find another way in order to keep its own interests productive and works with you as long as possible. Then, as a last resort, it forecloses to recover its investment, and the party that is living on the property moves out with losses. When there is money involved the most expensive thing is time. And when you are in foreclosure the last thing you usually can acquire is time. So I shall tell you how this tragic, painful and expensive event in the Rowell's life and the history of the Lyndonville Bank was avoided.

The Rowells owned a farm machinery dealership and also a large amount of land. We had grown up with the Rowells and had been friends and

Busload of supporters came to Rutland on December 16, 1993

neighbors for years. They were having financial troubles with the dealership, and their main creditor, the Chittenden Bank, had started foreclosure. The Rowells tried working with the Chittenden to sell some land to pay their debt, but the bank was not willing to do this. They then went to many other banks to try to arrange refinancing, but got nowhere. No other bank was interested. At the 11th hour, the day before the Bank took possession of the property, the Rowells contacted Noel and he got in touch with me. The Rowells had to come up with approximately $355,000 that day to save their real estate and personal property. We met with the Rowells and their attorney and Noel's attorney and came to an agreement. I would put up the money, and they would hire us to auction their real estate and personal property.

I borrowed the money and the repayment of this loan was my obligation. For putting up the money to pay the Chittenden and assuming the risk, we were to be paid a commission of 15%, plus advertising. We also agreed to guarantee that all creditors would be paid, which was another risk we assumed, hoping the auction would be successful. Everyone, including the attorneys, agreed to this. The auction turned out to be very successful. The government claims I hid Noel's interest in this transaction, but Noel's name was on all flyers and advertising, and the newspaper advertising was throughout the State, and parts of New England. After paying off the foreclosure and other creditors, the Rowells were left with their business, their homes and some land.

Again, everyone was happy except the government. I guess they would have rather seen the Rowells deprived of their business and land. There were four counts on the Rowell transaction, and I was convicted of only one count, and that was concealing Noel's interest.

That all of this could be arranged as an interlocking agreement with all parties, including their attorneys, is not an abuse of position but the actions of myself seeking to assist and work out what is a mutual community and individual financial problem.

Now when "The Whole of the United States of America" got us all to Court they said that it "appeared" that I borrowed the $355,000 from Caledonia Bank, where my brother was President, as some kind of favor. I could have borrowed it from any bank, and besides that I borrowed more money and had the liability.

As auctioneers we **guaranteed** the creditors that they would be made whole. If the items did not bring what was owed for them, then we guaranteed that we would cover the loss. Now that is some deal; we take all the risk, the creditors get paid, the Rowell Brothers salvaged their homes and some land and continued in business. All banks got paid and none of it went to Lyndonville, all lawyers got paid again, and the auctioneers got paid. Profits resulted from this agreement and auction, but it could have as easily been a loss. That is the nature of an auction. We could have lost, and we still would have been bound by the agreement to pay off the creditors with our money.

The deal turned out well for all because of a sound plan that was undertaken at some risk to me and for which I was paid. But stop and consider for a moment what it would have been like if I had not attempted this. Where would the finance companies, creditors, banks, and the Rowell Brothers be if this were not the case? They would have lost the home farm they salvaged, the banks would not have been paid, creditors not have been paid, lawyers would not have been paid probably (you never know for sure) and then, of course, I would not have been charged with this inside dealing. So it seems the only losses were assigned to me, personally. And "the Whole of the United States of America" would have had four less charges to print up and try.

And the only thing special about this unique to me was I got charged for all of this as a crime. Now Noel wasn't charged regarding this nor were any of the banks, credit companies, Ford credit, or suppliers, only me. And when the "Whole of the United States of America" brings Hollis Rowell into my trial, he testifies that Roger did everything he said he would and that if Roger hadn't become involved that three families would have been evicted, and they would also have lost the business. Of the government witnesses, he was among the briefest, helped my case, and I wish that the government had brought more like him. I never got to defend myself, but some of their witnesses gave it a good try.

Turning a "Case" into Help! The Provost Transaction

The Whole of the United States of America said that I created with my brother, Moe Provost and his father, Richard, the Provost Joint Venture. That I arranged for the Lyndonville Bank to sell the property to the Joint Venture for less than the amount owed to the bank, that I did not tell the bank of my interest in this Venture, that I profited $95,000 despite Lyndonville Bank's debt of $185,000, and that the Venture made a profit of $300,000.

Previously I have indicated what the Whole of the United States of America said that "I" had done — that in a twenty count indictment I had essentially dealt myself a helping of other's money from a position of trust, at their expense, and to my profit.

I denied this and told you that. Now I want to take one of the "big" cases and show it to you. You can see it from my perspective and make up your own mind. There are several other reasons for this:

- All of the people involved are still alive, and can speak for themselves.
- All can be contacted and verify what is represented to be the truth or tell you otherwise.
- All of the important documents are available and some are reproduced in the Exhibit section for you to consider.
- All parties to these agreements had their own attorneys present. (One was a former Attorney General of the State of Vermont) and none of the attorneys objected. Eventually not even the government of the United States, in the body of the Department of Agriculture, objected.

And then I want you to think how information is limited in this trial to what the Prosecutor (the Whole of the United States of America) used as part of this case to his benefit, while moving to exclude testimony beneficial to me. Again I remind you there was no defense presented, at the urging of my "Defense Attorney."

Finally I need to define for you some terms used and some consequences they usually imply:

Strict Foreclosure: In Vermont there is a law that allows what is called strict foreclosure. That means if someone has a mortgage on your property and you cannot pay it, they can foreclose on you, and the Court will grant them ownership. They own the whole of the property and can use it as they choose. Any profit, resulting from this use, is the mortgage holders, not yours.

Voluntary Foreclosure: asking the lender to foreclose in an orderly way to reduce the losses in time and money, and reduce those legal fees (more about legal fees later) all of which must be paid eventually. In a voluntary foreclosure you and your wife and children gather your personal things, clean the house and turn the assets over to the bank. The bank resells it and applies the money to your debt, which is reduced and someone else moves in and you move out. But losses to everyone except the lawyers are normal. The bank often loses, and wishes it never happened. The previous owner has lost his credit and wishes it never happened.

Bankruptcy: The event of being judged insolvent, without resources to meet your existing obligations. Now for an individual, the belief is the result will be the debt being extinguished by the bankruptcy court. But for the institution or company being owed the money bankruptcy also has the effect of extinguishing their right to collect. Any money that is available to be paid on the claims of creditors will be distributed among all of them. Often times many creditors receive nothing when bankruptcy is involved.

Dairy Termination Program: This was a federal Department of Agriculture program that was used to reduce milk production and pay dairy farmers to dispose of their milking herds for a five year period. The theory was you paid a farmer some of what he might earn for milking, on the condition he not have any dairy cows on the land he farmed. He could have crops growing, or raise beef cattle, but not a single dairy cow.

Now as I have said this was the most visible and most comprehensible of the indictments against me. And I present it to you now as if I was presenting the story and its cast of characters at your school play. It has drama, guys with hats, charges, and a good outcome for everyone except myself. So let's begin with the introductions.

The Cast in the Provost Matter

T his story has several parties to it; and in order of appearance they are:

- Maurice and Marilee Provost who operated a very large dairy farm. Maurice is nicknamed "Moe." Moe was a good crop farmer as well as operating one of the largest dairy farms in the State. He had been a regular customer of the Lyndonville Savings Bank for years.

- Then there is Moe's father, Richard. He is an elderly and very successful retired farmer, and Richard's brother is "Bucky." All of these Provosts lived in Orleans County and were involved, at one time or other, in agriculture and were doing as well as any one.

- Then there is the "Provost Joint Venture" which is an agreement formed by Richard Provost and Noel Lussier to seek the sale of some lands and be a legal vehicle for making agreements. This agreement was drawn by attorneys Anthony Aiossa for Noel and Bill Davies for Richard Provost. This Joint Venture had nothing to do with the Lyndonville Savings Bank.

- Roger Lussier is President of Lyndonville Savings Bank, the institution that holds a mortgage on the farm and is owed approximately $1,600,000 making it Moe's largest creditor. (Thereby being the institution facing the most to lose in bankruptcy)

- Andrew Field is the attorney for the bank. Jerome Diamond, Vermont's former Attorney General is attorney for Moe, and Carl Lisman is Marylee's attorney.

- Others in the cast are "Agway" also a creditor, David Turner, Vice President of Lyndonville Saving Bank, Ursula Johnson, of the local ASCS (Agricultural Stabilization Conservation Service) office, John McLaughry, who got the money released by the government, and several FDIC examiners during 1988.

There are other factors at play; the uncontrolled price of milk, which was falling, rising fuel prices, and high interest rates. The milk price had the most effect.

The last note. When this case was brought into my trial, the background, the circumstances, and the explanations that could have been offered were excluded from the jury. So here, probably for the first time, is the way it actually went. I will say so, the documents say so, and Moe himself will say so.

The indictments were brought in 1993, long after the events happened, as they occurred mostly from 1985 until 1988. And the intention that motivated all of these activities was to get everyone paid instead of taking a loss, and for Moe to be able to retain his family farm. It took a lot of work that never should have been necessary, and had the ASCS State Administrator not been worried about the lack of work in his office and its being closed, there never would have been a problem.

If we had not undertaken to recover the potential losses, all creditors would have gone unpaid, the farms would be sold at auction, the farmers would be out of business, and the examiners who encouraged us to take the loss and move on would have been pleased, I guess. Lyndonville's Board of Directors authorized me to attempt to find a solution, and I did. And as a result of all of these efforts everyone did get paid, the government finally honored its commitment, but never explained its delinquency in payment, and the family farm was retained. Now, later in another matter, the bank and the Whole of the United States of America accuse me of losing $426,000, but in this matter they did not seem to be concerned that we would lose $1,600,000 plus legal fees, and have a possible repayment of over a million dollars already paid from the termination program, of which Lyndonville was now "Moe's" Trustee. So it was not a surprise that at trial, the Whole of the United States of America would not allow this to be presented or discussed by its own witnesses.

Here we go again. In 1985-86 milk prices are falling, but not the cost of producing milk. Cows eat and need tending even if their product is not bringing back its cost. For a large farmer like "Moe" the existing herd of 2000 is costing daily more than they can produce. He and his wife decided to offer their herd to the Dairy Termination Program, a whole herd buyout program. Now to do this Moe must agree to slaughter or sell out of country the cows he has, and he must keep the land he was using free of replacement female bovine animals for 5 years. Secondly, Moe must offer a bid to the government for a price he will accept if they choose to accept his offer. Moe calculated how much he needed to pay off his creditors, checked with those in the industry regarding a bid price range, and because he needed to be accepted in order to avoid continued losses, he bid low, $9.89 a hundredweight. He was accepted for his low bid of $9.89 among a range of bids from his to $22.00 per hundredweight. That suggests he could have doubled the amount received, or that he "contributed" over a million dollars to his own government by his generous offer. He was accepted, the largest herd in the buyout program in Vermont.

Now Moe had numerous creditors. He came to me and asked if we could package his debt so everyone could be paid out of the "buyout proceeds" and that money would be marked for that purpose. Moe then could raise crops and sell some of his land for retail, to support himself, and his family, while the proceeds from the herd buy-out paid his creditors.

All parties agreed to establish a Trust Agreement[1], and since the Lyndonville Bank was the largest creditor, the bank was appointed Trustee. The parties to this agreement would be paid from the dairy buyout funds over the next five years. The creditors and approximate amounts due them were identified and the Trust account began receiving its funds; $1,249,177.18 was received in 1986, and was disbursed according to the Trust Agreement and Letter of Intent[2]. We went about our normal business until 1987 when the next payment of $78,073.57 was due but did not arrive.

As it turned out the ASCS had come to believe that Moe was not complying with the terms of his agreement with them, and they began the first of three investigations. When asked why the money had not arrived, Ursula Johnson of the Newport ASCS told me it was a "political" matter; and that the local board *had* voted to approve the payment. I had not known until then that cows had politics? That was a surprise, that a political matter among cows had brought this plan to help Moe and save his creditors large losses was being held up by cow politics. No, it was Washington politics, she explained. They, the local board, had voted to pay.

Now the consequences begin. (Remember that rhyme for lack of a nail a shoe is lost, for lack of a shoe a horse is lost, for lack of a horse a battle is lost…?)

For lack of an earned payment from the U.S. government, that they had agreed to make for five years, (the cows now already through the slaughter houses and could not be consulted) the mortgage becomes due, the creditors are asking about payments, and Moe's attorney is suggesting to Moe that he seek bankruptcy. And bankruptcy would have saved no one anything. (Would I be charged with that loss as well Mr. the Whole of the United States of America?)

It was at this time that Moe went to see his attorney and his attorney took him to a bankruptcy attorney. The bankruptcy attorney told Moe that he would need to come up with $100,000 up front. Moe told him he didn't have that amount on hand and the bankruptcy attorney told him to go out and sell whatever he could, even mortgaged property if he had to. Moe told him if he had the $100,000 he would use it to pay his creditors. At this time the bank had no choice but to start foreclosure proceedings. The bank entered into discussions with Moe, his wife and their attorneys about the foreclosure. With the possibility of bankruptcy in the background, the bank had to tread lightly with Moe and their attorneys. An agreement was reached for a quick foreclosure, but only after the bank agreed that Moe's father could buy the property back, if no one redeemed in the foreclosure, by paying the bank all of their expenses, including lawyer fees, real estate taxes, and costs that were not anticipated at that time, such as leases on land in the DTP program, the Agway settlement etc. Moe and Richard agreed to hold the bank harmless if the balance of the DTP checks (approximately $300,000) did not come in. The Bank also agreed to do what it could to try and get the balance of the DTP checks. Moe's father, Richard, and Richard's brother were going to buy the property back, but as the time grew near to purchase the property, Richard's brother got cold feet. Richard did not want to take on this large obligation by himself, so he and Moe got in touch with Noel.

Richard and Noel formed the Joint Venture (of which I am falsely accused of being a third member according to the Singer Aiossa) and then just before the sale of the land to Richard, Noel became concerned about his investment position as he did not want to tie his funds up for a long period. To keep the deal from failing, I loaned Noel $100,000 of my own money. Richard then purchased the land and Noel co-signed the note. An appraisal of the property was done, except for the Canadian property, and the appraiser took into account the restriction placed upon the land by the DTP, realizing that no cows could be there for five years. The land appraised for $973,000[3] as of August 11, 1988. Bored yet, it is simply that dry.

The Lyndonville Bank authorized a loan of $800,000, as part of the purchase price of $994,619.20. The loan was co-signed by Noel Lussier. *Then the cows had their political meeting in Washington,* the overdue money was finally paid (minus a $5,000 fine for one cow that could not be accounted for) and, upon receipt of the balance of those checks, the balance of the bank loans was paid to Lyndonville, and the remainder of the DTP checks was given to the Provosts as per the Agreement.

The Provost Joint Venture was extremely fortunate in finding a purchaser for two of the farms. That purchaser wanted to raise beef...a perfect match. Another parcel was sold for non-dairy use. So it all worked out. Richard and Noel made a profit in selling the farms, and Noel repaid his debt to me personally.

Out of all of this, the herd had been sold, and then unpaid for (temporarily) by the government of the U.S. in what turns out was an unexplained and unjustified suspension of the contract. The United States Attorney General was given a review of the whole thing and saw no reason to charge Moe with anything. All of the creditors listed in the Agreement were satisfied. The anticipated losses of $1,600,000 plus interest, lawyers, etc., were recovered.

The FDIC, expecting a loss, praised us with delight. I was satisfied the bank got paid, the creditors got paid, my loan was paid, and the Provosts kept their home and part of the land and buildings.

I think an important part to remember, in this whole affair, is that I had verbal authority from the Board of Directors at all times, while these negotiations were going on, and this verbal authority was verified when the Board of Directors signed an affidavit[4] that they had verbally given me this authority.

But none of this needed to happen and Moe was never given any explanation for why he was put through all of this. The person in the Burlington ASCS office, believed to have been responsible for such a poor federal performance, is no longer with them.

And I got indicted. Now if that isn't the American way, what is? The same government that could not explain its own actions now required me to explain mine.

Of course, there was more. Agway claimed it should have been ahead of everyone else as a creditor; as if that explained why they refused to participate in the creditor's plan. They had the same opportunity to buy out and redeem their position as anyone else. There were also disputes about debts to Moe's father, which had been promised to be repaid. And when it was all over Moe lost his farm in "quick" foreclosure, and the bank being fully paid sold it to his father. Fred Watson of the FDIC had said we would never recover the bank's money, and to write it off. I said we would recover the money and to "give me six month before we must write off the loss," and we did recover the funds. And then they said we were diverting money from his now divorcing wife. But again, a foreclosure is the loss of what you have, not the possibility of maybe eventually getting held up DTP funds. If the actions I have described had not been taken creditors would have lost out, lawyers be unpaid, banks be unpaid, farms still sold off with no possibility of buyback, and another family farm out of business. So I tried.[5]

Then there is ARDI (Applied Research & Development, Inc.), a Company of which I was the sole stockholder. Previously, it had been purchased from Space Research Corporation, and had been selling electronic business instruments. After that period it was simply my everyday business corporation, lawful, visible, and honest. But the Whole of The United States said that as the sole owner of the stock, I had concealed information from myself. Maybe I should have had Alzheimer's!

[1] See Exhibits pages 5-10 for Trust Agreement

[2] See Exhibits pages 11-14 for Letter of Intent

[3] See Exhibits page 15 for appraisal

[4] See Exhibits page 16 for Board affidavit

[5] See Exhibits pages 212-213 for Article on the Provost deal

The ARDI Loan

A RDI Borrowed $400,000 from Caledonia Bank and pledged 1000 shares of LBS stock worth over $500,000 to be used to pay for a farm. I sold the house and 10 acres of that farm before I had to pay for the farm so I didn't need all of the money I borrowed. After a few weeks I used some of the money from the loan to pay for the stocks that I had previously bought from Mr. & Mrs. Phil Bovee.(Phil was a former Director of the Lyndonville Savings Bank.) I had bought them some time before this but hadn't yet paid for them entirely. I did not have to pay for them at this time but Phil was seriously ill, and I wanted to pay him in case anything happened to him.

He was not charging me interest so it would have been to my advantage not to pay him at this time, rather than using loan proceeds that I was paying interest on. It was a little over a month after the loan before we made the first payment on the stock, and two months from the date of the loan when we paid the balance of the stock purchase. Brian Stirewalt from the federal Office of the Comptroller of the Currency was asked during my trial if there was any procedure for a change of mind of the borrower after the funds are borrowed, and he said none that he was aware of. The bank was paid in full plus interest. The intent of the questionnaire (Reg. U form) was to provide information regarding stocks purchased on margin, and was asked of persons using loan proceeds to purchase stocks or for loans secured by stock.

The charge against me was that I concealed the use of the funds on the Reg U form. I signed that form in blank, undated, and it was completed later by Robert Platka, the CEO of Caledonia Bank. Now he was not charged for this, and even when it was brought to Court the copy provided by the government was still undated.

So that is the summary of all of those pages and boxes and years.

- Adding to my defense, not simply me saying "not so" would have been the testimony of David Turner selected by the government, believing he supported their case, to say he would not have said what Van de Graaf (the Whole of the United States of America) said he would have said. "The Whole of the United States of America" said he was an essential witness for them, and they later chose to avoid him, going ahead on the Provost deal without him. Later, after his recovery from a disabling heart attack he swears an affidavit saying what he said. That is in the document section with the others who would contradict the "Whole of the United States of America".

(I keep using that phrase for a reason that reveals itself in a later motion in which I am upheld as "correct" when this mess gets to where it belongs. Maybe for a while I will make it one of those letter words: The Whole of the United States of America, all 280 some million of them, including my wife and children and grandchildren, will be identified as TWOTUSA.)

There was Attorney Andy Field waiting to testify, who later signed two affidavits[1]. Then there was the testimony of my brother Noel. He was available and was waiting to testify that the "cooperating witness was wrong" in the information he passed to the FBI, contrary to what they had been told by him. Noel would have said I had no knowledge of Noel's activities that had been attributed to me of the other matters; that I did not know about the Aiossa deal in advance; that he had set those events into motion without my knowledge and in disagreement with what that "cooperating witness" said that I said. The "Whole of the United States of America" had charged Doug Jolly and Noel Lussier and Charlie Kelton with crimes and had received their participation in the different investigations and trials, and had told the defense attorneys they would be used as witnesses against those clients, and me. And they did use Kelton and Jolly, but not Noel. In exchange for "considerations" in cooperating their millions and millions of dollars of crimes they admitted to; Charlie and Doug Jolly admitting to fleecing (the real USA) of over $100 MILLION that they admit to (plus were overlooked to a significant extent). The rest of us were pursued.

When it came to my trial Noel was not called. I assume "the Whole of the United States of America" knew he would not lie against me but would admit to his "deal" with "the Whole of the United States of America." That his testimony would conflict with the other "cooperating witness" Doug Jolly, who would admit, invent and create testimony that could have been shown to be untrue, and allowed to avoid significant consequences on his.

And, avoiding the absolute protection of the United States Constitution against self-incrimination, I would have taken the stand and been available for everyone to examine, and to explain and document what I affirmed. And "Mister Man," didn't I want to do so. But my "learned counsel" said, "No! Roger, they haven't proved a thing. We have them beat. Let it rest." A person charged in a Federal Court for 20 supposed crimes, a person charged who is a farmer-banker-auctioneer not familiar with the government's methods of overcharging in hopes of sticking you with something, a person facing a ruined lifetime of reputation, prison and possibly never returning home may feel like fighting with his attorney, may believe him wrong, but usually would accept his advice.

Usually you have evidence that the lawyer is prepared, (he admits in court he is not) has no conflict of interest, (deals made to exclude some of them, and some undiscovered until later) understands in detail the governments case, has filed motions for discovery, and has read and discussed with his client detailed refutation of the claims against the client. And he did not! Having a "big deal reputation" as a lawyer may be the same as having a "big deal reputation" as an auctioneer, or a banker. But in my work I worked for the outcomes, earned the fees, and produced the service. This lawyer…well, he looks good on television.

I had expected to now begin to reply in detail and with evidence to every claim against me, to provide the waiting witnesses, and take the stand myself. That is what I thought we were going to do. But the "Defense" rested. It rested before it pulled its load. Horses are normally rested after dragging a wagon up the hill, not usually before they leave the barn after a long night's sleep.

The "Defense" rested and this defendant then was found guilty. The outcome of all of this was actually foreshadowed in conversations with him the evening before, in conflicts of interest statements and sidebars, and of attorney conflict of interests evidence unrevealed until 2003. In conversations reported by another defendant regarding the strategy of "innocence" which he attributed to counsel saying, "You can't beat the Feds, you must plead to something, you can't win," he was advised. I was told we won, when we lost by default. If his views regarding beating the "Feds" had been a known attitude to me, I would never have hired that lawyer.

Earlier I was saying about indictments, that they provide the "warehouse" where the deals are made and never revealed. Now it may be that you can't beat the Whole of the United States of America, but that is no excuse for not presenting a defense. Who of my readers, anyone who has ever known me or dealt with me, would expect me to not defend myself and my family and this bank and community and country from something I believed was wrong? I never saw the charges coming, and when they came I was shocked. But I did not flee, stop business, close up shop, and run to Mexico.

I told my children and my wife what I knew, accepted the offer of an attorney (who had known I was to be charged and did not tell me) to represent me, and got ready for trial.

I did all of that again after my conviction, and did it again with a case not yet discussed, the Lyndonville Bank Theft case. And when I finally got to a jury, in the malpractice case, and could speak for myself, I was believed, even though I was called everything the lawyer could insert before lunch break, and still won.

Me agree to a deal? Never! I was offered a "deal" to avoid prison, even have my imprisonment reduced to house arrest if I agreed to work for them by an FBI agent. I was asked to agree to plead guilty when I knew I wasn't, not having cost anyone a dime, not losing anyone money, and making the bank 270 fold returns in its stock.

Run, lie, and quit! Well, I haven't, didn't and won't!

But using the "no defense, I'm resting method," I was convicted. I appealed (which is limited to the trial record and therefore containing no defense presented) and finally went to prison at age 65, perhaps to die there — certainly in danger of death, illness, separation from loved ones, and finding myself in the strangest world I have ever known.

Before this time the only run-ins I had with the law were for speeding tickets. I had many thousands of auctions in NY, NH, Mass. and Vermont and was never sued because of any of these auctions.

[1] See Exhibits pages 17-23 for Field's affidavits

The Criminal Trial

Think of a trial as a kind of an orchestrated "special town meeting." Everyone is invited to a place of honor to meet and see the presentation of this drama presented by the government. The different parts are announced and, after tryouts, the roles are assigned and the "meeting" takes place as a kind of presentation. Parts have been rehearsed by some of the potential actors (those cooperating witnesses again). The Conductor (Judge Billings) will lead the presentation throughout its script, and the different speeches and tunes for the orchestra will be announced, some parts sung and perhaps applauded. It begins with an opening, like in church, and a closing, like a movie. It has the features of drama, emotional conflict, and "right and wrong" polarization of the structure. A stack of "black and white hats" to be worn by the different actors are available for when they speak. A jury that is sitting like the choir tries to make up its mind about the quality of the contest and determine "thumbs up or down" in its verdict. Then the Conductor brings it to a conclusion with thanks to all parties for their citizenship assistance. Most go home and listen to the rebroadcast of the proceedings on TV and conclude it was a necessary effort and the Republic is safer now. Unless you lose!

Now I have already written that the actual "trial" of the alleged events is somewhat an event of the surviving results of all of the negotiations among parties that, prior to the trial, the lawyers, witnesses and evidence makers work out by a process of exchanges and replies. Those summaries for both sides reduce 80,000 pages of material to the brief pages. But is it accurate? The trial itself was another series of unexplained mistakes, and the 19 days of it are accounted for in:

- The Unprepared, Diverted, and Inattentive Defense
- The Use of Corrupted Testimony that was unchallenged
- The failure to call available rebuttal witnesses

So, come now to the entertainment prepared for all of us: The Whole of the United States vs. me!

My defense was unprepared, and stayed that way!

I had assumed the time and months between the indictments and trial would be filled with meetings with my attorney, and reading the "discovery" from the government regarding the evidence of their claims and its examination. I had expected this attorney to file pre-trial motions that would question the basis of the trial, its pretrial publicity, the location of the trial, and move to dismiss some of the charges or to consolidate them. There were several related trials being scheduled, and I had expected them in order of indictment, placing mine later so we could see what all of this was about. That did not happen. My attorney, in consultation with the court, sought "immediate" trial.

Usually a client's lawyer is presented the opposition's case in a process called "discovery," the ability to know in advance the details of what I must be able to defend myself against. And to my surprise I was spared all of the normal necessary preparation. Oct 14th – I received the witness list against me from Langrock, Nov 1st – to Rutland to conflict of interest hearing, Nov 23rd – interviews for character witnesses, Nov. 29th – pick jury, and Dec 1st – it began. Now usually it is necessary for the Court to wait until the findings of the jury to realize the trial verdict. In this, knowing what I have discovered, I can now say that this case never went to trial; trial was abandoned and the only response of the defense attorney to the charges was to call my "character witnesses" to say that I had been what I believed I was: decent, honest, and a helper of others.

The whole of the United States of America would say that Roger knew that a loan would benefit a failed attorney, named Aiossa. This same witness, together with another "cooperating witness," would name Roger as a conspirator against his own bank. These persons, who would benefit from saying what they were saying, were brought by the government to testify against me, both swearing to the lie to benefit their own agreed to guilty plea. The government, with a straight face, believes it can tell a man that he should say such and such, remind him that he has already pled guilty to a crime, and that his treatment will be conditioned upon how he performs in court and under oath. (Perjury doesn't seem to be a measurable count.) And this is supposed to be a believable testimony because the government has said he said he would tell the truth this time in order to benefit from his agreement. Like asking the cat with canary feathers protruding from its mouth to swear it was the mouse that ate the bird.

Vol. 1 page 10, noted later in the charge to the jury the judge said, "You should consider the testimony of such witnesses with great caution, they may have had reason to make up stories or exaggerate what others did in order to strike a good bargain with the government in their own cases..."

As is becoming a pattern, my attorney starts the defense with an apology, "I'm going to be going on for a while. It might be worthwhile to take a 5 minute break in all fairness." Then to my surprise, I learned for the first time that the government had been concerned about my business for over five years. Usually I would have expected to learn this beforehand. To my utter surprise my defense attorney told the jury that "the facts in this case for the most part are not in dispute."(Opening Vol. I page 33) The facts were in absolute dispute, but the damage was done.

Unprepared, uncomprehending of the opposition, unlearned about a case he had ignored while being in other cases throughout October and November, (Verified practice docket of Peter Langrock, cases active in 1993, Clerk of Courts, Rutland, Vermont) he rambled on about my character. My character had not been indicted as far as I knew. My actions and activities had been challenged and misrepresented. A reply to that was expected. It didn't happen. If I hadn't paid him I would have begun to wonder which side he was on. But he did agree that it was not a crime to borrow money, or not disclose, and that all of the charges against me required "intent to defraud or deceive." I hadn't defrauded nor deceived anyone so we went on and on for 20 unending days.

In fact during the earliest part of the trial, when he constantly asked the government about presented documents being entered into evidence, his un-preparedness is so blatant that the prosecuting attorney felt it necessary to announce to the judge (Vol. I-101), "Your Honor, just for the record, Mr. Langrock had access to these documents for the last several months. We didn't provide copies today because they are voluminous, but he has had access to them...." This was after so many references to not having seen the material that even the Whole of the United States of America got concerned that the jury would wonder if the government had surprised the defense. Can you imagine the impact of this faltering lurching around behavior? The effect it must have had upon them. On one hand, "The Whole of the United States of America" in orderly, prepared documents, with the apparent authority of the FDIC and FBI and clear exhibits were waiting, used and explained. Attackable conclusions were drawn for the jury. The "Defense" saying it had not known the government's case (in his opening statement Vol. I page 101 had not seen the documents, and then being reminded by the "Whole of the United States of America" that he had received all of them two months before the trial.

Already, you see the "handwriting upon the wall"...and it was not writing,

"Have a Happy Day"!

Of course it is possible to fault an attorney to avoid attention to my own plight. I have considered that, but the reading of the record clearly requires me to conclude otherwise. From the undisclosed and continuing conflicts of interest, to the time spent without preparation, to the evenings spent in dining and drinks before trial, my case was simply begun in a state of "ad lib…" and it was catch up ball at best …and we never did. He was in all components of trial preparation, unprepared.

As a consequence of that alone, it would have been enough for my conviction, and was also the direct cause of an additional nine trials (Two magistrate hearings, four appeals, two bank suits, one trial). It continued throughout the trial to the "summary" for the jury; impromptu, wandering, disconcerted…unbelieved.

And later when I suggested that I could have better defended myself pro se, he commented, "You wouldn't have done any worse."

And then there was the use of corrupted testimony; or

"The Trio Sings

"The Trio Sings"
A musical rendition by Jolly, Aiossa, and Kelton

Trials are perceived as a search for the truth which is revealed by a struggle among "facts and claims" before a jury which decides the outcome, subject to the instructed law as stated by the Judge. And great care is visibly taken to be sure everyone present is convinced that the information presented is itself credible. Care is demonstrated in how documents are created, if signatures were witnessed, if the person speaking was the one spoken to or is it "just" hearsay. That "hearsay" means unverified opinion as overheard in the beauty parlor. You see documents being labeled, named and questioned. Who wrote it? Where was it found? Is it authentic? You have persons asked to repeat what they heard, have them read what they said previously to see if their recall changed (as did some important witnesses in this case), and then everything and everyone is "sworn to tell the truth, the whole truth, and nothing but the truth, so help you God." That is how it is believed to go. But there are some worrisome problems.

What if they don't do so, can't do so, or have agreed for some other considerations to change role from witnesses to fact, to players of parts? What if they have a greater incentive to lie than is apparent to the jury? What if believing in God is against their religion? What if the need to please an unseen evaluator is greater than the fear of those at trial? Well then, you can return to my trial and listen to the singing of the guest "trio," Aiossa, Jolly and Kelton.

Their chosen song is, "Roger was there when we did not see him. We know it was him because someone said so who also did not see him, and our saying this will convict him but let us go free "la-la-la." This rendition may be sung to any circumstance, the benefit is in the singing and if you have tried hard to produce it you will get the reward, which is time off your own charges or case, the guilt to which you have already admitted in a signed "blank check" so to speak, with the Prosecutor's office. Now I would agree that the threat of additional prison, or its remission, is a great attention getter and motivator. But so far there is no evidence that such an arrangement would require you to tell the truth. Your usefulness is tied to what it is you will testify to. That is determined, in advance, by conversations with the person who has two powers over you, to punish and reward, and that person is the sole judge of your conduct. He has indicated what the passing answer, to the questions he has asked or is going to ask, is expected to be or you would not be necessary. This part of the rehearsal for singing is out of the sight of the jury, or anyone except the prosecution. You are not brought to court, if you are one of these singers, to tell the Court what *you* have done or how that may have contributed to something or someone else's problems. You are hired, so to speak, to sing a song as a witness to a specific something, your Song. Even the judge warns against these paid singers. Yet they are dragged out of the dark and brought into court as if they had been orphaned and virtue was their newly found father. Cheerfully they identify with the Prosecutor's solemn announcement that they have pleaded guilty to something, and if they don't perform well they will yet be punished.

Having heard this introductory music, they announce they are in the pay of the prosecution, that it will not go well with them if they don't perform well, and then they sing. Following their song they disappear from the record of the trial and the benefit and motive and compensation for their services is a separate and undisclosed matter as far as this trial is concerned. Perhaps their crimes are worse than those being currently tried, maybe (oh no) their losses and damages run into millions of dollars and the current trial is about none…it doesn't matter. It is their song and not justice that is the subject of their appearance.

So when the house is quiet, and the bailiff is done swearing them in, they sing.

Aiossa, the lying, deceiving, back-stabbing, false record-creating failed-attorney (as he so happily agreed) sings first.

But why? First, for this trial to work, someone needs to connect me with something that didn't happen. If someone lying says it is so, there is no "certainty" of proof. It is, "He said, she said." But if two or three persons have agreed to lie, then the "proof," without examination, is visibly established. And someone is placed in a spot where they were not, seemingly to agree to something they did not, and it is then presented to the others as if it was true…and the jury would accept it because it was not cross examined or exposed for the lie it was. Thus, the source of the word for the singer's songs: they said I was there so I was there even if I was not…lalala!

For some time there had been other bank scandals in the Northeast Kingdom, and they had several things in common:

- They were small banks that went bust,
- One of them had, as a president or major officer, the eventual president of the Lyndonville Savings Bank, Charlie Bucknam
- They also involved my brother Noel and Doug Gilmour, his partner, and they had loans that were legally involving the Lyndonville Savings Bank.
- And the singers were related to those other banks, and they had pled guilty to banking crimes.

And to enmesh the Lyndonville Bank and myself in what was presented as a conspiracy they needed to link my being present in meetings where "illegal deals" were hatched. To do this they relied upon lies of their own making, and of constructing agreements and partnerships out of other person's statements that implied a meaning that was not a fact. Now that is a song...lalala. But without cross-examination or contradictory evidence, which was available to be presented, it was believed because the liars said they were telling the truth, having admitted they were liars. What a strange spectacle!

Who is this Singer named Aiossa? First he was a lawyer admitted to the "bar" after reading it for several years. He moved to Hardwick and among his many new acquaintances and friendships was Noel Lussier, then President of the Caledonia National Bank. Aiossa described in his "grand jury" testimony and in my trial testimony his rather extended history of writing legal documents, entering into "nominee" loans on behalf of others, of making false entries in documents that were to be relied upon at the bank and among his many business interests. He also indicates he created his own fictitious entries, filled in amounts and provided "legal" documents for many businesses from which he personally benefited.

Now he and others had been creating fictitious entries in their activities for some time. And he prepared the joint venture documents involving Noel Lussier and Richard Provost. This undertaking was described earlier in the government's charges; and is misrepresented by The Whole of The United States of America to be an example of a conspiracy involving myself, who in fact knew nothing about it (Trial Record Vol. 1, pg. 174). Van De Graaf is quoted, "And I'm going to have preponderance of the evidence, proof that there was a conspiracy between Noel Lussier and Roger Lussier...that Roger Lussier and Noel Lussier were involved in this transaction together and that that is a conspiracy. Of course, the conspiracy doesn't have to be charged..." says The Whole of. To which the defense points out and my attorney asks, "As I understand it, a conspiracy has to be a factual arrangement of some sort to accomplish an inappropriate purpose...we don't think there's any basis for it." The Whole of the United States of America had this creator of false documents (as he admitted) and of false entries (which he admitted) and submitting formal documents that misled the examiners of his banking activities (which he admitted) now come forward and say that on the basis of his opinions and interpretations, and upon the hearsay of his admittedly uncertain recollection of a conversation with Noel, that he believed I was joined in with those he had known to be members. What a reach. And when confronted with the request for evidence the Whole of the United States of America simply says..."Your Honor, he may not remember the exact words. People can testify about the substance of a conversation." (vol. 1 page 177) Yes, but what if they lie and what if it didn't happen at all.

So he is allowed to answer, "I don't remember the exact wording of it, but it was that Roger was in the deal as a partner. That was the substance of it." This from the attorney who wrote the partnership agreement to which he was referring, and for which there was no evidence or witness to the claims he offered. In spite of the fact that Noel Lussier was available to the Whole of the United States of America as a witness, and could have been brought to court on their behalf. (They did bring his son, to also provide hearsay statements. Why not Noel?)

Then it gets hot! My attorney says, "…we have reason to believe that the government does not intend to call Noel Lussier *because he will not testify to having made the statement.* He will also testify – he has testified truthfully about this matter[1], that there was no such contract; that the government is trying to do away with our rights of confrontation – I think there is something more than that…I think the conduct of the government in trying to deal with the situation, where there're trying to – presentation of the situation when *they have substantial evidence to show that this is not the fact.*

> THE COURT: *You mean you're doubting what the Unites States attorney is saying?*
>
> Mr. Langrock: *I am doubting that the Unites States – the United States knows that Noel Lussier would not testify that there was a contract.*

(That is lawyer talk for "He's lying!")

They discuss that if the government had really believed that he would say such a thing they would have had him come and do so. But that knowing he would not, and that it had not happened, they would avoid bringing it into evidence in an appropriate presentation, and that this method of attacking me, using the absence of evidence as its own claim, that I must therefore have hidden my role is exactly what this was about. That is, my attorney was pointing out that The Whole of the United States of America was treating the role of evidence in this trial in exactly the same manner they had attributed to my own business conduct. He says (vol. 1- page 176), 'What they are trying to do is use a hearsay statement to put us in a position for which there was no evidence, and which could have been demonstrated to be untrue if they produced the supposed maker of that statement as a witness.' Instead, it becomes necessary for the imaginary conversation to be affirmed by a lying failed attorney as the source of the claim that then is used to link me into a partnership I was not a member of. They, in the absence of any evidence, call it a conspiracy.

Do you see the difficulty with the logic? You take an apparently active criminal that admits to self-interest and then give him the opportunity to involve others in his scheme, pretending it is "their" scheme, and reporting via his microphone his conclusion about them. Then in connecting false statements among two persons given immunity, you point to a connection with some other person not involved in the "cooperating witness conspiracy," and they are then "connected." And so it was with me.

---

[1] See Exhibits pages 24-26 for memo from Mitch Pearl (Langrock Associate) on what Noel would have testified to.

A CROOK DISCOVERS VIRTUE

Douglas Jolly emerges in this story as a person willing to sell anyone or do anything requested of him by the Whole of the United States of America in a desperate attempt to avoid prosecution for his actions in New York. He had been running what became seen as a Ponzi scheme and operating several corporations which promised investors extreme returns on their investments in agricultural related services or in tax sheltered cattle leasing.

He had several different attractions, including a firm called Microtech. And using this company, he indicated, could provide a computer supported farm management system that would allow farmers to compete and document their information so that all management decisions would become rational and profitable. He raised millions, and he defrauded persons of those millions. When he learned that his investors and their underwriter, James Good, were beginning to look into his operations and that the District Attorney in New York had secured a search warrant for Microtech records, he immediately sought the services of a criminal attorney. This well-experienced attorney "introduced" him to the services of the Whole of the United States of America, Assistant U.S. Attorney Van de Graaf, and **within three days** acquired an agreement of "immunity" from prosecution for his crimes in New York, in return for his services as a "cooperating witness" which meant doing anything his master asked.

He created schemes in which he attempted to invite "targets" to incriminate themselves. He scheduled meetings and was fitted with a wire recording or transmission system relaying the communications to the listening FBI agent. He would also admit to placing phone calls to persons they were interested in and, without that person knowing the call was being overheard, attempt to get them to incriminate themselves or admit to something they might have said. And since he knew his performance was being reviewed for value to the Whole of the United States of America, he would tell persons what he understood them to have been doing and reporting to his listener (usually John W. Hersh, of the FBI) what he knew they were attempting to avoid saying, so he said it for them. These "little soap operas" were written and recorded by the FBI, from the wire of Jolly and written up in a document called a "302." This would then become a form of evidence, with the statement or supposedly derived information being available to the prosecutor for use in his claims to crimes.

So it is not surprising that such a "Singer" was used by the Whole of the United States of America, but did they get their money's worth. The setting is strange. A man fleeing prosecution in New York approaches the Federal Prosecutor in Vermont and asks for protection in exchange for his perceived value to The Whole of the United States of America in investigating what was believed to be massive fraud in Vermont. In explaining to some of the people in New York, James and Mary Good, and some of their investors in the New York Teachers' Association, the prosecutor there explained to them it was necessary for the good of an important investigation in Vermont to overlook Jolly's crimes in New York. After all, what are *many millions* in New York State in the pursuit of an illegal $426,204.67 restitution in Vermont? So Jolly, within three days, is given broad and apparently blanket immunity for his many crimes if he will pose as a "fellow conspirator" with the group of individuals under investigation in Vermont. He is to create strategies to attract investors in his own scam in Florida. He is to make phone calls and make offers, and make appointments from the FBI office, get wired and participate in meetings. They are usually initiated by him, and then he plays the part or makes the connections, or interprets or places into the conversations statements that will incriminate.

Aiossa and Jolly were in business by fraud, creating false documents and misrepresenting positions and values in companies and investors to their clients. Then to get them out of their box they create lies about each other and me, and swear it to be true. After all, would liars lie? They said, "Roger said" something that no paper or document said. They did this in the presence of many documents saying the opposite. They say I was connected with ventures in which I was never a part. The government had an available witness who was among the other named parties available to them and named by their own "cooperating witnesses," but the government excludes that witness from my trials. They admit the testimony of Aiossa and Jolly, who simply declared what they said and had invented to be true, and the government refused to bring the other named person who would have contradicted their agreed-upon story.

Initially, and as it turns out erroneously, Jolly is perceived by the prosecutor in Vermont as significant and very important to his ability to investigate and produce incriminating evidence in the investigations under way in Vermont. Then that prosecutor begins to discover that Jolly himself actually "knows" very little, but has succeeded in striking a good deal for himself. The Acting U.S. Attorney in Vermont becomes embarrassed about his hasty deal, and finds it difficult to explain to the New York victims of Jolly's scams what he is doing for The Whole of the United States of America that is worth the cost.

So, failing to bring information, Jolly becomes a very busy meeting organizer and telephone recorder. He creates elaborate strategies for entrapment. He produces conversations pretending to be the gateway to South American drug money, all activities of a criminal nature if they were not being conducted with the permission of the Whole of the United States of America. Now if you do this it is a crime (lying to them as in Martha Stewart). When they do it then it is in the pursuit of Justice (pursuit: Does that mean justice is fleeing?).

And so it went for months with various victims gathered or enrolled to expand this evidence building scheme. It goes on for several years, with this "cooperating witness" creating stories or encounters, and warding off probes from New York by wrapping himself up in his patriotic duty to inform, and hoping all will be well.

He says he was told by the available actual witness who was excluded from the trial that I knew Aiossa was on a loan he should not have been. The attorney who held that document in his files said I had never seen it, the bank had never seen it, the Directors had never seen it. It had been taken from his files and planted later. And being available to testify he was not asked. He was also not called to say the truth. So the Tag Team of liars, Aiossa and Jolly, say, "he said such and such," and were not contradicted. They could have been...but the defense was resting, and they were not challenged. So in false testimony Aiossa says I knew about loans I did not. And by their testimony an innocent man is connected to events that others have already admitted as being criminal.

I had not known and would not admit and that becomes the bigger "crime." Insisting on innocence in the presence of false testimony will cost me dearly, and if the Whole of the United States were to have its way...cost us all. And the poor New York prosecutor is left holding his empty explanation of why this "small fish" (who turned out to have defrauded about $8 million) was so valuable. And there was no other evidence to connect their story to reality. None! And while the defense was "resting" the Whole of the United States of America was painting a picture of the efficiency of the FBI, the gathering of information and the implications you could draw from the sworn testimony of these two witnesses to ensnare me in their imaginations. And during the "rest period" at my trial that is what happened.

Aiossa said I knew he was the beneficiary of a loan he had made with the First National Bank of Vermont. That was not true. No document in our bank, or known to us would demonstrate that. We had witnesses that would contradict his testimony and documents to present in evidence that would contradict his testimony. They were not called. Jolly backed up Aiossa's testimony that I knew the payout was for Aiossa's benefit. These two singers performed in front of the jury, the Conductor of the song applauded, and I was harmed by their agreed upon lies. Even their testimony was rehearsed.

Terrie Paul, loan officer for the bank, testified that there was no document in the file from the original closing that showed the payout was for Aiossa's benefit. Ashley Jewell, the bank's auditor, also testified that he never saw any document showing that it was for Aiossa's benefit, and both Paul and Jewell testified that they knew the bank could have no business with Aiossa, and so would have been surprised to see that on Jolly's loan. FDIC examiner, Charles Paquin, testified that he showed a closing statement to the Board of Directors, which showed Aiossa's name, but the full Board signed an affidavit[1] that they had never seen the document, until 1994. It is still unknown how the document was put into the file.

[1] See Exhibits page 27 for Board affidavit

The Physical Journey of the Prisoner

With no defense presented what would you expect? The government presents its case, the jury had been given a jumbled box of jigsaw pieces, and everyone now sits down and is ready for the real business at hand. Andy Field, the long time legal associate of the bank is there and a willing witness, ready for engagement. The participants in the moneymaking loans are ready. The FBI agent that has been calling character witnesses, without my attorney's permission, until midnight of the night before is a hostile process witness. The thousands of pages of documents will now be examined and exposed. The Courtroom is quiet, waiting with the assembled families. The mood is expectant, waiting for a successful challenge, jury now open to hear and learn. The defendant is ready.

The familiar and distinguished defense attorney, facing the array of the opposed United States, so to speak, looks into the faces of the assembly (what were his thoughts; fear, dismay, shame?) and announces, "The defense rests!" Rests! Confusion and apprehension spreads among the Court. The jury still waits. The Prosecutor and the Judge see the comfortable conclusion and relax. Weeks of anticipation, of struggle and conflict over information and meaning evaporate, they can't believe it. The defense rests! What an easy thing to announce, the Defense Rests! As if it had been at labor. As if it had also prepared for weeks, researched details, made timely objections when evidence of witness tampering is displayed in court, as if it had listened to the evidence ready to be presented that would contradict that presented and erase it from the record of actual information regarding the alleged events. As if it has not wasted weeks of inattention, as if it had not been working on other cases the night before and socializing at drinks and dinner instead of trial preparation. What about "The Defense will now go to work and demolish this case. The Defense will now show you how the bank never lost a dime in this matter. The Defense will now show that this can be explained. The Defense will now demonstrate how the alleged deals can be understood. The Defense will now call Andy Fields, Arthur Elliott, Charles McGinnis, Charlie Howe, John McClaughry and place upon the stand its own client, Roger Lussier." Anything but the Defense rests. That comes after demonstration of the assembled evidence, after the witnesses have shown the lie, the governments has been reprimanded for using tainted testimony, after motion for a new trial and summary dismissal, after Roger has explained satisfactorily the bank's ability to earn when others failed is demonstrated, after clients who have been beneficiaries of this bank knock them over, complementing the witnesses as they testified to the truth. Testify, then you rest, go out to dinner with your client and have dinner and drinks, not the night before.

What is the attorney doing, to imagine the government is not prepared with a story (not the story) and allowing a client they have determined to prosecute go unexplained? Is "Defense" a synonym for the client is abandoned? The client is now abandoned, without a trial record for appeal, without error established and alternatives explained. The client is abandoned to unjustified fines, forfeiture, attachment of property, to confiscation of a lifetime of work, abandoned to jail, prison, chains, ridicule, and suffering; now married to a procession of other lawyers that will each attempt to create without a record the explanation of how the jury unjustly concluded its verdict, a consequence of "the defense abandons."

This defendant, capable in his own judgment, had placed himself, hands outstretched, in the care of his attorney, now resting, and finds himself with amazement having his hands tied together, chained, and himself acknowledged for slaughter, departing for prison with the real risk of never to return. Age, stress, a history of hemorrhage and a later tumor and lesions do pose that risk. Imagine yourself in this place. To imagine and foresee the consequences, to say goodbye to a beloved wife, (itself an increasing rare cultural event) and your grown children and growing grandchildren; to see your bedroom perhaps for the last time. The home and community you have resided in all your life in the rearview mirror for perhaps the last time. This all happened and all with indifference to the Court and your attorney, perhaps by now well rested and well paid.

Oh yes, it would take a few months of delay, of consideration of appeal, a few false starts and false hopes that what would happen might not, but to no avail. Without a record of the trial that contained the information from the "Defense" and defense record of objections to the interpretation and record, there is no chance of a change of outcome. The Court, the Prosecutor and the "resting" attorney knew the outcome in advance. You can only appeal the trial record, and if a defense record was not created that explains and proposes your position then the only result possible is to rely upon the record that was presented by your Prosecutor.

So at age 65, with everything in this world attached for forfeiture, including his home, with his wife's own personal property also illegally attached (as will come to be shown "illegally" attached by legal process) with his family gathered to share his pain and his sons offering to be imprisoned in his place, with every comfort taken from him, every asset seized, every claim to his reputation cast in doubt, with nothing but losses, he goes to prison, a new member in the Brotherhood of Job.

All lost save what could not be taken, the love of his family, the trust of his friends, his confidence in his own innocence, his religious faith unshaken, and a character of integrity.

And yet, while chasing to ground this guy in Vermont, out in Texas there was a group called Enron and Arthur Anderson that would have already set in motion the largest corporate theft in history. What do we do? Why we chase this guy in Vermont, and accept the contributions of Enron, and pretend we are doing justice. Along with her blindfold, Justice statues should be provided with a clothespin for her nose. The sight and smell of what is offered in her name is overwhelming even to a stone figure. Perhaps we once believed the blindfold was for impartiality, now we know it is to avoid seeing what is done in her name, not seeing her "scales" being rigged and her verdicts being occasions of entertainment. The current wave of TV shows, a variation on the old "Black Hat and White Hat" themes of the movies gives us a sense that justice can be bought. And without any knowledge of the documents and testimony of a perjured Detective, named Mark Furman, we know, without a doubt, that without his legal team then "O.J." would be in prison. How would his trial have gone with a local attorney, without research or the energy the Cochran team provided as his counsel? But what we overlook is the possibility of planted evidence, perjury and arranged testimony as a routine strategy in high-profile cases. And all of that happened in mine.

During the depression the geography of Vermont continued to provide a benefit of sorts. Traffic and economics that could use the proximity of the border with Canada did well. There was a town near here, called Danville that had its bank robbed. It was a hard time, and as we know that is where money is. This robbery must have proved to be a good example, because a former President of the Danville bank learned how it was done, and sixty years later it happened again. But this time there was an unexpected improvement of sorts on the standard robbery: this time the bank robbed its President. They robbed their President, took his money, attempted and failed to take his reputation, and absolutely flopped at convincing his community that he was their problem, not themselves nor their government.

But before you can rob even a President of your bank, there needs to be some value there to hoist, so to speak. So, how did a bank in a small Vermont town end up, according to the Bank Administration Institute, in the upper 10% of this country's banks, for its class, and make the Wall Street Journal? During my term, as President and Director, the Bank had grown from approximately $700,000.00 to over $16,000,000.00 in capital and Reserves, and the assets went from $7,265,039 in 1966 to $125,508,842 at the end of 1992. In 1987 the FDIC gave the Bank a rating of #2, which is next to the highest rating the FDIC gives any bank, and very few banks are given that high a rating. I retired in February 1993.

LSB Ratings by FDIC:

1987 — 2

1988 — 4

1989 — 3

1990 — 3

1991

1992 — 4

1993

1994 — Problem Bank

1995 — Troubled Bank

And then you vote to sue the former President for restitution of everything the bank lost as a personal liability while keeping the earnings advantage of the millions he made for the bank. That's how you rob a banker, and get paid for it.

The trial itself was the biggest trial in Vermont, in terms of monetary awards, and I could not even come to my own trial, everyone was invited but the defendant, it felt like being a hostage in your own country.

Then you spend over a million in legal fees (according to the present Chairman of the Board) covering it up and continuing to claim innocence, until finally they get to court in New York and the court finds out and announces that the bank is in the wrong court. The bank also originally claimed, under oath, to be a member of the Federal Reserve System, which they never had been, and which I believe to have constituted a fraud upon the Court. The bank did not retract this statement for over a year. And when the fraud is revealed, after four years and over 47,000 pages of documentation, repeated claims of the bank, the Directors and their lawyers, and with their banking regulators assistance, professional training by the now-President of the bank and his impressive articles of leadership and reassurance, say that it was all an "honest mistake." That while falsely claiming they were a member of the Federal Reserve, and after signing affidavits and verifying the complaint in their lawsuit, along with the impressive credentials of Hale & Dorr (the Boston firm that kept Nixon out of jail), and repeatedly announcing and extending and converting of restitution claims into civil judgments, then, at the direction of the Federal Appeals Court Judges; Cardamone, Sotomayor and Katzmann, the Bank's attorney, Richard Johnston, admits there is no "nucleus of operative facts, between the restitution order and the state law claims, which would have given the federal court jurisdiction to hear the bank's case. Federal Courts are courts of limited jurisdiction and according to the Second Circuit Court of Appeals the Federal Court had no jurisdiction to hear the bank's case. Judge Sotomayor asks Johnston five times what the nucleus of operative facts is between the restitution order and the bank's state law claims. Johnston can't answer that question. The Second Circuit Court of Appeals vacates the judgment of the U.S. District Court.

A reading of the transcript of the hearing before the Court of appeals, which is available, makes Johnston look like a little boy with his hand caught in the cookie jar. The Judge did not appear to be impressed by him at all.

The bank promptly runs off to the proper State Court, where they should have been at the beginning, and make their claims. A wish for a fact is the basis for their robbery. The bank uses the FDIC ban pretending to protect its stockholder's interest while losing them millions (something the former President never did) and asking to be praised for it...that is Yankee humor to the extreme. And they have done this.

Maybe there is more to this then we know. This story does get convoluted, and the "deals" need to be analyzed by name, but the actual events charged are about as hard to follow as a manure spreader being pulled up Main Street. It is in not expecting such a sight that causes most of the confusion. And having little experience with such an event most of you readers will think that what you think you are seeing can't be true because it is so unexpected, not because the smell is not valid evidence of what is before your eyes. That a man with an eighth grade education could provide the leadership to earn $16 million for the bank, and achieve business success while the nation's saving and loans (expertly led by professionals and former ambassadors, and attractive business school graduates) was costing us the largest losses in history. We did not understand that we needed training to wreck our institutions. We thought auditors and regulators were beneficial

I missed something there. I thought it was to be promotion of the fittest, not the most numerous of failings that qualified for advancement. Could, did this really happen? Well, pull your chair closer to the fire, get comfortable, and I will share with you this terrible tale. You won't be disappointed, there are deceit, lies, malicious prosecution, perjury, false witness, altered official records, neighbors and friends being misled, bank directors and executives swearing to a lie in triplicate, and becoming disgusted when they finally were not believed. More perjury, manipulation of testimony, perhaps a "purchased lawyer" or two (every story needs a villain, and this one did not need to invent one), loss of millions, ruination of a good community service by a protective government again, and all of those new directors mostly pleased with themselves. Some probably will even buy a copy of this for their children, and not even realize the author's intention.

LET THE PITYFUL SIGHING OF THE PRISONERS COME UNTO THEE, O LORD!

(Book of Common Prayer)

Without jail experience most of us cannot imagine the desperation and loss of meaning incarceration produces in a person. Our "James Cagney" big house prison movies in black and white with soulful Chaplains and Irish guards walking someone to the "chair" misses the reality. Nor are the prisoners always hatching plots to escape, confronting the stoolie for his betrayal of the prisoner's oath of non-cooperation. No, within the population about half of them could safely be in less restrictive and damaging environments with treatment for mental illness and addictions. And without that there is an almost guaranteed return for most.

Most in fact, spend the time in quiet grief, doing some job and standing in lines for every function from eating to getting your mail. The days are long, boring and repetitious. And mental depression and isolation are the most frequent experiences of the majority. The youngest seem to feel the need to put on a mental costume and posture around rehearsing made up lines for the amusement of their age group. The older persons have information about life that is unsought and everyone has some story of meaning to them. Many know exactly what went wrong and how it all came down on them, what they did what they did not, and exactly how it happened.

Some seem to be truly innocent but society cannot consider that easily. Just recall the uproar when a conservative Governor of Illinois concluded that there was just too much evidence, too much experience of distorted trials for him to continue to put inmates to death. He commuted the sentences of everyone on death row, saying the evidence of wrong doing by judicial process was more certain than the resulting convictions. Now those many, many men did not just arrive in Illinois and get found to have been disadvantaged upon arrival. They had been within that system for years...and continue to suffer. That is the way it is everywhere. We sentence persons to prison as punishment, not for punishment, but we expect it to mean for additional continuing punishment.

Separation from freedom is not enough. We usually seek retribution on them, and it changes those of you believing yourselves to be free as certainly as the prisoner. That ancient spiritual law of return: as ye sow, so shall ye reap. So our society continues this wasteful and destructive "tail chase." There are better ways...we do not want them.

What was most frequently displayed was the daily presentation of suffering persons trying to find meaning in a time frame that excluded that as a possibility. You would see persons who had been committed to long sentences being given opportunities to go to testify in other trials involving different persons and then receive some reduction in their sentence as a reward for that service. You'd see persons who are already physically disadvantaged try to comprehend the space that contained them; a blind prisoner being escorted around by another person and having the space and pathways described for him. You would see prisoners reading Bibles or the Koran and composing questions that might never have occurred to them in ordinary time. You'd see persons undergoing changes of thinking in hopes of demonstrating the insight or some new comprehension — of being saved, or learning that they are lost.

There was the sad and ironic display of a father and son in prison together. They shared a fraternity and calm analogy of experience while each was an example to the other of the end. Each was the other's witness to their personal tragedy. There were prisoners who had children or spouses or parents die, and they were unable to attend funerals or say, "Goodbye."

There were letters being composed to loved ones and to persons that were now leaving the marital or friendship circles and never wanted to "hear from you" again. There were angry letters written to protest and give witness to damages, perceived or real. There were amends being made in letters of apology. There were lines at the telephone walls where you stood for long periods of time waiting for the opportunity to make a brief but expensive call; each call preceded by a recorded announcement saying "this call is being placed by an inmate from a federal correctional facility, will you accept the charges?"

There are persons still in those facilities that will be there long after these pages are forgotten. Some of those persons now in my memory and on the verge of extinction and that time spent together will be lost in its entirety. There are persons who have been released and may return again because prison is in no way about rehabilitation, and the experience deprives many persons of any chance at a successful future.

The chains are not left at the door when you leave. They continue with you and function as a permanent handicap in your ability to support yourself or acquire a meaningful life. There were persons there, a former judge comes to mind, who was only required to be incarcerated for a brief time and found that horrible and spent all of his available time seeking legal reduction of the briefest of sentences. There were persons there who were accidental to the scene of the events of their incarceration and would be there for as long as anyone could foresee. There were floors to be mopped and baths to be cleaned and lawns to be cut and sod to be replaced, and stones loaded into wagons and fields over which sewerage was to be distributed. There was a large furniture factory that you could work in. Sewer and water resources repaired and light bulbs replaced and meals prepared and then eaten and prepared and eaten again. There were days spent waiting for mail and for replies to filed motions and disputed descriptions of circumstances. There were letters unanswered.

There was visitation and no visitation. There were families that drove for hundreds of miles, and at great expense, to find the visiting day canceled without explanation and turned from the doors to go back home. There were persons who could see loved ones arriving and not be able to talk to them or being held by them because of some rule infraction. There was mail that was returned and small packages of cookies or other gifts, usually from elderly relatives, that could not be received because they might contain some contraband or "tools" for escape. There were steps to sweep and always *the Count*: that every four hours ritual event of standing in an assigned spot and being counted to verify your being present and your continued incarceration.

There were sudden fights breaking out for no apparent cause or as a direct result of accumulated degradation in grievances untended. There was the life of the active psychotic, of the aggressive and the frightened. There were some trips to the guard stations at night to hear of some information conveyed or to be accused of some disciplinary infraction and then chained and taken to the "Hole."

There was the frequent lining up for sick call in hopes of finding some relief for pain or of receiving some attention to some physical concern. Sometimes the symptoms were faked in hopes of comfort...sometime their reality was overlooked...I almost bled to death once. There were trips to the parameters of the facility to do your work while glancing beyond fences to highways of cars moving, to the scenes of houses on distant hills. Of smoke rising from chimneys and the imagined pleasures of family and dinners together and the other routine delights in life from which we are now excluded.

And on appointed days each week new buses arrived full of persons beginning their adventures with us and collecting a few who were being transferred or relocated elsewhere. There was the arrival of Sheriff's cars from distant jurisdictions bringing new legal charges and issues for prisoners. Always the possibility of additional charges being brought against someone who believed they had already faced the worst. When you think all that is next is the time left, there is the frequent arrival of the distant Sheriff with additional suffering to be faced.

And rarely, but always as a sign of hope, there was someone who had received some portion of judicial relief from endless production of legal motions and research conducted by the prisoners themselves. That somehow something happened for the good.

One of the things that I did that helped me enormously was to conduct an activity that would be shared in the same time space with my family back home. We had every night the occasion of praying the rosary. A gathering of prisoners who met to pray the rosary and in some cases at the same time their own wives and families were doing the same thing. It was enormously helpful for all of us, and it continues as a source of respect and solidarity with those I have left behind. That was the one place during the day where we were with some measure of peace — where your mind could range freely over the things you needed to pray about, and you would be with others so that you could feel a part of the desired community, and you believed your prayers were heard. Before we began our prayers each night there was always some inventory of the day's activities. We would have messages about previous prisoners, some who had become ill or had died. That information had come back to one of us in our group. Occasionally there was a joyful message of some success or some good result that had happened to someone, and it was an occasion for all of us to rejoice.

We pray our Sorrowful mysteries, we pray our Joyful mysteries, we prayed for all those that had died and those who yet will. We prayed for other prisoners, for families, for peace in the world, for justice among nations, for children, for teachers, and we learned to pray for our guards and our Prosecutors, and for those judges that had sentenced us. We all were bound and in captivity…and we learned to pray for true freedom.

We learned to pray for all victims, and we learned to pray for ourselves. In some ways time stood still when we prayed, and we were mentally removed from our captivity and joined with others at home. Sometimes we could feel that the things that had brought us to this place never happened. But they did!

The particular facility of my incarceration was on the site of a former small Pennsylvania town that had been converted during World War II into a munitions plant for the Army. Most of the former houses had been removed but there were still the foundations of those wartime factories that we would bump into while working in the fields from time to time. The most persistent reminder of the previous years of living there were the remnants of that town's church. That building, made of stone and still containing stained glass windows dedicated to long departed pastors and Sunday school class teachers and others of blessed memory, stood apart from the main campus of the prison complete with its own cemetery and gravel pathway. This was a place that we could gather in each week and see ourselves differently than the descriptions assigned us by the courts. That in itself is "Good News" from the other days of the week. There were several different chaplains that attended us in the services, and they stay in my memory as kind, authentic and comprehending priests or clergy of several different denominations. Occasionally there were special programs provided by visiting choirs or other spiritual groups from outside offering to minister to us, and they did. During the holy seasons of the year there were special observances and for the most part prisoners benefited from this contact. We saw that place and those persons as a symbol of the larger reality that embraces all of this together. We would cut the grass at the cemetery and read the tombstones, the names of those that served in the Civil War that had been lost, or of husbands and then wives and departed children, gathered in these final resting places. And this sacred location gave us contact as well with lives that had been lived on this space before we did, before it became the prison that it now is. But the confidence of their lives, even in death, benefited us.

In prison everyone has to have a job. When I originally went to get a job I went to Jeff Wetzel, the Supervisor for the outdoor crew. I told him I would like to work outdoors. At first he told me he didn't want me, that I was too old, and that they wanted hard workers. I looked him in the eye and told him I would do my share, and if he wasn't happy with my work that I would go elsewhere. He was very happy with my work and said I was hardest worker he ever had. When I had about a year left to serve, a notice was put on the bulletin board that they were looking for workers for a new prison that was going to be built at Ft. Devens, Mass. Thinking that I would be closer to home if I could work there, I put my name in to go there. The supervisor said he wasn't going to lose his best worker, and that I couldn't go.

Our daily work was assigned to us from among a variety of jobs that were available; some perceived as more desirable than others but for the most part all of them "make work" and meaningless. Some of us as a matter of character performed the jobs as if they mattered and some performed their work as if they were not present at all. Overall it did not matter. There was nothing within the prison environment itself that gave confident meaning to your life's purpose. Those hours spent in continuing education, or special classes at night, or in the library, were all strings back to the other world, and they provided diversions and helped you escape from the reality of our enforced isolation, but had no practical meaning. Now I admit that there is some humor in going to a prison library and see a class assembled for the purposes of taking flying lessons ground school courses. But everybody understood that no one was flying anywhere soon and that the activity had no real purpose or performance possibility.

More than not, days were spent in meaningless boredom, seeking in the very small opportunities for divergent or unique ways to escape from the monotonous present, and some way to move you closer to the possibility, *if you survive*, of eventual release. Among all of us, a large group of over 700 persons, we were entirely interchangeable, involuntary in our associations, and not expected by anyone to achieve anything of significance or usefulness in a day or a week or a month or year or a number of years. And while I am out now myself, those that were left behind are doing exactly the same thing they were doing when we were all together. Presidents change and national debts go out of computation but the life of the prison is the same. One solution fits all!

So you can wander down the hallways in dormitory buildings filled with double decked beds, constant noise of over volume programs unending on TVs, slamming of doors, shouting of persons from one end of the building to the other in the absence of normal conversation and normal social rules, deprived of companionship and valued associations you simply breathe and pump your blood. The small cubicle you are assigned to live in is filled with the few acceptable articles from your previous life, a few photographs, or some letters that you have received. That space where you try to describe yourself differently from the announcement notice of your identity on the nametag at the entrance to your cubicle. Men sat on the edge of their bunks in the brief hours of respite and leisure. There is one still there whose name is gone from me now but the picture I recall is as clear as when I first saw it. He had a photograph of his wife and a child pasted to his locker door and underneath it was this question:

"How do you punish those whose remorse is already greater than the misdeed?"

During the time of my incarceration I had two additional trials: an appeal of my conviction itself and its illegal restitution decision (as determined by the Magistrate and the US District Court for Vermont), and a civil trial brought by the directors of the Lyndonville Savings Bank against me. The civil trial which was illegally brought against me in a federal court resulted in the largest award against an individual in Vermont history. By a combination of the bank's well-paid lawyers and bank officials I was charged in the wrong court knowingly by the attorneys who were eventually overturned upon appeal. (They still were well paid for their "mistake.")

The important part for me in all of that is that I was not allowed to attend my own trial. And that should be a concern for what can happen to you as well. To be judged as owing someone over $8 million and not being able to be present in those discussions sounds a bit one-sided to me.

The hearing of motions on my first criminal trial was held again back in Vermont, but it was not an occasion of simply being brought to trial and showing up for the arguments. To enter prison I was allowed to be driven by a family friend from Lyndonville to the Allenwood facility in the State of

Pennsylvania, a distance of 479.2 miles. I simply arrived, identified myself, and was admitted to that distinguished institution. But to be allowed to attend the appeal in Vermont once I was in the prison system I had to be returned to them and delivered in the most difficult, painful and extended method possible. My original trip from Lyndonville to Allenwood would take about 10 hours. A return trip consumed a total of 25 days. I was taken from Allenwood on a bus to another location, put on a "Con Air" plane that was flying cross-country and taken into Oklahoma City where the airplane was literally driven inside the prison and unloaded inside a secure hanger. All of us were packed and chained together, without severe weather clothing, and were very cold, hungry and suffering physically. The plane to Oklahoma City had about 25 percent of its passengers made up of women going to prison themselves, who were crying, leaving their children, being transported beyond areas of familiarity and probably scared to death. Two days later there is another small plane. The previous night having been spent huddled together in a small chamber, this day it is frequent landings as we picked up people and dropped off people, picked up more people and dropped off more people. While I waited on the plane, others were let off the plane on a chain line, then others were led back in on a chain line. Adding and subtracting. Then adding more, then some off, then lunch in a paper sack and finally landing in Bangor, Maine, where I was locked in and actually treated kindly. The next day I was flown to Burlington, Vermont, where I arrived with a blood pressure problem (the absence of blood pressure...there wasn't any) that was so severe I required medical attention and was taken to the hospital. Then following a brief hearing on the matter before the court the procedure was essentially reversed, and I disappeared from the presence of the court and the observation of my family (we could not touch) and was eventually returned to Allenwood with the same system of flights and buses and chains and countless isolations in small rooms that had been characteristic of the first of these trips. They are dangerous trips, as much for the prisoners as anyone. All prisoners are regarded as extremely violent and bent on escape. Every movement is monitored closely and any belief of infraction of procedure is dealt with severely. While I was in Otisville, on the way back, a person was killed in the dormitory next to mine. At one of the places it was raining and freezing. We were being transported between vehicles, and I had only a summer shirt to protect me. A Marshal inquired as to where my coat was. I told him I had not been given one. He gave me the coat off his back saying it would be easier for him to replace his than get one for me.

And it is that constant struggle, the fixed system, which is mechanical, impersonal, indifferent and lethal...and people like that unknown guard that had not lost all of his humanity, still seeing others as human and worthy of respect.

Travels Back to Vermont

The following is Evelyn's Diary at the time of my travels back to Vermont for appeals hearings:

Roger Lussier's Travels (1997):

While your dad was away at Allenwood Prison Camp in Montgomery PA, he was working very hard outside; driving tractor, digging up stones, clearing wood and debris from the fields, mowing and a lot of other manual labor. In the evening, after going to Rosary, he worked on legal papers and sometimes he had help from a couple of good friends he had made there.

He worked on the 2255 motion and the bank trials, read papers by flashlight after lights had to be out and read for hours and hours. Papers were sent back and forth from lawyer to lawyer, and on May 24, 1997 he was granted a hearing in Burlington, and he put in a request to be permitted to go for his own hearing.

Finally on Friday the 13th of June, he was granted that request and was told that he would be leaving Monday morning, the 16th of June 1997. On Sunday, June 15th he went to church as always; the priest blessed him and wished him the best of luck at his hearing. Roger went to Rosary that night and packed his legal papers. All other personal belongings were put into storage. Roger called me and said we would be seeing each other soon; how good that sounded.

Monday Morning, June 16: Roger left there at 6 am and arrived in Oklahoma late at night. Charles Gill called me at 8 am and told me he knew he was gone, and was in the custody of the U.S. Marshal's Service. Charles said he would be calling Dave at the office, or whichever boy was there, to find how things were going for him. I prayed for him tonight, and I know the family was also.

Tuesday, June 17: Roger called me from a prison in Oklahoma. He was flown there from Harrisburg, PA and was 15 hours in handcuffs and leg chains, and a bar in front of them. The handcuffs fastened to the bar so he couldn't lift his hands very much. He had only a little snack to eat. There were some women in the front of the plane, chained the same way. Roger said some were very young and crying. There was no getting up to go to the bathroom. Roger was very tired when they reached the prison and marched into their room for the night. He called me collect, and he sounded very drained. I was so happy to hear from him

Wednesday night, June 18: Roger called me from Bangor, Maine at 5 pm. They had to get up at 3 am and left at 6 am; was just up and down all day, picking up prisoners and letting some off. Chained as they were yesterday, very tired and again, not much to eat.

Thursday, June 19: Roger arrived at the Burlington, Vt. Correctional Center at 11 am, and he can call collect if time permits. He was put in the "hole," but we didn't know that at that time. It is a dreary place, not much to eat, no showers, same clothes.

Friday, June 20: Roger called me at 8:45 am and told me we could visit him tomorrow from 1 to 2:45 pm. How good that sounds.

Saturday, June 21: Reg & Heidi came and got me at 10:30 am and we went to Burlington to the Correctional Ctr. Met Richard there and they told us we couldn't see him as he had a TB shot and couldn't see anyone for 72 hours and that we should come back Monday. What a disappointment! They let him call me tonight; he was upset over it, you may be sure. Charles Gill called and said it was because they didn't want him to have contact with us, probably true; he was in with 8 others, tonight with 3.

Sunday, June 22: Didn't hear from Roger tonight. His lawyer, Peter DeTroy and Tom Majerison, the paralegal, are to be in Burlington tonight.

Monday, June 23: Reg and Heidi came at 1 pm and got me. We went to Burlington and got rooms at the Swiss Chalet. Dave came and got a room also. At 5 pm we went with the lawyers to their room at the Regency; they had been to see Rog a couple times. We discussed things about the hearing tomorrow, and what they had talked to him about. At 6:30 we could visit Roger. They told us only 3 at a time, so Reg, Dave and I went and then Heidi and I. It was so good to see him and give him a hug and receive one, but what an awful place, oh so noisy and the big old iron-barred doors closed behind you with a loud bang, enough to send shivers through your body. A lot of young people are in there and a lot visiting them. He said there was a fight last night. Also, last night, the guards took him to the hospital as his heart was beating so slow they were worried he was going to have a heart attack. They gave him a good check over, but he is so tired. He couldn't call and let us know, so he told us today. It makes me nervous knowing the strain he is having; it makes us all very uneasy.

Tuesday June 24: Burlington, Vt. 2255. Roger been gone 9 days from Allenwood. Reg, Heidi, Dave, Kathy, Steve, Richard and I met with the lawyers, Peter DeTroy and Tom Majerison this morning, and then in for the hearing. Roger had to come into the room in handcuffs, escorted by a couple deputies or whoever they were. That hit hard but hit Honi the hardest, to see her Pepere brought in that way; she hadn't seen him since he left home, she cried and cried. He was told not to make any contact by eyes or gestures, but he did in his own way and we noticed; it did seem good to see him in regular clothes, as they had him wear a white pullover shirt and gray pants. The lawyers talked with him after the hearing. They are preparing a motion to send to the Judge for a testimonial hearing and to see if Rog can stay in Burlington. He was in a room later there but they wouldn't let me in.

Ones that came to the hearing were: Andy Fields, John McClaughry, Dave Turner, Fay Young, Don & Bill Beattie, Bob & Edith Murray, Laurent & Bea Lussier, Lucille & Mona (Roger's sister and god-daughter), Dick & Julie Boera, Mavis Griswold and Marilyn Hughes, Don and Alan Fogg, Dick Axelrod, Reg & Heidi, Steve & Robert, Kathy, Holly & Honi, Richard, Ginny, Richa & Renee, Dave, Lisa and I.

Roger called me tonight, he was feeling pretty low and that was understandable. We all feel the same and feel so helpless.

Wednesday, June 25: Roger out of the "hole." We didn't know that. That was where they had kept him, caged up like an animal; just makes you boil. Now he is in a large room with about 35-40 others. He can shower when he wants and had a very good supper. He can also use the phones when available. What a horrible week he had and no one knew, but they didn't want him where he could talk. He called and said we could visit him tomorrow night. Charles Gill called Dave, at the office, to see what was taking place, a lot of others called tonight wondering.

Thursday, June 26: Roger called this morning. They let him go outside "in the pen." That was a treat and also to have a cigarette that one of the other guys gave him. He has to sign up for a time to go out, twice a day. He told me he needed some clothes as he has worn the same ones since leaving Allenwood, except on hearing day. I packed a bag and at 4:30 pm Richard, Ginny, the girls and I went to visit him, but when we got there, I couldn't take the bag in for now. He is in a different room, and we can go to visit him on Thurs. and Sat. Richa, Renee and I went in first, he was so happy to see them. He hugged them over and over. They were happy to see their Pepere, but a little uneasy, so noisy there and when the guards close that large iron-barred door, it closes with a terrific bang. It was nice being with him a short time. Then Richard and Ginny went in. We got home at 11:45 pm. It poured most of the way home.

Friday, June 27: Roger called Dave at the office at 5 pm and then called me about 8:30 pm. Dave received a copy of the paper from lawyer DeTroy asking the Judge if Roger can stay in Vermont.

Saturday, June 28: Our 45th Wedding Anniversary. Roger called this morning, but just at that time the guards were calling him to go outside. At 4 pm, Kathy, Ron and I went to visit him. We stopped first at Andy Field's to pick up a box of legal papers to bring back to the office.

Roger & Evelyn – 44ᵗʰ Wedding Anniversary, June 28, 1996, Allenwood FPC

I took back the bag of clothes he wanted but the guard wouldn't take it as he didn't have a slip for them (damn, damn). Twice I've taken them; he is still in the same clothes. He washes out his underwear and puts them back on; makes me feel so bad but can't do different.

While we were visiting him, there was a young couple that had a fight; the girl was worse, she was pounding on her boyfriend, who went up by the guards, and they had to take her out by force and told her she wouldn't be allowed back. Most of the ones in there were young people. Kathy hated to hear that door close and it did every time someone was let in or out. What a way to celebrate an anniversary, but we were together, even if in a jail.

Sunday, June 29: Roger called tonight. Andy Field went and visited him for two hours, about the bank case. It is supposed to go to trial in September. Andy is going to ask the judge if Roger can stay in Vt., now through August, to prepare for the trial.

Monday, June 30: Roger called and said he could have his clothes sent by UPS, so Marilyn took me to send them. I also sent him some money. I left money for him when I was there but he hasn't gotten it yet. They let him outside twice today, and he called tonight

Tuesday, July 1: Roger called tonight. He hasn't received his clothes or money.

Wednesday, July 2: Back to Otisville, NY. Roger called me at 7:12 am. The guards just came in and told him to pack up as he is leaving there in 10 minutes. He was lucky he could get a phone and call me; so quickly he didn't have any time to pack, his same clothes on his back, that's it. I stayed by the phone all day in case he might call but he didn't until tonight about 8:30 pm, and he is in Otisville, NY, near Port Jarvis. They told him he might be there a week. He said he was tired and hungry, hadn't had only a small snack today, and they told him there wouldn't be any food tonight; he said he was so tired that he didn't care. "What a life," no one knows, it is evident they didn't want him in the home area.

Thursday, July 3, Otisville: Rog called David at the office. Fay was in there so Dave let him talk to him. Harvey Stetson stopped to inquire of him, said he misses him, well, we all do, but it helps to hear from others that say they do also.

Tonight about 7 pm he called me. There is another young guy in with him. They are not locked in so he can go to other rooms and to the library, and they have a large gym. Roger borrowed a pencil and paper to write down the telephone numbers he wants.

Friday, July 4, Otisville: Rog called. There was a cookout for the inmates today, and they had a small band that played music. He missed out on breakfast. I took it he slept in and was told there wouldn't be any supper, so he said he filled up at the cookout all he could. "What a celebration!" It's hard to go to bed and sleep thinking of all this going on with us.

Saturday, July 5, Otisville: Rog called this morning. They have told him that there are some going to Allenwood next Thurs., and he may be one of them. He called tonight; he walked a lot today and his legs and back are stiff.

Sunday, July 6, Otisville: Roger has been gone 21 days from PA. He went to 2 pm Mass today. He called at 9 pm. He had just started talking and they called a count time, so he had to go. He called back at 10:30 pm, didn't talk but a few minutes as so many waiting to use the phone. He was outside some, said he was tired and hurt from walking and exercising yesterday. He hadn't been able to walk in Burlington, as just in a closed area.

Monday, July 7, Otisville: At 9:30 I walked over to the office. Reg was on the phone with his dad, so I talked also. Dave called the Court in Burlington to order a transcript from the hearing. Rog called at 9 pm to say good night and to wish Honi a happy birthday. She is 17 today.

Tuesday, July 8, Otisville: Rog called Dave; wanted some papers sent to Charles and to him in PA. so he would have them when he gets there. He called tonight and the officials had to tell him to pack up, he would be leaving in the morning. Well he still doesn't have anything to pack, still wearing the same clothes, same stockings (what's left of them). He doesn't know where he is going but hopes it is Allenwood; I do also. He asked if he would have something to eat and drink in morning, and they said yes.

Wednesday, July 9, Otisville: I was awake at 3 am wondering what was going to take place for him today. I pray and pray for him and cry & cry and wonder why all this torture, but then know there's others worse off. I'm very lucky to have my family all around; we will survive this. Roger called Dave at noon at the office. He was still in NY. He called tonight and said he is supposed to leave in the morning. Another night for all of us to wonder what will be.

Thursday, July 10, Allenwood: Rog called me at 6:30 am. He had been told he would be leaving at 7 am. I wondered all day and stayed close to the phone. Dave and I checked back and forth. Rog called me at 11 pm. He got there between 4:30 and 5 pm. They let him have his old cubby and get some supplies. He said the guys were all glad to see him, and he had a lot of handshakes and finally had a change of clothes. He was glad to get back there, if he couldn't come home. A relief for all of us also; he had been gone 25 days, same clothes.

Friday, July 11: I called Kathy before she went to work to tell her that her Dad was back at Allenwood; she was relieved to hear. Rog called about

9:30 pm. He said he had lots of mail waiting for him. They had saved it. He got his things out of storage today and has the weekend off.

Saturday, July 12: Lise called this morning and she and the kids are going to camp for the day and night, and asked if I couldn't go with them, so I did. The change was good, and good for my mind. Dave came tonight. As we sat on the porch we mentioned if Dad was here he would be out fishing. We all miss him so much and have to be careful in front of the twins, as they are only 9 years old. Rog called at 8 pm; he had been going through his papers and mail, sort of catching up.

Sunday, July 13: We were at camp today. We all cleaned and washed windows. Dave did the garage; he put everything outside except the woodpile, sure looked nice when he finished; he cleans like his dad does. Richard helped and tonight brought back a truckload of junk.

Rog called at 8 pm. He is depressed today; said it was very hot there. He rode to church. It rained all pm at camp and is raining tonight. Rog going to Rosary, hopefully that will help him.

Monday, July 14: Roger had to report back to work but it was so hot they had him work in the garage. He called Dave this morning and wanted him to find a letter Bucknam wrote the board; his wheels are still turning. I would think his mind would snap. He is going to Rosary and will call before count time.

Thursday, July 17: Rog called at 7 am as he couldn't get on phone last night. He called Dave at 7:30 to set up a conference call for him with Judge Meeker, Eric Parker and Gravel in Hyde Park. Dave did and they all talked about the Hammang case. The Judge gave Rog more time to get questions answered. Rog told the Judge that Parker did not send him material he had asked for. The Judge said LSB should pay for an attorney for Roger.

Friday, July 18: Roger had a conference call with lawyer Gravel on Hammang case. Steve made the call for him.

Saturday, July 19: Rog called at 9 am. He said he had read material on the Hammang case, until 2 am this morning, and he needs more papers. He called tonight; he had worked all day on the papers.

Sunday, July 20: Rog called this morning. He is going to church and then work on his papers.

Monday, July 21: Rog called in the later pm. There are a couple things he wants looked up. Richard will look for an article that lawyer Clausen wrote; the other, Hamel's letter, we will try to find. He called late tonight to say good night; it does make a good ending to the day.

Sunday, July 27: Dave visited his dad; he was very happy to see Dave, and they had a very good visit, and he could ask Dave questions that he can't on the phone. Dave had been to Davis auction in Conn.

Saturday, August 9: Andy Field visited Rog all day. Andy was telling him what he has prepared for bank trial. Rog feels good about it.

Sunday, August 10: Andy Field visited Roger all forenoon and left at 1 pm for home. Rog didn't sleep good last night as he was thinking of what he wanted to discuss with Andy today. It just seems so unfair that he has to be there. Things he's blamed for that he shouldn't be. I hope it can be proven soon.

Friday, August 29: Summary judgment at Vt. Superior Court in Montpelier on Guilmettes. Reg and Dave went; I couldn't as having that pain in my stomach. They were done at 11 am, and then they went and talked with Andy for a couple hours. Judge Meeker will make a decision within 30 days. Ones there were Reg and Dave, Gravel for the bank, Rubin for Elliott, the Guilmettes and Kilmartin on phone. Rog called tonight. He thought about it all day. He called in forenoon also but I hadn't heard from the boys.

Friday, September 5: Steve and I left the office at 9:15 am and drove to Conn., had lunch, gassed up and right through to White Deer Motel. We rested a short time and then up to visit Rog. It was so, so good to see him, hug him, hadn't seen him since June. We had a snack there with him, out of the machines. We visited until 8:30 and then back to motel, sure wished he could have gone too, but he had to go through body search and back to his quarters.

Saturday, September 6: Back up to visit Rog. He was outside watching for us to come and waved at us, but then they wouldn't let him come in until after count, as it was near that time, so we had to wait an hour, but we had a nice visit; had our snack with him. We were outside some, especially so he & Steve could smoke. Back to motel, there was a lot of deer and geese outside.

Sunday, September 7: Steve and I went back up to visit Rog. We had our coffee there with him. We sat out at the picnic table, but can't go off the patio. It did seem so good to be out there close to him. We left about 11 am as Rog wanted us to go to Andy Field's on way home, so said goodbye (both tearfully). I called Andy from the car phone, and he met us down street. Then we went on home and got there at 8:15 pm. I was too tired to even take a shower. Rog called after 9 pm so he knew we were home and all OK. He said after we left he worked on papers, Hammang and FDIC.

Thursday, September 11: Pre-trial hearing in Brattleboro on ARDI and the bank with Judge Murtha. Steve and Dave went. They felt the bank case leaned in Rog's favor but that ARDI was in Fed's favor. They feel the

Judge likes Andy. They all have to go and take Rog's deposition again at the prison. The Judge will make a ruling on today's hearing so we wait again.

Friday, September 12: Rog called Dave's house tonight and talked with Tricia and Aaron and wished them Happy Birthday, 9 years old. Their birthday is tomorrow. They were happy to talk to their Pepere and said, "we miss you so much." That didn't keep our eyes dry. He called me later at home.

Tuesday, September 23: Dave called at 5 pm. Andy had called and had heard from the bank's lawyers that the 2255 had been ruled on. Another hearing was denied but the restitution was thrown out. Dave called DeTroy; he hadn't heard, but called and found out and faxed paper to Dave. Rog called, so I told him to call Dave, as he might have more information.

Wednesday, September 24: Rog called tonight and Steve read the papers to him on the 2255 that we received. They discussed it. Bill and Sally Hill were here so Bill talked with him also.

Friday, September 26: Andy drove to Allenwood today, but was too tired to go up and talk with Rog tonight.

Saturday, September 27: Andy up and talked with Rog today. They are getting ready for the deposition on Monday, when the bank lawyers will be there. Rog wanted Dave to look up some things; one was the Rowell auction. Dave called Andy tonight at the White Deer Motel.

Sunday, September 28: Andy was up to work with Rog for the deposition tomorrow. Rog called tonight and had a couple things he wanted me to tell Dave. I called Dave at office and he was talking with Andy at that time at the White Deer, so Dave put the call on conference and I talked with Andy also. One thing Rog wanted was his retirement to the bank and list of his salary for the 27 years.

Monday September 29: Roger's deposition today at Allenwood. I didn't hear from him tonight.

Tuesday, September 30: Rog called this morning. He couldn't get a phone last night. He said yesterday that Gelbar, from the government, asked questions, and then Andy did,+ and the other lawyers just sat and listened. There were two Boston lawyers and of course, Charlie Bucknam. Today, Andy asked all the questions; Rog said he worked hard. He called tonight.

Wednesday, October 1: Rog's deposition continued on today by Andy and then by Johnston. Rog said Johnston got "huffy", but Andy got "huffy" right back at him. He was asking questions about the FDIC. They are done for this week, but told Rog they would be back a couple days next week.

Friday, October 3: Tonight when Rog called, Kathy was here and talked with him. Rog told her he had a letter from Judge Cook excusing himself from the Hammang case as he works with Kathy and likes her, was nice to hear.

Tuesday, October 7: Andy drove to PA. to White Deer Motel. Will see Rog tomorrow. He had sent Rog papers to work on.

Wednesday, October 8: Andy up to prison, worked with Rog for deposition tomorrow. He didn't call tonight.

Thursday, October 9: Rog called at 7 am. He couldn't get a phone last night; yesterday was payday so all the guys were waiting for phones. He called at 3:30 pm and said the deposition went pretty good. Andy was there, and Johnston, the bank's lawyer and Bucknam. Rog said he wouldn't look at Bucknam. He said that Johnston got "huffy" again. He wanted Rog to answer with a yes or no, said he tried to keep his cool.

Friday, October 10: Rog called at 3:30 pm and said the deposition went better. The bank lawyer finished, and he and Bucknam left. He said Andy feels good on how it went. Andy and Juanita left for home. I'm glad that's over and hope the rest will be soon. I know Roger's mind is tired but he's glad it's over.

Tuesday, October 14: Rog called at 7 am, said he couldn't get on phone last night. He cleaned his cubby, washed the walls etc. as they didn't work outside. Andy came to office and met with Fay, John Campbell, Dave Turner, and Wendy Davenport. David Lussier was there and when Kathy came from work, she and I went over. Rog called while we were there and he talked to Andy, Dave and I. Rog called at 9:30 tonight wondering how the meeting went; it went good and was on the bank trial.

Sunday, October 19: Reg went to visit his dad as he had an auction in Conn. yesterday for Davis. Rog called tonight. He was happy to see Reg and said they had a good visit and wished he could have rode home with him, we all do.

Monday, October 20: Rog called Dave a little after 11 am. Fay was there and talked with him. Fay had been looking up some things on the bank trial. Rog called tonight, he had talked with Andy, nothing different.

Wednesday, October 22: Rog had a tooth filled today and had his teeth cleaned, the first he's had a dentist appointment since he's been there (86 weeks). He has had his name in for a long time. Dave talked with Andy and told him the Judge had denied the bank's summary judgment.

Friday, October 24: Rog granted a testimonial hearing from Neidermier – thank God.

Monday, October 27: First day of the bank trial in Brattleboro. Dave, Lisa and I went. Bucknam on stand all day for the bank and questioned by his attorney. We ate lunch with Andy and Sara. After trial we stopped at their motel. Dave and Andy went over things and Andy gave Dave papers to give to some of our witnesses. Rog called tonight, just checking on it.

Tuesday, October 28: Second day of bank trial. Richard, Reg and I went to trial along with Marielle, Aunt Gay and Uncle Ernie from Mass. It was nice to see them. They went home at noon. We came home early as just Bucknam on – same old thing. We stopped at office and Rog called, he had been told to pack up his belongings as he is being moved. Dave called lawyer DeTroy's office. He hadn't heard anything. Dave called Andy at motel and DeTroy and they all talked by conference call, Richard was on Dave's other phone. Rog called at 7 pm, still there. DeTroy called the Marshal's office for them to call the Marshals in PA to leave Rog there, as they want to postpone the 2255 hearing to a later date and Nov. 5. Talk about an upsetting time, this was one; we don't know from one minute to another what will change. I can just imagine Rog's feelings.

Wednesday, October 29: Third day of bank trial. Kathy and I left at 6:30 am and were at the Courthouse at 8:30; saw Andy and Sara. Reg, Dave and Lise came. Andy cross-examined Charlie Howe and also Geo. Hopkins, Pearl Baird and Doug Nelson. He caught Howe, Geo and Pearl all in a lie as they were not at the bank meeting the day they were questioned about. Doug Nelson helped in his testimony. Andy then started cross-examining Bucknam until closing at 5 pm. Rog called me tonight. He is in Otisville, NY. I wondered where he would be. He left there by bus early this morning.

Thursday, October 30: First day in Otisville, Fourth day of bank trial: Dave stopped in this morning as Roger had called him at 7:45 am to hear how it went yesterday. I didn't go today. I was just plain tired and it is hard on my back as well as my mind, just so much with Rog being moved. Dave didn't go. Kathy went and Marilyn, Marielle and a friend came up from Mass. Bert, Bill Hill, Richard, Ginny & girls. Rog called tonight just as Kathy was here, so she told him of the day's events. Andy finished with Bucknam. He asked him to read a figure and Bucknam said he couldn't as it was too small and you would need a magnifying glass to see it. Andy said "I just happen to have one," and took it up to him. Bucknam said the figure was a zero that Grays owed bank and Bucknam was charging Roger for. Tom Thompson was in just a short time but didn't hurt. Elaine Smith was on, she didn't hurt, but two from the FDIC, of course, were against Roger. Johnston wanted them to explain what the FDIC was. The Judge told him he was a federal judge and knew, to get on with something else.

Friday, October 31: Second day in Otisville, Fifth day of bank trial: Reg and Dave went to the trial today. The bank's expert witnesses, Filipiak and Chandler, were on. Dave said Andy crucified Chandler, and Filipiak was a repeat. Also Bonnie Norway and Eileen Dunn said Roger made everyone nervous when he came in. They would stiffen up etc; of course Bucknam told them to say that. Rog called, he is still in NY prison, and he called Dave later.

Saturday, November 1: Third day in Otisville: Rog called at 8 am. He had tried to get Dave but it won't ring in, so Dave came here and Rog called back. He is going to use Dave's other number and that did work. I went back to the office with him. Reg and Richard were there, also, Fay Young, Dave Turner, John Campbell, Wendy Davenport, Kathy and Ron, and Lee Cleveland was in and out. Andy isn't using Lee as a witness. He interviewed them all and went over and over the testimony for Mon. At one time Fay got very upset, swore, and said he wasn't needed as a witness but he calmed down and was OK.

Rog called tonight. They were all locked in today as raining so hard. We don't know what's next for him or where he will be. It's been two months since I've seen him. The family anxious to see him also. What a mess!

Sunday, November 2: Fourth day at Otisville: Roger still in NY. Kathy and I left at noon for Brattleboro and Dave also. We got our rooms at the Motel and Dave went up to Andy's room. Andy and Sara worked with the witnesses, one on one. Lise, Mavis and Marilyn came. I called Steve at home in case Rog could call.

Monday, November 3: Fifth day at Otisville, Sixth day of bank trial: At the trial, Wendy was on first and did a great job. Arthur Elliott was then on and last was Fay Young. Dave Turner and John Campbell were there but Andy didn't want to use them so Sara sent Kathy out to tell them to leave. Dave went out and told them also. Andy rested his case, but the bank lawyers wanted to cross-examine Turner and Campbell. Ones at the trial were, Bert, Bernie, Bill Hill, Don and Catherine Beattie, Mavis, Marilyn, Esther Young, Jeannie Elliott, Reg, Steve, Kathy, Richard, Dave & Lise and I, and the reporter from the Caledonian Record. We went to Andy and Sara's room for a while and then went home. We just got in when Rog called, wondering how it went today. He is still in NY, so unfair. I hope he gets to Vermont soon.

Tuesday, November 4: Sixth day at Otisville: Roger has been having the hives, but he didn't tell me before. He says he is better; I'm not surprised. He called the office this morning and talked with Dave and Reg.

Wednesday, November 5: Seventh day at Otisville: Rog still in NY. He still has the hives. He is having medication night and morning. He wishes he could get out of there.

Thursday, November 6: Eighth day at Otisville: Rog called different times today. He is having a bad day. Dave talked to DeTroy and Tom Majerison and they are waiting for a call from the Marshals. I tried also at 4 pm. I know it's hard on Rog, but is also hard on us, and he needs time with his lawyers. I'm sure the Government doesn't want him to.

Friday, November 7: Ninth day at Otisville: Charles released today from Allenwood. He sent a letter to me to give Rog, whenever I see him. Rog called, he is doing better today. Dave talked with the Maine lawyers; they are doing what they can.

Saturday, November 8: Tenth day at Otisville: Rog called tonight and said his hives are better. He did go out awhile and walk. He said he was very stiff. He's done so good to try and keep up his health; I don't know how he has but I pray he will be OK. I will do my best here, I'm glad I have Steve and Rob here. It is good to have someone talking and in and out.

Monday, November 10: Twelfth day at Otisville: Rog called at 7:30 pm, his hives nearly gone. He saw one of the Marshals that was at his trial. He told Rog he did nothing wrong, just helped people too much. He can't find out when he is leaving. Dave talked to Tom Majerison and they are coming the last of the week.

Tuesday, November 11: Thirteenth day at Otisville: He called tonight. Honi was here so she talked with him, she was glad she was here. He was told tonight he will be leaving tomorrow, but doesn't know if Burlington or Rutland, or what time he will have to take his bedding to laundry.

Wednesday, November 12: Fourteenth day at Otisville: Rog has been incarcerated 89 weeks. I didn't hear from him all day or tonight; makes me wonder where he is, hard to settle down tonight.

Thursday, November 13: Rog called about 9 am. He is in Albany, NY. He said they left in a van yesterday morning and it took 12 hours to go to where it takes only 2 hours, to Albany. They got there about 4 pm, and he was given a lunch as they hadn't eaten all day. He didn't have a jacket and said he nearly froze and could feel a cold coming on. They were locked in the bullpen all night, with a bathroom stool in the middle of the room; at least they had one. They were let out this morning, then slept a little while. He called in the pm. He is at the Middlebury jail with about a dozen other guys. Tonight he said he had the best meal he's had in a very long time. He had a shower tonight, feels chilly. There is a guy, named Guillette, there from Island Pond. Tom Majerison, lawyer from Maine, at office today to interview Arthur and Andy. I could relax tonight and thanked God he was there.

Friday, November 14: First day in Middlebury: Rog called, he is tired but glad to be there. They are down in a room like a cellar, high ceilings with windows way up high; he said it is like a dungeon. There are little cubbies where they sleep and it is not pleasant, but nothing is in this kind of living.

Saturday, November 15: Second day at Middlebury: We left home at 8 am for Middlebury, Toby, Tiffany, Chad and I, to visit Rog. It was so good to see him, and the guards let us in to give him hugs and kisses, then we had to go back in a little room and visit through a screen; we do what we have to. The guard did a special favor for us to let us in first and give him a hug. I took him some clothes, maple syrup and honey. Toby brought him a carton of cigarettes and tea bags. He wants some tea with honey to drink for his cold. I took him Andy's papers of his 10 pages to Judge Murtha of why Rog should win the trial. We left at 11:45 am, relieved. The guard let us hug him goodbye. Rog called tonight and said we can come tomorrow.

Sunday, November 16: Third day at Middlebury: Kathy, Holly and I left at 8 am for Middlebury; it was stormy, but we made it OK. He was glad to see us. We visited until noon; the guard let us all have hugs and kisses. We couldn't help the tears, all of us. Richard, Ginny and girls went over, but didn't find the place, too bad and so close. Rog said they had pancakes this morning with real maple syrup; they have good meals.

Monday, November 17: Fourth day at Middlebury: Rog's hearing in Burlington for a new trial. Steve, I, Marilyn and Mavis left at 7 am for Burlington, also Ron and Kathy, Richard and Ginny, Reg, Dave and Donald Simpson. Lise came with Brenda and Smitty. The Sheriff brought Rog in in handcuffs. He said they took off the leg irons just before going in. God it was hard to see him treated like this. Mitch Pearl was the only one on stand. Langrock never showed up. The lawyers said they could go after him but knew he would lie on the stand, so decided not to. They also decided not to put Arthur Elliott, Andy, and Turner on stand, so was done by noon. The Magistrate will give an answer by the first of the year.

After, we met with lawyers and went over it all; of course Rog was taken to the inmate room. We couldn't go see him, and while in the courtroom they told him to just look straight ahead, not at anyone, but we did have eye contact.

He was in that room until 5 pm tonight and was very cold in there. The courtroom was very warm. His hives are bothering him tonight; I don't doubt it. It makes us all nervous. I came home with a headache. Rene Crete, an inmate at Otisville, called tonight to see how it went.

Those at the hearing were: Armand and Norma Morin, Pat and Paul Presault, Bert, Becky Sanville, Smitty and Brenda, Frank Temple, Fay and Esther, Arthur and Jeannie, Don Simpson, Dave Turner, Andy Field, Marilyn, Mavis, Reg, Steve, Richard and Ginny, Dave and Lise, Ron, Kathy and I.

Tuesday, November 18: Fifth day at Middlebury: I was tired this morning, was awake at 5 am till 7, and then slept till 8. I called the office but they hadn't heard from their Dad. In the pm, I was tired and didn't feel great, so sacked out on the couch and did sleep. As soon as I awoke, Roger called and he too had slept and he has a cold. The Doctor came there, and is coming back tomorrow with something for his hives, that hasn't all gone from his system. He called tonight and had a good beef stew for supper. It was so good, he said.

Wednesday, November 19: Sixth day at Middlebury: Rog called this morning. The Doctor came and gave him medication for his hives, and checked his ear that he has skin cancer on. Fay came in office and he and Dave and Reg read the 10 pages from the bank lawyers to Judge Murtha. Fay said he didn't say some of the things they said he did.

Thursday, November 20: Seventh day at Middlebury: Roger called at 8 am and said last night he took the medication and went to sleep and slept the night; the best sleep he's had for a long time. The Doctor is getting his record from St. J on his ear. He called tonight. His hives so much better; he had a very nice spaghetti supper.

Friday, November 21: Eighth day at Middlebury: I went over to the office. Rog called and gave me a list of things he needed me to bring Saturday. His hives all gone, but he is still on medication. It is awful being shut up like he is, especially when he doesn't deserve it, and at his age. It makes me feel very sad.

Saturday, November 22: Ninth day at Middlebury: Richard and I left at 10 am to visit Rog. We stopped at Beatties' store and got him a can of coffee, box of tea and cheese. Catherine sent him cookies. When we got to the jail, Bert and Sandy were visiting him. I told the guard we would wait, but he went and told Rog we were there, so Bert and Sandy came right out. We had a nice visit, but the room was cold where we had to sit, but warm on the side Rog was in. We had to talk through a screen. We had to leave at 3 pm.

Sunday, November 23: Tenth day at Middlebury: Lise called to see if I would ride to Barre with her to Sara Fields' as Wendy Davenport had a letter from the bank demanding she turn her notes over to them and take them to Gravel's office and transfer them from short hand to long hand. Wendy brought them here and we took them to Sara, as that's what Sara wanted done. We came right back; had been snowing. Rog called tonight, just to say good night.

Monday, November 24: Eleventh day at Middlebury: Dave went to Sara Field's office and copied Wendy's short hand notes. He has to go back tomorrow to finish. Rog called tonight; one of the guys gave him a haircut. He called Dave after. .

Tuesday, November 25: Twelfth day at Middlebury: I called the jail this morning to see when we can come again and can on Saturday. Rog called and things are the same. He's glad we can come Saturday.

Wednesday, November 26: Thirteenth day at Middlebury: Rog called tonight. He listens to the 6 pm news then the guys turn it. He would like to hear the national news but wouldn't say so. The Doctor checked his ear again and plans to take care of it next week.

Thursday, November 27: Thanksgiving Day: Fourteenth day at Middlebury: Rog called tonight about 9:30 pm. They had a nice Thanksgiving supper about 7:30. It's been two years we've been apart.

Friday, November 28: Fifteenth day at Middlebury: Rog called tonight. He had surgery done on his left ear, right at the jail. The Doctor is going to see if it's malignant and will be back Wednesday to take out the stitches. It's still numb tonight but I'm so glad they had the Doctor come there and check him.

Saturday, November 29: Sixteenth day at Middlebury: Reg came at 7:30 and we headed out. We stopped at McDonalds, for coffee and muffin, and ate on the way. The Sheriff took us upstairs to a room, like a conference room, with tables and nice easy chairs. He brought Roger right in there, it seemed so good not to have to visit through the screen and we could be together. Rog told him he appreciated that and we did also. He called tonight and mentioned it, also was so good for us.

Sunday, November 30: Seventeenth day at Middlebury: The family and I had our Thanksgiving here. All came, only Roger was missing. We miss him for the second year and pray he will be back with us next year. He called and wished he was here.

Monday, December 1: Eighteenth day at Middlebury: I called Middlebury jail for permission to visit again; they gave me Sunday. I went to the office to pay bills. Fay came in as Rog called so he talked with him. We sent papers to Rog that Tom Majerison wrote to Magistrate.

Tuesday, December 2: Nineteenth day at Middlebury: Roger called the office and talked with Dave and Richard. He called tonight. Kathy was here and talked. He received the papers we mailed yesterday from Andy. Herb Gray called and wants to go visit Rog. Rog will find out if he can.

Wednesday, December 3: Twentieth day at Middlebury: Rog called tonight. The Doctor came and took out the stitches from his ear. Rog can't look at it as there are no mirrors; they are not allowed, due to glass. Kathy called Brattleboro and got Judge Murtha's chambers and his law clerk. She asked if the LSB v Lussier trial case was decided and he said no and hung up. He has probably been getting calls. Been month today that it ended.

Thursday, December 4: Twenty-First day at Middlebury: Ron and Kathy were down tonight. They were here when Rog called and we all talked to him. He said his ear feels good. Doctor had to cut some of it out. They all went outside today and he said it seemed so good.

Friday, December 5: Twenty-Second day at Middlebury: Rog called. He thinks he is going to be moved as one of the head ones said tonight that some of you will be leaving Monday. I hope I see him first.

Saturday, December 6: Twenty-Third day at Middlebury: Rog called, nothing different.

Sunday, December 7: Twenty-Fourth day at Middlebury: Dave, Lise, the kids and I went to visit Rog. We were there at 1:15 pm. Laurent and Lucille were in visiting him. The Sheriff asked for more time as they had only been in there 10 minutes. After they left, Lise, Jess & Tricia went in for a half hour, and then Nate, Aaron and I went in. After that Dave and Herb Gray went in. That made 10 visitors. The Sheriff said he's a popular man. I hope he isn't moved and can stay there. His ear looked good to me. We couldn't give him hugs and kisses today, maybe because so many of us. Rog called tonight. He was so happy to see the grandchildren and wished he could have hugged them.

Monday, December 8: Twenty-Fifth day at Middlebury: Rog called this morning. They told him he will be leaving tomorrow, damn, damn. Here we go again. I wish he could have stayed in Vt. for the holidays and he likes it there. He was depressed tonight as all of us are. Will there ever be a break for us? I received a box from the US Justice Dept. – it was clothes that Rog wore at his hearing last June. All he wore was the pants rolled up 6", as too long, but the shoes and shirt they sent are nothing he wore and tags still on them. I won't pay to send them back.

Tuesday, December 9: Didn't hear from Rog this morning or tonight. He left Middlebury jail and was taken by bus to the Chester County, NH jail and put in solitary confinement. He couldn't wear a jacket. I didn't know this at the time, just wondered where he was and prayed he was OK.

Wednesday, December 10: Haven't heard from Rog, wonder where he is. I just stayed home by the phone. Didn't hear tonight, but later, that he was taken from West Minister to Manchester, NH, and put on plane to Otisville. There were 300 on the plane.

Thursday, December 11: Otisville: Roger called Dave this morning and then called me. He is at Otisville and got there at midnight. He said the Warden there in Otisville used to be at Allenwood. He shook hands with him. Rog called at 9:15 tonight and said he slept today and was pretty tired. He sounded better. Tonight he had played cards with some of them. His clothes came today he wore in Middlebury; what a funny feeling. This was the first laundry I've done for him for 22 months. It seemed good but also sad.

Friday, December 12: Otisville: I received a letter from the doctor that did surgery on Rog's ear at Middlebury. He said he got all the cancer but it should be checked in 3 months then every 3 months after. I sent copy to

Doctor in St. J. for records and will send to Rog to give Doctor in Allenwood. He called tonight, also Rene Crete to see how he's doing, so when I told him he's there in another section he will try to see him Monday just to wave and holler hello.

Saturday, December 13: Otisville: Dave came with the mail. My dividend came and was only half of it, on what Rog and I own together. We will check with Andy. Told Rog when he called. He slept a lot today; I'm sure he needed to. He called for just a couple minutes tonight as there was a long line, just to let me know he's OK. Thank God, and he knows we are.

Sunday, December 14: Otisville: Rog called tonight, things the same.

Monday, December 15: Otisville: Rog called tonight. He received his money order I sent him. Dave was checking out why he hadn't. It was there; they just hadn't posted it. He needed it to buy toilet articles; they did give him some clothes – that surprised us.

Tuesday, December 16: Otisville: Rog called me. He has been told he will be moving again tomorrow. I believe back to Allenwood. While he was talking to me someone stole his two cartons of cigarettes. Thieves. They would steal your clothes if they weren't buttoned on. He was very discouraged tonight; so are we.

Wednesday, December 17: Otisville. Rog called this morning, isn't sure what time he's leaving. Will call tonight if he can. Right now he doesn't remember his pin no. so will have to go to the office to find out. He called later. They don't think he will leave today. He said he's itching, maybe the hives coming back again.

Dave brought over Vandegraaf's response to Judge why he believes Roger should not receive a new trial, sure sounds like the Gov't. Rog reported his cigarettes were stolen, didn't do any good. They probably went to more that one person and they won't squeal on each other, or someone would get popped off – scary, but true. He didn't go today.

Thursday, December 18: I didn't hear from Rog all day or tonight. I'm sure he's on his way to Allenwood.

Friday, December 19: Rog called this morning and said he got to Allenwood at 3 pm yesterday. He couldn't call as the phone lines were being worked on. He went in one of their busses. They only chained his hands this time – that's enough. He has his same cubby. They gave him his things from storage, and he had to report for work at noon. He called me tonight at 8 pm. He said the guys were glad to see him again, shook hands and asked him about his hearing.

He was glad to be back there, if he couldn't be home. Charles had been released and had gone home; Roger was happy for him but missed him. His other good friend, Greg Walker, from PA, now helped him with his paperwork. They became very good friends.

This is what took place from June to December 1997, not a pleasant time for him or any of us. Neither he or I, or any of you, will ever forget it, but knowing all of you were helping him on this end, finding papers he needed, doing calls for him, contacting people for information he needed, getting the petition of over 2000 names to the judge and oh so many thing all of you did for me, meant he didn't have to worry about me, as he knew you all were keeping good tabs on me. The grandchildren writing him letters were a blessing for him, as he knew he was loved and realized how much he had to come home to. We all worked together and that's the beauty of family unity, and he did come home. Steve, Richard and I went for him and brought him back to St. Johnsbury, January 29, 1999 to the Lincoln Inn where all the family was waiting for him. He only had an hour there, and then Steve and I took him to fhe Correctional Ctr., but he was in our area. From there he was back home, at first for a half hour a day, and that time kept increasing until he was home for good. What a happy day that was for all of us. We survived, with all your help, the years he was away, the home confinement and the 2 years probation.

I still have the scars on my ankles from the chains that tied me to the others and I assume they will be with me forever. The experience of this type of imprisonment has not left the visible scars that you can find on my ankles but they are there upon me and upon my family, all of us just as certainly as the ones that had been around my hands and waist and chest and legs. I recall spending over 15 hours wearing handcuffs and those tied to a chain point on my belt. You can neither exercise your shoulders or your arms nor relieve yourself or probably escape.

I've been trying to describe to you a pitiful world of discarded persons who are for the most part out of sight and out of mind, and cannot be easily comprehended by anyone who has not experienced this shattering isolation and intrusion into your personality that incarceration itself brings. It is truly the experience of losing yourself. Nothing in my whole life prepared me for the changes brought upon me by imprisonment. It is a form of "social death," a way of visiting your grave in advance.

And it does not matter if the believed crimes were large, or small, violent, or of red in color or are purple. The owners of the system and the management of the process have concluded: **One size fits all!**

So far I believe I have accounted for you a boring story of life within prison. I have given some accounts of the noise, and the danger, the uncertainty of the most ordinary of events, the degradation of personality that you experience. I've indicated that there are many ways in which conflicts with individuals and society could be pursued without recourse to this primitive destruction;

mental health treatment and addiction treatment as the primary examples. But there is a whole side of this story yet to be told. That is the life of the families: those beloved individuals and relatives and community members who are also affected but not incarcerated directly. They also experience much of what the prisoner does but without the clarity of the roles being understood. Think of it more like the example of the tethered goat, an animal used as a target for another predator that is then captured in its own turn by the man doing the gathering. Can you imagine yourself tied up and contained while your own family members are socially abused or shunned or harmed on your behalf? That is a story often overlooked.

In my experience I had the absolute benefit of a loving wife and children, who were secure in their own identity and were supported by their own spouses and children. They were able to reassure and reinforce each other by being close and by being entirely informed regarding all of the circumstances and all of the facts and charges that led to my incarceration. We all were from a community that knew us well, and we had years and years of respect and trust. Friendships that had been tested over and again and found trustworthy and for the most part held the same opinion of us all from the beginning to the end of this miserable chapter. But many of the other prisoners whose plight I am reporting to you did not have the same generosity and security in their families and friendships that certainly was true for me. As I've indicated when mail call came around the holidays I would receive hundreds and hundreds of cards and letters. My remembrance is others received few if any. I would get letters from our social friends and from businesses and individuals recounting events to me; occasions of generosity and expressions of appreciation for things that had often been almost forgotten.

I never felt that I deserved being where I was and the behavior of all the others of my family and community were significant to me and assisted me greatly in retaining my self-respect and my belief that I was important to them. But for many others the information they received was in the form of letters from lawyers and announcements of divorce or separation or remarriage. There were notices of suspension of utilities at home for bills unpaid, loss of leases, repossessions of cars, attachments. These were all evidence of social distraction and social death. Now it was not as if I was unscathed or protected by a magic bullet. Our families were all seriously harmed economically by the unjust attachment of all family resources that Evelyn and I shared together as an extension of the bank's claims against me alone. All of us were forced to live with diminished or frozen resources. But obligations of our families continued as if it was business as usual. In spite of those difficulties my children were able to drive to Allenwood and see me on a regular basis during the visitation days. I was able to call home and talk with our children and my wife frequently. I was able to know that she was in the same house where we lived together and was not packing up and moving to an apartment somewhere that I had never seen. Our children were affected in their business by a proximate reputation I believe. People knew something had happened to me and I'd been found guilty of something but they weren't quite sure where the edges of all that were. Sometimes the children were looked upon in their businesses with suspicion and uncertainty. Could they be trusted? Was an auction in the Lussier name the same or different? Was it legal? Can their business deals be legal and stand scrutiny? But we were known and for the most part treated fairly, and as time passed the community understood that our family and the efforts of our children were as reliable and honest and as trustworthy as anyone else's and as ours had always been. I know that they each suffered, but I do not know in detail how each suffered or had them require of me an apology for what happened to them. But they suffered. I'm sure I will never know all of the harm done to them as a consequence of this prosecution. They have never presented me with a list of their damages or asked me to make things right for them. They have never come to me and told me they were ashamed of me or that I'd put them in difficult places. They've never told me about their personal fears for the future or the business costs or social costs they've had to pay as a result of all of this. But I know it was very bad, and I know they have suffered, and I know it was unjust for all of us. After I had been convicted and was in prison, my grandchildren had some problems in school. It seems that some of the other children would repeat what their parents or others might have said, not knowing the hurt they were causing. I was told of an instance where one of my grandchildren was in school when some of the others said things that confused, scared and hurt her, which began to affect her emotionally. Fortunately she had caring and understanding teachers that were quickly on top of the situation. The same situation existed for the grandchildren that were in high school. Caring teachers and trained counselors were aware of the circumstances and were on top of any problems that arose. One grandchild was in college and was very fortunate to have a wise and caring counselor that was always available just to talk and keep things in proper perspective. There were friends and even many strangers that helped our family during these troubled times, and they asked for nothing in return.

In spite of that, Steven would get in the car and drive his mother to Allenwood and wait for the visitation doors to open and then drive back afterwards and go to work. The other children did the same. There were births and baptisms and marriages and intentions to marry that were all decided in my absence but shared with me as loving children do with their parents. They would all come when they could and they did often, encouraging me and asking nothing for themselves.

As I looked around the visitation room past them, I heard the stories of other prisoner's family members. I heard of divorce, saw prisoners separated at trial from loved ones, heard stories of infidelity and affairs, of auctions and sheriff's seizures and of liquidation of assets and the collapse of those mutual hopes. I could see that indeed I was a man blessed by good fortune and the undisputed love of his family. Even if I died in prison I would die as a man loved by many. And that was a distinct difference from many of those around me who suffered as I did and perhaps suffered much more. For all I have said about the danger, boredom, and stress of being incarcerated, I will say that I believe it was far harder on my wife and children on the outside than it was personally for me on the inside. Once I realized that I could not help them further or do any useful thing for them the only resources available to me were resignation, trust that what they had learned previously would find them in good stead now, and commending them to a loving God that loves us all! It was terrible to be tethered, to know I could not help Evelyn as the bank pursued her illegally and unjustly for the control of her property and assets. It was difficult to see property that had been acquired so carefully lost to taxes because my assets were seized, and I could not pay the taxes as they became due. I always paid my bills promptly. But none of that probably was as difficult for me as life on the outside was for my wife, my children and their families. They suffered clearly without cause or justice, and there was nothing to be done about it. And Charlie Bucknam, who had earned none of the wealth of the bank he was now using as his own, attached – what came to be seen and found as an unjust "illegal" attachment – everything of Evelyn's in spite of the Vermont marital property laws, and his knowledge that the bank was not entitled to the legal course it was being driven to. And even now, after courts and signed documents have revealed his perjury and his deception, he wishes to be regarded as the defender of the bank's diminishing future.

I have mentioned how the religious life within the prison is a place where persons get to see and hear themselves described in other then judgmental terms. That what was true about us at our baptism was still true about us in our captivity. Now to be sure there were many persons who found "jail house religion" and perhaps they end up at the same place we all do. I don't know about that. But what I did find interesting is how the story from Christianity differs with that as told by society about us. Prior to incarceration I had grown up and continue to be a part of the Roman Catholic faith and have found that a satisfactory resource for all that has happened to me. I participate in and married into other religious beliefs as well. All of them are good...especially the Indians. At my trial Father Beauregard came daily and sat behind our family to give evidence of his understanding and support and regard for us. I'm grateful for that. After incarceration, other clergy from Lyndonville called Evelyn and indicated their respect for her and made themselves available to her if they could be of assistance. But there is another side of that that still confuses me.

There was a prior experience in Lyndonville of attending a church among whose members was the wife of someone else in prison earlier than myself. And within that congregation was a comment "how dare she come here when her husband is in prison!" Now one of the big problems that this story is circling around is how does society safely decide whom to judge and whom not to. Those perjuring "singers" that I mentioned were used by the judicial system to accomplish its own goals, and what they said was neither true nor valid evidence to be used to judge me. But they did. That collection of "singers" was forgiven over $100 million worth of admitted theft to society, and I was in prison the longest of any of them, when there was no loss claimed, on my part, by the Whole of the United States of America among us all. The most the Whole of the United States of America ever claimed I was responsible for was $426,000 and that was during the sentencing and was later found to be an illegal restitution order. The "singers" admitted theft was over $100,000,000. And that figure of $426,000 is disputed by me as a previously "written off" debt by the bank against normal operating experience and was not a loss to them by me. If corporate activity becomes simply "personal" then using that logic the profit by the bank of over $16 million should have been mine personally and not retained by the bank as theirs.

I believe the Indians who were native to this continent had it more correct when they saw the human being as an embodiment of both the spiritual dimensions and the physical dimensions in a person. Both are present. Their preferred methods for social control were strategies of conversation and consensus, not the strategies of death, isolation and war making. That is why a "Chief" spoke last, asked questions, and found ways of reconciliation. *War making and death giving was regarded as a failure and not an achievement*!

The "criminal justice system" is like a bully pushing a lady into the rushing river, running down stream and pulling her out...and expecting to be proclaimed a hero!

No other civilized culture has ever done this successfully.

There is something absolutely terrible beyond my own "guilt" or "innocence" when an "FBI" agent can feel free to say to me, and he did: "You didn't do anything wrong Roger. What you did was help too many poor people. Poor people are supposed to stay that way. That is what you did." Imagine, a sworn agent, a person promising to defend and uphold the constitution of the United States feeling and speaking that way against most of his fellow citizens. That is that "them and us" thinking of cheap politicians, too many law enforcement agents and prosecutors, and that for certain damned excuse of an "FBI" agent. Hersh, who do you think is paying for your rich retirement?

"DOMINION"

It was Easter morning; the announcing of the
Resurrection, claims of Hope and Victory and Life!
We, Roger and I, walked again to the Stone Church; an
anniversary of our captivity, citizens in this land of the
walking dead, proceeding to Church and the attending
to Statements and Claims and Blessings and Candles,
and Announcements and Declarations and Embarrasses
(the Peace) topped off with Wine and Bread and Water
at the door!

Standing upon the steps you oversee the waiting
cemetery. It is of those who once sought this place as
home, fought for it at Gettysburg (there they are now
rows of stone and flags) buried their children here and
then settled down among them later themselves to await
the awaiting, even now perhaps recalling that song:
"earth to earth, dust to dust, in the sure and certain
hope of life..." This was their place and it remains
awaiting in the shade of Oak and Conifer and quiet
grass, with squirrels a-play---all waiting, sons and
fathers, soldiers and wife, wife of another after waiting
for years; all planted in hope, all accounted for, Easter
upon Easter from farmland and home to now... as they
wait.

Beyond that place of grassy quiet another cemetery
announces itself with wire and walls to block sight
and sound and hope as certainly as nearby grass and
headstones. That other grave of steel and one way
entry, as certain and final as any sod site! IT stands in
arrogant announcement as tombstone of wire and wall:
one name fits all.

The yard before us is announced as waiting for another
change and buried in the sure and certain hope of
resurrection. It even expects it! That new yard brazen
with lights and sirens and steel coffins that open only

once at the door and closes upon you...is smug in the suffocation of the entrant...like a novice at the gate of the cloister: never to be seen again, never to be heard, never to emerge.

Both yards of death I see, standing at this House of Easter; both in sight and purpose joined, both at work with worm and time. A voice behind me says "they found the stone rolled away and the violated tomb still in shock at the invasion of Angels!" This grass asks quietly waiting its time: Is that true of me? The still walled Stone, unrolled and sealed replies: No! Go back to sleep. It is all a mistake! Don't you see my Seal and Flag intact?

There is no living here. Go! Go! We are the dead.

And so we are: the incarcerated in the land of the free.

Even in Hell there is Amusement!

My fellow prisoners were some of the most interesting persons I have ever met. Many probably are innocent, few deserving of what they received, and some absolutely needing to be where they were. Several were amusing, and some of this latter group I would like to present to you.

There was a fellow from Maine, nicknamed "the Rootman." He was good natured, friendly, usually alone, but approachable. His interest was horticulture. He was gentle and kind in manner and speech and did not seem a likely candidate for being where he was.

Everyone in prison is given a "job" which is more difficult to do than you might initially expect. With hundreds of persons to be occupied each day the meaning of the work is probably not as important as finding some differentiated task for everyone, getting them to it, and getting them back. So it was with "Rootman"! His specialty was gardening, and he could make things grow when others failed. So naturally he was placed in the greenhouse to grow plants, to start seedlings for the gardens, to raise tomatoes, lettuce and other produce which he sold, among other things, as a sideline.

Why was he there? He had been convicted of growing marijuana, which he admitted he did. It had been grown and used for medicinal purposes, and he had been part of a statewide effort in Maine to grow naturally-occurring in-the-wild marijuana domestically for its benefits to cancer and glaucoma patients, among others. You noted I said that marijuana can be found in nature. (ask a Vermont cow why they are so contented.) Well, hundreds of acres of fields in Pennsylvania had the same. And where did the plants find a comfortable winter home? The Greenhouses! And who is in charge of the Greenhouses? The Rootman! So he developed a profitable tomato business selling fresh produce to the inmates to combine with their "salads" also gathered from institutional resources. And his cultivation skill with the naturally occurring plant was noticed and appreciated by the staff and guards who bought his product and found it to be safe, inexpensive, and without legal dangers of a "busted" buy. Justice, adaptation, accommodation, or just getting his own back, I haven't decided.

Often I have heard people say that those in prison must deserve it or they wouldn't be there. And there is general agreement that it is a punishment, of which I have no doubt. But from time to time you meet persons there that seem to be truly happy with their plight and many, particularly the younger minorities, seem to have benefited from regular hours, clean living, and reasonably balanced meals. Now there was one person I recall that absolutely seemed to be pleased with his plight. And pardon me if I touch on some personal sexual material, but that also goes with such a place. This person, while in an all-male prison, regarded himself successfully as a female and such a conclusion was visibly advertised. "She" had a walk, a manner of speaking and eye movement, gestures and costumes that would have convinced you that the admitting physician had made a mistake in assignment. But this is not the point. When your mind is not challenged by the big events of the world then you have plenty of time to add up the small stuff and see the contradictions among us, like finding justice in a "justice system."

Now this person was supposed to be miserable and experiencing all of the believed benefits of being judged, jailed, and deprived of happiness. But for a person of his or her convictions where is the punishment in being confined with 700 other men, and you the only "female" available? Available! "He/she" had more attention, more privacy; more social life than most of us had altogether in our normal lives. We used to think that if they opened the gate and said "he/she" could leave that he would file a motion in Court to serve the entire sentence. Gifts! Love letters! Entertainment! No one seemed more pleased with the misfortune of being there, or made better use of the opportunity. It was just damned annoying to have a Saturday arrive after a hard week of working in the fields to come home to your cube and hear "her" singing in the shower…Saturday night, oh Saturday night! The rest of us had movies, that is, those without a date.

So if any of this was about seeking justice, or being somewhere where you are deprived of your meaning in life, then to put a practicing homosexual in jail and lock this person up with a herd of males is almost a travesty. The judge should have known better. "She" received free meals, free health care and free rent to boot. Now that is something. Where in Vermont could you get the same deal?

There was one man that I met in prison that was really upset after hearing my story. Bern Anderson knew people in the film industry and thought my story might make a good film. He wrote to these people[1], but did not hear back from them. His letter is an exhibit at the end of the book. He is one of many I met at Allenwood that was upset, but not really surprised, to learn to just what lengths the government would go to in order to make themselves look good. Justice means nothing to the government but publicity in their favor means everything.

Overall, mostly it is living among hundreds of men in large common rooms, (TV cells for privacy and protection are things imagined) surrounded with persons in varied states of misery and hurt. There would be those who never received mail or ever got a card, those that had no money for cigarettes or stamps, and those never able to move beyond just being contained.

There were people who prayed and said grace over their food... sometimes a real forced thanksgiving. There were people with what seemed like unlimited spending money for items from the "Store" and many without a cent. Not one! All of us together worked at prison jobs and were paid 20 cents an hour. If you were not a high school graduate you received .10 per hour and given a chance to get your education. I did and got the raise.

All days seemed the same: get up, get counted to see if you were still there, stand in line to eat, go to work, stand in line for lunch, work, go back and get counted again to see if you are still there, stand in line to eat, then an open evening to try and waste or use within the bounds of the place. There was also a wonderful and prayerful group of men at the nightly "Rosary." We listened to each other's account of the day, shared information about problems and good news, requests for prayer and remembering, and then we prayed...Mary, mother of God have mercy on us...and we believed she did. I cannot describe the noise, the constant tension among the prisoners, the endless hopes for legal relief, appeals and new court filings. (Like the lottery, you always heard about someone winning, but never anyone you knew or saw — urban legends) Conflicts of culture, habits, of talking and TV watching, grievances held among differing interests, and constant, unceasing demand for cigarettes, a loan, or a favor. Always the same clothes, the same colors, smells and subjects for discussion. Each new arrival begins it again, each departing person opens up again the loss and longing; memories of freedom beyond reach and sometimes even reason. It was just a large group of desperate men, isolated into helplessness and trying to find a way of surviving and passing time without going mad. Some managed, some lost.

All are forever affected and in no proportion to charges, guilt, ages, or character. One prison size fits all, very ecumenical. And later when some of those events, like constant and random harassment, chaining in transportation, isolation in holding tanks, are questioned, the reply is; that is what is supposed to happen. This is "Jail not Yale"! As if there had been any confusion about that. As if saying something absurd explained the absurd. It was doing its job, so they said. And to offer my reader some amusement from this I will describe for you something that seems so ludicrous and out of place as to be either "dark humor" or simply the silliest use of time imagined.

Now I am sure we have not forgotten that persons in prison are in a confined environment, and not expected to be going anywhere on their own, or freely. Now pick a subject of amusement and ask what might be the real time-waster. Advanced mathematics and theoretical physics? No! Could it be classes in home management, and alternative careers for when you are released? No. How to run a business and make a profit, classes in therapy, psychology and self-improvement? No!

How about flying lessons? Now think about that. A classroom filled with men, some never having touched a plane, taking ground school for flying instruction. The last people on earth going anywhere are studying lift, drag, weather and cross country navigation. There is no anticipation of any reality to their learning. It is a social form of denial and the suspension of facts for everyone; just a temporary evasion of our plight and an attempt at humor! A comedy in the coliseum of ancient Rome without the blood.

In my mind that rates right up there with "dressing up a corpse in his best suit" for the trip to the cemetery!

[1] See Exhibits pages 28-30 for Anderson letter

The Ninth Commandment

The attack upon the Northeast Kingdom by
lies, lies and more damn lies

When persons who have some awareness of the "Ten Commandments" are asked to recite them usually the list is incomplete. And if you were to ask those with partial accuracy to rank them, you often find certain statements about adultery, honoring your father and mother, and "going to church." It is unimportant here to note that there are actually several listings of the "10 Commandments," and that the list varies in order among the different denominations. To provide a common page for our inquiry, you may wish to see the list as translated in the "King James" version as quoted from the Book of Exodus: Chapter 20, verses 3-20.

(Go back and read this section in your family Bible. In colonial days this list often hung in the courthouse. It was believed to be an opportunity of instruction for the poorer class before the bar. Perhaps in fact it was there for the benefit of the lawyers and Judge and that point has just been forgotten. From my experience they currently neither hold that list nor the oath to tell the truth with any concern in this era)

So pause for a moment and ask yourself if you were to select the most damaging and most injurious to others of these to break which would it be?

Adultery may be seen as damaging and harmful to children, families and society. And certainly it is one of those we know the most about. And probably it is the one we wish most often had not been included in that list. We think of things like that as being personal, individualistic, often not "hurting anyone" and more a matter of embarrassment than of moral concern. Persons in adultery usually have some awareness they are harming someone, otherwise why the deceit, the necessity of it. But there is always some comedy when you make sex so important, so central to your values. It is almost like simply making sex a biological function alone, and you might just as well reduce the activity to "its ok anyone." You're not important or even know my name, mutual self-stimulation with deception. Which is usually the last argument used when discovered"…honey, she didn't mean anything to me…it was just sex." So while usually leading the popularity contest, even the practitioners of this activity deny it importance.

What about "graven idols?" We think of images of things, small and obscure; nothing like a Jaguar or Ford Explorer but those probably qualify!

"Honor your father and mother?" That is covered with cards sent and flowers delivered from California.

So why are we surprised, even disappointed, that when you get to Court the same game is played? How would it feel to you if you knew in advance of trial that the attorneys had, by a series of decisions, colluded to limit testimony to only one side, excluded beneficial evidence to the defendant, had his lawyers disguise their conflicts of interest, and then appear and announces to the contrary that it was not the case. What is it like for <u>any potential appeal</u> to be excluded in advance by the attorney resting his case when he should have been beginning to demolish the opposition with the waiting (and uncalled for) witnesses, documents, and facts?

How would you like to be sent to jail on the sworn testimony of persons who have agreed in advance to lie, misrepresent, exclude documents, and deny witnesses, and for all official parties to be aware of the contradictions. Then they solemnly require of each person in turn that they "swear to tell the truth, the whole truth, and nothing but the truth so help you God." Answering <u>Yes</u>, meaning <u>No</u>!

How would you feel then, as you now consider the Ninth commandment? Does it perhaps now seem more important? Well, the breaking of this commandment got me in prison, cost everyone a portion of their lives, harmed many innocent persons, and rewarded those commandment breakers. Won't those be interesting confessions to hear?

Our culture seems to be unable to grasp the differences among its methods of accountability. If something good happens usually we praise the American way of life, like success in the stock market or corporate profitability or some initial military success. If something bad happens <u>we avoid looking at the system</u> and search for an individual that is to blame for the whole. The "contra scandals," Enron, the savings and loan scandals almost now forgotten, the initial appraisal of "Watergate" as a third-rate burglary...unaware of its direct order by the highest elected official in the United States. We seem to be fixed in our cowboy movie mentality of "white hats" and "black hats" and we are told in advance the outcome so the stress of reality may be avoided.

What you begin to realize is that it is individual decisions and persons "dressed up" as the collective Whole of the United States of America that make the representations believable and decisions that are <u>passed off</u> as on behalf of the whole. But in fact it is the thousands of individuals in positions of trust, which have the capacity to misrepresent and betray on behalf of an abstract idea. And usually it is persons who presume to believe they are better informed or better to be trusted than others.

For example, if you go to the descriptions by the Whole of the United States of America for the necessity of the testimony of David Turner at the beginning of the federal criminal trial and the prosecutor's actual behavior you will see two entirely different and contradictory conclusions. As the trial is about to open the federal prosecutor's father has had a heart attack away from Vermont, and Turner has had a heart attack and is hospitalized within Vermont. The federal prosecutor previously announced that David Turner is their most essential witness without whose testimony the events that they alleged to be criminal couldn't be comprehended. They are so certain of this position that just as the trial is set to begin the prosecutor, the Whole of the United States of America, makes a motion to delay the trial and to have a continuance until David Turner's testimony is available. They said that Turner was absolutely essential to the Provost matter and important to a couple other counts. They did not make this motion out of generosity or of any concern for David Turner's own well being, but because they wished the public perception to be that his testimony is central, dramatic, and absolutely necessary.

The presiding judge indicates a willingness to consider the motion and seems surprised that the defense attorney does not know an opportunity when he hears one. The defense attorney has not become informed as to the extent of David Turner's testimony and probably has been himself misled about the nature of that testimony and concludes that it can only be harmful to his client. I told my attorney that Turner would not say what the government said he said and Langrock told me that the FBI and the government could get anybody to say anything they wanted them to. When in fact if you look at the affidavits[1] and Grand Jury testimony of David Turner in the Exhibit section of this book you will see that what he said to the Grand Jury and what he said in his affidavits would have absolutely benefited my defense and would have begun to expose the federal charges for the contradiction they were. When the offer for a continuance is declined and the defense attorney wishes to proceed, the Judge offers to separate the charges so that they can come back to those needing Turner's testimony and that offer is agreed upon. The following day the government changes its mind and said they would continue without Turner's testimony and the Judge told them they couldn't have it both ways, but finally agreed to go on with the trial. The government was able to give their version of Turner's testimony to the Judge without a chance for it to be challenged by the defense. He had successfully contaminated Turner as a favorable witness to myself and surprised my attorney into believing that David would be hostile to our own interest. Again when you read David Turner's sworn and truthful affidavits and Grand Jury testimony you see that he was in no way about to say what they alleged he would say, and they knew it. And this can easily be seen as speculation and as hearsay of the worst kind, because it was presented by an officer of the court and not challenged by another officer of the court and not regarded as speculative by the judge. Now begins the mystery.

One of our misleading assumptions is that there is evidence available to support a statement that is alleged to be the testimony of another person in a trial. And that such information is available for cross-examination. We are so impressed with the setting and the conduct of the "role players" in the court drama that we suspend judgment like we do when we go to a movie. We actually believe that <u>they</u> believe what clearly they do not! The prosecutor either had no idea what David Turner would say or knew what he would say and lied about it. After I was in prison my son, David, was talking with Turner, and Turner asked how I was doing. My son said I would be doing better if it hadn't been for what Turner had said. He then explained to Turner what the government said he would have said in Court. Turner said that was not true and signed a sworn affidavit as to what he would have said.

So this individual, a federal attorney, departed from what he had said was essential and he knew to be untrue, and is perceived by the Judge as credible because The Whole of the United States of America said it. That he was simply an individual misrepresenting the truth is not perceived in the federal magic show. Some magic show, I would say. Now you see it (essential witness), now you don't (we don't want to hear him). I doubt that the federal prosecutor regards himself as involved in theological matters when he is doing his trial preparation and determining whose testimony is essential and even decides for himself what they might say or should have said or will say when he gets them onstage. He will have many opportunities to affect that testimony or exclude it but I assume he believes those decisions are matters of strategy, not theology. I suggest that it is the heart of the ninth commandment; that he should not participate in false witness. A witness to an event is perceived as reliable testimony.

When he assured the Judge that David Turner would also represent what the prosecutor then proceeded to announce on his behalf, he was manufacturing conclusions and speaking beyond the range of his knowledge. He was giving false testimony under the guise of a well-informed and honest lawyer. He was breaking the ninth commandment. This also became some of the basis for a suit brought against the prosecutor by another attorney that had concluded the Whole of the United States of America was guilty of prosecutorial misconduct.

Cheryl Sturm, an attorney in Pennsylvania, represented me in a Rule 33 appeal, which is an appeal based on newly discovered evidence. We believed that the affidavits that David Turner signed about what his testimony would have been and an affidavit[2] signed by Arthur Elliott about threats from the FBI, along with the government hiding some 302's[3] from the defense, constituted newly discovered evidence. Langrock and Horstmann (Bailey's office) both signed affidavits that they had not been given some 302's. In a response to the government, Sturm stated "If the government's attorney feels that his testimony is essential to the outcome of the case, then his option is to withdraw from the case and testify. Otherwise he should be prohibited from acting as an unsworn witness immune from cross-examination." The Court did not agree with us that this evidence was newly discovered and turned down the appeal.

We then filed a Hazel-Atlas motion, which is a motion that claims there was fraud committed upon the Court by the prosecuting attorney. We claimed that he deliberately misled the court on what Turner's testimony would have been. We also claimed there was misconduct by the FBI in threatening Arthur Elliott. The Court did not agree that there was misconduct serious enough to warrant a new trial. They said that my original attorney could have and should have interviewed both Turner and Elliott himself to decide what their testimony would have been.

I might not have won these appeals, but Assistant US Attorney VandeGraaf certainly was kept busy trying to explain some of his more questionable actions in his so-called pursuit of justice.

Then there is the curious testimony of Charlie Howe. There are two Charlie Howes in this story, and I need to provide you a bit of a background for you to see the contrast between the periods of time involved. Charlie Howe was also a director of the Lyndonville Savings Bank during the time that I was on the board. Charlie's family had provided him with a sizable and significant inheritance and much of that had been invested as a "stockholder" in the Bank. Among all of the investing directors at Lyndonville Charlie and I and our families probably owned about half of the stock of that institution. So it would follow that we would have little incentive to harm the Bank or to see it into difficulties that would be so destructive to our own investments and our family's interest.

In any case Charlie Howe was considered as a candidate for the Chairman of the Board of Directors of the Bank, and the directors had approached him regarding that matter well before the difficulties identified in the trial had presented themselves. I had announced my intention to retire from the Bank two years before all of this had happened, and the Bank and the FDIC and anyone else who read our minutes knew that to be the case. I had been asked to continue serving the Bank as an outside consultant and wished to continue the availability of my medical insurance. The Directors extended such an arraignment to me when I did retire. But at the time that Charlie was approached to become the Chairman, his wife had become ill and then did unfortunately die from that illness leaving Charlie to care for his children. He requested that his acceptance of the Chairmanship of the bank be delayed for the time he needed to give attention to his children. He would continue as a director of the Bank during that period of time.

When you read the testimony presented by Charlie Howe at the criminal trial you will see that he assured the jury that I had not dominated the Bank, that the directors were individually capable of making their own decisions, and that they did. He also testified that I had kept the bank informed of conversations regarding potential loans, and that he saw no reason to criticize my role as President and Chairman or my performance on behalf of the Bank. He essentially confirmed what would have been my account of the events of the Bank if I had been able to present a defense that was available to the jury. Now remember Charlie, like myself, was a major investor in the Lyndonville Savings Bank and stood with me in jeopardy of loss if the decisions of the Bank had not been sound. Charlie's testimony at the criminal trial was consistent with the facts, and he swore the usual oath that he should be believed to be telling the truth. And he told the truth!

After my retirement[4] became effective Charlie remained on the Board of Directors and became Chairman. Like myself, he remained a primary investor in the stock of the Bank. The stock was selling for considerably more money per share then. Its value declined after I had left the bank and after my retirement, not before then.

In the document section you will see three conversations I had with Charlie Howe and can see how he changed his attitude over a very short period of time. He told me on September 2, 1995 the bank wasn't going to sue me and then voted on September 12, 1995 to sue me[5].

Now one of the things that Charlie Howe began seeing after I had been indicted was the power of the federal government to make things appear differently from time to time then he had believed them to be beforehand. You can see in the documents section several of the letters from the FDIC to Charlie, and the other directors, after he had become Chairman and was directing the affairs of the Bank following my retirement. You'll see that the FDIC tells him that my retirement had not brought about any improvement in the conditions of the Bank's operations. That must have been a surprise to everyone. I had been blamed for what was believed to be wrong, but certainly had not been given credit for the 16 million in profit the bank earned. For the next several years the Bank's directors continued to experience operational difficulty and there came a time during Charlie's term as Chairman when the FDIC threatened to fine him, and/or the Bank, $1 million a day every day until the FDIC was satisfied that the bank complied as the FDIC directed. Apparently the bank had not complied with some of the FDIC directives up to this point. Now a man who inherited many millions from his family's business success certainly might not be concerned about the cost of a cup of coffee or the increase in the menu price for a hamburger, but $1 million a

Lyndonville Bank Directors – L to R: John Campbell, Arthur Elliott, Charles Howe, Roger Lussier, Fredric Oeschger, Robert Beausoleil, Fay Young

day fine every day until someone else decided you were in compliance would begin to affect your enthusiasm for making up your own mind.

And Charlie also had the benefit of learning from my experience. He saw what could happen to a person, and that it could happen without a whole lot of provocation or explanation. Loss of $1 million a day helps focus the attention when it is your family's money at risk. Putting it bluntly, Charlie got the point.

And soon the directors of the Lyndonville Bank became the copy machine for the FDIC's vision of how the Bank was to operate. It was not to be an independent Bank licensed by the State of Vermont whose accounts were insured by the FDIC. It was to become a franchise operation of the federal government whose stockholders were to exercise no independent judgment regarding the safety of their investments, their own money, or of the community purposes of their Bank's charter. The Board of Directors was to become a large rubber stamp and its prepared message is inserted in Washington. And so it continues, even today.

But Charlie Howe clearly saw his duty now. He was to remain among a Board of Directors who had been successfully reduced to being spokesman for distant policy at the risk of being fined up to $1 million a day. Their insurance company, the FDIC, was in effect their controller. That they were not a federal institution and held a State of Vermont charter for their organization was simply ignored. The resulting litigation between myself and the Bank seeking illegal standing in a federal court to enforce the illegal restitution order became itself an extravagant deception upon the court and upon the stockholders of the Bank. The necessity "to jump, to clap and smile and pretend" and being encouraged to do so by their high-priced attorneys is simply seen as a necessity of survival. With their Chairman, and their expensive money-losing CEO, Charlie Bucknam, and a suitable change of all the Board of Directors, the Bank suddenly emerges as the aggrieved party in all of this matter. And it convinces itself that all of its difficulties are because Roger Lussier was or had been their president. The Bank now brings charges against me, Roger Lussier, and seeks to sue me for payment of an illegal restitution order and in the process of that attaches everything the Roger and Evelyn own. At that time we did not own our cemetery lots or I am sure those would have been attached as well.

Charlie Bucknam while continuing to spend an unrevealed amount of the stockholders money and perhaps believing he will be reimbursed for it by the Bank's insurance company, convinces the federal courts that he and the directors are what they are not. I had mentioned this in discussing the Bank's suit against me, and I mention it here again now only to show how Charlie Howe's testimony was tailored to fit the circumstances that he was facing. When I was on trial and before he was at risk for a million dollars a day fine he testified truthfully as would have been expected.

But after the Bank had decided that it could legally pursue a restitution order in the federal courts by misrepresenting their own institutional charter, Charlie Howe had to invent a new story. I have listed below excerpts of Howe's testimony at different times so that you can compare what he said in my criminal trial with what he said when he was unsuccessfully suing me for money to which he was not entitled, but mindful of the encouragement of the FDIC to do so he made up a new account. Now if a person tells two contradictory stories about essentially the same events at least one of those stories must be incorrect. And when this was pointed out to Charlie by the judge he said that he simply didn't know in his first testimony what he knew in his second testimony. He had been on the Board with me for four years at that time. Which leaves the question of course to be – so how do you know now in your second testimony that it is to be more believed than perhaps what will become your third testimony?

---

[1] See Exhibits pages 31-41 for Turner affidavits

[2] See Exhibits pages 42-44 for Elliott affidavit

[3] See Exhibits pages 45-50 for Skeet 302 & Exhibits pages 51-54 are Langrock & Horstman affidavits on 302's

[4] See Exhibits pages 55-60 for my retirement letter to Directors

[5] See Exhibits page 61 for conversations with Howe

Howe Testimony in Criminal Trial (Dec 93)

Questioned by Langrock:

Page 56;

Q. Has there been any single figure that's dominated the board since you've been on it?

A. No. I think we're all very independent people. We – when we're discussing loans or policies, we actually have some fairly rigorous arguments. And then when the vote is taken, we regroup as a team.

Q. In observing RRL on the board, how would you describe his influence on the board?

A. Well, Roger, all the time that I was on the board with Roger, Roger was the chair. And Roger also did have a lot to say, and it was very important material and everyone listened. But when the votes were taken, each person had one vote.

Questioned by VandeGraaf:

Page 61:

Q. Would you agree that he had a lot of influence? (RRL)

A. I wouldn't agree that he had more influence than other board members.

Q. Sir, did he have a lot of influence over you?

A. No

Now see what he says in his deposition in 1997 when questioned by my attorney, Andrew Field:

Pages 10 – 12:

Q. Did Roger Lussier ever tell you how to vote as a director?

A. Roger would frequently tell directors how they should vote.

Q. Tell me what directors did Roger tell how to vote?

A. He told the board to vote for certain loans.

Q. You mean he recommended that certain loans be approved?

A. Roger would say things, such as goddamn it, this is a good loan, approve it.

Q. Regardless of what RRL said as you indicated, did you feel compelled or under pressure to approve any particular loan?

A. Not to my recollection.

Page 19:

Q. Do you ever recall voting to approve a loan to Ryan to finance the Roundhouse?

A. At this point my position as being director was really one of observing what was going on. I had been elected to the board the previous February and knew nothing of the bank's operation and was advised by Roger Lussier to watch what was going on and after awhile I would catch on. I did not vote for the loan or against the loan, but I did not abstain either.

The Ryan loan was approved in June 1989. According to the minutes of 4/4/90 he was appointed with Arthur Elliott to review and make any changes necessary to the Memo of Understanding. On 9/12/90 he was authorized by Directors to negotiate with the Guilmettes on their problems. On 2/13/91 He informed the Directors that he was taking a course at UVM on Funds Management for Commercial Banks. On 7/22/92 he worked on the testing of the Mardon property. On 11/1/92 He was appointed to help write a CRA (Community Reinvestment Act) program for the bank. It would seem he was doing a little more than just observing.

Page 26:

Q. I understand that you were an observer rather than voting at this period of time as you have indicated. Can you tell us, by the way, how long you continued to observe as a director rather than vote?

A. It was an evolving process.

Q. Tell us how it evolved and when you started voting.

A. It started evolving the day I first became a director, and as I continued to learn more and more, I took a more active part in discussion, I took and active part in questioning some loans. When did that evolution absolutely complete itself, I'm not sure it ever has Andy. I think it's a learning process that one never ends.

Page 66:

Q. I'm asking you do you generally recall anything. You apparently don't recall anything.

A. I will not sit here and take that type of comment from anyone.

Q. Well, I think —

A. And with further comments such as that, I will excuse myself from this room.

And now look at his testimony in the Bank's suit against me:

Volume 3:

Page 7 by Johnston, LSB attorney:

Q. Mr. Howe, were you ever made aware that Noel Lussier had a dealer reserve account at the bank that was intended to guarantee obligations that he had at the bank?

A. No, I was not. *(Board meetings on Noel's reserve at which Howe attended, 12/27/89, 6/19/91, 11/27/91, 12/4/91, 12/27/91, 4/1/92, 5/27/92)*

Pages 60 – 62 by Field:

Q. You testified on questions asked by your attorney on February 15th, 1990, you attended a board meeting. And at that board meeting it concerned a $300,000 refinance loan of the Walker Brothers. And you testified in response to a question that you never saw the business plan. Correct?

A. That is correct.

Q. You testified that there was a presentation by a loan officer or Roger, you weren't quite certain, but that you were certain that in any event, that Roger spoke.

A. What I was not clear on was who brought it. Roger did make the presentation and spoke on it, yes.

Q. And at that meeting you stated that there was no information presented to the board of directors to substantiate the loan. Do you recall that, that testimony?

A. The information that was provided - - again, are we talking about written or verbal?

Q. Either way. Suit yourself.

A. Roger stated that there was sufficient collateral to make the loan. Did I see something in writing? No.

Q. Now, will you turn to Exhibit 632, please?

A. Yes.

Q. You, George Hopkins, and Pearl Baird were absent from that meeting according to the records. Do you see it there? And the following directors were present - -

A. Yes

Q. - - Bob Bosely, Fay Young Jr, Arthur Elliott, John Campbell and Roger Lussier appeared. George Hopkins, Charles Howe, and Pearl Baird were absent. Do you see that?

A. Yes, sir.

Q. So what you've been talking about, everything that was revealed to you at that meeting, you couldn't possibly have heard?"

A. That would be correct.

Q. And you were asked as to whether or not that was shown to the board of directors at that meeting when they considered that $200,000 loan (Harrison) Do you recall that question?

A. Yes, I do.

Q. Do you recall your answer, we were not shown this? Do you recall that?

A. Yes, I do.

Q. Why don't you turn to Exhibit 529, please. Do you have it before you?

A. Yes, I do.

Q. You weren't even at the meeting, were you?

A. That's correct.

And even the judge had questions about his change of testimony from the criminal trial in 1993 to the civil trial in 1997:

Volume III pages 65 – 66:

The Court: Before you start Mr. Johnston, Mr. Field has brought up some testimony that you gave at the criminal trial of Mr. Lussier which appears to conflict with what you said here. Does it?

Witness (Howe):   It does not conflict with what I'm saying here, because it was point-in-time testimony. During the time that I was on the board with Roger, I had complete and absolute faith in Roger. I believed he knew what he was doing and that he was – what he was doing was in the best interests of the bank

Court: All right. And so I still don't quite understand.

Witness: Since that time, through different suits against the bank and certainly this suit, I have discovered just endless amount of information showing that Roger was --- was, one, not disclosing to the board, or at least to me, his involvement with almost every single loan that we're discussing, that there was personal involvement; that he was intimately involved in every detail at a personal level, financially at a personal level. I never knew that before.

Court: So when did you testify, do you remember, at the trial?

Witness: Oh, when was that?

Mr. Field: I'll get the date, your Honor. It was December 16, 1993.

Witness: '93. So it was ---

Mr. Field: And I have the transcript here, if the court wishes to have a copy.

Court: That's all right. So in December of 1993 when you made – when you gave the testimony, particularly about the influence of Mr. Lussier upon the board, how's that different from now?

Witness: Well, knowledge is power. And Roger was telling us – I speak only for myself. He was telling me at the board only what he wanted me to know so that I would vote along with him. What I know now is there was a great deal more information that never was disclosed. Had that information been disclosed to me at that time, my reaction would have been 180 degrees opposite.

Charlie then testified at the malpractice trial. Bailey's lawyer wanted Charlie to testify that the restitution order had nothing to do with the Bank's decision to sue me in Federal court. As could be expected, Charlie's testimony again disagreed with the facts as shown below. This testimony was on May 6, 2003. I would have thought that the bank, after settling with me and getting my stock at a reduced price, would be truthful in their dealings with me, but it seems that once you start lying it is much easier to continue to do so.

Howe is being questioned by Bailey's lawyer, Eric Poehlmann:
Page 78:

Q. Okay. What role did the restitution order play in your decision to bring suit?

A. The restitution order played no role in our decision to bring suit. What did play a role is we were running up against the Statute of Limitations and if we let it go by, that we would lose the ability to try to recapture money that had been lost. The Statute – the restitution had only recently been in place and the Statute of Limitations on that was somewhere way out in the future, so that was not a major factor.

Q. And I take it that the restitution order had no effect on the Bank' decision to bring suit at that time, at that particular time?

A. That's correct. It was included in the suit.

Q. All right.

A. But it was not the reason for bringing suit at that time.

Pages 97 & 98:

Q. Okay. Sir, my final question is this: I guess final two questions. Did the Bank ever consider bringing suit just for the restitution order?

A. No.

Q. And why is that?

A. We weren't concerned about the restitution order at that time. We were more concerned about the other items of the suit that we did file because of the Statute of Limitations. The Statute of Limitations on the restitution order, as I stated this morning, was way out there in the future.

Now he is questioned by Roger's lawyer, Dave Williams:

Pages 98 – 106:

Q. As I understand it, the Bank had two federal questions in its federal lawsuit; is that correct?

A. Two.

Q. Two federal questions; it wanted to enforce a criminal restitution order, correct?

A. Yes.

Q. And the Bank was seeking damages based on Roger Lussier's being an officer or a director in a Federal Reserve member bank, correct?

A. No. It does state that; yes.

Q. And we know now that the Federal Reserve banking claim was false?

A. That's correct.

Q. You weren't a member of the Federal Reserve – the Lyndonville Savings Bank was never – has never been and is not now a member of the Federal Reserve banking system, correct?

A. Certainly not at this time – at that time or at this time.

Q. Never were?

A. No.

Q. Now, you stated that the Bank was not concerned about the restitution order when it filed its federal lawsuit?

A. We included it.

Q. And I think your testimony was also that the restitution order was not a major factor in deciding to file the lawsuit?

A. That's correct.

Q. All right. Sir, you remember filing an affidavit in the United States District Court in Lyndonville Savings Bank v. Roger Lussier and Evelyn Lussier, Defendants?

A. Could I see it?

Q. You don't remember filing it?

A. We filed many.

Q. Back in November 17th, 1995, do you recall making the following statement under oath: Primary among the reasons for the board of directors making this decision – that is a decision to file suit against Roger Lussier – was the affirmance of Mr. Lussier's criminal conviction by the Second Circuit Court of Appeals and the existence of a valid restitution order in favor of the Bank as issued by the United States District Court as a result of that conviction?

A. I don't remember that specifically, but I'm sure it's correct if it's in there; but I think what the meaning of it was –

Q. Sir, if you could – first of all, if you could refresh your recollection of that statement?

A. Yes.

Q. You made that statement under oath?

A. I did.

- - - - -

Q. All right. It was a special board meeting called for the purpose of meeting with Attorney Richard Johnston of Hale and Dorr to discuss the strategy to be applied to secure payment of $426,000 from Roger Lussier as required under his criminal conviction; is that correct?

A. That was part of it; yes.

Q. And the Bank board did not approve naming Mrs. Lussier as a defendant, did it?

A. I don't believe it did at that meeting.

Q. Sir, in your affidavit filed with the United States District for the District of Vermont, you told the judge that the board of directors voted to commence this litigation against Roger Lussier and Evelyn Lussier at a meeting of the board of directors held on September 12th, 1995. Do you remember saying that?

A. If that's what it says, then that's what I said. I would want to read the minutes of that meeting.

Q. So your statement in your affidavit is inaccurate?

A. Technically, yes.

Q. Sure. You, your chairman of the board of directors, Mr. Bucknam, and your boss and lawyers weren't going to pull any punches in this litigation against Mr. Roger Lussier, were you?

A. We certainly went into litigation to win.

Q. In fact, you and your colleagues attached the marital home of Roger and Evelyn Lussier, correct?

A. It was held in joint; it was joint; yes.

Q. And you attached it?

A. Yes

Q. With the sort of threat that if Mr. Lussier lost the lawsuit, you were going to evict them from their Lyndonville home, correct?

A. I don't think that was ever said.

While the stock was high and his family's money was doing well on the dividends earned by the Lyndonville Savings Bank, Charlie was a most contented director. But after presiding over the Bank for several years with Charlie Bucknam providing him insight into their losses Charlie Howe began to see things differently. The FDIC letter threatening the million dollars a day fine was not addressed to the period of time he served with me on the Board of Directors. It was addressed to his period of time as Chairman. Rather than taking responsibility for what they were and what they had become Charlie Howe and his "cronies" began to invent an elaborate deception calling the Bank something it was not and swearing to the truth of their lie. He votes to pursue me for my stock in a federal court and shortly after, Bucknam made the decision to also bring suit against my wife so that they could go after all our stock and assets. They were lying to judges, creating false documents, swearing to the truth of their lie, and hoping to convince the stockholders that they were doing well.

Prior to his service with the Lyndonville Bank, Charlie Howe had served the University of Vermont as its Registrar. Among the responsibilities of that office, amid all of the organizing of courses and registering of students for credit hours, is the responsibility to report on the truthfulness of documents. It is the Registrar's signature and seal that attests to the validity of degrees and the granting of credits. It is the Registrar that validates the claims of education and hours earned. And it is shameful to see him make untruthful claims regarding the bank being a "member of the Federal Reserve System" and entitled to an imaginary standing in a Federal Court. The two Charlie's (Bucknam and Howe) and their high-priced attorneys pretended they were something they were not. If you would ask Charlie Howe if there were consequences to the Registrar's office swearing to a false claim he would probably say yes. It should not be done. It is against the law. Your mother would be ashamed of you, Charlie.

But he was willing to do so, as Chairman of the Bank, when faced with the necessity of pleasing its absentee owner. I guess every man has his price and yours must be around the million dollars a day. Myself, I would have found that too much to pay and would simply have resigned my responsibilities, and placed my money elsewhere.

If I had enough money to be at risk to that kind of a fine I wouldn't need to be working in a Bank.

And in forcing a settlement of my personal stock as part of the bank's false assertions he enriched himself personally, increasing the value of his own stock without earning it. A shameful twist of fate – that both Charlie's among themselves profit from inside dealing, manipulation of the sale of assets and making decisions that affect stock price – the very things they had falsely claimed against me. In a normal conscience that would be shameful, it became for the present bank business as usual. (There is a matter of the inside purchase of property in Hardwick, by Charlie Bucknam from the Caledonia Bank, but that is another matter).

Charlie Bucknam's testimony differed depending on what case he was testifying in. When he testified in the bank's case against Roger his testimony was slanted one way and changed when he testified in cases where the bank was being sued.

In February 1996 he was deposed in the Hammang case where the bank was being sued, so naturally he had to be extremely careful to put the bank and Roger in the best light possible. Andrew Field had sent a letter to Gravel[1], the bank's attorney in April 1995 explaining Roger's role and success in negotiations with GE and Koster for the purchase of the finished goods and equipment. Below are excerpts from his deposition:

Questioned by bank's attorney John Gravel:

Pages 5 – 8:

Q: From your review of the file did you think that everyone involved used their best efforts in trying to obtain as much money as possible from GE for those assets?

A. Yes.

Q. Including Roger Lussier?

A. Yes.

Pages 11 – 13:

Q. You have reviewed the files as they concern the sale of Mardon assets to Koster Industries?

A. Yes.

Q. And was the approach taken to sell the assets to Koster for a fixed price of $1,475,000. Was that prudent banking?

A. I believe that it was in that instance.

Q. And you are also aware that when Koster finally sold those assets at auction that they obtained from the auction price significantly less than the $1,475,000?

A. Yes.

Pages 18 – 20:

Q. During your review of board minutes in this file – in this case and in other cases, have you obtained a fairly good working knowledge of how the board of LSB worked in the late 80's and early 90's?

A. Yes.

Q. How would you categorize the way they approached the banking business?

A. Well, the board I think placed a great deal of reliance upon real estate for collateral purposes and they considered themselves experts in evaluating real estate. Several of them were realtors or former realtors. They took some pride, I think, in being responsive to customers and making credit decisions upon their knowledge of their history and personal relationships with people.

Q. Would you also categorize their dealings as directors as fairly casual?

A. Yes.

Q. Certainly more casual than they are today?

A. Yes.

Q. Is that unusual in the banking community in the Northeast Kingdom?

A. It was not unusual in certain banks in the Northeast Kingdom. I think it was more casual than banking practice in general during that period of time, but it was a way of doing business at that point

Q. Was it unusual during that period to time for a customer, to receive an expeditious unsecured loan?

A. No, it was not unusual.

Then in late 1996 when he is deposed by Roger's first attorney in the banks suit against Roger, he is still following the same line that the bank was quite informal in the late 80's and early 90's and that the economy was beginning to go sour. Below are excerpts from that deposition on 11/25/96:

Questioned by John Pacht:

Page 52:

Q. Do you think it is fair to say that perhaps greater risks might have been taken with customers back in the mid to upper 80's than would be taken today based on the real estate being the collateral for the loan?

A. Yes.

Page 102:

Q. Given your experience as a banker, would you agree that banks generally were somewhat more relaxed in 86 about underwriting standards than say in 93?

A. Yes.

Q. And those were banks that went beyond Caledonia and LSB, isn't that right?

A. Yes

Pages 128 & 129:

Q. Would you agree this time period was a difficult time for banks in general, 1991 time frame?

A. Yes, I would agree that a lot of banks were feeling strains on their loan portfolio.

Q. And had there been a significant economic slowdown by that time?

A. Yes.

Q. And that put a significant strain on all of the Vt. area banks, did it not?

A. Yes, I think earnings deteriorated for most Vt. banks in that period. Loan delinquencies increased and losses increased.

Then on the second day of being deposed by Roger's attorney, John Pacht, Charlie is trying to be a little more cautious in answering especially on things that might explain some of Roger's actions. The below excerpts were taking from his deposition on 11/26/96:

Page 68:

Q. But do you understand the bank took the position, that is LSB, the bank for which you serve as President, that in fact, RRL was not heavily involved in operations at the bank?

A. Yes, I do recall that the board or – at least made that argument, yes.

Q. And the board made it in a letter which was signed by Tom Thompson as CEO for the Company?

A. That may be. I may have seen the letter. I don't recall.

Pages 74 – 76:

Q. Are you aware that Wendy and others on the board have stated that, in fact, board members did discuss issues relating to cash flow of the customers?

A. I don't recall the specifics of the deposition. She may well have.

Q. Do you know, one way or another, whether board members discussed cash flow of the borrowers in this case.

A. No, I don't.

Q. Do you know, one way or another, if the board discussed financial statements of borrowers in this case?

A. In some cases – well at least in one case, the Ryan case, there was reference in the minutes to them reviewing Ryan's financial statements.

Bucknam is then deposed by Roger's second attorney, Andrew Field, on 7/16/97 and has a hard time citing actual facts to form the bank's many accusations against Roger. He apparently made many assumptions as shown by the excerpts listed below:

Page 22:

Q. Do you know whether or not a local broker was in fact, contacted on or before the date of closing of the $700,000 transaction?

A. I don't – I don't believe – I believe if a local broker was called and I don't remember specifically, that the information – the information that came back from the local broker was negative. They couldn't determine the value, and the investigation for the value of the stock I – I didn't see evidence of that until after the loan had gone into default.

Pages 24 – 26:

Q. And as I understand your testimony, that you made an assumption that he recommended to the Board the $700,000 loan, but there's no factual material –

A. I don't recall writing or anything that would say that.

Pages 28 – 30:

Q. Well, I'm concerned at the time the loan is made. As I understand your expression here, Roger concealed from the Board, and I'm trying to find out what he concealed. Can you tell me what he concealed from the Board with respect to the $700,000 loan?

A. I believe that Roger knew that McCormick did not have any operating money and this was the only way he was going to get it to keep payments current on his loan to Gray and LSB. There is nothing documenting that in the file. That's one of the problems with the file.

Pages 38 – 39

Q. You agree with me there's nothing in the minutes of the Board or there's nothing written in the file that indicates that Roger recommended to the Board that they lend this money?

A. I didn't see anything in writing, that's correct.

Page 44:

Q. Well, you don't know whether it was disclosed orally or not, do you? (interest in Hamel)

A. No.

Q. Did Mr. Campbell ever indicate to you that he was not aware of Roger's interest in the Hamel property at the time that loan was approved?

A. No. As I say, I don't remember specifically which directors indicated that they knew of some relationship. So my feeling – my recollection is that some did, but none were aware of the extent of the relationship.

Pages 47 – 52:

Q. You don't know whether or not an oral disclosure was made; do you, at the time that the loan was approved?

A. No, I don't.

Pages 56 – 57:

Q. You have a statement here that on 9/21 Roger recommended that the Board approve a loan in the amount of $1,950,000. (Gray) What's the factual basis that you have for saying that Roger recommended that that loan be approved by the Board?

A. Well, again there is a lack of information specifically in the file, but in reviewing the file and the history, Roger is the only one that had the information on this loan.

Q. Is that what the file indicated, that Roger was the only one that had any information?

A. That's what I concluded from my – my review. I found no evidence that there was anybody else ever involved in this loan, either a loan officer at that time or another board member.

Q. What does the file show you, that Roger recommended the loan at the time it was approved?

A. The file does not specifically show that.

Q. Is than an assumption on your part?

A. Yes

Pages 70 – 79:

Q. Do you recall whether or not – did you lose any potential buyers as a result of that environmental contamination?

A. No, I don't believe we lost the buyer. In fact, I believe the original – the buyer that had made the original offer ended up buying it. He did end up buying it for less money.

Q. And was it less money because of the environmental impact on the property?

A. Yes

Q. Do you feel that Roger had any fault with respect to the environmental matter?

A. No. No. There are normal procedures when you finance commercial properties you would like to go through including site assessments and so on. A site assessment was never done on that property when it was – when the loan was originated, but at that time it was not quite the general practice that it became later on, so I would not fault him for that.

Q. Any reason why you would not have made inquiries of the Board and Lee Cleveland with respect to what you felt was improper conduct on the part of Roger?

A. Well, for one thing, I felt that in this process we would learn about Mr. Cleveland and what his input was. My focus was on the document – documentary evidence and I was trying to review files and draw conclusions from what I could find in written form.

Q. So that you made no inquiry of these original board members that were involved in the approval of the loan prior to filing the Complaint – the bank's filing the Complaint?

A. I didn't make specific inquiries but they had ample opportunity to contribute and review things that were said about the loan and to have their input prior to the filing of the Complaint.

Q. You found that out subsequent to your affidavit, didn't you? I notice in your affidavit you stated there was no financial analysis of the – that there was no financial statements reviewed by Roger. What did you do, subsequently discover that the board did, in fact, review the financial statements?

A. I don't recall. I may have found the reference in the minutes subsequently.

Pages 87 – 102:

Q. As you sit here today, you don't know whether Lussier Auction Service got a commission for auctioning the LSB property or not, do you?

A. No, I don't, and that's why I used probably in my statement.

Q. You don't know what properties the $53,000 commission approved by the court applied to?

A. I suspect that it applied to the Bank of Boston properties, but there is nothing in the record to show what if any commission was paid to Roger for the sale of the Lyndonville properties.

Page 115:

Q. I notice the Board approved this – is that pretty much it in substance, Charlie(Walker Bros)

A. Yes, it's an underwriting issue.

Q. I notice the Board approved this on 1/20/88, a couple days before it was consummated. Did you have or have you had any conversations at all with any of the members of the board at that time in connection with the underwriting of this $300,000 loan? And to refresh your recollection, I'll tell you who the board members were. They were Pearl, Bob, John, Arthur, George, Doug and Roger. With respect to any of those board members, at any time prior to the filing of the bank's complaint, did you have any conversations with any one of them as concerns the deficiency matters with respect to underwriting that initial $300,000 loan?

A. No, I didn't. I felt that the deficiencies were apparent on their face because they were not in the – there was no evidence in the file. The other – the other one that I didn't mention initially that I should mention is the fact that Roger did not disclose his business relationships with his brother, Noel, at that time.

Now we get to the actual trial on 10/27/97 and we can see that Charlie is beginning to do a complete turnaround, as he is now blaming Roger for not doing an environmental check on properties that did have a small problem before they could be sold etc. Below are excerpts of his trial testimony in the case LSB v Roger and Evelyn Lussier:

Volume I: Direct by bank's attorney, Johnston:

Pages 160 – 161:

Q. Was there any evidence that Roger or anyone else at LSB had an environmental consultant check the property before taking the deed back from Gray, for contamination?

A. No. There was no evidence that such a study was done prior to accepting a deed in lieu.

Q. From your experience in banking, during the end of 91 was it customary for banks to do environmental analyses of commercial properties before taking them back or before lending money?

A. Well, for that type of property in particular, because it was an auto dealership and because an auto dealership would have occasion to have underground storage tanks. And, in fact, one of the potential buyers of that dealership, prior to signing a purchase and sale agreement did an investigation. And that's when it was discovered. So in the course of their doing their due diligence, they did the study.

Q. But LSB had done no due diligence before taking the properties back and releasing Gray from the deficiency?

A. That's right.

Page 133:

Q. Did you find any evidence of an analysis of milk production or cash flow? (Hamel)

A. No, I did not.

(Arthur Elliott disputes this in his testimony as does Fay Young in his deposition. They both say they gave an oral report on the Hamel's application)

Now he is cross-examined by Roger's attorney, Andy Field:
Page 198:

Q. Now you agree with me that with respect to every one of these seven loans, you have absolutely no personal knowledge whatsoever as to how those loans were underwritten or approved?

A. That's right. I was not present at that time.

Pages 206 – 208:

Q. Are you aware then that as soon as the bank received the complaint, that they had a board meeting and two directors were authorized to go to Florida and check out the quality and condition of the cows? Do you remember that?

A. I remember wording to that effect, yeah.

Q. And do you know that they did?

A. I believe – I believe that I understood that they did, yes.

Pages 210 – 211:

Q. It was a board decision was it not, to defer? The bank voted to do that? *(Not to go after Gilmour and Noel until after the bankruptcy in Florida)*

A. It appeared to be, yes.

Q. Well, it would appear to be. Was it or was it not? You looked at the file. Was there not, in fact, a board meeting at which the board considered this?

A. Well, the minutes are not in the file. I'm trying to recall what the letter said that I did see that indicated action would be deferred against the guarantors until the bankruptcy matter was settled.

Q. And that came about as a result of a board vote?

Volume IV

Bucknam Cross-examined by Field:

Page 10:

Q. Does this form (Reg U) – this is in writing, and I think you always look for things in writing. Does not this form, in all fairness, Mr. Bucknam, convey to your mind that somebody consulted at more than one investment firm to determine the value of that stock? Isn't that what this form says?

A. Well, it would indicate that –

Page 15:

Q. That's a document taken from the Lyndonville Savings Bank file(Purchase & Sale, Gray to McCormick)

A. It's a document that we came across in the process of discovery. It was not in the loan file. That was my testimony.

Page 26:

Q. The point is, Charlie, that when you testified that no additional security was given to the bank when it made the $380,000 loan, is it not true that the – those loan documents in possession of the bank show that additional parties were made liable, Ryan's Roundhouse – Ryan's Express, and that personal property owned by them to a large extent was added to the security for the bank? Is that not true?

A. It would appear to be, from reviewing this security document.

The bank has two expert witness in the suit against Roger and, as shown below in their testimony, apparently a good part of what was in their report was what they had been shown or told by Charlie Bucknam and apparently some things that should have been in the file were withheld from them especially Clark Chandler. He must have been a little embarrassed about things he wasn't shown etc: The other expert is Michael Filipiak, who happened to be the former President and Chairman of the Board of Independent Bank Group that Charlie Bucknam was also associated with when he was with Caledonia National Bank.

Chandler Cross examined by Field:

Volume V:

Page 73:

Q. When you were searching those files to find documentation to support – factual matters to support your expert opinions here, did you also include establishing facts based on what other people told you?

A. The only person at the bank with which I discussed what I found in the loan files was with Mr. Bucknam, to insure that I had seen, in fact, the entirety of the loan file.

Q. Did Mr. Bucknam show you anything – documentation of any kind that would support his statement to you in that regard?

A. No, I don't believe he did.

Page 77:

Q. And would you believe me if I told you that the board did, in fact, ratify that loan by vote? (Walker Brothers)

A. That's inconsistent with what I had found out, but—

Q. That is Exhibit No. 623 that we have in this case, which is a copy of the board of director's minutes ratifying that loan. That was a significant statement to make, was it not, that that was never approved by the board of directors that charges Roger Lussier with making a loan that they never approved?

A. That was one of the statements that I made here. You're correct.

Q. That's part of the – a piece of the facts that you relied upon to render your opinions and conclusions in this matter. Isn't that true?

A. If, in fact, if this loan was approved by the board, it would not have changed my conclusions.

Q. Not asking whether it would have changed your conclusion. When you talk about fiduciary responsibilities and gross negligence, isn't it significant when you state a fact that Mr. Lussier went out and made a loan that the board never approved for $225,000? Isn't that a significant fact?

A. It – from what you've described to me, it represents a mistake in my report.

Page 81 & 82:

Q. When you looked at that file, didn't you find a certificate of title – title opinion issued by Attorney Pepin? (Hamel)

A. I have since seen that opinion, but it was not in the file prior to June of 1997.

Q. All right. This is another situation where there was a document, an important document that was simply not in the file when you looked at the file. Is that correct?

A. That's correct. Not one which, by itself, would have changed my conclusion, but an important document.

Page 84:

Q. When you reviewed the minutes of the board of directors, I would assume that you failed to find any board minutes in September that approved such a loan.

A. Mr. Field, I believe this particular statement is an error that, in fact, on September 13th, there was an indication of approval for a $375,000 loan to the Ryans on that date.

Page 90:

Q. Did you consider the 1,450,000 note one that was bound by equipment terms? Wasn't this the financing of a leasehold estate? (Ryan)

A. Yes it was.

Q. That's not an accurate statement in there, is it?

A. No, it's not.

Q. And it's not a fair one either, is it?

A. It's not accurate.

Pages 94 & 95:

Q. Is it possible, rather than reading that deposition, that somebody at the bank may have told you about the deposition and what he was alleging? (Harrison)

A. That is possible

Q. And then the next line down you say that Lussier instructs Harrison to write a $75,000 check to Ryan. Do you see that?

A. Yes, I do.

Q. And you apparently either read that in a deposition or somebody at the bank told you about it. Correct?

A. It was either one of those two sources, yes.

Q. Uh-huh. There was nothing written in the files to that effect, was there?

A. There was nothing in the loan files to that effect. That's correct.

Pages 97, 98, & 99:

Q. How did you know about those, were they in the file or did somebody tell you about that?(Harrison bankruptcy petition)

A. I was informed of those.

Q. Were you also informed that the federal bankruptcy court twice had to throw his petitions out for bad faith and for lying about where he lived?

A. No, I was not aware of that.

Q. It would be most unusual, would it not, for a lender to make loans of this magnitude and not obtain a lien on the real estate?

A. I did not see any evidence of any lien on this particular loan.

Q. Didn't see any title insurance?

A. No, I did not.

Q. Didn't see any attorney's opinion?

A. No, I did not.

Q. You were not aware that a title insurance policy had been issued in this case on those properties?

A. I did not know that.

Q. It wasn't in the file?

A. It was not in the file.

Filipiak Cross examined by Field:

Volume V:

Page 127:

Q. You never had a conversation with anybody, did you, that was personally involved in the origination and the approval of these loans?

A. I don't – no, I did not.

Q. The only information you had in connection with these loans is what you may or may not have found in the loan files, what you may have seen in FDIC examinations, and what other people told you?

A. It's what I saw in the files, what I saw in the documents I reviewed other than the loan files, and what I was told by Mr. Bucknam.

Pages 133 & 134:

Q. Will you agree with me that it's a sales agreement?

A. It's a sales agreement between the buyer, Ralph Wright, and Lyndonville Savings Bank by Roger Lussier.

Q. Yes. He's the auctioneer to that – of this. It says, "Lyndonville sold to" ---

A. Correct

Q. Is this a situation where you simply didn't see it in the file?

A. I certainly didn't see it.

Q. And that's why you so reported it?

A. That's correct.

Q. There are a number of documents you didn't see in the file, weren't there?

A. Yes, there were.

Q. What support do you have for making such a statement, that he gained a commission from the sale of those two lots? What did you find that told you he got a commission?

A. There was some document in the file with regard to a commission for the sale.

Q. Was there a document in the file?

A. To the best of my recollection, there was. I believe I had to make it on some basis.

Q. So somebody must have told you that?

A. Would somebody have told me?

Q. Yes.

A. I presume they could have. It would be Mr. –

Q. Probably Mr. Bucknam.

A. Bucknam

Now in 1998 he testifies in a trial where the bank is being sued and we want to make the bank and the director's actions look good again, so we have to be careful, as seen below:

Bucknam being questioned by bank's attorney, John Gravel:

Pages 34 – 36:

Q. Did the Board operate in a banking context in an extremely formal manner?

A. No, I would say that it was very informal.

Q. Did members of the Board of Directors bring business to the Bank?

A. Yes, they did. They were – a number of Directors at that time were quite active in soliciting and bringing potential customers to the Bank.

Q. Did the Bank in late 80's and early 90's place a reliance on the value of the security given in granting a customer a loan?

A. Yes.

Q. Was that in fact one of the main conditions of the borrower, prospective borrower, that the bank would look at in granting loans?

A. Yes, I think so. I think there was actually an over-reliance on the value of collateral and to a much lesser degree, a reliance upon cash flow or potential cash flow of a borrower.

Q. Was – in that respect was the Lyndonville Bank any different than any other bank in Northeast Vermont at that point in time?

A. Well I think there was the tendency certainly at that time in the 80's to rely very heavily on collateral to support a loan. I do think that some banks were quicker to react to a weakening economy and to regulate a request and suggestion that it should be looking more at cash flow.

Page 78:

Q. Was ratification by the members of the board of directors an unusual method of doing business in the late 80's, early 90's?

A. No.

Q. They did it for Marden Industries, did they not?

A. Yes.

Q. They did it for Mr. Palmisano, did they not?

A. Yes.

Q. Did they do it for other customers, as well?

A. Yes

Charlie Bucknam would have you believe that he is a paragon of virtue but some of his actions would certainly lead you to question that belief. In

December 1987, he and his wife purchased a building in Hardwick, Vt. from the Caledonia National Bank, his employer, for $75,000.00. They knew that the Town of Hardwick was interested in this building, but that it would take some time before the Town could get their approvals and paperwork in order, so the Bucknams bought it. They sold it to the Town of Hardwick in August 1988 for a selling price of $99,500.00. When they purchased the building there was no personal property involved in the sale but when they sold it to the Town they showed $10,000.00 of the purchase price to be personal property, which cut down the amount of tax they would have to pay. Sometimes when Charlie Bucknam speaks I am reminded of some old sayings, such as, it's like the pot calling the kettle black or he speaks out of both sides of his mouth, or people who live in glass houses shouldn't throw stones.

We now arrive in the year 2000 and the bank is suing Roger again, this time in Caledonia Superior Court, after having been thrown out of Federal Court, and his lies seem to now be coming home to roost. Roger's attorney, David Williams and Evelyn's attorney, Lisa Chalidze really bear down on him, and it is almost pitiful listening to his answers. Below is his testimony at the attachment hearing in Caledonia Superior Court and notice near the end of his testimony when Lisa Chalidze gets into the unconscionable aspects of the bank's actions:

10/24/00:
Bucknam by Williams:
Page 87:

Q. If the board had followed the recommendations of the FDIC, would any of the loans been approved? It's yes or no.

A. I would say no.

Page 107:

Q. Are you aware, sir, of any criticism that Mr. Howe voiced at any of the shareholder, the annual shareholder meetings about the direction of the board and its decisions?

A. Not in that time frame, 1988, '92.

Bucknam by Chalidze:
Page 160:

Q. Thank you. And so in that particular record, it was of import to the bank, was it not, whether the bank was being considered as a state chartered bank? (Bucknam memo of 8/15/94)(see other memos that show Bucknam knew difference be State and Federal chartered banks)[2]

A. Or a national bank, in the eyes of the FDIC, yes.

October 25:
Bucknam by Williams:
Page 5:

Q. Sir, would you read into the record paragraph 77 of the verified complaint?

A. The conveyances of the stock and stock interests were without adequate consideration.

Q. You swore to the truth of that assertion. What evidence were you relying on to make that assertion under oath?

A. I could find no evidence in the bank records.

Page 20:

Q. Right. And the reason that the bank wanted to issue that stock in Roger Lussier's name alone is so that you could, you, meaning the bank, could ask this Court to issue a writ of attachment without dragging Evelyn Lussier into the case; isn't that a fair statement?

A. Yes.

Page 23:

Q. And what the banks' decision in May really did, May of 2000, really did was deprive Mrs. Lussier of her joint tenancy in over one million dollars' worth of bank shares; correct?

A. Yes.

Bucknam by Chalidze:
Page 40:

Q. What exactly do you mean by stock records, what exactly did you look at before making that affirmation under oath?

A. I looked at the stock transfer records, and I was primarily looking at dates of transfer.

Q. What information is contained in these stock records as to how much money is paid for stocks in a given transfer?

A. Usually none.

(On 2/23/94 LSB receives a letter from the FDIC saying there is no prohibition against Roger selling his stock , so Bucknam knew at this time that Roger was trying to sell stock but did nothing about it or try to stop Roger from selling his stock in 1994. See Exhibit for letter from FDIC)

Bucknam is now questioned by bank's attorney Gravel:

Page 61:

Q. What happened to the money in the reserve account?

A. Money in the dealer reserve account by then was totaling some ninety seven thousand dollars. That money was released to Noel Lussier and Doug Gilmour, and Roger Lussier did not require that that be applied to reduce the defaulted Walker Brothers note. *(The minutes of 5/27/92 state: VOTED: To apply the balance of Noel's reserve account of approximately $9,000 to the Walker's note.) (All money in the reserve account always went to notes that Noel had with bank)*

Q. What does the last box or column on the document indicate?

A. The last document, the last item on this document shows how the transaction with the Walker Brothers was finalized. They had defaulted, the dealer reserve account was dissipated to the guarantors without any benefit to the LSB. Roger Lussier had not protected the bank's interest under the bankruptcy in Florida and Roger Lussier recommended that and actually released Noel and Doug Gilmour as guarantors allowed the transfer of assets owned by Noel Lussier and Doug Gilmour to Roger Lussier's nephews. *(As shown above the money in the reserve always went to notes that Noel was responsible for)(In the minutes of 11/6/91 the Board approved accepting interest on the Walker Bros. and Hawthorne farm in the amount of $30,000. Pending FDIC approval. We still hadn't received FDIC approval by 11/20/91 meeting and the Board directed Turner to call the FDIC saying that payment was in jeopardy because of lawsuits against Gilmour and Noel. See letter[4]from Hale & Dorr associate to Gilmour's attorney reference possible action against Gilmour and Roger. By this time Noel and Gilmour didn't have the money anymore. Turner didn't dare accept the money before FDIC approval as he had been fined by them for doing this once before.)*

Bucknam by Williams:

Page 123:

Q. After becoming president of the bank, did you suggest to the board of directors that they take action to pursue the guarantors of that loan, Mr. Gilmour and Mr. Noel Lussier?

A. No.

Q. And certainly the statute of limitations for such action had not run by the time you took over the bank in 1994?

A. Correct, but they had been released in their assets transfer.

Q. But they were guarantors on a loan that had gone into default, correct? Is that correct?

A. The loan had gone into default and it was charged off, yes.

Q. Charged off. And as guarantors, they, the court, the bank could have proceeded in court against the guarantors of that loan for any losses?

A. Except my recollection was that they were released from responsibility as guarantors.

Q. By?

A. Roger Lussier.

(Minutes of 11/20/91: The Bank will not pursue the personal guarantees of Noel and Gilmour on the Walker notes at the present time due to the Walker's bankruptcy situation. Lussier and Gilmour are reluctant to give us financial statements at this point in time because of the pending lawsuits against them.)(Noel and Gilmour were never released while Roger was on the Board of Directors)

Bucknam by Chalidze:

Page 129:

Q. Now, in regard to the stock transfers in 92 and 94 that form the basis of bank's fraudulent conveyance count in the federal court, isn't it true that the bank was telling Mr. Lussier as late as 1995 that it did not want to sue him?

A. There may have been some discussion with a board member and Roger Lussier.

Q. All right. And that information that you didn't want to bring suit against Mr. Lussier was being conveyed to him as late as 1995; isn't that true?

A. Yes.

Pages 142 &143:

Q. Was Mrs. Lussier pro se in that matter?

A. In the original complaint? Yes, I believe she was.

Q. And also when she turned her stock over to you, she was pro se?

A. Yes, yes.

Q. You think it's important for a party to have an attorney in litigation?

A. I think it's a decision that the party makes.

Q. And your decision is to have two, right?

A. Right.

Q. Don't blame you.

Q. Did you think you had any evidence indicating that Mrs. Lussier had engaged in conduct that was illegal or improper?

A. No.

Page 144:

Q. Did you know how Mrs. Lussier was going to keep body and soul together with her husband in jail and no job outside the home –

Gravel: Objection.

Lisa C: -- and no stock

Court: We're getting to the unconscionable advantage, so, yes, I'll let the witness answer.

Witness: Again, what's the question?

Q. Sure. Did you know how Mrs. Lussier was going to keep body and soul together with her husband in jail and all his assets attached, even her home, no job outside the home, and no stock?

A. No.

Q. Did you ever stop to think about that?

A. I don't recall, but I gave it any thought.

One final item on Bucknam. In 1996, the bank was co-executor with two other people on the Bob Beausoliel estate. Bob had been a Director at LSB. The other two executors wanted Reginald Lussier to conduct the auction for the estate, but Bucknam, as President of the Bank wrote a letter to the Caledonia County Probate Judge objecting to the engagement of Lussier

Auction Service as he mentioned in his letter to the Judge, he thought it might seem inappropriate, since they were suing Roger, to have his son hold the auction.

I have never been able to understand why Charlie Bucknam hated me so much that he would lie and distort the truth, keep information from the stockholders, and get rid of the former officers and directors. In the exhibit section I have shown the officers and directors that have left the bank[5]and also a memo from Bucknam to the Directors about Turner signing an affidavit in my favor and that he recommends Turner be terminated immediately.[6] I can only assume that he was in bed with the FDIC and the Vermont Banking Department. If you look at his testimony when the bank sued my wife and I and then his depositions and testimony in some of the lawsuits against the bank, it is quite obvious that Charlie is a master of speaking out of both sides of his mouth.

[1] See Exhibits pages 62-63 for letter

[2] See Exhibits pages 64-67 for Bucknam memos

[3] See Exhibits page 68 for FDIC letter

[4] See Exhibits pages 69-71 for letters

[5] See Exhibits page 72

[6] See Exhibits page 73 for memo to fire Turner

Whose Body is This

Wouldn't you think that the Lyndonville Savings Bank would know its parents? That a bank that thought enough of itself to operate a trust department on behalf of its depositors would know where it came from, what it was. An institution that held first mortgages on millions of dollars of property and that employed over 50 people and had a value of over $16 million would at least know what its legal charter was. Now that is such a simple matter that it is really testing our credibility to be asked to believe that it, the Lyndonville Bank, doesn't know its parents!

How can it be that an institution that has been in Lyndonville for over 100 years and has made thousand of loans and has maintained complicated financial records and has reported to federal institutions and state institutions and has paid taxes would make such a simple, enormous mistake? What am I talking about?

While much of what I've told you in this story would appear to be complicated and require the assistance of judges and legal experts the simple question of the character and legal status of the Lyndonville Savings Bank is instantly determined by asking the Commissioner of Banking in Vermont who they are? But suddenly, after years of knowing they were a State bank you can see them fitting exactly the description I have giving you above regarding the fraudulent pretense of the Bank: to have been born in Washington of federal parents. After a hundred years of local residence they suddenly carry on a masquerade in Lyndonville of being born of noble parents from Washington. They continued this until their birth certificate was produced denouncing their claim and proving them to be the sham that they are. And as if that was not enough of an insult when their birth certificate is produced in federal court and shows them to have been born in this beloved State of Vermont they pretend that all of their previous claims were a mistake.

And so it was in this tortured case of the civil suits of that bank of "unknown and disputed" parentage. That after five years of misleading, deceptive and perjured statements, having the resources of those highly paid endorsers of untruth, signed statements now seen as frauds upon the court and myself, they found out, thanks to the Second Appeals Court, they were "sleeping with" the wrong body, that their legal recourse was the Vermont Superior Court, not the Whole of the United States of America.

Sorry does not explain or repair what the parasite lawyers sitting in bigger richer offices in Boston and Burlington did to me and my children and their families. It does not explain Charlie's seizing of my wife's sole means of support while I am headed for prison, our stock, and our property, as security for his false claim. Does a bank robber make an "honest mistake" when he loots a bank? How about a bank president looting the resources of a citizen… pretending to be a child "Federal born" when in fact he comes from here.

So let's look at how "bodies" get created. It would seem to be self-explanatory if I had not learned better. Imagine; sex education at my age. What a lesson.

It goes like this. One method of creating a "body" is more or less familiar to us. There are a series of activities among persons of separate genders, usually married or at least about to discover that they will be so, and after a quiet period of at least nine months a person is born. This is usually regarded as an occasion of joy, all family members gather to welcome the new child. Gifts are given. Parents are congratulated (or will be following a meeting with their dads and a local preacher) and the life cycle continues. We are so familiar with this system of creation, and often so embarrassed at some unexpected deviation that we seldom consider that there is another way of creating persons, legal entity persons, here in Vermont. Yes, our children are born to us here, our pride and joy are given names, placed within our families and given their place in our hearts, and we are delighted. But there is this other form of body, just as valid and more enduring.

The State of Vermont creates these "children" itself. Imagine that. The State in the business of creating bodies. It is referred to by scholars of the law as a "legal fiction" which seems to mean we have agreed to act as if something that we know is fundamentally untrue is in fact to be believed as if it were true. We allow, upon common agreement to believe, that a "person" can be created by the payment of a fee to the Secretary of State in Montpelier. Forms are filled out giving a name to this fiction, and by placing the State Seal upon all of these papers a new legal body is born. It can be a body to sell cars, or a body created to run a restaurant or sell groceries. It can be body to operate an airport, or create a bank. The State of Vermont is the geographic home, within this Constitutional nation, of persons living here as natural citizens and as "legal fiction citizens." They are in every way to be regarded and treated just as a natural citizen would be, having a name, paying taxes and living in this State of Vermont. And this introduction is exactly the necessary setting for understanding how a Vermont Citizen, the Lyndonville Saving Bank, posed as a Federal citizen fraudulently, and carried on that impersonation until exposed for the only thing it ever was, a legal citizen of the State of Vermont, and returned home to a Vermont Court to face the music…and be judged.

We assume a bank knows what it is, what it does, and can be trusted to tell the truth. Where did we get such an idea? Because for the most of us, the bank we do business with has been where it is for some time, and is composed of persons running it that we have grown up with. It is started by successful local persons and is usually a part of some of our earliest memories. "Going to the bank" is like going to the post office. And I assume you can easily remember when your parents took you to the "bank" and opened a savings account for you, explaining that saving was often the route to getting your dreams to come true. The Bank was a place you knew your money could be deposited with safety, where they knew who you were, and didn't lose things. It took care of your money, loaned you some money for something you needed that would last, took your payments and seemed to know you had done well with your decisions. It helped you buy cars, houses and farms and shared the risk of raising cows and dairy products. It loaned you money for your children, and was just part of your town landscape. It seemed to just be there forever.

I have been proud to be among those community members that provided service and leadership to the Lyndonville Savings Bank during its hundred years in Lyndonville. I had not grown up in a banking family, but had chosen much of what my father had taught me to be my way of earning a living. I had learned how to buy cattle and sell them in Boston. I had learned how to choose good dairy cows, how to care for them and see them as top producers. I learned how to judge farms for value and how to buy and sell land. And I had become an auctioneer and established my own business, currently reflected in the careers of some of my own children. So it was as a successful farmer, dairyman, auctioneer and land manager that I was asked by a previous President of the Lyndonville Savings Bank to become a Director of that bank. One of several, not the only one! I was asked to be part of a gathering of selected persons risking their own interests, time and assets to assist that institution. The Board of Directors is a legal requirement of the State of Vermont in creating a legal body of a corporation. Every natural body has a brain to manage and control it, and it is the same with a legal body. The Board of Directors is the mind of that body. And having become successful in my own personal businesses, I saw serving as a Director the continuation of my interests in the well-being of the community itself. I never needed the bank, any bank, to become successful in business. That came first, was already established when asked to be a Director. And while it may seem to you a rather prideful thing to say, it is for you to know that as the events during my period of leadership develop.

When I came to the Lyndonville Board of Directors, the bank was worth about $700,000.00. When I left being President in 1993, after establishing suitable reserves and writing off normal business losses, employing almost sixty persons in three locations, the bank was worth $16,000,000. There were no dividends paid and very little growth for four years immediately following my retirement. In November 1994 the bank was still being criticized by the FDIC.[1] The FDIC said that the management and Board of the Bank had been unable to resolve problem loans and to identify emerging credit weaknesses, and still had unacceptable underwriting and monitoring practices. Bucknam was President of the bank at this time and had been for a while. Now just a brief reading of those FDIC letters to the next management after I left the Board will show this is no exaggeration. And as I have said, all you need to do is try and get a loan for anything there now to see how it is changed. But I can say simply, that the bank I left and turned over to others was an institution to be proud of, serving this community, making good loans, serving credit-worthy people, and actually caring about its customers. And while now I wish I had never agreed to serve it, that I did so and did it well is an achievement that I see nothing to rival it in the remains of that institution. And how can that happen? It seems to have two explanations.

How could a small bank in rural Vermont become such a lightning rod, be the site of such interest and attention? Well, now over these past ten years I have reviewed every document associated with this event, I have spoken to hundreds of persons regarding it, have had all possible explanations considered and have concluded the following. It was during this time that hundreds of banks nationally went "broke" (see the geographic chart in the documents section)[2] and seems to reflect a pattern of numerical reduction. There were too many small independent banks for the "big" boys who wanted more market share. The FDIC used almost any pretext to consolidate or dissolve local independent banks. In my case they even issued a phony "fraud alert" alleging I had "broken" the IBG banks...to which I was entirely unrelated, and they knew it. But the FDIC had been stung by an article appearing in the *Wall Street Journal*[3] regarding this prosecution and our local success, in the presence of larger banks failing. So they put out a story regarding me, related me to banks I had no stock in, and to whom did not even owe a dollar. They even leaked a story to the press that a "bank director might be removed from office." So again in the context of a time when the government is closing banks all over the country, and rushing to reassure others that they are significant to the survival of banks (a premise the FDIC has never proved was that their oversight matters) it seems that Lyndonville Savings Bank offered them a sought-for opportunity. Some of the reasons may be that:

1. It was entirely the result of a prosecutor's ambition and seizing of opportunity in the aftermath of the national "saving and loan scandals" and it was the mistaken belief that with a similarity in names of their Presidents, two separate and entirely different institutions were perceived as operating as the same.
   And it seems it all could have been avoided if only I had been willing to plead guilty to something, and go to work for the

government as an unknown conduit for information among my many friendships in the Northeast Kingdom.

2. It may have had some "nudge" from other departments or interests of the federal government in matters involving Space Research Corporation.

3. It may have been prompted by some rumors and some erroneous belief that I had banking interests and resources "overseas." To that I can say, I never did! And I am certain that with all of the resources of investigation of my background and activities, if the phone taps and bank record investigations and travel reports revealed no such activity. It simply was not there.

4. The bank case against me, seeking eventually $8,700,000, was the willful decision of persons motivated by greed, the opportunity to collect unearned money, and to avoid the scrutiny of their own conflicts of interest and unearned assets. They were seeking to profit at my expense for decisions made while I was there that they knew were legal, corporate in nature, and involving the whole of the Lyndonville Savings Bank – not simply Roger Lussier, citizen of Vermont.

For whatever else you can say about me, I have always known who my parents are.

And it is their shame that they pretended they did not!

To be sure the Bank did not go from its high profitability to losing money for the next few years, simply because I chose to resign. When I was completing my last term as President and had announced my intention to resign the stock was well regarded. The stock was selling for over $500 per share and there were few shares available, though highly desirable for purchase.

I had indicated my desire to resign and had been asked by the Board of Directors to continue as an outside consultant with one of the benefits being the retention of my health insurance. Charlie Howe was busy with his own family interests and the board certainly understood that. They chose William Rockford, a former Commissioner of Banking for the State of Vermont, as their next President. Now if our Bank had been such a problem to the State of Vermont, the State that had granted its charter in the first place, he certainly would have known that. He was very well informed regarding banking throughout the State and he certainly knew the Lyndonville Savings Bank. And that knowledge was very favorable to his reputation and our prospects for continuing as a profitable institution respected by the community. We were always sound financially. and he was in a position to know. There were other invisible players in this comedy. The issues involved in this narrative are not simply those of the employed personnel of the bank, or the personalities of the Directors, and examiners from the FDIC, or even the presence of the "Whole of the United States" in the person of one of its prosecutors. There were changes occurring in the banking industry that were nationwide in scope, and politically managed as a result of other difficulties far from the geography of the Northeast Kingdom of Vermont. I call them invisible because they did not appear in the reporting of the trial or in the testimony of the examiners. But they can be seen in the larger context referred to when you read about the banking scandals of that era, particularly the affairs involving losses in the Savings and Loan industry. There emerges a change in the culture and purposes and the control of these institutions themselves. The "invisible" and undisclosed issue behind all of this was a change in the history of these institutions within American culture and the role of government posing as "protector and defender."

Prior to the arrival of the 1980s, and a then different federal banking system, the accumulation of capital in small communities was very much a local affair. Farmers and businessmen that had done well in the 19th and 20th centuries, who had contributed to the building of railroads and expansion of markets, were frequently the source of the savings capital necessary to create such an organization. Doctors, farmers, dairymen and small-business owners gathered their resources and formed banking companies and provided those services to the community. This was usually a local effort among stockholders that had known each other and had experienced growth with the others of that specific community in all areas of local industry. The primary ingredient for success at that time was stability, familiarity with clients of the institution, and the willingness of the owners of the bank stock to invest. They used their experience, their own money, and their own judgment in both the clients and the stock of the institution itself. The Lyndonville Savings Bank and thousands of others like it across the United States were typical of this period of time. Sometimes they lost money, frequently there were small-scale scandals, but for the most part these banks were successful. This was possible because of their attention to changes in conditions or reputations locally, and they had something at stake themselves in the outcome. I did! We did!

We had local contact and immediate feedback regarding the circumstances of our markets and our customers. If a farmer's barn burned, the Bank knew it immediately and could assess the consequences to all parties and proper decisions could be made. People made loans with people they knew. Loan officers and clients, in advance of going to an auction or needing to make a purchase, could anticipate the desire for a loan, and our approval. We were in things together. Loan officers could make loans on their own authority and if necessary could always contact some Directors if a loan request was over the officer's lending authority. Service to the customer was the important thing. And there were many very good reasons to conduct our business that way. Just look at the results in our banking profitability. Choices and decisions and loans were good. You needed to wait until "after Roger" to lose money in the most profitable period for banking in this country's history, and stonewall the stockholders when they asked their expensive Chief Executive for information.

Listed in the next chapter are loans that were charged off before Bucknam came to the bank. One important thing to remember is that except for the McCormick loan, all of the others had real estate and/or personal property, securing the loans, that could have been sold to lower the loss, but Bucknam and cronies had no idea of the value of these properties and just sold them for pennies on the dollar, knowing that they were going to charge the losses to me.

[1] See Exhibits pages 74-76 for FDIC letter

[2] See Exhibits page 77 for map of banks closed by FDIC

[3] See Exhibits page 78 for Article

Charge Off's Before Bucknam Came to Bank

			Charged Off
McCormick			
12/27/89	c/o	$410,000.00	
2/28/90	c/o	To charge off McCormick Loan (all charged off) (No chance of any recovery)	$700,000.00

Walker Brothers			
7/1/92	c/o	82,866.76 & 246,058.31 (all charged off) (Still had Gilmour & Noel on this note)	$328,925.07

Ryan			
6/19/91	c/o	(Took back Roundhouse real estate lease and equipment which should have covered balance of loan.)	
7/1/92	c/o	$403,540.63	
7/1/92	c/o	$75,000.00	
10/7/92	c/o	$25,604.93	$504,145.56

Harrison			
12/18/91	c/o	$290,000.00 (Had real estate and equipment with title insurance on it)	
12/9/92	c/o	$100,000.00	$390,000.00

Jasmin			
12/28/90	c/o	$337,256.93 (Had real estate worth more than this amount & had Mr.& Mrs. Kelton personally on this note)	
7/1/92	c/o	$250,000.00	
7/7/93	c/o	$250,000.00	$837,256.00

Guilmette			
12/18/91	c/o	$343,378.32 (Had real estate worth more than the balance due)	
7/1/92	c/o	$497,243.13	$840,621.45

Beck & Beck			
7/1/92	c/o	$233,000.00 (Had big granite factory in Barre plus equipment as security for the balance)	$233,000.00

Total charged off before Bucknam came to Bank   **$3,833,948.08**

We charged off as much as we could because we could use the tax write-off and after these write-offs, the bank should have made a profit, or at least broke even, after selling the collateral that secured these loans, except for McCormick, which was fraud. The Bank settled with Jasmin, against my wishes, and even went so far as to indemnify him if I sued him. The bank agreed to indemnify Jasmin at the same board meeting that they voted to bring suit against me.[1] All of the real estate was appraised by professional real estate appraisers for more than was owed on it.

2/29/92: Statement of Assets and Liabilities on Officers Questionnaire for FDIC signed by Elaine Beliveau as Treasurer of LSB showing:

Capital Account	$14,568,611.28
Unearned Discount	318,382.73
Reserve for Loan loss	1,494,215.04
IRS Tax refund	518,180.00
	$16,899,389.05[2]

This is RRL's Opinion of Bank worth (as of 2/29/92) plus bank building and equipment which was worth more than the depreciated value that they were carried on the bank's book for.

Before 1993, when LSB had foreclosed on property and had to sell it, the Directors were aware of property values and were most often able to sell it for what they had appraised it for, or more, and did the work themselves. Now the Directors rely on Senior Management to make these decisions, and they do not have the knowledge or ability to obtain reasonable values. For many years this was not a problem for them as they figured that any loss they had they would just add on to what they were trying to get in Court from Roger.

A prime example of this is a farm property in Coventry.[3] This farmer had sold approximately 106 acres in 4 parcels for between $900 and $1,000 per acre. The land that this farmer sold was not crop land, it was cut off wood land on the back side of his farm. An appraisal was done in November 1991 and the real estate was appraised for $728,500 for the buildings and 600 acres.

He deeded back approximately 300 acres to the bank to lower his debt load.

The Bank sold the 300 acres for an average of 407.20 per acre, including a mobile home and barn. One of the buyers then sold the mobile home and some land and his net investment was lowered to 248.00 per acre. This was mostly crop land and there was an owner of adjacent land that had been paying up to $3,000 per acre for crop land like this.

One of the former directors of the bank, who was also a real estate broker, went to get a listing from the bank, and when he saw the price he asked if it was OK for him to purchase it himself. They said they didn't care. He purchased 20 acres for $9,300 and sold it for 28,000.

This certainly does not appear to be making money for the stockholders.

The Bank foreclosed on the North Country Motors property in Derby. They had an offer of $450,000 in March 1994 from a bona fide buyer for cash and turned it down. They then put it up for sealed bids and one of the Directors[4] and a partner, after notifying the Board he was interested, put in a bid of $408,000 cash which was accepted by the Directors. Shortly thereafter Bucknam convinced the Directors not to accept this bid. In 1997 they settled for $350,000 and financed it. During this time they had to pay insurance and taxes etc. This property was in a prime location on the main commercial strip between Newport and Derby.

There was a lot and mobile home in Sheffield that they had foreclosed on. They had a cash offer in 1994 of $7,500 that they turned down. They then sold it to the brother-in-law of one of the directors in 1995 for $3,000.

But unfortunately the banking environment began to change in the late 1980s as a consequence of the scandals in the Savings and Loan industry. And as a consequence of electronic interconnection capacity to cross over boundaries of geography and the circle of relationships that had previously made "personal knowledge" so important. This was also a time of extensive banking expansion and consolidation. Regional banks became "nationwide" banks by way of computers and purchase of rival companies in their range of influence. South Dakota became the credit card processing capital of the country simply as a function of time zone processing. What had once been a distant New York bank like City Bank of New York became a household name, Citibank, nationwide as a result of their entrance into credit card fields and banking services that had previously been denied them by regulation. The borders of local knowledge that used to ensure profitability of loans were overwhelmed by the ability of the Banks to use three credit reporting agencies in distant locations within the United States as their primary source of information. Creditworthiness became less a matter of knowledge and judgment regarding an individual by a local loan officer. The credit history of a particular individual was and is now not even determined exclusively in Vermont.

The Congress is the place where the interests of these banks are managed. The Congress, and lobbyists attending to that body, is the place where extreme differences in financial policy are controlled. But as we saw from the Savings and Loan scandal which, until the time of Enron, was the largest single loss in the history of this country as an industry, the regulations were always more noble in their language than effective in their application. There were federal banks and state banks and they each fared about the same regardless of their legal parentage. The Great Depression brought a significant change in the role of the federal government's participation in the banking industry. Its new role would be to ensure local credit availability and insure depositor's investment. The use of the federal role to achieve some uniformity in the management of banking companies was dramatically increased with the extension of credit and insurance to those institutions, and the ability to borrow from the federal treasury by the use of the Federal Reserve System. That beginning period of regulation began to increase the size of the FDIC, and its presence has increased over and over again. Its regulations have been extended into almost every institution for banking in the United States. Its representatives have arrived unexpectedly time and time again at the doors of local banks. They collected information and made reports to all parties involved and have also increased the cost of managing these banks. But in fact the actual benefit of this believed service has never been demonstrated. Banks have continued to fail in some cases by the manipulation of dishonest officers or Boards of Directors. Some have been caught and many have not. But the actual role of the banking examiners discovering danger to the institutions or helping them avoid some scandal has in fact not been demonstrated. When disasters have struck these institutions, the FDIC has been good for insuring that the taxpayer will cover the loss to the accounts up to the amount set from time to time. (Some depositors might also lose.) But they probably have done very little to bring about a change of environment when either market forces or intentional fraud emerges in these institutions. And like much of government, we are led to believe that the appearance of the FDIC plaque or the announcement that our accounts are insured is dealing with the problem. It is not. But it does give us some assurance, and a new tax bill.

Following the billions of dollars of loss to the taxpayers from the Savings and Loan scandal, with most of the diverted wealth not recovered, it became necessary for the government to reassure its customers that this environment was indeed well managed and safe. So following this period of time there was an exercise in searching for demonstrations that were converted into the form of a public circus, as an entertainment method for reassuring the uninformed. In the document section there is the chart of "failed banks" – some 500 banks failing in Texas and 100 failing in Oklahoma. But the States they focus on and pursue are those in Vermont and New Hampshire and Massachusetts. A vigorous effort to identify problem banks and problem institutions begins in the late '80s and is itself contradicted by its own previous reporting of those institutions on the list as satisfactory. Banks that the FDIC had been regularly visiting from the '40s and '50s and '60s and '70s and into the '80s suddenly become problem banks in the middle '80s and most are now out of business by 2000. Why?

The joint interest of the large banks to reduce competition and the federal government to have fewer entities to be concerned about served the interest of both of those parties. But it becomes a disaster to the thousands of local community banks that the farmer and the home buyers and small businesses could rely upon as a source of credit and a sympathetic ear if there was a crop failure in the fields that year or a down-turn in the economy. Banking became a matter of matching credit scores and numbers from distant reporting bureaus that had no accountability and little visibility to the borrower and Board of Directors. Previously-exercised independent judgment, regarding their own investments in their own stock, is now seen to be an obstacle to uniformity. The "insurance agent" government, with no investment of its own at stake, defines for that client institution what it is to lose, what it is to recover, and how soon it is to do what is required.

The value of the Lyndonville Saving Bank stock in the 1980s is a reflection of that bank's management of its opportunities, its earnings and expenses, and its experience and judgment. The value of that stock today is a reflection of its experience as a "federal insurance client" offering you some return on your investment. The value of the stock today is approximately the same as it was 10 years ago. There has been no growth in the value of the stock. This increase of regulations and the cost of regulation and the use of the bank's in-house CEO-president, and the changing role of the Board of Directors to a rubber stamp committee of the whole, changes it entirely. It is now a franchise mailbox outlet for a check-clearing company.

If you are looking for a good investment in Lyndonville to begin the 21st century, I doubt that you are looking to purchase that stock. The lack of growth in that value, from 1993 until today, is just about what all of that governmental supervision is worth, and the pretenses of local directors and their hired CEO, even less. It takes a lot of hard work to wreck a good business for the community, but they have done it.

Now that background is inserted as a way of beginning to understand that what happened to the Lyndonville Savings Bank and the directors that were part of that institution during my presidency represents an entirely different method and an entirely different purpose than what is present in that institution today. The present Lyndonville Savings Bank and similar institutions are currently operating primarily as individual retail stores for checking and credit card services serving the interests of the Federal Deposit Insurance Corp. And the large banks like Citicorp have made credit card use the primary device for extending lending services and managing active accounts. Previously, the Lyndonville Savings Bank made a modest profit out of investing its deposits into federal securities. It also made significant loans that might expand the local economy or provide someone with a business opportunity. It was mostly our money that we, the decision-makers, were risking, and we knew what we were doing and with whom. But now it is not a place that you would still seek investment or to expect your stock to return significant profit.

In 1990 we were able to provide the financing for the new Lyndon Town grade school in the amount of $5.3 million. We were in the position of having the funds available to lend, and we could also use the tax advantage of a municipal loan. We provided the full financing and did not require the guarantee of the State, which saved the school district money.

But actions like that to save the town money and benefit the community that must repay it is no longer possible. It is now a banking McDonald's or banking Subway, providing a menu of services decided upon elsewhere at a price that you will become accustomed to. An example of the change in purpose can be seen in overdrawn checking account charges, charges which are seen by many banks as a primary source of profit, since the cost of those services electronically is almost 0, and of no significant loss.

By the time I had been indicted, banks like Lyndonville had been pretty well identified as places for the expansion of federal control and the reduction of local options in their management. And the desire to get the Roger Lussiers of the world that demonstrated independent ability to make their banks profitable could be seen as an explicit goal of the federal regulators. During the early 80's I attended a banking conference in California. One of the presenters at the conference, speaking to similar banking institutions like our own, told us very clearly that we should expect to sell our stock and get out of the business. He said the federal government intended to reduce the thousands of local banks to about 18 nationwide banks that could range across the economic opportunities of the whole United States and control both the market and the product for banking services, and that these banks would do this with the assistance of the federal government. A strange and continuing partnership of those two different institutions was hard to believe – the government helping banks make money and defeating competition. Putting banks like us out of our traditional business was to be seen as the American way. And they've done so. Move over Indians, you have company.

Large banks can do what they will and seem to do so. Small banks are regulated to the point of exhaustion and are never able to accumulate the wealth that would be necessary to challenge the competition. The use of regulation can be shown to serve not only the insurance interests of the FDIC but also the emerging nationwide banking companies. We can now see the use of the benefits of regulation authority of the federal government to the advantage of the huge institutions that have emerged, like Wells Fargo and Bank of America and Citicorp. The government becomes the working servant of those banking institutions that then benefit their political patrons.

Meanwhile back in Lyndonville, the former Commissioner of Banking for Vermont has decided that his own personal interests are no longer to be the President of the Bank. Charlie Howe is Chairman of the Board of Directors and Charlie Bucknam is now appointed a hired president rather than holding that office as an investor. As a man well known to the government during his employment in other failed banks, the regulating body of the FDIC immediately approves him for that position and together they began shaping the Board of Directors to become the rubber stamp that it was intended to be. The primary affairs of the Bank are managed on a daily basis by a hired employee who has no community roots, and no family knowledge of the traditional customers of the Lyndonville Savings Bank. He initially had no investment, and today only marginal investment in it as a stockholder. He is concerned first and foremost with his relationship with the Bank's lawyers, the Bank's insurance company lawyers, and the Federal Deposit Insurance

Corp. Some members of the Board of Directors resigned, all of the others are simply not re-elected. And within a reasonable period of time, by 1995, the Bank is the visible servant of its new master, The FDIC.

Returning to the federal trial now there are two matters that will continue to follow this story throughout the period of my imprisonment and will result successfully in my favor only after I have served an unjustified sentence and been subjected to the loss of hundreds of thousands of dollars.

They are:

(1) The illegal imposition of a restitution order attached to my sentencing by Judge Billings and

(2) The fraudulent and systematic attempt by the successor Board of Directors and President of the Lyndonville Savings Bank and expensive lawyers to misrepresent the bank's status as that of a federal institution.

The purpose of that misrepresentation was to allow them to attempt to sue me in a federal court and to allow my conviction in a federal court to give them the appearance of being an injured party. This would have entitled them to funds which had been awarded to them illegally in the first place. And they knew at the time this began that this was fraud upon the court. And the lawyers and Officers later admit that they knew it to be so, but said they had made a mistake. The Bank continued to know it through all of the thousands of pages of their representations to the federal court, and they know it now. They knew it was an issue for contention before I ever went to prison. And most of their efforts during that time were to conceal from the stockholders and from the federal court itself the truth of their pleading. They also failed to provide information when a petition signed by 20 stockholders asked for information. Now why would a Board of Directors do this?

When you read Charlie Howe's testimony at the criminal trial he continues to speak favorably about both the Board of Directors of Lyndonville as a competent body of persons among which Roger Lussier is a member and a stockholder. He affirms actions of the Board as a whole, acting as informed directors, but that Roger neither stacked the deck in favor of his interests nor did he dominate the directors as is later charged. He said what they did was done collectively, and they never found any problems with anything they were doing collectively. In early 1992 the FDIC had requested the bank to do a management plan, and we hired HAS Associates Inc,[5] to do this for the Bank. They returned their report on April 11, 1992. On June 15, 1992 I had received a notice from the FDIC seeking my voluntary removal as President and member of the Board and the Directors signed a resolution[6] refusing to accept my resignation. Charlie Howe was one of the Directors that signed that resolution. And one of the big surprises in all of this is that after my retirement, the Bank was to divide from a whole corporation into winning and losing teams.

All historic successes were now seen to be a collaborative effort of the directors and staff and customers, and any of its difficulties and losses were mine alone. That any of the conditions that allowed this Bank to earn the $16 million that we had acquired during my presidency were to be regarded as collective wisdom and any losses that we ever incurred in the normal process of business were to be seen as mine alone, personally. And one of the remaining questions in this whole matter is just at what point did the corporate body of the Lyndonville Savings Bank see itself to be different from the personal body of Roger Lussier, a citizen of Vermont.

As we have discussed one of the primary identities of the Corporation is to be a body of its directors. A director may speak on behalf of the whole, but that director is not the whole. That's why they call a corporation a body, and not a person. It never was "Roger's Bank" but the Lyndonville Savings Bank, a corporation formed in the State of Vermont. It was a corporation. And that corporation also had insurance that insured the services of its directors and officers. And the insurance for that corporate body became a very significant interest of the new Board of Directors, to see profit out of their current situation.

The directors retained some of the country's most experienced and expensive lawyers in Boston and Vermont and began looking in every direction for opportunities to attach blame individually upon Roger Lussier. Perhaps they believed they would be able to recover their expenses and even profit from the litigation to the banks benefit. That they intended to profit from it is most clearly demonstrated by their suit in the Federal Court for an $8 million verdict against me for no demonstrated loss. The Bank lost that suit, but one of its highly paid lawyers, who was found on all sides of the misrepresentations to the courts, still retains that unjustified award as one of his marketing claims to success on his web site. You can find it at: vtlawoffices.com.

So as Charlie Howe and Charlie Bucknam begin their service with the Bank you began seeing them focus their attention on retaining high-priced lawyers and initiating the version that led them to commit fraud upon the Courts and the State and the Bank and myself. The requirements of the FDIC, now their master, with the threat of $1 million a day fines, motivated Charlie Howe to invent a new "sworn testimony" in direct contradiction to his previous "sworn testimony" and without explaining the difference he begins to sing the new national anthem, "Oh-FDIC."

Now the restitution order had come about in a most unexpected way. As Judge Billings was adding up all of the counts that I had been convicted of he announced apparently to everyone's surprise that I was to repay as "restitution" the amount of $426,204.67 to the FDIC for losses incurred. The federal prosecutor, that "Whole of the United States," gently reminds the Judge that the FDIC and the Whole of the United States had not lost $426,204.67 in this matter, and they could not be awarded the restitution. Judge Billings accepts this modest correction and then announces the restitution will be paid to Lyndonville Savings Bank, who had not lost it either but does know a gift when it shows up. My defense attorney, now well rested but having been previously provided a pre-sentencing report by the federal government that identified that amount as restitution, did not challenge that conclusion. He later said, in his deposition on the malpractice case, equally illogically, that it would irritate the judge to raise it, but hoped that it would be eventually covered at the appeal

It was widely discussed at that time as an *illegal restitution requirement* because the federal statute did not allow that to be attached to relevant conduct;, that is, conduct for which I was not charged. Now at this point what does it matter to be splitting legal niceties like "an illegal order etc.," after all of the work they had gone to? But the prospects of collecting $426,000 of my money while the bank is spending millions of our money as stockholders to be diverted to lawyers and the "fire sale" of assets was just too pleasant a prospect for the existing directors and their hired president. They then claimed in federal court that I had wrongfully abused them and that I "owed" them the restitution. Both Charlie's have a good eye for money from others.

Another matter not discussed in public was the role of the bank's insurance. In what way would the insurance companies, that the lawyers were relying upon to pay for costs to the Bank, become obliged to pay the bank's claims. The evidence of those discussions is out of public sight. Their behavior is not. They even refused to provide this information to stockholders – while gleefully spending their money. In 2000 twenty stockholders signed a petition[7] asking to inspect the Bank's accounting records to determine what the Bank had spent in legal fees. The Bank declined to make these records available. So what the bank chose to say is that the Judge said they were entitled to his (illegal) restitution order, in spite of nothing to "restitute." It begins defending its position of actually being entitled to this restitution; its arrangements to do so are for the most part out of sight and not part of public record. The Bank was insured but the payments by the insurance company to the Bank are unknown to the public record. But probably the bank spent more on its lawyers during this period of time and spent more of the stockholders money for lawyers, including mine of course, than it recovered. It was a good try for the Bank and allowed it to pose in front of the community and stockholders as the injured party, while in fact placing the stock at great danger for losses, with millions of dollars going to lawyers who were willing to continue to dance for them as long as they were very well paid.

Now it is beyond logic to explain why a Federal judge who is supposed to know the law apparently did not do so at the time of my sentencing. It is beyond my ability to explain why the Whole of the United States of America, having achieved my conviction and unavoidable trip to prison would have found it necessary to assist in the fraud. The FDIC testified at the bank trial where the Vermont Department of Banking and Insurance was also involved. Yet neither one of them said the Bank was a State Chartered Bank, and they certainly knew.

The Commissioner for the Vermont Department of Banking and Insurance at that time was Elizabeth Costle. She was an attorney with the firm of Arnold & Porter in Washington, DC before moving to Vermont. She joined the Department of Banking, Insurance and Securities and became Commissioner after an unknown shake-up in the Department. She was Commissioner of Banking, Insurance and Securities when I had my criminal trial, and she wrote a letter to Judge Billings[8] regarding my sentencing. After reading her letter, which is attached as an exhibit, I would have thought that she would have asked to testify at my trial, under oath, but apparently she didn't want to be cross-examined. And she didn't want to be under oath, because if she was she wouldn't have been able to say what she did and get by with it.

She says that I claimed my dealings caused no harm. In my criminal trial there was no loss to anyone.

She says that in my dealings with Kelton that I allowed him to engage in a massive check kiting scheme, failed to report the check kiting, lied to bank examiners, funneled loans to Kelton through nominee borrowers, and made loans to Kelton in excess of the statutory lending limit of the bank. The complete history of the Kelton check kiting charges is told earlier in this story, and it refutes most of what Costle wrote in her letter. The one thing not listed earlier about Costle's charges is lending in excess of statutory limits. This was not so and was shown as being a false claim by Andrew Field when he discussed the "basket clause," which, under the law, allowed for this type of loan. The check kiting was stopped long before the State and Federal regulators got involved. When she says I lied to examiners, I believe she is referring to my saying that I had never met John Barry, the President of First Vt. Bank. I had never met him. I had only talked to him on the phone and that is what Barry testified to at my trial, and he was a government witness. The FDIC examiner, Mitchell, said at my trial that he thought I had told him I met Barry at Kelton's complex, but I didn't. I only talked to him on the phone.

She then states that I refused to cooperate. The only times I refused to cooperate with regulators was when they wanted us to sign and open-ended Memorandum of Understanding, and then it was only because it had no termination date, and since I was going to retire I did not want to be responsible after I left the bank. Tom Thompson, the CEO at that time had told the Directors that he had taken care of this MOU. But the Directors found out that he hadn't, and we asked for his resignation shortly after this. When we were having troubles with the FDIC I told Tom that he wouldn't be getting a raise[9] until we got things straightened out with them. I did not want to sign the Cease and Desist Order, but the bank's attorney, Bob Gensburg, said we should sign it because we had to live with them. If we didn't sign it, they would be miserable to live with. He felt we could win if we fought it, but that it wasn't worth it. I also refused, for a time, to pay a bill from the Banking and Insurance Department because I took it to be extortion.[10] That letter was dated 10/27/92 and read in part "Please let me know if the Bank proposes to pay these expenses as part of a settlement that would give the Bank cease and desist language that is more to its liking."

She then states that I violated Vermont banking law on a scale that this Department has never before seen, yet she fails to state which laws I violated. The FDIC never claimed I violated any laws. This would have been a good time for her to have been under oath, but then the truth probably never mattered to her so it wouldn't have made any difference if she had been under oath.

Finally she says I controlled the bank and the Directors. I have copied affidavits from many of the Directors, officers and an employee that dispute this statement. They are listed in the Exhibits section of this book.

She obviously went out of her way to try to increase the harshness of the penalty I suffered from the court. It's too bad that she was considerably less aggressive with respect to a huge expansion project at Burlington's Fletcher Allen Health Care, the state's largest hospital, in 2001-2003.

In addition to regulating banking, Costle is charged with protecting the general interest of the public from excessive costs resulting from new health care facilities. When the FAHC project came to her department in 2001, she sued FAHC to get regulatory control over the project's proposed parking garage. FAHC caved in and settled the litigation in June 2002, in return for the Department's declaration that the huge project would be "uncontested."

Costle's "expedited review" whistled through FAHC's application. Not long after her approval, it turned out that FAHC CEO, William Boettcher, had contrived to misstate or suppress the true costs of the project – some $362 million in place of the announced $170 million. The ensuing scandal costs Boettcher his job, resulted in the resignation of almost all of the FAHC directors, saddled patients, premium payers and the state with sharply increased charges, and finally led to a FAHC suit against its legal counsel, Downs Rachlin and Martin. In April 2004 the law firm agreed to pay FAHC $2 million in settlement. Meanwhile, the Attorney General fined FAHC $1 million for its wrongdoing – but of course the Renaissance Project went forward as planned. Costle was terminated when the Douglas Administration took office in January 2003.

If Costle had been as aggressive in protecting the public's interest in this $362 million scandal as she was in urging the court to punish me, the people of the state would have been a lot better off.

It is easy to see why the average person mistrusts their government and its leaders when, as is shown above, they do not feel they are bound by the expected rules of society such as telling the truth and by virtue of their position, to be held to a higher standard than the average person. To me Elizabeth Costle makes Martha Stewart look like a saint. I am thankful that the new Governor did not reappoint her when he was elected.

In December 1991 before Costle was Commissioner, she, along with other members of the Department and the FDIC, met with many local legislators.[11] They were worried that the publicity from the FDIC and the Vt. Department of Banking would hurt LSB and make obtaining credit harder for the local businessman.

It makes you wonder who you can trust. It is perhaps understandable why the new Board of Directors of Lyndonville could be convinced to sue me upon the advice and self-interest of its highly paid lawyers and insurance company (and using my money to pay them). In May of 1995, the bank's attorneys, Gravel & Johnston, met with me at my office and discussed some of the lawsuits against the bank[12]. We also discussed the FDIC position towards me at that time. I asked them many times if the bank planned to sue me. You can read the excerpts from that conversation in the exhibit section. Then in August 1995, Johnston of Hale & Dorr sends a letter to the bank's insurance company[13] outlining why the bank believes I did nothing wrong and why the insurance company should pay. In October 1995, about a month after the bank brought suit against me, Gravel had written a letter to Andy Field[14] asking for comments on the banks lawsuit against me. In early November, Andy answered the letter and voiced his concerns about the bank bringing this suit.

But it was not beyond the ability of a Magistrate and the federal court to say absolutely and without reservation that the restitution wasn't a legal order and that all of the consequences derivative of that order should be extinguished. The Bank and its lawyers were embarrassed when asked, "What was the nucleus of operative facts" that allowed them to so deceive themselves and others? After repeatedly being asked this question by the appellate judge their boastful and expensive lawyer had to admit that there was none.

Now you would think that upon exposure to the harsh light of reality that the Bank would realize the game was up and would return to doing for the

Lyndonville community what its charter had expected. But they did not. They took their fabricated case and their notarized perjury and then with obvious public enthusiasm went to the State court and set up shop all over again. Making the same claims and making the same deceitful misrepresentations.

When LSB first brought suit against me in State court, I did not have a lawyer and Mark Whitney wrote a Motion[15] for me to file pro se. We felt this Motion would get the Bank's State lawsuit dismissed. When I hired David Williams, I showed him the Motion that Mark had written, but he didn't want to use it. I can only assume he felt he was much smarter than Mark and would do his own paperwork. As it turned out I should have gone with Mark's Motion.

Now you would think at this point that a citizen who had been twice found to be harmed and aggrieved by the actions of the Lyndonville Savings Bank's directors, lawyers, and also the media, and so carefully supervised by the FDIC would now be required to repair the damage that they had created. After all, that was the basis of their original claim, that I had caused them damage, and they lost money because of me. But they did not say, "We are found wrong. We owe Roger restitution for what we have done to him." But now being a different Board of Directors with a different agenda to protect themselves and an FDIC owner, they simply said it was all a misunderstanding, and they should be understood as being the decent and reasonable people, even though their actions and the record shows otherwise.

And since there was no mechanism for me to force an accounting, and since they continued to deny to the stockholders details of this and other legal expenses over the years, they have continued to collect their salaries. Since they could avoid explaining why they had done such outrageous things they simply chose to do so.

So we have this remarkable display of legal talents defending for almost eight years the clearly visibly illegal positions of the Lyndonville Savings Bank masquerading as a federal institution while simply holding a charter from the State of Vermont. Two citizens of Vermont, Lyndonville Savings Bank and Roger Lussier, one a legal fiction and the other a natural citizen are both equal before the State court. But to recover even a fraction of the damages I received it would be necessary for me to sue the lawyers, which I did, and to win that suit which I did, rather than to be able to bring actions against the Lyndonville Savings Bank itself.

I believe I still had a good case against the bank, but my attorney at that time, who had done nothing to prepare a proper suit against the bank, such as taking depositions, told me he would need an extra $218,000 within nine days or he would file a motion to get out of the case. The case had been set for trial, and there were only so many days available for preparation and depositions and pleadings for documents available. I had already paid him $100,000, and could not come up with the extra $218,000 within that period of time, as my assets were still tied up by the bank. By forcing me to come up with this extra money, he forced me to drop my case against the bank.

Now return again today to the bank's history of profitability and you'll observe the following. The bank value increases every year that our previous directors and myself were related to it. Our money collectively was at risk, not the governments'. We made our decisions, paid our bills, employed over 50 people, provided credit as appropriate and invested in the community. My compensation as President was a modest contribution in place of the wealth I could have earned as an independent investor. We had occasional losses as every institution does which is offset by significant earnings, placing our Bank among the most respected in the country. Now look at it today.

After my retirement and a change in the Directors and hiring of a president at the highest salary ever paid by the Bank, they lost money for a time, didn't pay any dividends for four years, and had very little growth. This litigation settlement was delayed by the Bank itself to the enrichment of lawyers at the cost of the stockholders. At every stockholders meeting, since the meeting in 1996, the Bank has refused to provide any meaningful details about expenses to the stockholders. With indicators down Charlie Bucknam sings them a lullaby as to how well they're doing. How do you measure that Charlie?

What is to be believed now with every annual report offering the same slick distortion of the realities of the Bank you offered the courts? With those notarized statements from you and the lawyers attesting to your imagined status. That after all of the money spent and pages of testimony and lawyers that rehearsed you, you would now claim that it was all simply an honest mistake. Charlie, it was neither a mistake nor was it honest. The exhibits that characterized your claims in the federal and state courts were summarized by you and your lawyers as "simply an honest mistake." Of course, Charlie, it would not surprise you to read in the testimony from banking experts at the Federal Reserve Bank and Dartmouth College that your testimony, as to you not knowing that the Bank you serve was a state chartered Bank and not a federal institution and never had been, was unbelievable. Those persons said they found it most improbable you could not have, did not know. Charlie when I put that alongside some of your inside dealings in property, and your liquidation of assets of the Bank for pennies on the dollar, when all that was needed to recover profitable investments was knowledge and your own effort, it would appear to me that you are simply the fox inside the hen house. You are blaming the farmer that built it for letting you in the forced-open door. Deception, misrepresentation, fraud, perjury and inside dealings may in fact be the recent history of the Lyndonville Savings Bank. But that now can be seen to be a history that was only introduced after my retirement from the Bank. It is something that clearly came into existence during your watch. To call such explicit deception an honest mistake is to prove the point; it was neither honest nor a mistake.

But your ability to distort and misrepresent may be to your advantage if you seek public office. We have, as you know, lowered the standards. Now isn't that a situation!

[1] See Exhibits pages 79-80 for Board Minutes to sue me

[2] See Exhibits page 81 for LSB growth chart

[3] See Exhibits page 82 for Hamel land transfers

[4] See Exhibits pages 83-86 for excerpts of Fred Oeschger deposition

[5] See Exhibits pages 87-91 for excerpt of HAS Report

[6] See Exhibits pages 92-93 for Board Resolution

[7] See Exhibits page 94 for Stockholder petition

[8] See Exhibits pages 95-97 for Costle letter

[9] See Exhibits pages 98-99 for Board Minutes where Thompson did not get raise

[10] See Exhibits page 100 for letter from State

[11] See Exhibits page 101 for excerpt of meeting

[12] See Exhibits pages 102-103 for excerpts of meeting

[13] See Exhibits pages 104-121 for copy of letter

[14] See Exhibits page 122 for copy of letter

[15] See Exhibits pages 123-165 for Motion

Affidavits and Depositions

Any narrative of events relies upon some source for evidence supporting the opinions and conclusions presented, and contradictory conclusions are frequent. In the matters relating to this trial you have second parties quoting first parties. You have the "Whole of the United States of America" mind reading my intentions and interpreting to a jury his certainty as to what I "intended" in actions that were in some cases over five years old.

You see elaborate attempts to create meaning out of things that were just ordinary and normal and familiar, though the Whole of the United States created elaborate structures out of desire – far more than out of fact. So I'll want to be sure that my readers have access to as much of the primary material as possible, in order for them to reach their own conclusions. Those pages tell a story when you read them. Of course they are somewhat stale reading but they will reward you if you take the time.

Now in the federal trials most of the records used in the trial are available in some historic form but they're not always easily accessible. The documents from the court in this matter are stored in a Federal warehouse in Woburn, MA. but can be viewed there upon application if you travel to that place.

Of greater convenience to you might be the housing of all the documents that I have collected in Lyndonville. There you will find boxes and boxes of indexed documents that will also allow you to conclude that my account of these activities is based upon the normal reading of available documents. I knew I had to have them available in addition to those sources I am including. This account includes complete reproductions of some of the most significant depositions that were available but unused by the "resting defense." And these affidavits and depositions are intact and self-explanatory. They attempt to answer several questions that we assumed would be raised during the trial. And in the later "Bank Trial" they show that Charlie Bucknam and Charlie Howe swore as the truth contradictory statements; one set of them swearing to a known lie! (With Richard Johnston, Esq. of Hale and Dorr, and John Gravel, Esq., their local crony, joining and encouraging them.) You cannot read their statements and conclude otherwise.

One of the more bewildering issues raised by the "Whole of the United States" and later by the bank itself was that the bank's own decisions and the complete record of those decisions contradicts what they then filed as true. Their records convict them of their fraud and deception, continuing as long as possible and then "self-forgiven" as a mistake. Mistake Hell! Lies, lies and more damn lies are what they are and did!

I found the records and minutes of the bank could be relied upon to be true because the actions of the bank were taken and reported correctly, as Wendy Davenport, Executive Secretary of the Corporation, affirmed and swore in her attached affidavits[1]. She swore and announced that there was no undue influence regarding those loans, as affirmed in the actions of the Board of Directors and myself.

The Whole of United States of America concluded that all of the other directors and officers of the bank were essentially spineless and mindless, and that they were incapable of speaking their own minds. That their voices and votes recorded in an explanation of the business of the bank were not to be believed, that their testimony was distorted by my dominance. They did not know that but the prosecutor could see into their minds, and he knew what they did not.

Now if you go back and look at the membership of the bank's Board of Directors I believe it would be difficult for anyone familiar with any of these individuals to be able to convince people that I was indeed so persuasive. And if you asked them if they had the ability to differ with Roger Lussier as a Board of Directors they said they did. Apparently, after the federal prosecutor read their minds only then did they discover he was doing all of their thinking for them? They themselves probably would regard that conclusion as extremely unbelievable.

Does anyone really think that John Campbell is not capable of speaking his own mind or having his own vote recorded? Does anyone believe that Fay Young is so spineless as to require my assistance for him to reach his own conclusions? You mean that Doug Nelson and George Hopkins were not doing their own thinking? Have you ever attempted to argue with Andrew Field when he is absolutely convinced of the correctness of his position? Do you really think that John McClaughry is so shy that he would require my thoughts and defer to my judgment as a substitute for his own? Do you think Arthur Elliott could not speak or write for himself, or Phil Bovee, or Bob Beausoleil? Well go read the affidavits[2]. They said what they said under oath and were exposed to danger of perjury if it could be shown otherwise. And unlike what you will learn from the "cooperating witnesses," they were not rewarded by the government for their testimony.

During the period from 1986 through 1992 The Board minutes will show that the Directors voted against my position a total of 170 times and prevailed.[3] That doesn't do much for the domination theory, does it?

The attached and displayed affidavits show you clearly that their authors believed themselves to be informed and speaking in that mind when they voted their conclusions and when they presented information. Charlie Howe's testimony even contradicts himself later in the civil trial. And Charlie Bucknam signed as "true" contradictions as to what was the legal structure of the bank of which he is the hired President. Now which of those positions was my mind dominating for him?

You have the affidavit of Arthur Elliott affirming that the FBI threatened to make his life "a living hell." He would have been a useful witness. You have an affidavit of Wendy Davenport affirming all of the other director's statements as being true and her description of the relationship of decision-making by the bank to Roger Lussier. Read the affidavit of Andrew Field who was very critical of the processes used in decision-making by the defense attorney in the trial. He was prepared to testify in my defense and very aggressively. He was not allowed to be heard. You have the bank's own request for findings of facts[4] and letters from John McClaughry.[5] You have the signatures of 2000 persons, six of them lawyers, regarding the outcome of the trial itself that are summarized in the petition for rehearing or dismissal. Page after page of information that should have been heard and now can be seen in its entirety.

So look at the affidavits displayed here and ask yourself what these persons themselves said they believed. And ask if that information would have been useful to the jury, which did not get to hear or see this testimony. Ask if this information would have harmed the "Whole of the United States" case against me. Then ask yourself why it was not allowed to be heard. Ask why it was important to exclude it from the evidence of the trial and the knowledge of the jury. With all of this available how could it be accidental that it was not used?

In addition to the affidavits that I regard as supporting my position there are also some curious documents you might want to read involving individuals that are hostile to my position. When they were exposed in the course of hearings to have perjured themselves, they did not like it.

The evidence of their conspiracy is displayed where you have a curious exchange in the bank suit against me. George Hopkins and Pearl Beard were asked separately about a matter involving my presence at a meeting. This was one of those moments when both appear to have agreed in advance to a version of the story. Each told the "same story" separately and each was discredited upon examination in court by Andy Field's asking them when they heard me say something. Each was absolutely sure that it had happened at exactly the same time and place. They were each referring to a director's meeting in which they said they had heard me say such and such. As it turned out, they each separately, having sworn to the truthfulness of their statements, discovered that they were not present at the meeting itself according to the official minutes as recorded.

Now how can such a strange thing occur? How is it possible to spontaneously hear two stories told separately, both be found to be untrue, and still ask the judge to believe them even after they were forced to admit that the record of the meeting contradicted them? Odd? Well, look at the testimony for yourself and try and figure it out. My own view is that they got together on a story and sold the story as true in spite of the evidence to the contrary. Like all of the "bank case" it was "their story and they're sticking to it..." even if it is a lie!

That was a strange role for Pearl. She had been a longtime employee of the bank working in the trust department before I ever entered the Board of Directors. Prior to coming to work for Lyndonville she had been with Attorneys McShane and Graves and had been placed by previous directors in a position in the trust department; which always lost money for the bank. I imagine now she kind of regrets having sent me a letter in January of 1983[6] thanking me for all I had done for her upon the occasion of her retirement, and commending me for being a helpful director and a good listener. In any case her belief was that the losses in the trust department were offset by their eventual conversion to an investment in the bank at sometime in the future. That never happened.

One day she came to my office and said she had been talking with some of the employees, and she felt that unless we put a woman on the Board of Directors that they might sue us for discrimination. She insisted that she wanted to go on the Board of Directors. I went to see the largest stockholder at that time, Mrs. Howe, and asked her how she would feel about putting Pearl on the Board. Now since Mrs. Howe was the largest stockholder of our Corporation and she was undeniably a woman I felt that having her opinion on the matter would certainly be fair to Pearl. Mrs. Howe had been anticipating her son Charlie taking over her interest within several years but she said she didn't mind Pearl doing so until then. She liked Pearl, and she felt she did good job handling the trust account. She felt it would be OK for a few years until her son was ready to go on the Board. So I brought up putting Pearl on as a director and most of the Board members, except George Hopkins, were against this idea. So after talking awhile about not having a woman on the Board I told them that she might be able to help the Board as she was very familiar with the internal workings of the bank and we, as directors, were not. Now maybe that is where they got the idea that I was dominating the Board because after a short discussion she was selected.

When Pearl became a director she began taking the minutes of the meetings until Wendy Davenport took over that job, having been named executive secretary of the Corporation. But Pearl did go with directors on occasions involving appraisals and other bank affairs. When the time came for Charlie Howe to become a director and to begin to represent his family stock in the Corporation we felt it was time for Pearl to leave. She was very upset about leaving the Board and was not altogether pleased when we determined to make her a director emeritus, giving her a voice but not vote in the bank's affairs.

After I was no longer a director and the bank had decided to sue me as an individual for the actions of the whole Corporation during my presidency, Pearl became a hostile witness against me in my criminal case and also in the Lyndonville bank case. Now here it gets amusing. As I have said previously, she and George Hopkins both told exactly the same lie separately, and they each swore exactly as to what they had heard at that director's meeting. But then my attorney, Andy Field, showed them the minutes of the meeting and had them admit that they'd never attended that meeting at all. So in some way George Hopkins who wanted her on the board and Pearl Baird who never wanted off the Board are found together in common cause – lying on behalf of the bank at the truth's expense. Their perjury was exposed in court and I assume they felt as foolish as they looked. I was surprised somewhat at their opposition to me because we had many associations over a number of years. I had done an auction for Pearl and her husband when they were farming and I considered her husband a very good friend of mine. It's beside the point to note I sold them the farm where she is living now. Just goes to prove I had no favorites.

Listed here are excerpts of Pearl's and George's testimony in the bank's suit against me showing that they weren't at the meeting where they said they heard me say certain things.

Hopkins, Cross-examined by Field:

Volume III

Page 119 – 124:

Q. Well, is it your understanding – let's see – that that - - that on 9/21/88, that the loan to Gray to finance the dealership had already been consummated?

A. That's what my understanding was.

Q. Your understanding. All right. Would you believe me if I told you it wasn't consummated September 23rd?

A. I have no reason to disbelieve you.

Q. All right. Why don't you turn to an exhibit that's identified as Exhibit # 13. It's in the same book that you have there, sir. You have it before you, sir?

A. Yes, I do.

Q. On the first page it indicates in the minutes who was in attendance at that meeting. Do you see it there?

A. Yes, I do.

Q. You weren't there, were you?

A. No, I was not.

Q. Phil Bovee was there, wasn't he?

A. Yes, he was.

Q. Do you recall now that when you attended a board meeting on 9/21, the purpose of that meeting was to correct a board minute to reflect that the loan was really $1,950,000 and not two million nine?

A. I noticed the difference.

Q. That's why it had to be so called ratified. Isn't that right?

A. Yes

Q. And it was the meeting on 9/13, as evidenced by this exhibit # 13 – rather, 9/18/88. Wasn't that the meeting where that loan was reviewed and approved and underwritten by the Board?

A. It would appear that way from the minutes.

Q. All in your absence. Isn't that right?

A. That's right.

Page: 129:

Q. If you were not in attendance at those two meetings, would it be fair to say that you don't know what was presented or how the loan was underwritten, do you? (Harrison note)

A. Unless it's in the minutes.

Baird Direct by Johnston:
Volume III:
Page 139:

Q. Ms Baird, did you typically receive a package of information with respect to each loan when you arrived?

A. No. (*There was always a sheet from Lee and Turner about the loan applications*)

Baird Cross by Field:
Volume III:
Page 158 – 161:

Q. Pearl, you just, in response to a number of questions asked by the attorney for the bank, indicated that – with respect to the McCormick loan transactions, that's the $700,000 one, and a two hundred - - there were two approvals. One of our board minutes showed there was a $2 million approval of a loan to McCormick to purchase the dealerships that was never consummated. And, subsequently, he assumed those dealerships, dealership obligations. And then there was a $700,000 loan for working capital purposes that the board approved for Mr. McCormick in his operation of the dealerships. Now, my question to you is this: As I understand your testimony, at those meetings Roger told you that you don't have to worry about him - -

A. That's right

Q. - - referring to McCormick. And you've also testified that Roger presented those loans to the board of directors.

A. That's true.

Q. And he did that in your presence?

A. I'm not sure that I was there for one of those.

Q. You weren't there for either of them.

A. Yeah. But they were - -

Q. And the minutes so reflected.

A. They were discussed - - -

Q. When the loan was presented, you weren't there so you really don't know what transpired, do you?

A. On this one right.

Q. When the board met to consider a $700,000 loan to McCormick for working capital purposes with respect to the two dealerships. Now the director's minutes for 10/26 states that Pearl Baird was absent.

A. That's true.

Q. So when you testify that Roger did not disclose certain things to you and that you did not have to worry about somebody, and that he made presentations of these McCormick loans, that really is not true, because you were not at the meeting?

A. On those two things, you're right.

The Court: So how did you know about the loans?

The Witness: It was discussed, because I can remember it very vividly. So whether – it wasn't in these two minutes, but we did discuss it and he did make that statement. And he did say that McCormick was related to the McCormick-Deering family. And I remember that very vividly. *(John Campbell is the Director that said he was related to the McCormick-Deering family)*

Another curious thing about the bank and the whole of United States of America is the willingness of the government and the bank to avoid other official records, <u>even denied the testimony of their own record keeper</u>. It's kind of a funny thing when the person that you rely upon to truthfully report Board actions does so, and her conclusions based upon the evidence of the meetings that she is certifying contradicted your later desires. So you change the story and accuse the record keeper of not having known in advance the necessity of your lie. Wendy Davenport's testimony demonstrates this in great detail. And then there is contradictory testimony by the now Chairman of the Board, Charlie Howe, who said one thing in the criminal trial and then changed his story.

I indicated when they threatened him with fines for his own conduct in the bank, that he changed his testimony to what is more acceptable to his new boss, the FDIC. There are two documents you should probably read: the memorandum to the Board of Directors which says well after my departure that they have violations and that they have no one on their staff that has the experience necessary to function as a senior loan official. The FDIC noted that their officers were weak in financial analysis and that none of their existing lenders would qualify. They did not exclude Charlie Bucknam in that category. There is also the document from the FDIC threatening Charlie Howe and the other directors with up to a million dollars a day in fines if they didn't do what they were told. If every man has his price, we now know his. But if you can afford that kind of money at risk, why bother with it all in the first place?

[1] See Exhibits pages 166-169 for Wendy's affidavits

[2] See Exhibits pages 170-185 for Director affidavits

[3] See Exhibits page 186 for Director votes

[4] See Exhibits pages 187-194 for Request for Findings of fact

[5] See Exhibits page 195 for McClaughry letter

[6] See Exhibits Page 196 for Pearl's letter

SCALES OF JUSTICE

A gain the picture we are familiar with is the blindfolded lady holding an unbalanced scale; the verdict is weighted and visible. So it seems strange to see the scales in this case absolutely reversed: $400,000 outweighs $100 MILLION. That the Whole of the United States reached deals with persons who admitted to crimes in excess of $100,000,000 in pursuit of myself.

Can you put yourself in my place for a minute, everything derogatory that can be said about you is being said, and you must listen to it, but may not reply. Your family sits there and listens as well. You must listen to errors, lies, self-serving distortions, and persons who have sat with you at dinner now saying things that both parties know are untrue.

You must watch a jury return a verdict based upon only one side of a many-sided matter. You watch yourself being sentenced and know the verdict is both legal and unjustified in fact. You watch lawyers leave you behind having deposited their checks and going on to the next "case." (Impressions of helping, great sincerity of purpose, self-important mumbling about working on it hard, going deep, etc.) And after that the next! Then after some initial appealing of a non-existent record, you face saying goodbye to your home and wife and family, familiar smells of clothes and the town you have lived and worked in, and believed you served well, and get in a friend's car and watch your life leave you in the rear-view mirror...to prison.

Then in the strange world of prison with its constant danger, noise, abuse in language and process, you try again to appeal. You spend years and borrow money for further appeals again for what is finally seen as judicial error, and be seen as the victim of the present bank's perjury, fraud on the court, misleading stockholders and down-right lying. Charlie Bucknam's signed memos which are reproduced in the documents section (August 1994) and two in January of 1995 where he showed he lied by explaining to his so-called directors the difference between a State chartered bank and federally chartered banks. He was of the first, and he frequently and continuously misrepresented himself as being the other. A "wantabe" fed posing before his mirror and this community and Courts as such, knowing all of the time he was a fraud, and doing fraud upon us all. But until exposed by the 2nd Circuit Court of Appeals in New York as the manager of this deception, he caused harm and distorted justice at every opportunity.

But finally, after all of the thousands of prayers and tears, of thousands of nights in torment and danger and exhaustion, after money spent and thousands of pages submitted, and phone calls, and visits from friends and one faithful lawyer serving me as both, we get to Court again. This time it is discovered that the bank, and its lawyers having been paid millions, and its officers running scared from their fraud, are shown to be in the wrong court from the beginning. This was not a Federal case; it was a State case of one Vermont citizen with another as a corporate citizen. The Lyndonville Savings Bank was a State chartered bank, and everyone knew that. The Charter hangs right there in the bank. But as a price for participation in their conspiracy of fraud, they had said otherwise, written otherwise, claimed an $8,700,000 verdict against me, and crowed about it. One lawyer even put it on his website, where it remains in advertising dishonesty to this day, and then lost.

Then they went to the State Court, filed, had several hearings, kept delaying the "trial" and after arbitration, my wife and I were forced to settle. So after all of this, and the harm to my children and grandchildren, the theft of my money and reputation and life, after all of their shouting, my voice was heard. Slowly, the flawed and distorted scales of Justice righted themselves.

Allenwood Prison
to St. J. Correctional Center
to Home

(As told by Evelyn Lussier)

On Sunday, January 24, 1999, Roger attended Mass as he did every Sunday, but this Sunday the Priest knew that Roger would be leaving on Friday, so he gave him his blessing, shook his hand and wished him the best. I feel he knew the good man Roger was and was happy that he was returning home to his family. Roger went to Rosary every night there and was always asking the guys to go also. He participated in all the religious events he could. Some nights, when it was possible, many family members would say their Rosary at home the same time we knew he was, it was a feeling of closeness and serenity.

That same Sunday night he had his personal items stolen while he was sleeping, he didn't have them locked up or under the bed covers. That night there were many new inmates admitted who probably had no money and knew he was soon leaving so as he slept they crept in and helped themselves, but before bedtime, after the Rosary, some of the guys gave him a party sharing whatever they had for a snack. Roger appreciated them doing this, and they were happy for him.

He called Monday and said he was having a week's vacation, "big deal," He would rather have worked to take up his mind.

He had a team meeting and was given papers to sign; he didn't know what they were or why he was signing them and the officials wouldn't tell him. This made him and us very nervous. Later he signed more papers on being released to St. Johnsbury Correctional Center, and I told him he had been denied home confinement, a big disappointment for him and us at home. It didn't help our nerves, but we knew that he would be nearer to home.

Wednesday the 27th: He called during the day, and tonight we are all tense. I told him we would be leaving in the morning and would be there to visit him tomorrow night. We had the car all checked out today and new tires put on. On Thursday, Jan 28, we woke to a snowy morning and Steve, Richard and I left home at 8:30 am. We drove through McDonalds for coffee and a breakfast snack and ate on the way. Our next stop was in Conn. for gas, a snack, a restroom and then on our way again. Roger called Dave during the day to see if everything was OK. He told Dad we were on the way and we had our cell phone so we were in contact with Dave.

After reaching our motel, I needed to rest for a short time after the long ride and being so tense and nervous. The boys were smoking one cigarette after another, and I knew they were also a little nervous. We went up to the prison, did all our usual paperwork to check in. As we were called in, I prayed to God this would be the last time for all of us here, especially for Roger, and as he came through the back door, after being searched and had his ID checked, here we were, all thinking the same. We had something to eat from the machines and he and the boys, Richard and Steve, were in and out to smoke; we were all very tense.

Later that night more of the guys, inmates, gave him a going-home party. They were happy for him as he was the old man in the group. They all shook hands patted his back and wished him well. He became close to some of the guys and they to him. None of us slept very well tonight.

Friday, January 29, 1999 – Release Day: Steve & Richard went up to the prison at 8:30, the time they were told to be there for their dad. I waited at the motel, my stomach churning. The owners of the Motel were very nice and caring people; they came & hugged me and wished us well. They always had a room for me and my family. They were more than just the owners, and I felt they knew we were "good" people also. She had let Roger call and leave messages for me. I was waiting and praying all would go as agreed. It seemed like hours but was just a short time when I saw them coming and yes my husband was with his sons. I had my overnight bag already outside and wasn't very long getting into the car. Crying and happy we embraced and clung to each other. We went to a small restaurant just below the motel as none of us had eaten, and Roger could sit down and order anything he wanted, but we couldn't seem to make an order, so had coffee and something light, and then were on our way again. We knew we had to be at the Correctional Center, in St. J. at 6:30 pm, now out of the hands of the US Marshals. The car was making us nervous as it was shaking and rattling, and we only stopped for gas and to go to the restroom, get a cold drink or coffee and on our way. As we drove into the parking lot at the Lincoln Inn in St. Johnsbury, Vt. out rushed the family, lots of hugs, tears, and kisses. What a happy reunion, even the owner had tears. He had food all set up, and he had been a great supporter from the start.

Roger didn't really eat very much, as he was trying to talk to each one; some hadn't seen him since he left three years ago, as only so many could be on the list. Time went very quickly and was soon time to have him at the Correctional Center. Steve and I took him there once more, to leave him locked-up. I wasn't happy, but was relieved we had reached this point.

February 1, 1999: Richard and I visited him – jail is jail – none are pleasant to visit but at least we could sit at a table across from each other. It was very hard to see him treated this way as he didn't deserve it. The family went to visit when time was allowed. I prayed that they would let him come home soon. He is still under lock and key. I get angry and hurt again thinking of the ones that have done this to us, especially some of them we have known and knew their families and they have lied and cheated. I can see their faces and eyes as I watched them at annual meetings and in Court. It makes my stomach burn and burn. One of these young guy's father visited me one day, and he had a lot to say. He was not feeling well and knew his time on earth was getting short. He told me what he thought about the situation. He had always worked hard, an outstanding man in his community, a farmer and a business man. He has a very nice wife and raised a family. He didn't like the way the Bank treated Roger. He knew Roger was an honest man and didn't deserve this treatment. He had a son on the board of directors, one that called Roger several times asking to be on the board and when the time was right, Roger helped put him on. The father was hurt to think his son became a "yes" man, one that voted to sue Roger. This man is now deceased but I was glad that he talked with me, and he also talked with Roger one day. I don't know about that discussion.

Friday, Feb 4, 1999: Roger was allowed to come home from 1:00 to 3:00 pm. My daughter-in-law and I went for him. She dropped the two of us off at our door, and as we walked in, he was dizzy for a few minutes and needed a little support. Here we were, in our own surroundings, holding on to each other, in the home he had to leave over 3 years ago. We got our bearings. He said things were blurry at first, but soon he was walking from room to room, upstairs and down, even down cellar and in the garage. He was reading the signs the children and grandchildren had put up, welcoming signs for their Dad and their "Pepere," saying how much they loved him. I fixed us some lunch but he couldn't eat very much, and soon the family came. Then it was time to return to the Correctional Center. He had a good friend, a retired Sheriff and a farmer for many years, and asked if he could go for Roger mornings and bring him home; he did this and the family brought him back.

March 1, 1999: His probation officer allowed him to come home to stay; she was here when he came and put a bracelet on his ankle. Richard and David were here to listen to her instructions. They had to hang up cords to reach the monitor. The officer went up and down stairs and down cellar and in the garage to make sure the monitor range was right so they would know at all times if he was in or out. She allowed him to go to his office and come home for lunch and then go back. He had to be home at 3:00 pm and at that time he had to stay inside the house. When he would leave for the office, the monitor would beep 82 times and stop as soon as he stepped inside the office. It was very annoying, but we had no choice. He had many friends stop at the office and here at home. The room would be full, a lot of hand shaking and back slapping friends, how good it was to see and hear this.

On Thursday nights we were allowed to go grocery shopping at the Price Chopper in St. Johnsbury. We were given 2 hours and this was the first time he was allowed to drive his car. I don't drive so therefore they let him; it seemed so good just the two of us, almost like dating all over again. There were always a few in the store that would recognize Roger and would come to shake his hand and say how glad they were he was back home, and that they knew he was given a raw deal and he shouldn't of ever had to go to prison.

He was allowed to go to his granddaughter's high school graduation and to her home for a family get-together and then be home by 2:00 pm. He wasn't allowed to go to a granddaughter's graduation from law school; he has missed 4 grandchildren's graduations.

On June 28th: Our 47th wedding anniversary, he was to become free from home confinement but no official came all day or called, and no one did the next day. On the third day, about 3:30 pm, Roger called their headquarters and they replied "Oh, we thought someone called you," and he said, "no and it's over 3 days, what now?" They said "you can cut off the ankle bracelet and unplug the monitor." I had the honor of cutting off that bracelet and unplugging the monitor; what a wonderful feeling that was.

Roger shook his leg, walked around and said let's go celebrate our anniversary in more ways than one, and this we did. We went to a small friendly restaurant we used to go to before, and as we walked into the room, several there, upon seeing him, rushed over to shake his hand and tell him how glad they were to see him back, and that he never should have been incarcerated in the first place, how unfair it was. It was a very pleasant evening.

Now for two years of probation, but we will survive it.

RETURNING TO SOCIETY
...The grateful life of a "dead" man!

I was having dinner, now years later with friends when one asked me, "What was the food you missed most and wished for first when you got out?" I replied "ice cream." But the simple question of what I missed and what got restored never can describe the losses, damage and harm suffered during and following incarceration. In our fantasy world of "law and order" we always have sudden conclusions. He served his time, he paid his debt, and it is over now. Welcome back, we are even.

In fact, you are branded forever in computers and references, placed in a series of "steps" toward social freedom, given electronic monitors, local jails to return to at night following a day at work, limitations on friends and communications, a "parole officer" moves into your life like a wife, limitations on travel, and the endless repeating to persons who don't want to ask, "What happened, or Where have you been?" In my case it began with some of our children driving to Allenwood prison in Pennsylvania and picking me up to redeliver me to a jail in Vermont. I was released to them, and we were given 9 hours to be in Saint Johnsbury, Vermont. It had been planned that my other family members would meet at a restaurant near the jail, we would have dinner together, then say "Goodnight" and hear the doors slam shut again. And so after years of fears that I would not live to see this return together, and having survived some possibilities of that happening, we were rejoined. And it was wonderful.

We had known that the accusations and trial would affect us all, and each family member had paid some price associated with the trial, some terribly. Jobs had been lost, houses and businesses lost and forfeited, social reputations strained, public confidence questioning their business legitimacy continued, others left off associating with us. Everyone in my family paid for something they had not purchased. Some still have the scars. And yet those payments were made by my family without hesitation. They attended every minute of the trials, attended two I was not allowed to be present at, and read every page of evidence and all newspaper articles, and listened to anything said. And they had concluded that we were in the midst of a tragedy, and that we would all be participants. When the sentence to prison was announced my "boys" offered to divide up the time and like a "civil war soldier" go in my place.

Some of the simple reasons for our eventual success as a family and our family businesses were local experience, hard work with others, being fair in business and following every opportunity that was presented. I had been born here and knew every one from childhood. They also lived here. Here was a place we loved and where we belonged. There was no greener pasture, only a head start in heaven. When I chose a wife, and was chosen by her, I did not need to go to Boston to find a treasure. She was here, as was her family before her. We worked together, and I milked cows seven days a week, a lot of cows. We began an auction business and auctioned off everything needing auctioning, and we would go anywhere. We sold and saved. We started before dawn and kept going, saved our money, bought more property here, sold more and bought again, and knew everyone. The children came along and helped us and did the same. They stayed here, worked hard, helped the family, chose to live here also, and so it is with their children. All of our generations are here. And all of us participated in a way of life that seems to be passing. We knew each other, cared for the whole of it, and tried to help others as much as ourselves. I gave "money back guarantees" on things sold at auctions; imagine that! We weren't looking for all that we could get, but a reasonable share acquired by earning it with our labor. And all of our children seemed to share in the good regard and respect of this community. Before the "charges" there was no anticipation that any of us would ever do much more differently than we had done, and that we would all be together in a mutual effort to care for ourselves and this community and State. As the indictments began being developed none of us perceived that everything we held dear was to be shaken. We knew nothing that justified any accusation, and we believed naively that if you weren't guilty you couldn't be found guilty. That was yet to be learned. That naivety was replaced with the awareness that things had happened that were fundamentally unjust to everyone and could never be made right. And in such a simple setting of events the message of my story, that love prevails and even transforms persons, is now recounted. For to tell another dismal criminal story and attempt to give it some meaning is impossible. There is none.

The system that has been created has no insight, no memory of days without pain, and no imagination of the purposes for our creation. It is simply a product grinder which has been hijacked as a solution when it is itself the problem. The system that was created and is used increasingly as the resolution of social conflict and created injustices does what it does. It is a method of social killing, isolation and stigmatization, which can be used for political or social purposes just as well as for clearly criminal concerns. It can be used by any government against <u>any one of you as well.</u> If a government is so rich in resources and underemployed lawyer talent as to make such an enormous effort at prosecution in the rural Northeast Kingdom of Vermont, and come up so short on damages, crimes, losses, and harm, overriding jurisdictions and separations of powers and State obligations, then this will happen and is already happening elsewhere. If the "fair and impartial" operators of this destructive system will " forgive and give immunity" to those who admittedly claimed over $100 million in order to secure their manufactured testimony against me, and only claim against evidence of no losses, that I must have cost someone $426,204.67, then any one and every one is in danger. This was the amount the bank charged off on property we had taken back in lieu of foreclosure, with the concurrence of the FDIC. It was appraised for more than we allowed for it. We had it under contract, but when it was tested, contamination was found and the contract was voided. This amount was charged off after I left the bank. If a federal employee representing himself as the Whole of the United States of America will participate in the construction of this judicial fraud upon the Courts (lying under oath, perjury, tampering with evidence and witnesses, and false witness...)

My family learned to know this was true, and in my case made their own choices, together with those thousands of others who came to understand my case as their own. They came to see that in the pretense of justice their community's capacity for local credit was harmed, that foreclosures and loans now moved beyond local control to somewhere else. They came to see the stock value of their bank decrease after my conviction and not because of it. They saw familiar and trusted employees disappear into unemployment. A long time customer with a $30,000 certificate of deposit in the Lyndonville Bank is denied a loan of $4,000 of his own money. The new loan officer taking the application could not see how a farmer without a salary could pay it back.

The bank never was the primary source of my income and earnings, only the beneficiary of it. When I came to the bank it had a worth of $700,000. When I departed it had been paying taxes, paying dividends, employing a staff, and worth about $16,000,000, including loan loss reserves. I put my own money into stock and risked it there. Charlie Bucknam wisely avoided buying some, and then only a bit, knowing what a risk he was taking with his own management. Having previously failed as a leader in other banks, his career was rescued from an additional disaster selling precious metals in a family business. He was rushed into this new "Presidency" for this pending failure by a rushed vetting by the FDIC, itself a money losing venture, who found him to be a man they could count on to hit the rocks. He continues to "fire sale" good assets, taking losses he need not have. The Bank is no longer regarded by its previous banking competitors in this region as significant competition. But that is something you can test yourself. Just go and apply for a loan.

I grieve for the harm this brings our community. I had bought our stock in that bank out of earnings from real estate and my auction business success, and a lifetime of 7 days a week enterprises. I had milked and shoveled for that money and then invested it in the community bank, Lyndonville Savings Bank, and saw it to be successful. I ended up, with other community members owning a significant percentage of stock, and we earned the dividends from good loans and helping others. We were helping the community and investing in our neighbors, and having mutual success. We found ways for families to stay in their homes when property values declined, when milk prices went south, when men went to war, and when our customers could not pay their bills on time. We worked it out legally, and we benefited when they benefited. So the value of stock went up, this bank became noted by and reported in the *Wall Street Journal* as one of the best capitalized and most consistently profitable small banks in the country. It was after this article came out that the FDIC issued their "phony" fraud alert which was mentioned earlier. We made money. We spent money. We took an occasional loss, wrote it off, and loaned again when the circumstances justified it. We could do this because all of the Directors of the bank knew the people using the bank, knew the business of farming and cows and crops, and we knew that you did not need "flood plain insurance" when you placed a loan on a farm on Kirby Mountain. (This was one of the criticisms by the FDIC when asking me about "missing" information on a local loan. "Where is your flood plain insurance?") We earned our money. The Directors invested their personal and family money in the bank, the bank in the people, and the people earned a return on their labor and repaid the bank. In 1988 the Directors owned or controlled 67% of the stock in the bank. Eventually we came to understand that was considered a crime in some parts of the country.

The bank itself, at its most profitable time, never paid me anything like the salary it is now paying its president. But in my day it was the expectation that the Directors find customers and investment opportunities for the bank, not use the bank for their own income or wealth. The bank did not make me wealthy; my judgment in business, my conduct in business, and my experience and stamina allowed me to earn what I had. And then I invested it again into the Bank to benefit others as well as receive a dividend. Had I never been invited to join the board of the Lyndonville Savings Bank, I probably would have earned far more using that time for myself than I was ever paid by the bank, and I would have never gone to prison and completed my interrupted high school education. Or probably write a book. Or learn that the "criminal" justice system is just that; a criminal system. But I did and that is exactly what I learned.

Returning to this community following imprisonment has provided me with some additional discoveries. I have more friends now than before. Now I must admit I am a bit surprised myself. I never expected it and I can't really explain it. But while in prison at every holiday period I received mail and cards out of all proportion to what others around me experienced. For many in prison, that time is as if they were dead. No one calls, no one writes, and no one sends birthday and Christmas cards. The mail call is silent to their name, the locker doors and shelves are empty. Like a graveyard for the unloved and hopeless. Then they would call "Roger Lussier" and for the next ten minutes would be passing me mail. On one occasion I received 350 cards when the average per person was 3. I even had another prisoner go for me and get the mail, just for the vicarious experience of getting a letter, any letter, even if addressed to another. In the midst of desperation and despair my cards, letters, encouragements, photos and prayers continued to affirm that I was valued and not forgotten. That was wonderful, and it happened again and again. When I was released from prison I went to the Postmaster to change my address and mentioned that on some days he must have up to a thousand pounds of mail. He looked me in the eye and then told me it would be a hell of a lot less when I left.

And then there was the "Petition"[1] begun by my son Reggie. Reggie has followed my trade as an auctioneer and is very good at it. Somewhere in all of this, people began speaking to him about the miscarriage of justice, the lies told about Roger, etc., and suggested that ancient Constitutional right to petition. So after the press had done the "reporting" for the Whole of the United States of America, after the Whole of the United States of America had presented its case, after my lawyer had rested his defense without using it, after sentencing, and <u>after I was already in prison</u>, over 2000 citizens of Ethan Allen's modern Vermont, and some from other states, signed a petition asking for retrial or release. It worried the prison system, when they read my mail and in talking with a prison official, he said he couldn't believe it as he doubted that President Clinton could get 2000 people to sign a petition for him, if he was in jail. See what fear is invoked when someone notices that some citizens have noticed something. The authority is afraid of the prisoner ...who is quietly repairing tractors or working pulling up rocks.

Well, in that list of citizens there were lawyers, a priest, customers of the bank, people I had conducted auctions for, even people signed it that had been sued for collection by the bank when they could not pay their loans.

It did not change the Courts, and no authority in office cared about what the basis for it might be, but it told my family, my children and friends that they had support and the confidence of their fellow citizens. That was wonderful. Maybe I should run for something!

---

[*] See Exhibits page 197 for article on petition

The Lawyer's "merry-go-round"
(And around, and around, and around again)

merry-go-round: a machine in an amusement park, with a circular revolving platform...

The New Lexicon Webster's Dictionary, 1990, NY

As a consequence of my indictment and the bank filing a self-serving claim to illegal restitution, I have had to employ or defend myself from over 28 lawyers and associates related to the events described to you in this book. I have been required to purchase thousands of pages of official transcripts and organize the filing, storage and recovery of enough paper to stock a small library in Vermont. Out of necessity I have had to devote hundreds of thousands of hours in legal review and travel thousands of miles to attend hearings, and to give and receive depositions and confer again and again and again regarding conclusions and positions to be offered to a whole variety of courts. And it was necessary that I do this simply to make available to me the basic documents and records that support any claims I may have made regarding the events and statements made at our trials. This "discovery" undiscovered, verifications, witnesses, and related links to the layers of evidence are necessary to this story. I have had to do this at enormous expense, and I have had to pay personally. My family has suffered the loss of those resources that were required of us simply as a consequence of the trial, the trial method, and the legal "lawyer dominated system" of conflict management.

There is a strange phenomenon that has occurred that might confuse you as you ponder its implications. I have been represented by some of the finest lawyers and some of the poorest lawyers in Vermont and elsewhere, and I have represented myself "pro se" in numerous pleadings of my own. The outcome is curious. All of the hearings and proceedings in which attorneys represented me, save two decisions, were lost, while all of those in which I represented myself were won. And not thinking of myself as an "orator" well-schooled at the law, I have decided that the difference is in the perception of my motive and the truth in the matter. That a jury of Vermont citizens listening to the presentations before them is able to discern within the testimony the elements of truth, and they are convinced by my testimony and by my manner. That I am being forthright, without guile and actually believing to be true what I have said. That when I am confused I appear confused. That when I am certain of whatever I have been asked or am testifying to that it is clear that I am certain, and that in matters of conflicting testimony I am believed. That is what the Vermont jury decided as we successfully sued the attorneys who were responsible for the appeal of my criminal conviction. The Vermont jury listens to all the legal experts and believed me. There were many years of devastating legal struggles and hundreds of thousands of pages of testimony at a cost of close to $1 million in legal fees. There were over three years in prison of being chained and convicted and paraded in the press as a person who should be thrown into prison and the key thrown in behind him. During my criminal trial the jury was not sequestered, and the jury was able to read all the bad publicity on a daily basis. I believe this is the one of reasons I was convicted.

The highly paid and skillful attorneys who had so willingly charged me their fees and had so reluctantly provided me their best services were simply not performing at the standard you should expect for a competent State of Vermont lawyer. (Their verdict did not address the standard of competence for those other states of New York and Massachusetts.) And if you've been following this dismal picture you see that everything that happens to a person in the legal "criminal justice system" is a consequence of all that went before it. So starting out with a non-defending lawyer that produced no appeal of the trial record, we end up with a descending list of attorneys who repeatedly attempt to make more of less. They move among the possibilities for challenge in their futile attempts to rescue what should have been there to begin with... a trial and defense record. It is like bailing out the whirlpool below Niagara Falls. Now how can this be?

How can events which are presented as so clear and so simple and so easy to understand by a prosecutor to a jury of ordinary Vermont citizens end up requiring so many lawyers and so much effort to be able to finally conclude what any sober attendee at the trial or reader of the transcript can realize for himself? How can this be?

That was a question I addressed to one of my worst lawyers and it was the only time he gave me a satisfactory reply after relieving me of several hundred thousand dollars: "trials aren't about the truth. If you want the truth to come out you will need to write a book." My conclusions then, at the end of this bitter history of false conviction, are the following:

1. Charges and accusations of a criminal nature do not need to be true or be proved to utterly destroy the social, family, financial and mental well being of the person charged.

2. The "legal entertainers," lawyers, judges, etc., are in a "legal process" and function as participants in a monopoly, and their primary loyalty is really not their client. The client is used to further the operation of their cartel. A "just" outcome or a presentation of truth in their productions is not the primary

activity of their enterprise. The maintenance of their standing as the officers of the court is the purpose of all of their activity.

3. They bear no responsibility and suffer no consequence for unfair or corrupt or untrue results from the operation of their system. It cost me millions of dollars and years of my life defending myself from something that they let happen out of negligence, indifference, corruption, or simple incompetence, to say little of "ego" or love of their part in the theater.

4. Since they hold the monopoly within society in both method and execution of resolution, there is no way that a person like myself can reform or experience justice in that system. It is committed to its own pleasures. You may be snared by this system entirely by accident and you will be the only one that ever clearly understands how you ended up in the slaughterhouse as a sacrifice to the gods they hold dear, themselves!

We have known for hundreds of years that lawyers or barristers or attorneys, or counselors at law are not held in society's highest regard. As Shakespeare said, "They are a parasitic intrusion into our wellbeing." To my own experience over these thousands of hours and many years to discover that you need a lawyer is something like discovering you have a fatal disease. The further away you can stay from them the healthier you are likely to be. And as they get closer to you the more probable it is that you are about to fall seriously ill and become tangled in a web of irreversible consequence. That is my conclusion: something like a disease, the further away from them you can stay the better.

In each case, as one of my attorneys and their paralegals followed the other, the initial meetings were always the same.

It begins characterized by sorrowful and displayed outrage over the previous circumstances that brought us together. That is coupled with solemn assurances that the previous outcome would not have been the case if the current representative of that profession had been retained. The outrage is detailed in citations and legal language, and proposed pleadings and while no specific outcome is ever guaranteed one is led to believe that this time you are most probably going to find an open gate in the chute on the way to the slaughter house, that this time it will be different. You continue to hear that until you reach the point where your throat is cut. This time also turns out to be, after many thousands of dollars of retained counsel, a false hope. You begin to look for the exit from this "Merry-Go-Round" when, after a brief stop, another passenger appears walking towards you.

This turns out to be the next representative of this profession. He appears and having discovered some additional and overlooked and unconsidered event in the preceding documents, the process is repeated, expectations are raised, money is paid, expectations are not realized for some unanticipated reason, and the consequences fall upon the individual who retained the counselor. They get paid, but again they do not know how it will turn out for you.

The system of "law" cannot be examined in advance to see what the definite consequences are to be. And an experienced Judge, like Judge Billings sitting in his own Court, can enter an unlawful restitution order that will have enormous consequences, additional jail time, and cost me more lawsuits and thousands of dollars and further loss of property. He renders a finding based upon a written law, and HE gets it wrong…but I pay.[1] And when finally overturned in his opinion he will suffer no consequence.

This monopoly system of players and defendants allows all burdens and obligations and costs to fall upon the defendant. So that even an experienced sitting Judge, with no pressures upon him, cannot predictably interpret the law – requiring more lawyers and appeals. And when found incorrect, he suffers no consequence. This system assures its participants in the Court Cast of Players that their decisions will be without consequence to them personally. This comedy of helpers would like to be regarded in our society as significant, but their relationship is more parasitic than contributory. We pretend they are profound and necessary. We as a society say it takes a jury of non-lawyers to convict a defendant. The lawyers pretend like a chef in a dining room, that their presentation is of more value than the dinner, and that the jury is an afterthought. No one certainly will be asking *them* questions about perjury, false witness, or the Ninth Commandment. The practice of law is one of the oldest professions and among the four traditional professions requiring an oath of trust and accountability. But in fact lawyers get to exempt themselves from both the experience of their practice, and, unlike real professionals, never have to participate in the impending tragedy.

A competent surgeon must not only graduate from medical school but must also complete the satisfactory experiences of internship and residency and have his work reviewed and the consequences of his decisions assessed and widely shared.

Passing an exam qualifies a lawyer, but demonstrated competence is required of other professions. The captain of an airliner has extremely realistic simulator time that allows him to experience all of the drama of engine failures and structural failure or the collapse of a tire or engine. And he practices under supervision for thousands of hours as a trainee and co-pilot before he may himself determine the fate of hundreds of passengers, AND he usually must share their fate. And so it is with seagoing ships and their captains. Practice in command, in fires, or collisions at sea with engines burning, lifeboats smashed. He must practice and experience the possible before he is rated to command. He works his way through those lessons with his decisions evaluated, and he himself breaking out in deep sweat. He also is at risk to share the fate of those he controls, and is expected to be the last to leave his ship…not the first!

When you need a lawyer the most, you are already at the greatest disadvantage. Your need interferes with your judgment. And they arrive alongside you in the new legal matter, never seeing that they themselves have created most of the bind themselves!

[1] See Exhibits page 198 for Letter to Editor on Judge Billings

A Sample of the "Advice" I received, and paid for at least twice!

I will include some of the advice that I received over the thousands of hours of consultation among these many attorneys and myself. The order of the information presented is of no particular significance, and I will not attribute the recollections of advice. I believe it is more merciful, and a higher purpose served in protecting the identity of the guilty. The advice provided was often harmful to me, always expensive, and frequently incorrect, as it turned out. So return again to the mental image of a "merry-go-round," that platform of the horses endlessly chasing the other's tail, going up and down in stately movement, going nowhere but having a great time while listening to lovely distracting music.

After I began the process of appeal, I searched for another attorney. I retained one who had a unique view of wealth distribution. He acknowledged very clearly that the transcripts of my federal trial showed anyone reading them that the trial was conducted as a one-sided affair. That a reader, without having been given an explanation for the "resting," might even think it was rigged. In any case he chose to offer his services and construct an elaborate appeal of the bank case with its illegal restitution. Then following a number of motions and conversations and some discovery, he announced to me that *I should give him all of my money*[1] – that the courts or the bank or some other lawyer was going to get all of it anyhow so I might as well make him the beneficiary. He actually said that to me. You should give me all of your assets because you're going to lose them all one way or another. He was not the only advisor that reached the conclusion that I would lose everything, but he was unique in asking me for it straight out – instead of by the hour. I wrote him a letter suggesting his proposal was indecent. He was outraged when later a Judge in another court learned of his proposal. That Judge was disturbed at the lawyer, who himself was offended that such a proposal had come to knowledge. I had not understood that I was the only one expected to be embarrassed by his conduct.

Then there was a lawyer who promised me complete and reasonably instant recovery from the bank's fraudulent suit. He created a reasonably logical and then incomprehensible series of pleadings, which began with calling my initial attorney to task for representation that he (they) then blamed upon one of the appellant attorneys. They then blamed other appellant lawyers for even poorer representation, and then decided that the bank was the culprit. That the bank, with its new Board of Directors in its newly found zeal for assisting the federal government and helping itself to profit at my expense, had intentionally brought about a frivolous and fraudulent case. The bank case had cost me enormous amounts of time and money and the Bank and its attorneys should be sued for their role in damages, for loss of value to my stock, loss of use of my land, and for malicious misrepresentation.

Finally when all of this was ready to go to trial he concluded that the firm that had the least to do with the mistakes at appeal was probably the most guilty, and that the other lawyers had miraculously discovered a "magical bullet" as he called it. He went to the attorneys of all of the other people he planned to sue and suggested that the other firm with the least involvement should be responsible for all of the millions of dollars I had lost or been cheated out of. They were all guilty, but the previous attorneys and their firms and their insurance companies and the bank should be dropped from the suit and the one firm with the least culpability pursued. I protested and said I didn't want to do it. Then I learned that the client's view, if he disagrees with the attorney's previously negotiated one and not presented until the last possible minute, will be sacrificed. I told him I did not want to do it. He told me, with a further demand for an additional $218,000.00 dollars, that I must accept his offer or he would drop all of his proceedings already paid for and I would need another lawyer. And that for what he had said was a slam dunk case.

Then there was a lawyer who, when offered a delay for trial preparation and an essential witness, said that the federal government was not prepared in its case before the jury and that he believed it would be better to have a quick trial. He would catch them "with their pants down; they wouldn't be ready;they hadn't prove a thing." I got 4 years in prison and an illegal restitution order. God knows what I would have received if the prosecution had been prepared.

Then there were the other appeals. After the federal trial when it was obvious an appeal was necessary and that the trial record had been allowed to be closed without detail of my defense available to it, I declined using that law firm further. I chose the well-respected firm of F. Lee Bailey in Boston to represent me. Of all of the lawyers that I retained he was among **_three_** of them (Field and DeTroy the others) that provided me with honest service. When mistakes were made he admitted them and indicated that he would help me recover from those mistakes. At the time he'd been preoccupied with some other difficulties and did not provide me with the standard of care that he had promised. Now for that level of honesty he was seized upon as the "identified sacrifice" by his brother attorneys who saw both his prominence and his willingness to acknowledge a mistake as their opportunity. And we successfully sued him for the malpractice that we claimed also existed among everyone else's representation as well.

Shortly after my sentencing, I was subpoenaed to appear before a Grand Jury on Arthur Elliott by Assistant US Attorney VandeGraaf on 7/7/94.

Fishman, from Bailey's office, got the subpoena quashed twice, but I finally had to appear on 10/20/94. Fishman and Horstman were there and Fishman told me that if there was any question that I had a hard time answering, that I had the right to leave the Grand Jury room and go out and ask them about the question. After I was sworn in and identified myself to the Grand Jury, VandeGraaf asked me if I knew Arthur Elliott. I told him I had known Arthur for many years. I had known him when he was Town selectman, when he was Town Lister and when he was on the Bank's Board of Directors. I told him that Arthur was the most honest man I had ever met. After saying this VandeGraaf wanted me out of there. I asked the Grand Jury if they had any questions, and then I left. That was the end of this, but it did cost me approximately $4,000 to have the attorneys prepare for and attend this hearing.

I can't make any sense out of that but perhaps some of my readers will have insights that have so far escaped me in this matter. The bank had the expensive and unsuccessful assistance of a prominent Boston firm, with a local affiliate, actively assisting them in repeated misrepresentation and fraud upon the courts and myself. They filed claims, which they acknowledged were generated by the opportunity to profit from the illegal restitution order. They sought "safe-haven" in Federal Court until they were tossed out. The bank's lawyers knowingly and with the certain knowledge of its hired President, Charlie Bucknam, and the Board of Directors "had or should have known" their legal charter was misstated over and over again.

They filed documents that they certainly knew to be untrue or incorrect, probably both. They seemed to be extremely well paid and highly praised for their unsuccessful campaign. After I was vindicated and the unprecedented award against me was set aside, one of their Vermont cronies still maintains the initial award of $8.7 million against me as one of the credits on his web site.

Another one of the attorneys had arranged to have what he himself regarded as conflicts of interest excluded from knowledge in one of my trials; however, he never indicated to anyone, as far as I'm aware, that he had multiple conflicts with the IBG involving Bucknam, and my brother Noel, and the Patrick matter. These involved inside information, allowed him to see the strategy of the federal prosecutor in what became derivative prosecution, which was far more damaging than anything that he'd indicated to us might be a conflict. He made strenuous efforts to be sure that the agreed upon exclusion, concerning conflict of interest on Hill, was protected throughout my trial, which was agreed to by the Government. Duncan Kilmartin, an attorney representing a client suing myself and the bank, stated in writing to Langrock that Langrock had severe conflicts of interest concerning representing myself and Arthur Elliott at this time, especially in the criminal trial.[2] We did not know we were following an elephant. These conflicts were only discovered much later. The size of the conflict and his awareness of the interests and activities of the federal prosecutor's office for several years prior to my indictment are a far more damaging matter. Damaging to me that is. He was not concerned about its existence, only its revelation.

And then as I began requiring explanations and information from my attorneys, they went and retained their attorneys to protect them. So I began seeing more "horses" added to the merry-go-around."

And when you get to the appellate Judges you begin discovering that some of them have relationships with those pleading before them. We went before the Second Circuit Court of Appeals charging that the original trial had been flawed by numerous errors and by defects in the defense counsel's conduct. Imagine how that sounded to that particular Appellate Judge, hearing his former partner, Langrock, so described. I believe this Judge had a more severe conflict of interest than Langrock and should have excused himself. They are all married to each other. My early appeal of the federal convictions to the Second Circuit Appellate Court was vigorously presented by my newly retained prominent attorney from Boston.

At the time all of this was beginning to happen I thought that such experiences were unique, unusual and extremely rare. Only later, to my dismay, did I discover that they were frequent, ordinary, well understood, and to be expected. During the time that I was attending that federal graduate school at "State Pen" I also had the companionship in incarceration of numerous attorneys. Several were former prosecutors themselves who had experienced some difficulties with cocaine that led them into questionable relationships, or had misused trust funds provided by others for their safe keeping. All had miserable stories to tell. The one thing they had in common was that they all agreed that they knew the grievances that I've identified in these pages, and that they were frequent in occurrence. They are anticipated by all parties and as far as the legal system was concerned of no significance. One former prosecutor pointing to a large phone book in the library said with certainty of belief, "Open it to any page you choose; put your finger on any name you choose; the government can have that person in prison within the year if it wants to."

We have come to see how some of that really can happen since "9-11." Now it is possible to arrest a citizen without charges, holding him out of sight and unknown. We have seen that the system is primarily managed by arbitrary political influence, and the criminal part of the justice system is just that. It may be used for criminal purposes by those who are entrusted to its operation and management. Books have been written about that subject alone so I commend you to the library or to the Web where you can find such titles as "mad dog prosecutors," documenting that conclusion. Franklin's book *"__lies and the lying liars that tell__* " takes us beyond just the administration of prosecution to the world of misrepresented public policy. The intentional use of the deception in the chasing of mass weapons is simply a further application of the individual being set up by "collaborating witnesses."

And then there were the attempts of others to have the Whole of the United States of America, that federal prosecutor in Vermont, explain his preference for giving full immunity to Doug Jolly in the absence of any real benefit and purpose. When citizens who had been defrauded of significant amounts of money went to see the Whole of United States, they found the Vermont prosecutor barely willing to listen to their claim that Jolly had done these things. He sat sideways at his desk snapping rubber bands at his computer letting the clock run out the time he had made available to these defrauded citizens. He regarded them as there to help defend me, rather than understand they were after his cooperating witness. Announcing he was done listening to them he was later surprised to find that they were bringing investigations, in Washington, regarding his own conduct. That didn't go anywhere either, but it did create an awful lot of smoke and windy explanations.

So you have a closed system of self-interest riding a merry-go-round of brightly painted horses going up and down moving together to the sound of the music, but going nowhere. The horses carry loads of clients around and around before dumping them off into the gulags, themselves simply going round and round and up and down watching their bank accounts grow.

I would not have believed any of this possible. I always wanted to believe that the federal system was reasonably free from influence and corruption. But there were too many of my fellow classmates at "Federal University" with similar stories. And the libraries and law books are filled with so many similar accounts that I know my experiences are not unique. And while you will still probably remain skeptical that the system is as devious and corrupt as I allege, please remember when it comes around to you that "Uncle Roger" tried to tell you so.

But out of "governmental necessity" something becomes something it was not. The banking regulators could have sat down and said, "Well, boys, we have made a mess of the saving and loan industry. We must clean up the information procedures that have worked fine for years[3]. Roger, we know you have already resigned and will be leaving the bank. Now is a chance to bring about the changes necessary for the future. So sit down with us, we need to work it out!" And we would have done so. I would have sold my stock and gone back to working for myself, and none of this would have happened. But that was not their intention.

THEY COULD HAVE. AND THEY DID NOT WANT TO DO SO...
THEY WERE MORE INTERESTED IN SENDING A MESSAGE
AND GETTING THE ATTENTION OFF OF THEIR FAILURES

You reach the conclusion that it is clear to most persons now that justice in this country can be bought. For the most part the rich get off, and the poor go to jail. Or those soon to be poor by attempting to defend themselves against a government that has unlimited resources and the will to use it – and by public officials that themselves have no moral compass. Its sole purpose is to "send messages" and rule from fear to make its point. Just look at the difference in sentencing and the periods of imprisonment received by the persons in this narrative.

Anthony Aiossa received two years of probation, 100 hours of community service, no fine, and no restitution.

John Howard received two years probation and $60,000.00 restitution to the FDIC, and no fine.

Charlie Kelton received six months in prison, three years supervised release, $2,300,000.00 restitution and no fine.

Robert Platka received six months home confinement, three years probation, $10,000.00 fine and $286,000.00 restitution to FDIC.

Doug Jolly received blanket immunity, with no fine and no restitution.

If you invent, lie and cooperate you get off lightly. If you accept your constitutional right to trial you are punished for requiring the government to run the risk of embarrassment. With that power to punish anyone, and to serve any vanity of their personality or political expediency they simply take a citizen, point to his name in the phone book and say, "Your life is mine to use – and your children's as well."

[1] See Exhibits pages 199-200 for letter to Attorney on money issue

[2] See Exhibits pages 201-206 for Kilmartin letters to Langrock

[3] See Exhibits pages 208-211 for letters from Sen. Illuzzi and John McClaughry

Appeals

Now there is a matter of the four appeals of the original conviction. In the normal course of events in our working lives we are normally able to go back and make a correction if we see something going wrong . We are able to start over to where the error began. But in the legal business, corrections are neither automatic nor are they necessarily timely or even possible. If in Vermont, for example, you were building a barn and you began to discover that some of the load bearing beams were out of plumb or had shifted, you could stop your work and go back to the place where the beam could be corrected and correct it. From that point of correction you could continue with the building of your barn. In the legal process you're not permitted to go back and make a correction of one mistake if you continued with any action or activity or testimony beyond that point. And I've indicated several times now that if the matter was excluded from the original trial it cannot at any point be included subsequent to the closure of that record.

And that is how my appeals worked. The only thing that can be appealed is the record that was allowed into the trial and not what could or should have been introduced. The assumption is that if it could have been introduced it would have been, which can easily be seen as a very dubious conclusion. And if the decision-makers are collaborating with each other or presenting a chosen rendition of events as the whole story, then you end up in difficulty. Well, when my federal trial had concluded with a resting defense and my conviction, I believed I could successfully appeal the process I'd been through. But I discovered that the process itself was not up for review. In resting my case before a defense had been presented the appellate record could not be attached to present information that would have been available, but can only deal with information that had been presented by the Whole of the United States of America. My attorney at that time, now well rested, proposed to appeal to the Second Circuit where he believed he would have more success. If I had truly appreciated that his former law partner was now one of the Judges for that appeal's court I might actually have regarded that as a reasonable proposal. But still not understanding how the game was played and believing that the goal of all parties was to get the truth out, I looked around for a capable law firm whose reputation commended them. F. Lee Bailey was chosen and agreed to handle my defense and appeal.

The Bailey firm attempted to appeal a flawed record and itself overlooked the obvious claim of illegal restitution in spite of the fact that it had been pointed out to them during the time of cooperation. It was the initial firm that had the responsibility to provide a record that could show the arbitrary nature of the government.

The Bailey and Langrock firms also made a mistake in failing to observe the mandatory seven-day period of filing an appeal of the sentence itself.

I always felt that while F. Lee Bailey and his firm inherited an unnecessary legal confusion when they decided to represent me, they admittedly made mistakes that turned out to be costly, and for which they paid. Starting with the failure to connect the pre-sentencing report and Judge Billings announcement of restitution in the absence of legal authority to do so, representations frequently overlooked the obvious. All of the Lyndonville Bank's actions against myself were admitted by Lyndonville later to be consequences of the restitution order.

Winning a case of ineffective counsel – now this latter successful claim is actually one of the most painful for a person trying to follow reasonable logic. It began simply enough with a lawyer successfully representing me in appealing the Lyndonville Savings Bank's claim of $8.7 million against me. This case ovioously was found to be in the wrong jurisdiction. Having extinguished the right of the bank to sue me in federal court and attach everything my wife and I owned and having harmed the value of my property by that attachment, it was now overdue to look at the whole history of my legal representation. And that is where the logic gets funny. If the bank had never been offered that illegal windfall, and had not deceived itself and been deceived by its high-priced attorneys to pursue that judgment and attempt to collect it regardless of its merits and their lack of loss, much of the damage to my family and to the assets of my lifetime of labor would have been avoided. But with the time served for the federal trial my life was still tangled up on the lawyer's merry-go-around by the greed and by the illusions of the Lyndonville Board of Directors.

My belief has always been that the decisions made for the defense against the original indictments by the whole of the United States was the area of initial legal malpractice. That all of the consequences of the bank's actions to myself had been the bank's own self-illusions and were based on this initial failure. The consequences of that was the illegal restitution attempt. Under pressure from the FDIC, and with the natural appearance of self-righteousness and greed on behalf of the new Board of Directors of the Lyndonville Savings Bank, the opportunity to collect insurance and assets from me and my family proved irresistible. It is an irony of ownership that since I owned about a fourth of the stock in the Lyndonville Bank, I was actually contributing to the fund to sue myself. It was my money in stock that was used to fund all of the high-priced lawyers for the bank who were seeking to do two things at once: get our personal money and get our ownership of the stock itself at our expense. Now how is that for being on both sides of the issue? I get to pay the banks attorneys and also the attorneys I hired to defend myself from them. Get the point. Well my bank account certainly did!

So looking at the whole of this legal landscape by the next attorney's logic we will say that all of those lawyers in sequence did it to you. But if F. Lee Bailey had been successful upon appeal it all would've been stopped, so we will let those who came before him and after him off entirely. We will send him the complete bill for the already agreed upon costs for all of the others. Then my lawyer wanted me to settle the case that he argued so firmly was worth millions to me. He wanted me to dismiss the bank entirely when in fact it was the bank that did far more harm to my family and my finances and my ability to defend myself than any other single party, and he invented some kind of magic bullet theory that said if one lawyer somewhere did get off then the others should get off as well. The Judge to whom he presented this novel opinion asked him if that was really what he intended to do and felt that was fair enough. Then he expected to collect millions from F. Lee Bailey's insurance company that he said was liable. Then he wanted me to take a settlement way below the demonstrated cost of damages to me, and of that amount give him a third. Now isn't that a sporting proposal. It seemed to bother him that I felt that a private agreement he had made with the other attorneys, to which I had not been informed, might be more important than what I wanted to do in my own case.

When it was all over a Vermont jury said that I had not been represented by my attorneys at the level of practice that should be expected and that they were guilty of malpractice. I got to testify, as I told you for the first time in 18 years, to all of these events, and when I did so, the jury believed me and found in my favor. They found in my favor in spite of the opposition saying that I was a convicted felon, guilty of every fraud known to man. The jury listened to them and believed me. Then they got back on the lawyer merry-go-round for a few more turns for some more lawyer stuff among themselves. I was eventually awarded for the misconduct on their part with a small portion of the funds that I had expended on my own defense in no small part because of the conversion of an illegal restitution into a self-serving and greedy federal claim by Lyndonville Bank. To my lawyer's disgust I declined to accept the agreement to settle with the bank. He then threatened to withdraw from my case if I would not give him another $218,000 within nine days to do what he had originally agreed to do in the first place. Then in order to protect my family from further life-absorbing stress and irritation and more trips to the lawyer merry-go-around, we entered into a one-sided agreement upon his suggestion and recommendation, and the bank was assured it would never again be held accountable by me in legal proceedings for the shameful conduct that this record demonstrates.

When we did settle with the bank, my wife and I were pressured by our lawyers to accept the settlement. It was the worst settlement I have ever seen. The settlement said that we were to be paid on or before September 15, 2002. When we weren't paid by that date I wanted to break the agreement as the bank had not lived up to their part. That really upset our lawyers as they wanted us to settle. By this time another quarter had passed and another dividend on the stock was due. I told them we would only settle if the bank paid us the extra dividend due, which amounted to $16,032.95. They paid. As part of the jury award in the malpractice case, the jury awarded me $40,400.00 for lost dividends, but the judge struck those dividends from the final judgment as he said the settlement with the bank had taken care of those dividends.

Earlier in the malpractice case the judge had tossed out the possibility of collecting on the land that had been attached. My lawyer had said that we would be able to collect on the value of the land that had been attached at 1% per month. This amount would have been approximately $1,700,000. I spent several thousand dollars having John Stevens appraise these properties to establish a value. The judge decided that it was the bank and not the lawyers that were responsible for the wrongful attachment, and we could not collect from the lawyers. I had told my lawyer that we should try to collect from the bank, and that I would pay him the same amount that he would get from the malpractice case, which would have been a third of any settlement. But he did not want to do this. There must be a universal law here. The obviously guilty get to collect a mistake and those whose guilt is manufactured by perjury, cooperating witnesses, exaggerated and convoluted interpretation of business practices, and down right fraudulent perjury and false documents, get to call it all a mistake.

Fellow citizens, fellow countrymen I would never have believed this possible. Ten years ago I regarded it all as somehow a correctable mistake, and all of us would end at seeing the truth for what it is, and it would never happen again. Well look around you now. See how the word citizen has come to mean subject, being fitted for ball and chain. Look at the similarity in the events of my prosecution and the manipulation of all of the components of circumstance and the adventure by the bank in its self-serving desire to profit at my misfortune.

So in what context do we affirm our lives, extend hope to others?

*Nothing that is worth doing cannot be achieved in our lifetime;
therefore we must be saved by* **hope***.*

*Nothing, which is true or beautiful or good, makes complete sense
in any immediate context of history; therefore we must be saved
by* **faith***.*

*Nothing we do, however virtuous, can be accomplished alone;
therefore we must be saved by* **love***.*

Reinhold Niebuhr

Step outside of the harm and pain my account of the events at "trial" I have described and just think about living your life for a while. I am sure all of us wish much earlier that we had the secrets of how to live long, and live well. All of us share more in common in a common plight of living than we share in disagreement. And we all seem best described as sharing a journey, with an unclear destination, but one that does end!

We remember our favorite teachers, and those that scared us. We mark "turning points" as we age, as our faces look more and more like our parents. We begin to become like them somehow.

Now I have reached an age where I can consider many, many things I have been surprised to experience, and going to prison was not the only one. I look around my familiar portion of Vermont where I have known almost every farm family, driven every lane picking up cattle or bringing feed. I remember auctions and have most of the records of them. Evelyn has folders of receipts and pictures of sales from homes coming to an end with change of circumstances or tragedy. I have seen piles of cordwood, mud roads, and have seen business and small manufacturing replace plows and herds. I sold at auction most of what had been previously bought, and knew almost every person present in the gathering. I have met important people, and those that thought they were. There is a difference. And I have seldom been surprised at the human events we celebrate or create for ourselves or those we love.

A little over two years ago our children pulled a surprise on Evelyn and me. We are a large family with longevity on all sides, and we love to be together. But this occasion was our own 50th wedding anniversary. Unknown to us the children had reserved the very hall which held our original wedding reception, organized a catered dinner, gathered a band and located copies of the same music played upon our original wedding day. What a lovely evening

— the hall decorated, our children and grandchildren all dressed up, and over three hundred and fifty people who have known us and cared about us all gathered to share that evening. I could not believe it was organized without our knowledge

Friends from Vermont and some from away were all gathered to eat, listen to music and dance. We are and have been blessed. Fifty years ago to the very day our Maid of Honor and my Best Man attended our wedding. Fifty years later they joined us again and shared in the renewal of our wedding vows, with the Rev. Ted Ruggles officiating. That was a tender moment for us. Then Evelyn and I danced...just like then, all feelings of those years gathered and then our grown children and their partners, then their children joined us, then our friends from everywhere...and the band played on. Walking among the persons we loved and seeing others happy in living, rejoicing in our good fortune and the joy of our families, those other harmful and destructive days could be seen in better perspective. They were not and have not been the most important thing to happen to me, to us. Many of those friends gathered with us took the opportunity to speak a few words about happenings in our lives that they had shared, mostly humorous, while some brought tears to our eyes. Those people here with us now were the evidence that love outlasts and eventually defeats Evil.

Pause for a moment and consider how little we knew when we made that original decision. Evelyn and I knew each other when she was in high school. When my father became ill I decided to drop out of school and practice what he had taught me. For those days that was not all bad. He had showed us by his example of work and his love of people how to be successful, and we just did as we had learned. Evelyn and I married, and we stayed that way. That has not been a burden but continues as the joy of my existence. Our children worked along side us, and I am sure there were days when another potato field would be the last thing they would ever want to see again. But we all worked together, and we all loved being with each other. Their families and their children are all different to be sure, but they truly enjoy and stay near each other, and are available for us all. Many persons have never known the pleasure of that, a family that actually likes each other. And we do.

They danced, the band played, and I felt myself getting younger with delight. The hall that night had been decorated with pictures taken at different times in our 50 years. Some were very young and hopeful, some in middle years with the children, some of our parents now deceased, locations, trips, auctions, memories by the thousands. And we could see how much we had shared and were grateful. And around us there were over three hundred and fifty persons who knew us well, knew all about some of the hard events of the trial and jail and they could have been elsewhere – they were there. A priest talked a moment about love overcoming evil, and steel bars and prisons walls. He knew what he was talking about. Nothing in those events – that jail and prison and chains and shame and humiliation – had been able to stop Evelyn's love of me. Nothing stopped or weakened my love for her. Our children suffered and sacrificed with her, and their love for each other and their love for me reached past locked doors and restrictions and attached property – a family kept going by its love and not its wealth. They were all there, the band played, the lights blended into memories and some tears. Evelyn looked like a bride and danced with me across all of those years, and I never loved her more! She is beautiful. Oh Mister Man! Life cannot be better than what we have, all of it! I know from my experience that evil loses to love.

Never had we anticipated on that lovely day 50 years ago some of our experiences. We probably never expected to be as successful. We have more friends now than before prison. We never expected to leave the Northeast Kingdom except on vacation, and we were right about that. We never joined the bank to make money; my taxes before I did were higher than the earning of the bank itself. But in doing so, I could and I believe I did help a lot of people. Those cards and the petitions were not just things to put up a good front, they were from persons who knew me and found our association a desired thing.

Evelyn and I never for a moment expected when we married that I would, in the course of our life together, go to prison. But when that became fact it did not have the power to split us. (Several people did suggest to Evelyn that a divorce would benefit her.) She never moved from my side and my heart. Now that is the meaning of those wonderful words in our promises to each other: I take thee for better or worse, in sickness and in health...! We are joined, we promised each other and God to be so, and we are glad of it! I could have died during several periods of illness in prison. Well, that is a scary thing to remember, but it did not happen. And each day now that I live, I see more clearly what a gift each day is. Passing the cemetery in Sheffield I realize I did survive what some hoped would kill me. I can only thank a loving God and my family and friends, and Love itself for each of these days.

If nothing else in this story interests you then at least consider what I believe can be learned along the way. We don't know the future. We have the opportunity to share our life's adventures with many persons and some of it will be painful, mostly it will be a delight. Harm and evil will tempt us to give up. Love is the product of our good choices and seems to be from the universe itself. Love is adequate to anything that happens. So there is my sermon, fellows, and I believe it.

Those guys in the prison rosary have learned that, I have lived that, and you are invited.

Well the evening wore on and Evelyn and I seemed to have stayed around and danced more and talked more than I remember from the first time....the effect is the same and eventually we did go home!.

You can feel the gifts of that love in everything you do, and I just can't imagine a better way to demonstrate what I believe is important than to point to that evening which was itself a gift from our children and friends and say, "That is the heart of the matter". God Bless us all! He has, he certainly has!

For I am persuaded that neither death, nor life, nor powers shall separate us from the love of God.

Exhibits

 **BANK OF BOSTON**
NORTHERN REGION

March 9, 1988

Mr. Charlie Kelton
Kelton Motors, Inc.
Route 14, Box 1100
White River Junction, Vermont 05001

Dear Charlie,

With respect to our recent discussions, please find below an outline
of a proposed financing package for Kelton Motors, Inc.

Facility 1

Borrower:	Kelton's Inc. and Charlie and Shirley Kelton.
Purpose:	Refinance existing mortgage with Lyndonville Savings Bank.
Amount:	$4,280,000 Term financing.
Rate:	Floating at Bank of Boston's Base rate plus 1.25% or fixed at Bank of Boston's five year Cost of Funds plus 2%.
Structure:	5 year note, with 20 year amortization.
Fee:	1/2 point, payable at loan closing.
Security:	First mortgage on property owned by Kelton's Inc., located in White River Junction, Vermont. First mortgage also on property currently mortgaged to the Lyndonville Bank including the Adams Farm, Manning property, Michels property, Murphy property, Smith property, and the Twin State Warehouse property.
Guarantee:	Unlimited personal guarantees of Charlie and Shirley Kelton for the property owned by Kelton's Inc.

Facility 2

Borrower:	Kelton Motors, Inc.
Purpose:	Refinance existing notes payable.
Amount: ·	$5,000,000 working capital line of credit.
Rate:	Floating at Bank of Boston Base plus 1%.
Structure:	Demand.
Borrowing Base:	On a formula basis of 80% of 60 day receivables plus 50% of used car and truck and parts inventory, with an inventory cap of $4MM.
Guarantee:	Unlimited personal guarantee of Charlie and Shirley Kelton.
Security:	All Corporate assets, except GMC and Volvo/White new vehicle inventory.

Facility 3

Borrower:	Kelton Motors, Inc.
Purpose:	Refinance existing notes payable.
Amount:	$700,000 term financing.
Rate:	Floating at Bank of Boston Base plus 1 1/4% or Fixed at Bank of Boston's 3 year Cost of Funds plus 2%.
Structure:	3 year note, with 7 year amortization.
Security:	All Corporate assets including equipment, company vehicles and leasehold improvements located at White River Junction and Burlington, except new vehicle inventory from GMC and Volvo/White.
Guarantee:	Unlimited of Charlie and Shirley Kelton.

Facility 4

Borrower:	Kelton Motors, Inc.
Amount:	$3,000,000 floor planning line of credit.
Rate:	Floating at Bank of Boston base plus 1%.
Structure:	Demand.
Borrowing Base:	100% of new vehicles invoice.
Security:	All Corporate assets, except new vehicle inventory of GMC and Volvo/White.
Total Lines of Credit:	$12,980M.
Covenants:	Full range of covenants including, but not limited to, minimum net worth, minimum current ratio, minimum debt coverage, minimum working capital, restrictions on acquisitions, capital expenditures, owners withdrawals and bonuses, other restrictions on material ownership changes and additional Bank and floor planning debt. All loans to be cross collateralized and cross defaulted.
Other Conditions:	–Annual certified audit by an accountant acceptable to the Bank. –Monthly agings of accounts receivable. –Minimum of three annual examinations by the Bank of receivables and inventory. –Monthly dealer – financial statements on all dealerships owned by Charlie Kelton.

This proposal is subject to approval by the Bank's Credit Committee and Policy Committee, a satisfactory examination of receivables and inventory by the Bank's examiners and a satisfactory review of the appraisal dated 3/3/88 by the Bank's Real Estate Group.

As discussed, we consider this proposal as the first of several financing stages for the Kelton dealerships and for the personal financing needs of the Kelton family.

Our intention is to assist in the separation of the financing needs of the Kelton Corporate activities from those of the Kelton family. With this in mind, we shall be shortly introducing our Private Banking Group to yourself. This group provides financing and other products and services to entrepreneurs and their families.

We will also be recommending several independent accountants to yourself in order to prepare certified statements.

Finally, it is our intention to consider the financing of the other Kelton dealerships at a later point in time. We believe that the financing proposal outlined in this letter provides a substantial base upon which additional business between ourselves can be developed.

We hope that this financing proposal meets with your approval. If so, please sign and return the attached copy of this letter.

Please do not hesitate to call if you have any questions.

We have enjoyed our discussions with yourselves and we look forward working with you on this transaction.

Sincerely yours,

Andrew D. Colby
Vice President

Sara M. Dean
Assistant Vice President

ACCEPTED

_____   DATE_____

TELEPHONE CALLS FROM LYNDONVILLE TO CITY BANK - 1988

Date	Time	Number	Duration
Thu. June 30	10:46 a.m.	542-9586	2 min.
Thu. June 30	12:39 p.m.	543-0111	8 min.
Thu. June 30	12:51 p.m.	543-0111	4 min.
Thu. July 14	9:56 a.m.	543-0111	1 min.
Tue. July 19	4:44 p.m.	543-0111	24 min.
Fri. July 22	9:33 a.m.	543-0111	1 min.
Fri. July 22	11:03 a.m.	543-0111	14 min.
Wed. Aug. 10	10:26 a.m.	542-9586	4 min.
Fri. Sept 9	4:04 p.m.	543-0111	3 min.

TELEPHONE CALLS FROM CITY BANK TO LYNDONVILLE - 1988

Date	Time	Number	Duration
Wed. July 13	3:50 p.m.	626-8121	1 min.
Thu. July 14	9:41 a.m.	626-8121	1 min.
Thu. July 14	10:43 a.m.	626-8121	12 min.
Thu. July 19	11:48 a.m.	626-8121	1 min.
Thu. July 19	1:50 p.m.	626-8121	1 min.
Wed. July 20	2:00 p.m.	626-8121	1 min.
Wed. July 20	2:25 p.m.	626-8121	6 min.
Fri. July 22	9:59 a.m.	626-8121	1 min.
Fri. Sept 9	2:25 p.m.	626-8121	4 min.
Fri. Sept 9	4:11 p.m.	626-8121	21 min.

TRUST AGREEMENT

THIS AGREEMENT entered into as of the ₁₅th day of May, 1986, by and between Maurice Provost and Marylee Provost, d/b/a Provost Farms, of Derby, Vermont (herein collectively called "Producer") and Lyndonville Savings Bank and Trust Company of Lyndonville, Vermont (herein called "Trustee").

WITNESSETH, That

WHEREAS, Producer is indebted to Trustee evidenced by a Promissory Note dated March 19, 1984, secured by a Mortgage Deed and Security Agreement (as combined and consolidated) of even date therewith on certain lands and property located in the Towns of Derby, Morgan and Holland, Vermont; and Producer desires to modify and otherwise amend the terms for repayment of said Note and Trustee is agreeable to the same in consideration of the within Agreement; and

WHEREAS, Producer has entered into a "Contract to Partici-pate in the Dairy Termination Program" (herein the "Contract") with the Commodity Credit Corporation, an agency of the United States Department of Agriculture (herein CCC), a copy of which contract is appended hereto and identified as Exhibit A; and

WHEREAS, Producer will be the recipient of approximately $1,561,471.14 under the Contract, payable over the next five (5) years subsequent to the "contract disposal period," on the basis of 80% in the first year of the contract of about $1,249,977.00, and in four (4) equal installments of $78,073.57 for each subsequent four (4) year period (herein the "Payments"); and

WHEREAS, Producer anticipates the receipt of about $400,000 from the sale for slaughter of Producer's dairy herds at auction, required to be so sold under the Contract and applicable regula-tion of CCC, (herein called "Sale Proceeds"); and

WHEREAS, Producer desires Trustee to receive and disburse the Payments and Sale Proceeds as in this Agreement hereinafter provided, and to that end has executed and delivered to Trustee an "Assignment of Payment -- Dairy Termination Program" of the Payments, a copy of which assignment is appended hereto and identified as Exhibit B, and also hereby assigns and sets over unto Trustee all of the net Sale Proceeds; and

WHEREAS, Trustee is agreeable to acting as Trustee herein of the Payments and Sale Proceeds, and to disburse the same as hereinafter provided to the extent thereof.

NOW THEREFORE, in consideration of the foregoing and for other good and valuable consideration, Producer hereby designates Trustee to accept and disburse the Payments and Sale Proceeds, subject to and in accordance with the following terms and pro-visions, with the understanding that Trustee as a creditor of Producer of pre-existing indebtedness incurred by Producer in conducting their dairy farming operations, shall be a beneficiary recipient for its own account of Payments and Sale Proceeds to be disbursed by Trustee; all as hereinafter provided:

1. Producer agrees to comply at all times with the provisions of the Contract and regulations of CCC applicable
thereto, including the requisite periodic certifications
of compliance, copies of which certifications shall be
submitted to Trustee.

2. Appended hereto and identified as Exhibit C is a
listing of all persons entitled to recieve disbursements
of Sale Proceeds and Payments, and amounts owed by
Producers to each as indicated. Further, Producer
represents that such persons and amounts are representative of pre-existing obligations owed by Producers arising
out of Producer's farming operation. Producer, at the
request of Trustee, shall furnish written confirmation
from the aforementioned persons as to the amounts owed
by Producer.

3. Appended hereto and identified as Exhibit D are
copies of Producer's dairy farm leases, which leases under
the terms of the Contract and applicable CCC regulations
are required to be maintained in full force and effect
by Producer for a minimum period of five (5) years from
the date of the "contract disposal period" to assure that
the subject land and premises are not used to maintain
dairy cattle thereon or devoted to the production of milk.
Producer hereby confirms that rent required to be paid
under said leases is current. Attached as Exhibit D-1 is
a listing of periodic rent payments required to be paid by
Producer over the subject five (5) year period, together
with a projected estimate of other pecuniary obligations
of Producer required under the terms of said leases. Producer's aforementioned obligations shall be paid from the
Payments to the extent of the availability thereof, and
otherwise from any income source available to Producer including any income derived from the subject land and
premises.

4. Trustee shall administer the disbursement of all funds
actually received by it from the Proceeds, the Sale Proceeds, and as otherwise made available by Producer, to the
persons specifically identified in Exhibit C and to the
Landlords under the leases identified in Exhibit D, and
in that respect, appended hereto and identified as Exhibit
C is a listing of the funds and periodic payments required
to be disbursed to each person so identified to the extent of
available funds. Trustee shall have the right to disburse
to itself for its own account as a credit on the indebtedness
owed to it by Producer from first available funds, a sum sufficient to reduce said indebtedness to a principal balance of
not less than $750,000.00 with interest current thereon.

Further, Trustee shall not be responsible for allocating available funds on the basis of any priority among the aforementioned persons entitled to receive disbursements.

5.   The within agreement is undertaken by Trustee as an accommodation to Producer and without any consideration paid to Trustee for acting as such, it being the intention of Producer to undertake the within agreement for the purpose of establishing an independent depository, as it were, to administer the disbursements of funds to numerous creditors and obligees of Producer as herein specifically provided, to the end result that said creditors and obligees may be paid to the extent of available funds. Further, the agreement is intended by the Trustee and Producer to be enforceable only as between them and not by any other party.

6.   It is understood and agreed that subsequent to the application of the assigned proceeds to the mortgage note indebtedness owed by Producer to Trustee as in paragraph 4 hereof provided, the resulting unpaid balance of the indebtedness owed by Producer to Trustee shall be payable in annual installments of not less than $75,000.00 over the succeeding five (5) years applied first to interest accrued and the balance to principal, and any then remaining unpaid balance shall be reamortized and payable in monthly installments of principal and interest over the remaining term of the subject mortgage note at the rate of interest set forth in said note.   All security now held by Trustee securing the repayment of said indebtedness shall be and remain in full force and effect.   Further, Producer and Trustee agree to execute a new mortgage note to amend and replace the existing note to reflect the foregoing terms of payment, including an amendment of Producer's mortgage on all secured real estate to provide that in the event there is a default and the Trustee takes the property back or secures it through foreclosure or by other means, there shall not be any sale or use of the real estate for dairy purposes as limited by the federal whole herd buyout program, e.g. no female bovine animals, for such time that is necessary to ensure that the Producers do not default in their commitments to the federal whole herd buyout program.

Further, Trustee shall have the right for its own account to disburse to itself from Payments hereby assigned, as a credit to the aforementioned indebtedness of Producer, the annual sum of $75,000.00 required to be paid as set forth above in this Section 6.

7.   Producers hereby constitute and appoint Trustee their attorney in fact and in their name to collect and receive all Sale Proceeds and Payments and to endorse checks and drafts for collection representing the same for the purpose of enabling Trustee to effect disbursements required to be made hereunder.

8. Unless otherwise provided above, Producer shall furnish
to Trustee the following:

   a.   Listing of Producer's Secured Creditors, nature of
        security and amounts owing.

   b.   Listing of Producer's creditors having attachments,
        nature of property attached and amounts owing.

   c.   Listing of Producer's judgment and unsecured creditors
        and amounts owing.

   d.   Written consents of Secured Creditors to Producer's
        Dairy Termination Program ("The Program"), the amounts
        to be paid to creditors from initial proceeds, and
        agreed upon terms for repayment of balance of secured
        loan.

   e.   Listing of all parties to be paid from the sale of
        cows and initial proceeds under the Program, and
        amounts to be paid in installments from balance of
        the Program proceeds, and terms of payments.

   f.   Written consents to terminate cattle leases, and the
        costs to be paid to each lessor therefore, and
        source of funds.

   g.   Copies of leases of leased farms, non-cancellable
        during period of Program conditions (5 years), and
        source of funds to pay rent and maintenances of
        leased property over 5 year term.

   h.   Satisfactory assurances to Lyndonville Savings Bank
        and Trust Company by legal opinion or otherwise, to
        the effect that the assignment to it of the Program
        funds and the parties and amounts to be paid therefrom
        will not contravene any applicable laws of the State
        of Vermont or that such payments may be subject to
        being set aside or otherwise voided.

9. Subject to Producer's obligations owed to Trustee under the
terms of their mortgage note and security given therefore, as
amended aforementioned, the within Agreement shall not constitute a waiver or cession by and between Maurice Provost
and Marylee Provost of their respective rights, if any, to
pay or receive maintenance, child support, or property in
or under their pending divorce action.

10. In consideration of the pre-existing indebtedness owed by
Producer to Trustee and the modification thereof and the mortgage securing the same as herein provided, the within appointment of Lyndonville Savings Bank and Trust Company as Trustee
herewith, shall be irrevocable so long as Trustee is in compliance

with its obligations hereunder and said indebtedness remains unpaid and outstanding.

11. Subject only to the modification of payment terms of the mortgage note and mortgage aforementioned made and delivered by Producer to Trustee, the same, together with any and all other indebtedness and security therefor made and delivered by Producers, or either of them, shall be and remain in full force and effect and subject to all of the terms and conditions thereof.

12. Further, should Producer fail to maintain the leases identified in Exhibit D to preclude default or anticipated default under the Contract and applicable CCC regulations, then, in that event, Trustee shall have the right, but not the obligation, in its own name or that of Producer to advance such funds and take such action as may be necessary to preclude any default by Producer under said Contract and CCC regulations, and any such funds shall be payable on demand with interest at the annual rate of the then highest New York City bank prime rate of interest plus 2% as reported in the Wall Street Journal, and the same shall be and are hereby secured by (i) the Producer's Mortgage Deed and Security Agreement dated March 19, 1984 aforementioned, and (ii) the Producer's Leasehold Estate in the particular lease for which funds may have been advanced to cure or preclude any default as aforementioned.

13. Subject to the terms and provisions of this Agreement, should Producer have insufficient funds to pay all or any part of the first annual lease rent of its lease from Tukker Fox N.V., then, in that event, Producer hereby authorizes Trustee to make available such funds from the Proceeds remitted to and received by Trustee under the Contract during the year 1987.

14. It is understood and agreed that the language of the within Agreement is a result of negotiations between the parties hereto, all being represented by Counsel, and accordingly, the same shall not be construed more strictly against one party than the other.

IN WITNESS WHEREOF, the parties hereto have executed this Agreement as of the day and year first above written.

In the presence of (as to all)

_____   Maurice Provost

_____   MaryLee Provost

LYNDONVILLE SAVINGS BANK AND
TRUST COMPANY

By: _____ VP

STATE OF VERMONT   )
)
COUNTY OF ORLEANS) ss.

At _____Newport_____ on July 3, 1986, in said County, personally
appeared Maurice Provost and Marylee Provost, known to me to be
of age and sound mind and to be such and the same persons who
under due and lawful oath, swore and acknowledged to me that
the making, signing and execution by them of the within Agreement and the Power of Attorney therein set forth was and is their
own free act and deed.

                                    Before me,

                                         _____
                                           Notary Public

STATE OF VERMONT   )
)
COUNTY OF ORLEANS) ss.

At _Newport_, on July 3, 1986, in said County, personally
appeared _David M. Turner_, _Vice President_ of
Lyndonville Savings Bank and Trust Company, and he acknowledged
that the making, signing and execution by him of the within Agreement was and is his free act and deed as such officer and the
free act and deed of said Bank.

                                    Before me,

                                         _____
                                           Notary Public

ASSIGNMENT
LETTER OF INTENT

NOW COME MAURICE PROVOST, MARYLEE PROVOST, and THE LYNDONVILLE SAVINGS BANK, and enter into this letter of intent to provide for said bank to receive funds by assignment and to act as trustee in the disbursement of said funds.

WHEREAS, Maurice and Marylee Provost, d/b/a Provost Farms have entered the federal whole herd buyout program and will receive approximately $1,561,471.14 over the next five years, including eighty percent (80%) in the first year of the program, or approximately $1,249,177.00 in the first year; and,

WHEREAS, Provost Farms will also receive approximately $400,000.00 from the slaughter of beef; and,

WHEREAS, Maurice and Marylee Provost want to assign these monies for the purposes of guaranteeing certain payments which are absolutely necessary to the fulfillment of conditions necessary to qualify for admission to the whole herd buyout program; and,

NOW THEREFORE BE IT RESOLVED THAT:

1. All monies to be received by Maurice and Marylee Provost from the whole herd buyout program and the slaughter of beef shall be assigned to The Lyndonville Savings Bank.

2. The Lyndonville Savings Bank agrees to act as Trustee and administer disbursement of the funds in the following manner,(all figures approximate):

    a. $725,000.00 to the Lyndonville Savings Bank.
    b. $ 20,000.00 to Marcel Roberts
    c. $ 50,000.00 to Rod Barrup
    d. $ 53,000.00 to Production Credit Association
    e. $ 30,000.00 to Bradford National Bank
    f. $114,900.00 to FICA & Property Taxes
    g. $ 58,851.44 to Insufficient Funds Checks
    h. $275,000.00 to Caledonia Leasing Co.
    i. $148,000.00 to National Cattle Co.
    j. $162,500.00 to North Star Cattle Co.
    k. $146,300.00 to Regina Operating Co.
    l. $ 25,000.00 to Petit Farms
    m. $ 60,000.00 to Tukker Fox

3. The remaining $300,000.00 that will come to the LSB over the next five years in increments of $75,000.00 per year, shall be applied to interest first and principal second, on the remaining mortgage debt held by the LSB on all Provost real

DIAMOND &
ASSOCIATES, P.C.
ATTORNEYS AT LAW
MONTPELIER AND
BURLINGTON

DRAWER D
MONTPELIER, VERMONT.
05602

(802) 223-6166

-1-

NOTE MRP mP

estate. No other payments on the mortgage shall be required during the five year period. However, any sale of Provost real estate over the next five years, shall be applied to reduce the principal amount of the LSB mortgage on Provost real estate, in such amounts as agreed to by the parties at such dates.

4. In return for the acceptance of $725,000.00 by the LSB, the Lyndonville Savings Bank agrees to an amendment of their mortgage on all Provost real estate to provide that in the event there is a default and the LSB takes the property back or secures it through foreclosure or by other means, there shall not be any sale or use of the real estate for dairy purposes **AS** (no female bovine animals) for such time that is necessary to ensure that the Provosts do not default in their commitments to the federal whole herd buyout program.

5. The above described payments required to be made by the Provosts amount to approximately $200,000.00 more than is available for payment. For that reason, the actual payments by the LSB may have to be modified, and contributions toward the payments will come from final milk check proceeds, renegotiated amounts due the above creditors, and increased proceeds from the sale of beef.

6. The foregoing is subject to being setforth in a mutually satisfactory agreement including compliance with those conditions setforth in Exhibit A attached.

Dated at Montpelier, Vermont, this 15 day of May, 1986.

_____
MAURICE R. PROVOST

_____
MARYLEE PROVOST

_____
LYNDONVILLE SAVINGS BANK
By Its Duly Authorized Agent

WITNESS:

_____
M. JEROME DIAMOND

_____
ANDREW FIELD

_____
CARL LISMAN

DIAMOND &
ASSOCIATES, P.C.
ATTORNEYS AT LAW
MONTPELIER AND
BURLINGTON

DRAWER D
MONTPELIER, VERMONT,
05602

(802) 223-6166

7. *The foregoing is not a waiver or cession by Maurice and Marylee Provost of their rights, if any, to pay or receive maintenance, child support or property in their pending divorce proceedings.* MRP

EXHIBIT A

1. Listing of Producer's Secured Creditors, nature of security and amounts owing.

2. Listing of Producer's creditors having attachments, nature of property attached and amounts owing.

3. Listing of Producer's judgment and unsecured creditors and amounts owing.

4. Written consents of Secured Creditors to Producer's Dairy Termination Program ("The Program"), the amounts to be paid to creditors from initial proceeds, and agreed upon terms for repayment of balance of secured loand.

5. Listing of all parties to be paid from the sale of cows and initial proceeds under the Program, and amounts to be paid in installments from balance of the Program proceeds, and terms of payments.

6. Written consents to terminate cattle leases, and the costs to be paid to each lessor therefor, and source of funds.

DIAMOND &
ASSOCIATES, P.C.
ATTORNEYS AT LAW
MONTPELIER AND
BURLINGTON
———
DRAWER D
MONTPELIER, VERMONT.
05602
———
(802) 223-6166

7. Copies of leases of leased farms, non-cancellable during period of Program conditions (5 years), and source of funds to pay rent and maintenances of leased property over 5 year term.

8.   Satisfactory assurances to Lyndonville Savings Bank
and Trust Company by legal opinion or otherwise, to the effect,
that the assingment to it of the Program funds and the parties
and amounts to be paid therefrom, will not contravene any applicable
laws of the State of Vermont or [constitute a preference among
creditors of the same class under bankruptcy law or] that such
payments may be subject to being set aside or otherwise voided.

f OND &
C TES, P.C.
'S AT LAW
JER AND
TON
CHER D
VERMONT.

L-6166

Mr. Roger R. Lussier, Pres.
Lyndonville Savings Bank & Trust Company
Lyndonville, Vt 05851

Dear Sir:

In accordance with your request, I have inspected and made an appraisal of the property of Maurice and Marilee Provost located in the towns of Derby, Morgan and Holland, Vt., which were involved in foreclosure action by Lyndonville Savings Bank & Trust Company.

Neither my employment nor fee were contingent on the valuation estimate of this appraisal.

I have appraised farms and rural properties in Vermont and New Hampshire for the past 32 years for the Federal Land Bank of Springfield and the Farmers Production Credit Association of St. Johnsbury.

The indicated market value of the five properties involved after taking into consideration the restrictions placed on them by being signed up in USDA whole herd buyout and the problems and delays of subdividing in Vermont, as of August 11, 1988, is $973,000.

Yours truly,

Franklin Temple

EXHIBIT "A"

AFFIDAVIT

THIS AFFIDAVIT IS FILED IN AID OF ROGER LUSSIER'S JUNE
21, 1994, SENTENCING IN UNITED STATES DISTRICT COURT FOR THE
DISTRICT OF VERMONT, NO.93-50-01.

Under penalties of perjury, the undersigned declares that
at all times relevant to this matter, he was a member of
Lyndonville Savings Bank's Board of Directors ("The Board").

Then LSB President Roger lussier ("Lussier") represented
to The Board that he believed he could obtain approximately
$1,000,000 for the Provost Farms ("The Property"). Accordingly,
The Board said "If you can sell it for $1,000,000 then sell it."
The Board specifically authorized Lussier to obtain no less
than approximately $1,000,000 for the Property and to finance
no more than approximately $800,000 of any such transaction.

ROBERT BEAUSOLEIL
Lyndonville, Vermont

ARTHUR ELLIOTT
Lyndonville, Vermont

DOUGLAS NELSON
Derby, Vermont

JOHN CAMPBELL
Newport, Vermont

DATE   6/14/94

PHILIP BOVEE
St. Johnsbury, Vermont
Director Emeritus

STATE OF VERMONT   )
)
WASHINGTON COUNTY) ss.

AFFIDAVIT
OF
ANDREW R. FIELD

    NOW COMES Andrew R. Field, and after being duly sworn and under oath, deposes and says as follows:

    1. I am a resident of Montpelier, Vermont and have been engaged in the practice of law in Vermont for the past 37 years.

    2. In large measure, my practice of law has involved my representing a number of Vermont banking institutions, private financial corporations, and insurance companies, in documenting and closing large farm, commercial and industrial loan transactions, and the collection and liquidation of such loans.

    3. Beginning in 1985, I represented, from time to time, the Lyndonville Savings Bank and Trust Company (herein the Bank) on documenting and closing many of the Bank's large farm, commercial and industrial loans, and on occasion the collection and liquidation thereof, and in that capacity, I have known and dealt directly with Roger Lussier as President of the Bank.

    4. In criminal proceedings brought by the United States of America v. Roger Lussier in the United States District Court, the District of Vermont, Case No. 93-50-1 , as a result of an indictment that had issued against Roger Lussier, I was listed by

both the government and Mr. Lussier's attorney of record, Peter
Langrock, as a witness who might be called to testify. The
reason for listing me as a possible witness was apparently
because (i) I represented the Bank in documenting and closing
many of the loan transactions that allegedly gave rise to
wrongful conduct on the part of Roger Lussier, with whom, among
other representatives of the Bank, I had direct contact in con-
summating the transactions, and (ii) I was present at a Board of
Directors meeting and gave legal advice as concerns alleged
"kiting activity" undertaken by one "Kelton," which allegedly
also gave rise to wrongful conduct on the part of Mr. Lussier.
Mr. Lussier was subsequently convicted and judgment entered
against him based upon the aforementioned wrongful conduct.

5. Although I was available and willing to appear as a
witness in the aforementioned proceedings, I was never called
to testify, notwithstanding the fact that I could and would have
given testimony based upon personal knowledge most favorable to
Mr. Lussier's conduct, particularly as concerns what became known
as the (i) Provost transaction, (ii) Jolly/Skeet/Aiossa transaction, and (iii) the Kelton Kite. Further, I believe my testimony
based upon personal observations would have also served to effectively rebut that portion of the government's case charging that
Mr. Lussier dominated and controlled the Bank's Board of Directors.

6. I clearly made known to Mr. Lussier's trial attorney the
nature of my testimony; however, for reasons unknown to me, he

never elected to call me as a witness, either on direct or in rebuttal, nor was I, understandably, never called to testify by the government.

7.   I attended the relevant testimony stage of the trial sitting in a motel room, not far from the courthouse. The one comment made by Mr. Lussier's trial attorney to me at the time was that he feared the government's attorney would, in effect, have a field day, as it were, in conducting a "devastating" cross examination of me as the Bank's "general counsel," who as such should have been aware of various internal Bank matters concerning Mr. Lussier, and he then demonstrated the same by a rapid-fire series of "let's pretend" questions, with no time for answers shortly after which I left the motel, but not before expressing my utter amazement to trial counsel that after all the time in preparation of the case, he had not yet discovered or grasped the fact that the Bank was only one of many financial institutions I represented in documenting and closing loans, that I was never general counsel for the Bank, or for any bank, nor did I have any familiarity of the day-to-day internal workings of the Bank and its officers; hence, for any examiner to portray or examine me as though I was general counsel to the Bank would have been error made manifest and demonstrably a display of ignorance of facts on the part of the examiner and a matter of embarrassment before a jury.

Dated at Barre, Vermont this the 31st day of July, 1996.

_____
Andrew R. Field

Sworn to and subscribed in my presence by Andrew R. Field, this the 31st day of July 1996.

Before me,

_____
Notary Public

UNITED STATES COURT OF APPEALS
FOR THE DISTRICT OF VERMONT

UNITED STATES OF AMERICA   )
)
v.   )   CRIMINAL CASE NUMBER 93-50-01
)
ROGER LUSSIER,   )
      Defendant   )

AFFIDAVIT OF ANDREW R. FIELD

I, Andrew R. Field, Esq., being duly sworn, hereby depose
and state as follows:

1. I am a licensed attorney in the State of Vermont and have
practiced law in Vermont for the past 37 years.

2. My practice of law has concentrated in representing a number
of Vermont banking institutions, private financial corporations,
and insurance companies in a variety of business and commercial
matters.

3. Beginning in 1985, I represented the Lyndonville Savings Bank
and Trust Company (hereinafter "LSB") from time to time on a
case-by-case basis. My representation of LSB concerned documenting and closing farm, commercial and industrial loans made
by LSB, and the collection and liquidation of these same types
of loans. Thereafter, around 1990, I represented LSB before
the FDIC as concerns certain "cease and desist orders" proposed
to be issued by the FDIC.

4. Through my representation of LSB, I generally dealt directly
with Roger Lussier in his capacity as President of LSB.

5. In view of my having represented LSB in documenting, closing
and liquidating certain mortgage loans, I was listed as a
potential witness by both the Government and the Defendant in
the criminal matter of United States v. Roger Lussier, Docket
No. 93-50-1

5. Prior to the commencement of the criminal trial of Roger Lussier, I had not met with Roger Lussier's attorney, Peter Langrock, to discuss my testimony or the facts of the criminal case.

7. After the Government closed its case-in-chief in the criminal trial of Roger Lussier, Peter Langrock finally met with me toward the end of the Defendant's case-in-chief, and at the place of trial, to discuss my testimony in the above-captioned criminal case. At that time, I informed Attorney Langrock in substance, that I would testify, among other matters that appeared to be relevant, that:

(a) I closed the Provost loan for LSB and subsequently provided legal services to LSB in liquidating the same; further, during the liquidation period, Roger Lussier, in my presence and in the presence of the Provost principals and others, stated that he would help the Provosts to reacquire their farm homestead, but that his primary concern and goal was to make sure that LSB was made whole and did not suffer any losses whatsoever in the matter.

(b) Roger Lussier did not dominate members of the LSB Board of Directors; on the contrary, board members did not hesitate to disagree with him on a number of occasions.

(c) I was present at Board of Directors' meetings in which the Kelton check-kiting problem was discussed.

(d) I gave legal advice to the Board of Directors regarding handling of the Kelton check-kiting problem, namely the decision whether to file an apparent crime report.

(e) I was present at Board of Directors' meetings in which the Aiossa FDIC "cease-and-desist" order was discussed.

(f) I gave legal advice to the Board of Directors regarding handling of FDIC "cease-and-desist" orders, including that invovling Aiossa.

(g) I alone documented and closed an LSB commercial loan known as the "Jolly-Skeet" loan, in which closing one Aiossa did not participate as local counsel or otherwise for the borrowers, nor was he a necessary party thereto except that a corporate resolution of an out-of-state co-maker appeared to have been drafted by Aiossa and was delivered by the co-maker at the closing. To my knowledge, Roger Lussier was not aware of any involvement by Aiossa in the loan transaction, nor was there any discussion concerning Aiossa between myself and Roger Lussier.

8. Based upon my experience as a lawyer and personal involvement, it is my opinion and belief that my testimony would have been relevant and probative in raising a reasonable doubt as to Roger Lussier's allegedly criminal actions with regard to the Provost loan, the Kelton check-kiting problem, and certain related transactions and issues.

9. I was present and available for testimony during the criminal trial of Roger Lussier. During the course of the trial, as stated in paragraph 7. above, Attorney Langrock briefly met with me and stated, in substance, that he did not intend to call me because the Assistant United States Attorney may conduct a "devastating" cross examination of me "as LSB's general counsel."

10. I have never been the LSB's general counsel, or the general counsel of any banking institution, and have never represented to any person that I am or have been LSB's general counsel.

11. Attorney Langrock's statement to me that I would be subject to "devastating" cross-examination as LSB's general counsel indicated to me that Attorney Langrock did not understand the actual factual nature of the transactions that were the basis for the criminal charges. Attorney Langrock's statement also indicated to me that he did not understand my position or role with respect to LSB's banking business as concerns relevant matters that were the subject of the criminal proceedings against the Defendant, Roger Lussier.

Dated: January 9, 1997

_____
Andrew R. Field, Esq.

STATE OF FLORIDA)
ST. LUCIE COUNTY) ss.

Personally appeared before me the above-named Andrew R. Field and made oath that the foregoing statements made by him are true and correct to his own pesonal knowledge

_____
Notary Public
Kevin J. Smith

- 2 -

MEMORANDUM

24 November 1993

TO: Roger Lussier File

FROM: MLP

RE: Conversation with Noel Lussier, November 24, 1993

****

This morning I had a three way conversation between Rick Davis and Noel Lussier. Rick represents Noel in connection with the Federal Indictment. Noel has pled guilty to four counts and claims to have an agreement with the government that they will not call him as a witness against Roger. He did however, sign a stipulation of facts in connection with his own case that contains material about the Provost transaction. Interestingly, he did not plead to counts involving the Provost transaction, nor are either Provost or Rowell part of Noel Lussier's indictment.

Noel indicated to me that when Dick Davis was alive he had been inclined to "fight the bastards" but has run out of money and lost his patience or inclination to fight the thing. He said he wanted to get it over with.

Noel sounds much like Roger on the phone and indicated he wanted to do anything he could to help Roger. I told him that it was unlikely we would want him as a witness but Noel said that he would be willing to testify for Roger if we wanted.

ROWELL

According to Noel, Roger was going to go to the Passumpsic Bank to borrow the money necessary to pay the Chittenden. Noel convinced Roger to go to Caledonia National Bank (in Danville) despite the fact that Roger had done no business with them in quite some time. Noel said that the Board had discussed Roger on several occasions and had asked Noel to try to get some of Roger's business because it knew Roger and thought he would be a good customer. Noel thinks that the Board had pre-approved Roger a substantial line of credit prior to the Rowell application, even though Roger had never asked the Bank to do so, merely as an enticement to get some of Roger's business. Noel was able to convince Roger to go to Caledonia, in part, because Caledonia had recently hired Robert Platka, who Roger liked.

According to Noel, Noel went with Roger to the Bank to secure the $355,000 loan. The application process was handled by Judy Nudd, who is on the government's witness list. Noel says he was either in the room with Roger and Ms. Nudd or in and about the Bank during this time. Noel said that he had authority to approve loans in that amount and that such loans would not have required any other approval. He does not know whether Roger told Ms. Nudd explicitly the purpose of the loan, but says that everyone knew that he and Roger were partners on the Rowell matter and thinks it would have been obvious what the purpose of the loan was given the circumstances under which Noel and Roger came to the bank.

Noel says the loan was paid off with no loss to the bank.

Noel also stated that Roger could have gone to any bank he wanted and certainly did not need to pay a "bribe" to anyone. Noel also indicated, as is obvious, that he put considerable amount of time and expense into the auction itself, which was run by Noel Lussier, Inc. Thus any profits he made were legitimate profits and not a "bribe."

PROVOST

Noel says he has told the following to Paul Van De Graaf, but he "just does not believe me".

Noel concurs with Roger's view of the transaction, in general. He says that he had been discussing the deal with Pinky Provost for some time and spent several days looking at the land. Because LSB wanted a substantial down payment, among other reasons, Noel was ready to back out of the deal until Roger offered to loan him personally the $100,000. According to Noel, Roger told Noel that he (Roger) really needed this to go through to get the Bank out of a bad position and that he thought Noel could make money on it. According to Noel, Roger told him that if he couldn't sell some of the parcels, Roger would buy them and thus Noel believed he was in a no lose situation.

Noel entered the joint venture agreement with Pinky which was drafted by Aiossa with Pinky represented by Bill Davies. Pinky was adamant that he did not want to lose any money, and wanted to be paid on his $150,000 (approx.) second mortgage to Moe. Accordingly, the agreement provides that all losses will be sustained by Noel, but that Noel would get two/thirds of the profit. Noel is clear that the reason he was to get two/thirds of the profit was because he was assuming all risk of loss.

Noel then says that he spent three to four weeks of his time promoting the property and even set up an office there to do so. He said they were very lucky in selling parcels for substantial profit.

With regard to Noel's payments to Roger, Noel says that Roger had been good to him on a number of different matters and that "it was just time to divvy up". Noel is clear that the amounts paid were not quite one-half of his profits on the

Provost deal, as Noel had drawn other funds from the joint venture for his own use of which no payments were made to Roger. Noel says that Roger had done quite a bit of work taking care of family, had given family parties, and had let Noel use his plane in connection with the Maine land deal. Also, there was no separate interest payments on the $100,000 loan.

Noel is clear that there was no agreement ahead of time to pay Roger in connection with the Provost deal. However he says that Aiossa, Matt Lussier, and Jack Howard (who was a real estate broker with Noel) may have gotten the impression that Roger was involved. Noel is sure that he never told any of these individuals that Roger was involved, but also says that he never told them that Roger was not involved. Aiossa, Howard and Matt Lussier on the government's witness list.

EXHIBIT "A"

AFFIDAVIT

THIS AFFIDAVIT IS FILED IN AID OF ROGER LUSSIER'S
JUNE 21, 1994, SENTENCING IN UNITED STATES DISTRICT COURT
FOR THE DISTRICT OF VERMONT, NO. 93-50-01.

Under penalties of perjury, the undersigned declares
that at all times relevant to this matter, he was a member
of Lyndonville Savings Bank's Board of Directors ("The
Board").

Attached to this affidavit is a true and accurate
copy of a document from the files of First National Bank
of Vermont. This document was a Government Trial Exhibit.
The Government's purpose in submitting this document was to
demonstrate that Lyndonville Savings Bank made an improper,
indirect loan to Anthony J. Aiossa. The undersigned disagrees
with the testimony of FDIC Examiner Charles Paquin. Mr.
Paquin testified that the attached document was shown to
The Board in connection with Douglas Jolly's application
for a loan. However, the undersigned states that Jolly
never submitted the attached document to The Board. Moreover,
the undersigned did not see the attached document until 1994.

FAY YOUNG   6/14/94
Lyndonville, Vermont

CHARLIE HOWE   6/15/94
Colchester, Vermont

ARTHUR ELLIOTT   6/16/94
Lyndonville, Vermont

I do not recall ever having seen
the Anthony Aiossa loan payoff
document.
JOHN CAMPBELL   6/15/99
Newport, Vermont

ROBERT BEAUSOLEIL   6/15/94
Lyndonville, Vermont

November 8, 1998

Mr. Thomas Clohessy   Phone: 516-676-5839
Something Great Productions   Fax: 2605
9 High Meadow Court
Old Brookville, NY 11545

If there are 850 men here there are at least 845 stories with at
least 845² gradients of bullshit. If one listens carefully, checks,
reads, re-checks, and allows a compassionate gut-reaction to drive
reason - there are 4 or 5 people and/or situations that boggle the
mind and are clearly beyond any semblance of human decency.

The facts, background, and "personage" do not, in these cases,
resemble the minimal expectations I hope we all share regarding
justice in a democracy. The particular story that I am highlighting
to you is a least a dramatic example of prosecutorial and judicial
abuse, where facts and reality become twisted beyond recognition.
Seemingly well-intentioned processes became twisted and David not
only gets crushed by Goliath - he is treated to heart-wrenching,
expensive, mindless, necrophilia.

The "story" reads like fiction. Unfortunately, the human being is
very non-fiction. He is here, has been here, or on his way here,
for a long time. His life, and other's, have been ravaged beyond
repair. But, like some Melville character, (Billy Budd?) he stands
proud; will not lie; believes in his country, democracy, and justice;
and wants to be heard, not just for himself, but, to prevent others
from suffering the same fate.   The man himself is a real, live,
"Noble Man". What happened, may in the end, be best understood
by the Wall Street Journal article (enclosed). Maybe it's a sureal
example of culture-clash. Careful study has moved us to use
"Kafkaesque" as apt characterization.

What I am proposing here is providing a forum on up-scale TV news
or "News Magazine" for this story. We all owe something to this
victim - and the message could artfully stimulate some belated
justice for him, and might - just might - expose a juggernaut
that people are starting to realize has become a danger to a demo-
cratic nation and consciousness.

We have spent a good deal of time with this story. Fortunately,
the necessary resources for this project are abundant at Allenwood
FPC.   We have plenty of time, access to Roger Lussier, Roger's
trust and confidence, and a rather volumnious amount or rather
carefully arranged documentation.

With that in mind, here is a brief overview of "the story."

     In September of 1993 the USA indicted/charged Roger Lussier
with some 20 counts of bank fraud with a potential of earning him
$5 million in fines and up to 120 years in jail. Basically, these
charges involve perceptions/realities (?) of "self-dealing", that

these"suspect" activities occurred while Mr. Lussier playedaa
leading role in creating a highly-competitive, rural-user-
friendly, successful banking operation, is a story by itself.

The Lyndonsville Savings Bank (LSB) received national
attention for its successes in making fiscal opportunities available
to a historically underserved (and perhaps discriminated- against)
population. That this enterprise became competitive with the more
conventional banking networks and systems most probably fostered
a "lurking risk" for the citizen, farmer, auctioneer, yankee
entrepenuer, who has, for 40 months, bunked at "camp fed."

His trial, conviction, and sentencing are curious and sinister.
Access to competent counsel, exculpatory evidence, due process, so
on and so on -- were not operative forces in this situation. Yet,
Roger maintained his innocence.

The Goliath, called the US Justice Department, the FBI, FDIC,
ect. rumbled on. By the time he was convicted, in a trial that
was farcial in the cruelest of senses - he was only left with his
pride and the will to appeal.

Strangely, even this, Rule 33 (appealing for a new trial),
2255 (right to appeal based on inadequate counsel), and ex post
facto request for "compassionate release", failed.

His legal representation went from the worst to F. Lee Bailey -
who was preoccupied with his own problems and dropped the ball over
the issue of restitution -- the momentum and the evil was, seemingly,
too powerful.

The attention his case commanded was very interesting. Victims
proclaiming that they were'nt and aren't victims. Witnesses who
were claimed to be witnesses, never made to appear, and denied
Rogers guilt in sworn depositions.

Truely,(it goes on and on) amazing:(so does Roger) Certainly
wise befond his presentation. but just as certainly a natural,
gentle, honest yankee -- and a citizen of the country that let some
of its miscreants destroy him.

We are "proferring" a sampler of some of the documents. The man,
you have to meet.

We have briefly commented on each item of the sampler to help
organize your interest and thoughts.

The "index-sampler" is attached to the front of the package of
documents.

Mr. Lussier has authorized us to send you these documents which
constitute the "tip of an iceberg". He understands their potential
use by you and will makethe iceberg and any other information
available to you through his son.

> David Lussier   802-626-9541
> Box 892
> Lyndonville, VT. 05851

David has been apprised of the project and will receive a copy of this.

An absolute must in this situation, to capture the justice/injustice involved is to share time, thoughts and feelings with Roger. It and he, are dramatic and, if artfully presented, representative of what America shouldn't be...or become.

Sincerely

(signature)   *(signature)*

(Mike Knoph)   (Bern Anderson)

I have been aware of this project from the beginning. This information is as it was presented to these individuals and I have contacted my son as they have stated.

(signature) _____November 8, 1998

Roger Lussier

UNITED STATES DISTRICT COURT
FOR THE DISTRICT OF VERMONT

UNITED STATES OF AMERICA,	)	
	)	
v.	)	Criminal Case No.: 93-50-01
	)	
ROGER LUSSIER,	)	
	)	
Defendant	)	

AFFIDAVIT OF DAVID TURNER

I, David Turner, being duly sworn, hereby depose and state as follows:

1. I, David Turner, am a resident of Vermont, and previously was the Vice-President and Manager of the Derby, Vt. branch of the Lyndonville Savings Bank (*hereinafter* LSB);

2. On July 3, 1986, I was present on behalf of LSB to handle the Trust Agreement between LSB and Richard Provost, dated July 3, 1986;

3. On August 11, 1988, I was present on behalf of LSB to handle the Purchase and Sale Agreement between LSB and Richard and Regina Provost which was closed on September 1, 1988;

4. I testified before a Federal Grand Jury on July 9, 1992 and April 22, 1993, transcripts of said testimony are attached as Exhibit A and Exhibit B respectively and are incorporated herein by reference;

5. I met with FBI Agent McGinnis and Assistant United States Attorney Van de Graaf and discussed my knowledge and the facts of this case prior to my testimony before the grand jury;

6. On other occasions, I met FBI Agent McGinnis and discussed my knowledge and the facts of this case;

7. I have reviewed the Government's Motion for Continuance dated December 3, 1993, and the transcript of telephone conference regarding the Motion for

Continuance which was held on December 1-2, 1993. The Motion for Continuance is attached as Exhibit C and incorporated herein by reference. The transcript of the telephone conference is attached as Exhibit D and incorporated herein by reference;

8. The Government's Motion for Continuance (Exhibit C) misrepresents what my testimony would have been if I had been called as a witness;

9. If I had been called as a witness, I would have testified contrary to the Government's representations contained in Exhibits C & D;

10. If I had been called as a witness, I would have testified, in substance, that

    (a) Roger Lussier was not a participant in the Provost transaction;
    (b) Roger Lussier did not have an interest in the Provost transaction;
    (c) The joint venture in the Provost transaction involved Noel Lussier and Richard Provost;
    (d) Roger Lussier did not set the price of the land sold in the Provost transaction;
    (e) I have no knowledge of any false entries in LSB's records;
    (f) I completed the Provost loan based upon my knowledge of the approval of the Board of Directors of LSB, my conversations with Directors other than Roger Lussier, and an affidavit of the LSB Board of Directors.

12. I was never contacted, in advance of trial, by Attorney Peter Langrock or any person acting on behalf of Attorney Peter Langrock.

DATED: _1-8-97_   _David M. Turner_

                                       David Turner

STATE OF Vermont
Caledonia County, SS. Town of Derby   _David Turner_

    Personally appeared before me the above-named David Turner and made oath that the foregoing statements made by him are true and correct to his own personal knowledge.

                                         Notary Public/Attorney-At-Law

UNITED STATES DISTRICT COURT

DISTRICT OF VERMONT

United States of America,   )

       Plaintiff,   )

)

       v.   )   Cr. No. 93-50-01

)

Roger Lussier,   )

       Defendant.   )

Roger Lussier,   )

       Petitioner,   )

)

       v.   )   Cv. No. _____

)

United States of America,   )

       Respondent.   )

SWORN DECLARATION OF DAVID TURNER

1). That I am David Turner, previously Vice-President and Manager of the Derby Branch of the Lyndonville Savings and Trust Company, of Lyndonville.

2). That I am the David Turner who appeared before the Federal Grand Jury on July 9th, 1992; and April 22, 1993.

3). That I am the David Turner who was described by the Government as an essential witness, critical to and the only witness present at events alledged in Counts 1 through 6, and 20, of the charges against Roger Lussier, and I am the person described as David Turner in the Memorandum at Law filed by the Government on December 3rd, 1993, and the person who was subject to the government's statements regarding my importance in their case against Roger Lussier, when the Government argued for a continuing motion prior to trial on December 1st and 2nd, by phone and in court before Judge Billings.

4). That I associate and recognize my previous testimony as true as offered in the above accounts, that I agree with the government in it's assertions that I was the only person present and party to the events the government

- 1 -

4). (continued) claimed within my knowledge in it's attached copy of the Memorandum at Law, filed with the Court.

5). But that I deny and have no knowledge that would have allowed the government to portray my probable answers in these matters as they have described them.

6). And that I believe that the government relied upon my sudden illness to present to the Court information that the government knew to be contrary to what I had provided them in the meetings with the Grand Jury; and in personal interviews and meetings with FBI Agent McGinnis and US Attorney Van de Graff. That the representations made to the court, unknown to me until October of 1996, are directly contradictory to my information and testimony and do not reflect the facts known to me, they contradict the information provided in interviews with the US Attorney, and they distort the written records regarding the "Provost" loans, the authority for payments, the ownership of funds, and they allow the government to describe these events in ways that are absolutely untrue to fact, contrary to the written records and memory of these events, and allow an uninformed person to conclude guilt and suggest fraud when none occurred.

7). That the narrative presented by the government in it's opening statements and concluding statements at Mr. Lussier's trial did not reflect the events of the "Provost" deal known to me and would have been contridicted by my testimoney were I able to have attended trial.

8). That the US Attorney correctly informed the court as to my importance to a just understanding of these events at trial; but that he himself knew, or should have known, that the testimony he offered as mine in his memorandum would have contridicted his conclusions that he offered the Court, that I would have denied what he concluded I would affirm, and I do not know why he presented such inflated and extreme conclusion to the court; as to be assumed to be my knowledge.

9). And that I was not interviewed by him or his office following my recovery, and never provided any copy of our mutual meeting notes or "302s" to correct or sign. Yet I met with the US Attorney at his office immediately before the trial.

10). That my understanding of the "Provost" deal is contained in this continuing narrative and is made part of this statement:

10). (continued) "... that were I called to trial I would have said then and I do say that my understanding and memory of the details of the "Provost" deal, also affirmed by the quoted and attached records, is that..."

A. That in 1985 Mr. Provost began to get into financial difficulties as milk prices dropped. At that time he owned the Lyndonville Savings Bank about $1,500,000. He sought the advice of Attorney Jerry Diamond who recommended that Mr. Provost consider bankrupcy. The attorney to whom he was referred requested $100,000 up front; Mr. Provost said that if he had money like that he would pay his bills rather than hire an attorney.

B. Lyndonville chose to work with him and attempted to avoid bankruptcy. If bankruptcy could be avoided, all secured parties could be paid and this was accomplished by working closely with Mr. Provost, attorneys and the bank. To accomplish this Mr. Provost, and Lyndonville entered into the attached agreement of July 3rd, 1986, titled TRUST AGREEMENT, signed by Maurice Provost, Marylee Provost, and DAVID TURNER, VP., on behalf of Lyndonville Savings Bank and Trust Co. This TRUST AGREEMENT and a Letter of Intent and Assignment, also signed by Maurice and Marylee Provost, on May 15th, 1986, (attached) among other things that Lyndonville would operate as an Agent and Trustee for the Provost agreement:

1. All monies would be assigned to Lyndonville, including the whole-herd buyout.

2. Identified obligations and allowed Lyndonville to disburse the funds, including money from sale of real estate.

3. Amended the mortgage to provide for acceptance of $725,000 by LSB, to take back property if there is a default, to not default the whole-herd buyout agreement, identified proposed disbursements, and changed the time table for paying the shortfall, and allowed for any renegotiation necessary with creditors. This (par. 12) required $95,000 additional fees paid to creditors in 1989 to retain contract and avoid loss of $1,250,000 to LSB.

4. This agreement provided detailed provisions covering several pages of provisions for the TRUSTEE to act to the interest of LSB or the Provost interests. This included the right to advance funds on behalf of this effort.

5. And that this TRUST relationship shall <u>continue</u> and remain in force and effect for the time necessary to accomplish this agreement, beyond the year 1986. This is the foundation document of the relationship, but to my memory it was not introduced or discussed as an authorization for subsequent actions.

C. Following this agreement the government, independent of any cause related to LSB, suspended Provost from the whole-herd buyout program, resulting in severe cash flow problems. There were several attempts to resolve this conflict before LSB was forced to foreclose upon this property.

D. Within the methods stated in the TRUSTEE AGREEMENT quoted above, LSB began discussions regarding sale, with the assurance to the Provosts that the bank's interest, as agreed, would be for LSB to be paid in full,

D. (continued) and if no other creditors would pay the bank off then they could have the real estate for what the bank was owed including interest, late fees, etc.

E. That on the 11th of August, 1988, I was present to witness a "Purchase and Sale Agreement" between LSB and Richard and Regina Provost to buy the listed property, to pay $994,619.29 for it, to close before September 1st, 1988, with Attorney Field. As part of the agreement Noel Lussier was added to personally and unconditionally guarantee payment of said note involving some of the property in Canada, if LSB could not collect the money at a Canadian court. There were documents signed on August 10th, 1988, outlining the schedule for payments by Obligors and Noel Lussier that I was a signature witness to completion. (attached)

F. On August 2, 1989, I witnessed a document signed by LSB and Richard Provost, accepting $95,196.73 received by LSB from the Canadian land sale, but paid to Provost as a result of the signed Agreement of the 10th of August, 1988.

G. The LSB was paid in full, including fees and attorney charges. For Provost there remained cash on deposit as security and the diversion check balance, after final LSB charges, returned to Provost as the contract of 1986 required.

11). Contrary to statements in the government's Memorandum of Law filed December 1st, 1993, I state that I do not know that Roger Lussier was a secret participant in the Joint Venture. To my knowledge the Joint Venture was Noel Lussier and Richard Provost. I have never seen any agreement saying he was.

12). Contrary to statements in the government's Memorandum of Law filed December 1st, 1993, I do not know that Roger Lussier set the price of the land sold.

13). Contrary to statements in the government's Memorandum of Law filed December 1st, 1993, I do not know that Roger Lussier steered other LSB property to the Joint Venture.

14). That contrary to the statements in the government's Memorandum of Law, filed December 1st, 1993, I do not know that Roger Lussier created false entries in LSB's records.

15). Contrary to the statement on page 6 of the government's Memorandum of Law, filed December 1st, 1993, I have seen and believe the signed Affidavit of five members of the LSB Board of Directors giving direction and permission for Roger Lussier to sell and place a loan for the Provost Farms.

16). Contrary to the statement on page 7 of the government's Memorandum of Law, filed December 1st, 1993, I would testify that the payment to Northern Ag. was authorized under the terms of the Purchase and Sell agreement.

17). In response to the statement on page 7 of the government's Memorandum of Law, filed December 1st, 1993, I would state that I completed the loan based upon my knowledge that the Directors had approved this. This knowledge is based upon conversations with other Directors and the above mentioned Affidavit of Directors.

Executed under the pains and penalties of perjury pursuant to 28 USC § 1746 this _19th_ day of November, 1996, at _Newark_ , Vermont

David M Turner

DAVID TURNER

At _Derby_ , Vermont, this _29th_ day of November, 1996, David Turner, personally appeared and acknowledged this instrument, by him sealed and subscribed to be his free act and deed.

Before me _Dale A. Guerin_

Notary Public

My commission expires
_2/10/99_

- 5 -

UNITED STATES DISTRICT COURT
DISTRICT OF VERMONT

Lyndonville Savings Bank and Trust Company., Plaintiff,	))))	
v.	))	Civil Dkt. No. 95-CV-287
Roger Lussier and Evelyn Lussier, Defendants.	)))	

AFFIDAVIT OF DAVID TURNER

The undersigned, DAVID TURNER, hereby states the following to be true based on my actual knowledge of the circumstances surrounding the activities of the Lyndonville Savings Bank and Trust Company during the time relevant to the above captioned matter.

1. I have been an employee of the Lyndonville Savings Bank ("the Bank") since 1981. I am presently the Bank's Vice President. During my entire career with the Bank I have worked out of the Bank's Derby, Vermont branch office.

2. If asked, I will testify that I am the person who referred the *Palmisano, Beauregard, Roberts* and *Jolly* loan proposals to the Bank's full Board of Directors. This would occur whenever a particular loan request exceeded my personal lending authority and that of the Derby Advisory Board.

3. I would often attend meetings of the Bank's full Board of Directors. I personally witnessed and often responded to the questions of individual Board members. I would characterize the Board as very independent.

1

4. I personally witnessed Roger Lussier presiding over many Board meetings. At no time did I ever witness Roger Lussier strong-arming, manipulating or attempting to unduly influence the decision making function of the Board.

5. To me, the Board acted in a manner that is consistent with what a reasonable person would typically expect a responsible Board to act.

Executed under the pains and penalties of perjury pursuant to 28 U.S.C. § 1746(1) this _13_- November, 1995.

DAVE TURNER

AFFIDAVIT of

DAVID TURNER

NOW COMES DAVID TURNER, and after being duly sworn and under oath, deposes and says as follows:

(1). In criminal proceedings brought by the United States of America v. Roger Lussier in the United States District Court, the District of Vermont, Case No. 93-50-1, as a result of an indictment that had issued against Roger Lussier, I was named as a witness who might be called to testify for the government.

(2). That on November 30th, 1993, I suffered a heart attack and the government was informed I would be unavailable for at least two weeks and "absolutely will not be able to testify for at least a month". [1.]

(3). That I am the David Turner identified in a Memorandum Of Law in Support of the Government's Motion to Postpone The Trial. [2.] That motion, filed on December 2, 1993, requested a delay in trial that was to begin on the next day and requesting a delay until early January, 1994. In that document filed with the Court the government described me as "an essential witness" [3.] It further stated through 11 pages that my testimony "occupied a central place in the facts underlying three of the six events"; that I could testify that "Roger Lussier was a secret participant in the Joint Venture, that Lussier set the price of the land sold...that he steered other property to the Joint Venture, and that he created false entries in LSB's records to cover up his actions." [4.] I was further identified as the sole witness who can testify to most of this information. [5.]

The above named document filed with the Court was heard in open hearing, and denied. Only during the week of October 20th, 1996 did I see and read the document argued as to my importance and as to my probable testimony by James Gelber, Assistant U.S. Attorney, and lead Attorney, Assistant U. S. Attorney Paul Van de Graaf. In this document each of the charges against Roger Lussier, as to be affected by my testimony was identified and my conclusions offered.

AFFIDAVIT OF DAVID TURNER, continued, page two

(4).That I was unable to participate in the trial; but if I
had been able to participate my testimony would have been to deny
the positions and knowledge alledged to me by the government.
In reference to the pages of the named document I would have and do
deny the conclusions proposed for me by the government on page 2;
as to the creation of a false document on page 4; as to the Provost
Scheme on page 5, 67, and as to "E" of page 8. This material and
the statements anticipated by the government only came to my knowledge
as stated during, October of 1996, and the conclusions offered in
them as they anticipate my testimony are denied as true to my
knowledge.

(5).That the government presented me as their "essential witness",
"obviously crucial to the jury's understanding of the Provost scheme",
"crucial to establishing Roger Lussier's use of his power as LSB
president, an essential witness under the Speedy Trial Act, and
that I (he) "alone handled a number of aspects of those transactions.
For these reasons, Mr. Turner's testimony is essential to the
Government's proof at trial," is their assessment of the importance
of my testimony. I have no ability to make their assessment as other
than they stated: essential!

(6). Were I to have been able to testify during the trial,
I would testify to deny the statements proposed for me by the
government.

(7). My knowledge of these events would be favorable to the
accounts offered by Roger Lussier as true and reflecting the actions
and motives that moved these events.

Dated at. Lyndon, Vermont, this day the 1st of NOVEMBER, 1996

David M Turner

DAVID TURNER

Sworn to and subscribed in my presence by David Turner, this 1st day
of, November , 1996.   Before me,

Attc: footnote page

UNITED STATES DISTRICT COURT
FOR THE DISTRICT OF VERMONT

UNITED STATES OF AMERICA,	)	
	)	
v.	)	Criminal Case No.: 93-50-01
	)	
ROGER LUSSIER,	)	
	)	
Defendant	)	

AFFIDAVIT OF ARTHUR ELLIOTT

I, Arthur Elliott, being duly sworn, hereby depose and state as follows:

1. I, Arthur Elliott, am a resident of the State of Vermont.

2. From 1985-1993, I served as a Director of the Lyndonville Savings Bank and Trust Company (hereinafter "LSB").

3. During my tenure as a Director, the Board of Directors approved the Provost loan, the Collonade loan, the Rowell loan, and handled the various issues posed by the Kelton check-kiting scheme.

4. During my tenure as a Director, I participated in various events relating to the Provost, Rowell, Collonade, and Kelton transactions.

5. During my tenure as a Director, I participated in ratification of loans to Carol and Alfred Kelton.

6. At the time of Roger Lussier's indictment, I was represented by Attorney Peter Langrock in a lawsuit in which Roger Lussier was also a defendant. The lawsuit was entitled, *Guillmette, et al. v. Elliott & Lussier*, Washington County Superior Court docket no. s600-92.

7. Attorney Langrock's representation of me in the lawsuit began on or about September 22, 1992.

8. Attorney Langrock continued to represent me until May 11, 1994, which was subsequent to Roger Lussier's trial and conviction.

9. *Guillmette, et al. v. Elliott & Lussier* arose out of Roger Lussier's and my capacities as directors of LSB. Since the lawsuit was related to our service on the Board of Directors, LSB paid for our representation by Attorney Langrock and LSB controlled the litigation.

10. I have no recollection of meeting with Attorney Langrock or anyone acting on behalf of Attorney Langrock with respect to the criminal charges against Roger Lussier or the possibility of my being called as a witness at the criminal trial of Roger Lussier.

11. Prior to, and following the conviction of Roger Lussier, Special Agent McGinnis of the Federal Bureau of Investigation met with me frequently. S/A McGinnis repeatedly told me that Roger Lussier was "going down," and that if I did not cooperate with the government, my life would be made a "living hell."

12. I believe that S/A McGinnis was aware that I was represented by Attorney Langrock in the civil case of *Guillmette, et al. v. Elliott & Lussier.*

13. During this time period, I also met with Assistance United States Attorney Paul Van de Graaf regarding the criminal case.

14. Prior to and following Roger Lussier's criminal trial and conviction, it was my understanding that I may be charged with crimes arising out of my service as a Director of LSB.

15. If I was called as a witness at the criminal trial of Roger Lussier, I would have testified, in substance, that:

    a. Roger Lussier was not involved in the Collonade transaction prior to the approval of the loan by the LSB board;

    b. Roger Lussier was not a silent or secret partner in the Collonade transaction prior to the approval of the loan by the LSB board;

    c. Roger Lussier did not influence, or attempt to influence, the decision of the LSB board with respect to the Collonade transaction loan;

    d. Prior to consideration of the Collonade transaction loan, I fully disclosed my interest in the Collonade loan to the LSB board;

    e. Roger Lussier never controlled or dominated the Board of Directors of LSB;

f. The Directors of LSB were independent-minded people who exercised their own judgment and discretion in loan and business decisions.

16. To the best of my knowledge, Roger Lussier never carried out an official act on behalf of LSB without the board's full approval, and always acted in the best interests of the bank.

17. To the best of my knowledge, Roger Lussier and the entire Board of Directors acted conscientiously and in the best interests of LSB and its stockholders.

DATED: ___1/11/97___   _____
                                           Arthur Elliott

STATE OF Vermont
Caledonia County SS. town of Lyndon   Arthur Elliott

Personally appeared before me the above-named Arthur Elliott and made oath that the foregoing statements made by him are true and correct to his own personal knowledge.

                            _____
                            Notary Public/Attorney-At-Law

rv. 3-10-82)

- 1 -

FEDERAL BUREAU OF INVESTIGATION

Date of transcription   3/31/93

        DOUGLAS G SKEET, white male, date of birth, July 18
1940, place of birth, Buffalo. New York, Social Security Account
Number 097-30-9215 was interviewed, at his request, in the
presence of his attorney, PHILIP H. WHITE of Montpelier, Vermont
and Assistant United States Attorney (AUSA) PAUL J. VAN DE GRAAF
at the United States Attorney's Office for the District of
Vermont, Burlington, Vermont. After being advised of the
identity of the interviewing Agent, SKEET provided the following
information:

        SKEET stated that he currently resides in Rochester,
New York and is a school principal within the Greece School
District in Rochester, New York. In this regard, SKEET advised
that he is the principal at the Apoll Middle School, 750 Maiden
Lane, Rochester, New York 14615, telephone number (716) 865-1000,
and added that he could be contacted at extension 2100.

        Regarding his investments in the State of Vermont with
K. DOUGLAS JOLLY, SKEET stated that he became aware of JOLLY
through another principal within the Greece School District,
Rochester, New York by the name of BILL CLICQUENNOI. SKEET
remembers CLICQUENNOI referring to JOLLY as the "Vermont Cow
Man", referring to several investments JOLLY had in Vermont
dealing mainly with farms and cattle. Prior to investing in the
State of Vermont with JOLLY, SKEET advised that he purchased and
rented out apartments for investment purposes however, as this
investment began to take up a lot of his personal time, he
decided to invest in other ventures with JOLLY.

        Prior to investing with JOLLY in the State of Vermont,
SKEET was aware that CLICQUENNOI was involved in short term
investing with JOLLY. Through CLICQUENNOI, SKEET advised that he
became aware of the Chase deal and Marine deal, and these deals
pertained to investments in dairy farms and cattle in the State
of Vermont, whereby JOLLY would be buying out cattle and
returning pretty good money to investors. SKEET added that he
did get involved with JOLLY prior to investing in Vermont by
granting money and/or personal notes to JOLLY as investments.

_____

ation on 3/11/93 a _____   at Burlington, Vermont   File # 29B-AL-34828 _____
                    29B-AL-34838, 29A-AL-31328, 29B-AL-3438, SUB 4

SA CHARLES MC GINNIS, JR./vep _____   Date dictated 3/17/93 _____

-AL-34828

tion of FD-302 of ___DOUGLAS G. SKEET_____ . On ___3/11/93___ . Page ___2___

SKEET stated that when he began investing in the State
of Vermont with JOLLY, he was getting a very nice return on his
investments up until January, 1991. In this regard, SKEET stated
that he received between 20 % to 25% as a profit on his investments, and had heard through other associates in the Rochester,
New York area that investments with JOLLY resulted in a 30% to
40% return.

SKEET became concerned in January, 1991, when he
stopped receiving profits on his investments with JOLLY in the
State of Vermont. SKEET explained that he had used tax sheltered
annuities and had borrowed money to invest with JOLLY, and had
lost many tax benefits and paid severe penalties for withdrawing
funds to invest with JOLLY. When his profits stopped in January,
1991, SKEET explained that he was in financial difficulty and
money became tight due to other loans and commitments he had with
financial institutions. As an explanation for no return on his
investments, SKEET explained that JOLLY told him that it was
because of new bank regulations as a result of the S & L
failures, and SKEET was told by JOLLY that since several of the
financial institutions throughout the country had gone "belly
up", so did the opportunity for JOLLY to make a profit on his
investments in the State of Vermont. SKEET also remembers that
JOLLY stated to him that young bank regulators were causing a
problem with his investments, and remembers JOLLY talking about
the banks "up north" or "northern banks". In this regard, SKEET
advised that this was the first time that JOLLY had mentioned the
LYNDONVILLE SAVINGS BANK AND TRUST COMPANY (LSBTC), Lyndonville,
Vermont as a financial institution with which he had an
affiliation in the State of Vermont. SKEET remembers that JOLLY
told him that once the "heat" was off with the banks in Vermont,
the restructuring of farm loans could be begin and profits could
be once again returned on investments in Vermont.

SKEET went on to explain how JOLLY had planned to restructure investments in the State of Vermont, and specifically
listed four separate phases which JOLLY told SKEET would
eventually return the original money invested by SKEET. SKEET
remembers that as the phases increased, JOLLY told him that more
money would be invested, more investors would become involved and
both JOLLY and SKEET would be made "whole". In this regard,
SKEET advised that the restructuring plan began in May, 1991, and
in August, 1991, JOLLY and SKEET obtained a loan in the amount of
$775,000.00 from LSBTC. SKEET advised that he was told by JOLLY

?9B-AL-34828

tinuation of FD—302 of   DOUGLAS G. SKEET   . On   3/11/93 . Page   3

that this was first of four phases in the restructuring plan. SKEET remembers that JOLLY told him that the second phase would occur within two or three weeks of the signing for this loan at LSBTC, and at that time all of the money invested by SKEET would be returned. SKEET stated that by signing for the loan at LSBTC he would receive $50,000.00 cash, and in addition, a CD in the amount of $100,000.00, put up as collateral for this loan at LSBTC, would be given to SKEET in the second phase of the restructuring plan thereby returning all of the original investment money to SKEET. However, SKEET advised that phase two never took place, and that phases three and four, involving the purchase of farms and cattle in Florida and Vermont, possibly involving NOEL L. LUSSIER, never occurred.

SKEET advised that in the Spring and Summer of 1991, after the returns on his investments stopped, he began to talk to JOLLY about the plan to restructure. Up until this time, SKEET stated that he thought JOLLY owned the farms and cattle that he had invested in. However, SKEET learned that JOLLY was a broker and merely passing on the money made for being involved with the purchase and sale of cattle. In addition, SKEET advised that he became aware that JOLLY held second, third and fourth positions on several mortgages and not first positions as was explained to him. SKEET stated that he was rather confused when he became aware of this situation, inasmuch as in 1989, he had invested $25,000.00 and received $30,000.00 from JOLLY, and in addition, remembers investing $50,000.00 and receiving $60,000.00 in return from JOLLY. More specifically, SKEET remembers that in 1989 he invested $100,000.00 with JOLLY and received $150,000.00 in return and added that his return amounted to approximately $5,000.00 per month.

SKEET stated that when the $775,000.00 loan from LSBTC was obtained, he was of the understanding that this loan was obtained to make SKEET "whole". SKEET described his initial contact with LSBTC as beginning in May, 1991, when he submitted paperwork to LSBTC while the loan with JOLLY was being processed. However, the first time SKEET had personal contact regarding the loan obtained from LSBTC was on the evening of the closing for this loan, which occurred in the law office of Attorney ANDY FIELD in Montpelier, Vermont. Prior to this closing, SKEET stated that the only person he discussed this loan with was JOLLY. Based upon the discussions with JOLLY, SKEET understood that the loan was to refinance assets in which both he and JOLLY

29B-AL-34828

tinuation of FD-302 of __DOUGLAS G. SKEET_____ . On ____3/11/93__ . Page ___4___

had an interest, and in addition, to acquire income producing investment property. SKEET believed that security for the loan consisted of a first mortgage on the SMOKE HOUSE HILL FARM, which is a 100 acre farm located in Salem, New York, and in addition, thought security agreements had been reached concerning cattle, crops and farm equipment. SKEET stated that he was told by JOLLY that he would receive $50,000.00 in cash and a $100,000.00 CD, which was put up as collateral on the note, would belong to SKEET during the second phase of the restructuring plan. SKEET remembers that he and JOLLY were to purchase 200 cows for approximately $200,000.00 and lease these cows to the HAMILTON BROTHERS FARM, which SKEET learned was in bankruptcy and efforts were underway to re-structure the finances of the farm as well. SKEET remembers that he was under the impression that the cows would be purchased from MARCEL ROBERTS, however, learned that the cattle were purchased from an individual by the name of STANLEY MCLENITHAN who had himself purchased the cows from MARCEL ROBERTS.

SKEET advised that approximately four weeks prior to the interview he had received a telephone call from ROGER R. LUSSIER, who was in Florida at the time. SKEET remembers that LUSSIER was looking for JOLLY and attempts to contact JOLLY had been negative. Therefore, LUSSIER was inquiring of SKEET where JOLLY could be located. During the conversation, SKEET advised that LUSSIER told him that he, LUSSIER, was having problems with the "feds" regarding the $775,000.00 loan obtained from LSBTC. SKEET remembers that LUSSIER told him during this telephone conversation that proceeds of the loan went to ANTHONY AIOSSA in violation of a Cease and Desist Order issued by the Federal Deposit Insurance Corporation (FDIC). SKEET stated that LUSSIER told him that he, LUSSIER, did not know that any of the proceeds went to AIOSSA during the time the loan was processed, presented before the Board of Directors at LSBTC and approved.

SKEET remembers that when this loan was closed in the late evening at the office of FIELD in Montpelier, Vermont, the atmosphere was rather helter, skelter, and documents were being exchanged back and forth between participants because they were not correct or needed to be changed. SKEET remembers that the closing was rather chaotic, and being late at night, SKEET felt that this was a rather unusual way to close on a $775,000.00 loan. SKEET advised that those in attendance, in addition to himself and FIELD included JOLLY and ROGER R. LUSSIER. SKEET

!9B-AL-34828

stated that FIELD took complete control of the closing and that
ROGER R. LUSSIER played a lesser role that evening. SKEET
described FIELD as being rather assertive at the closing and had
all the documents in order and correct prior to signing. SKEET
felt that it was rather unusual that this loan was being closed
with no loan officers representing LSBTC being in attendance.

Regarding the 200 head of cattle leased to the HAMILTON
BROTHERS FARM, SKEET later learned that this farm was run by a
father, son and two uncles, who were in their early sixties.
SKEET also learned that the HAMILTON BROTHERS FARM refinanced
their farm with JOLLY, and as a commission for this refinancing,
heard that JOLLY obtained approximately 300 acres of farm
property. As a result of the refinancing and JOLLY receiving 300
acres, SKEET heard that the HAMILTON BROTHERS FARM held a clean
note on remaining balances owed. In this regard, SKEET learned
that the HAMILTON BROTHERS FARM owed JOLLY approximately
$150,000.00 and JOLLY held a lien on farm equipment to secure
this money. SKEET was of the belief that this farm equipment was
"clean" and that the $150,000.00 was put up as collateral for the
note he obtained with JOLLY. SKEET advised that the cows were
leased to PAUL HAMILTON and SKEET, and the payments per month to
LSBTC totaled approximately $9,000.00. SKEET admitted during the
interview that he had no idea of his role in leasing these cattle
or how the cattle would be handled. SKEET remembers receiving
calls from JOLLY and subsequently faxing documentation to ROGER
R. LUSSIER for approval of releasing a certain amount of money
for these cattle. SKEET does not ever remember. receiving
receipts from STANLEY MCLENITHAN for the purchase of the cattle
which were currently on the HAMILTON BROTHERS FARM. In this
regard, SKEET stated that the first time he met STANLEY
MCLENITHAN was in July, 1991, when SKEET first visited the
HAMILTON BROTHERS FARM in Salem, New York.

SKEET advised that in July, 1992, he was contacted by
DAVID TURNER, the Vice President of LSBTC, assigned to the Derby
Branch, regarding the fact that no money had been paid to LSBTC
regarding the loan with JOLLY. SKEET remembers that he then
called JOLLY, and JOLLY explained to him that there was a problem
with the WHITMAN FEED COMPANY which was charging double payments
for supplies. In addition, SKEET remembers that JOLLY told him
there was a problem with milk receipts involving the coop. JOLLY
explained to SKEET that there was a problem with a name change at
the coop, and therefore, checks were not being assigned

'B-AL-34828

ₐₐₜᵢₒₙ of FD-302 of   DOUGLAS G. SKEET   , Oₙ   3/11/93 , Pₐgₑ   6

correctly. SKEET thought this was a rather flimsy excuse to note. In addition, SKEET was aware that milk production was down at the HAMILTON BROTHERS FARM, even though the same number of cows should have been producing milk at the time. SKEET was under the impression that the milk production was down due to the fact that he, SKEET, believes that JOLLY sold off some of the cattle that were being leased at the HAMILTON BROTHERS FARM. In this regard, SKEET stated that he called JEFF LOURIE at a farm located in West Rupert, Vermont, to inquire about any reason why milk production would be down on HAMILTON BROTHERS FARM. SKEET explained that LOURIE was a nephew of JOLLY. After discussing the situation with LOURIE, SKEET stated that LOURIE told him that it would make sense that if the cows were sold from the farm, that milk production would be down. SKEET remembers mentioning to LOURIE that ROGER R. LUSSIER was under "heat" regarding the note that SKEET and JOLLY obtained from LSBTC. SKEET advised that LOURIE told him that proceeds from this loan went to pay off a note at the FIRST NATIONAL BANK OF VERMONT located in Spring-ᶦield, Vermont and that this bank is affiliated with NOEL L. ᴸSSIER. SKEET admitted that this was the first time that he had heard that proceeds from the loan he obtained with JOLLY paid off a note at the FIRST NATIONAL BANK OF VERMONT.

SKEET advised that within the last week he has heard that JOLLY has purchased and/or placed an additional 40 head of cattle on the HAMILTON BROTHERS FARM in Salem, New York. In addition, SKEET has received word through JOLLY not to worry about the loan in default at LSBTC and that in fact the loan was covered. In this regard, SKEET advised that he and CLICQUENNOI were traveling to Utica, New York within the next few days to meet with JOLLY and attempt to determine the specific circum-stances surrounding the note which is in default at LSBTC. In particular, SKEET is pursuing the specific information pertaining to the cattle on the HAMILTON BROTHERS FARM located in Salem, New York.

At the conclusion of the interview, SKEET advised that an individual by the name of JIM GOOD of Rochester, New York has also been involved extensively in investments with JOLLY and should be contacted regarding investment schemes that GOOD has experienced with JOLLY.

UNITED STATES DISTRICT COURT
FOR THE DISTRICT OF VERMONT

UNITED STATES OF AMERICA,	)
	)
v.	) Criminal No.: 93-50-1
	)
ROGER LUSSIER.	)
	)

AFFIDAVIT OF PETER LANGROCK, ESQUIRE

I, Peter Langrock, depose and state the following:

1.   I am an attorney and partner in the law firm of Langrock, Sperry & Wool,

P.O. Box 351, Middlebury, Vermont 05753-0351.

2.   I make this Affidavit in support of Defendant Roger Lussier's Motion for

New Trial.

3.   I was lead counsel for Roger Lussier at the trial of the above-referenced

indictment.

4.   I have reviewed FBI 302s, dated 7/14/93 and 7/21/93 purporting to describe

interviews with a cooperating witness (Douglas Jolly) and an FBI 302, dated 3/11/93,

purporting to describe an interview with Douglas G. Skeet.

5.   It is my belief that none of the FBI 302s described above were provided to

defense counsel prior to or during Mr. Lussier's trial.

6.   I have caused a review of our files and have determined that we are not

presently in possession of the FBI 302s.

7.   I am certain that had this material been made available to defense counsel at trial, it would have been used in cross-examining government witnesses regarding exculpatory statements made by Mr. Lussier.

8.   I would probably have called Douglas G. Skeet to testify at trial regarding the exculpatory statements made by Mr. Lussier to Mr. Skeet.

9.   Additionally, advance notice of the exculpatory statements of Mr. Lussier would have influenced our defense strategy.

SINGED UNDER THE PAINS AND PENALTIES OF PERJURY THIS 4th DAY OF NOVEMBER, 1994.

_____

Peter Langrock, Esquire

UNITED STATES DISTRICT COURT
FOR THE DISTRICT OF VERMONT

UNITED STATES OF AMERICA,)	
)	
v.)	Criminal No.: 93-50-1
)	
ROGER LUSSIER)	

AFFIDAVIT OF PETER CHARLES HORSTMANN, ESQUIRE

I, Peter Charles Horstmann, Esquire, depose and state the following

1.   I am an associate attorney with the Law Offices of Bailey, Fishman & Leonard, 66 Long Wharf, Boston, Massachusetts 02110, attorneys for the Defendant in the instant matter and on appeal of his conviction to the United states Court of Appeals for the Second Circuit.

2.   On August 30, 1994, I received copies of Jenck's Act material from Mr. Lussier's trial counsel, Langrock, Sperry & Wool, which was provided to trial counsel by the Government and related to Government witness Douglas Jolly.

3.   On or about September 1, 1994, I received a package of materials concerning Government witness Douglas Jolly which included several FBI 302s which had not been provided to this firm by trial counsel.

4.   Thereafter, I spoke with Mitchell Pearl, Esquire of Langrock, Sperry & Wool, who was co-counsel to Peter Langrock, Esquire at Mr. Lussier's trial, to inquire as to whether there was any additional Jenck's Act material which he had not sent to me.

5.   I subsequently sent copies of three specific FBI 302s, dated July 14, 1993, July 21, 1993 and March 11, 1993, to Mr. Pearl for the purpose of his determining whether he could locate them in his files and to determine whether he had seen them previously.

6.   Mr. Pearl subsequently responded that he could not locate these particular FBI 302s in his files and that he did not recall having seen these reports previously in the material which was provided to him by the Government prior to trial.

7.   On October 14, 1994, I travelled to Mr. Pearl's office for the purpose of reviewing his file.

8.   I reviewed the entire file in Mr. Pearl's possession relating to the trial and could not locate any of the subject FBI 302s in Mr. Pearl's file.

9.   I subsequently spoke with Assistant United States Attorney Paul Van de Graaf about this matter and was advised that the Government would take the position that it had turned over all three of these reports with its pretrial disclosures.

SIGNED UNDER THE PAINS AND PENALTIES OF PERJURY THIS _7th_ DAY OF NOVEMBER, 1994.

Peter Charles Horstmann, Esquire

2

Lyndonville
Savings Bank & Trust Co.

98 Broad Street, Lyndonville, Vermont 05851   (802) 626-8121
Office Of The President

February 24, 1993

To: The Board of Directors
     Lyndonville Savings Bank & Trust Company
     Lyndonville, Vermont 05851

In light of my retirement as President and Chairman of the Board there are
a few things I would like to highlight from the past and a few things that might
be helpful for future days.

It took a year and a half for me to accept the position of Director of
Lyndonville Savings Bank after being asked several times by the Directors of the
Bank during the last part of 1964. The reasons for my reluctance was my lack
of experience and education in the banking field and, at the time, my own business
was taking most of my time. They told me they wanted a Director who had a good
reputation and had the respect of the working people so, in 1966, I became a
Director. In 1976 they asked me to be President and Chairman of the Board. I
refused saying I didn't want it, but again in 1977 they urged me to accept and
claimed it would not take any more of my time than being a Director. I finally
agreed to take the position for three years. Those three years, however, turned
into sixteen.

With the exception of the past year I never worked full time for the bank and
never worked inside the bank at all. The Chief Executive Officer was always in
charge of the internal affairs of the bank as had been the case during the terms
of the last three presidents, Mr. Hopkins, Mr. Pearce and Mr. Russell. As you all
now I gave notice two years ago that I would retire at age 60. Everything was well
planned for my replacement and the entire Board agreed that Charlie Howe would be
my successor. We all know that due to the death of Charlie's wife, plans changed
and I was asked to continue until his children graduated from school at which time
he would take the office. I did so and have no complaints except you all know

The Board of Directors   - 2 -   February 24, 1993

what my wife and I have been through these past two years. *I believe this was uncalled for as my reputation in the State of Vermont was second to none and was the reason my personal business prospered.* I find it difficult to understand why public officials and the press have been so prejudiced against me and have discriminated against me. In fact, have gone out of their way to hurt me and my family to a great degree to the point that many people, including some attorneys, have come to believe these stories to be the truth. I have not pushed the issue as I was President and Chairman of the Board but now that I am retiring and free to think of myself and not just the bank, I will paraphrase what the press has often said, "There may be other charges coming." with "There may be some charges going as well as coming!".

The negative publicity has hurt me both financially and physically and is why I am holding the bank to its agreement for my retirement. I have lived up to my contract. For several years I refused pay raises as, at the time, my business was doing well. I furnished my own car, telephone, secretary and office machines

was always willing to do so. By doing so I felt I was doing all I could to help this bank prosper as I have always done.

On the bright side, I am very proud to have worked with an excellent Board of Directors who all had minds of their own and, despite the feuds that came up occasionally, everyone was working for the sole benefit of the bank. I have asked a lot of you Directors, often "above the call of duty", and none of you have ever failed to do more than your share. That is the reason this bank has been so prosperous. It was the great loyalty and wisdom you have had which has made it so successful. I have great confidence that you will carry on as a great team. I hope my departure will make it easier for you to get along with the regulators.

I believe that Attorney Kilmartin has had a lot to do with turning the F.D.I.C., the Commissioner of Banking and the press against us. He has tried many times to discredit the bank and me personally which has resulted in a grand jury investigation against me. In truth, the investigation should be against him for the frivolous suits he has brought against the bank – the Maxwell case, the Beauregard case, Regina Mead and, of course, John McCormick just to name a few. When you have an over-
icated crook and an overeducated nut with a vicious mind and unknown connections, he can injure many innocent people, businesses and towns.

I feel sad that we were unable to find another C.E.O. and President before my departure. We have worked hard in doing so and I wish you the very best of luck in finding a man that you will be comfortable working with. I feel you will succeed in doing so. This bank has been known to be the workingman's bank and I hope it

To: The Board of Directors   - 3 -   February 24, 1993

doesn't lose that reputation. I believe this bank has served the community well.

I feel we owe Ashley Jewell a lot of recognition for replacing Mr. Thompson as I guess none of us realized as a Board, that Mr. Thompson was not qualified to be a chief executive officer. This created a lot of hard work for Ashley from policies to compliances which we believed were put in place by Mr. Thompson but were not. What bothered me the most was the fact that Mr. Thompson was ordered by the Board to stop cashing checks on Charlie Kelton's uncollected funds but continued to cash them. I twice reminded him and insisted he stop but was obviously ignored.

I know that Mr. Thompson, Marguerite Beane and George Hopkins had a lot to do with the internal management of the bank. Mr. Hopkins was Vice President and a Director but was in the bank almost every day communicating with Marguerite and Tom. He did very little outside the bank as his primary interest seemed to be internal business.

I don't understand why the Government is trying to blame me personally for the problems with Charlie Kelton's checking account. We were the first bank to top him from writing checks even though the other banks should have known better than us what was going on. Several times we called them and were told the checks were good and that Charlie was an excellent customer. As for the Beauregard suit, I'll be glad to help you in any way I can although I don't know very much about them. Mr. Nelson took great pride in bringing them into the bank as a customer and Mr. Hopkins knew Mr. Beauregard's partner. Mr. Bovee and, I believe Pearl Baird, were the ones that found him out of trust on cars. Bob Gensburg is representing us in this case. This makes me a little nervous as he has changed his strategy three times and said he would take the case at $85.00 per hour and is now charging $125.00 per hour. I have my doubts that Mr. Gensburg is qualified to take on such a vicious individual as Attorney Kilmartin. Someone should at least hold him down on expenses as his charges are very unreasonable.

It seems rather odd to me that we have three major lawsuits pending which are three car dealers, each of whom has been in the car business for a long time. It also seems odd that they have all been able to find an attorney with whom to file a lawsuit against this bank because we made them a loan. It should be illegal for attorneys to bring such cases and attorneys representing us are profiting very uch from them. They claim we are insured for such lawsuits, however, I don't feel insurance companies should be ripped off in such a manner as it results in making it harder and more expensive every time to obtain coverage.

As far as Attorney Field is concerned, he has worked hard and with great

LSB 2:40

To: The Board of Directors   — 4 —   February 24, 1993

interest for this bank and has devoted all the time we needed for more than a reasonable price. I have had great comments from the F.D.I.C. on Attorney Field on the quality of his legal work. They have said we were fortunate to have someone who had his excellence in legal documentation. I hope the next C.E.O. will not find it necessary to have any lawyers at all since they are all too expensive.

I have a great personal respect for all the employees as I am sure you all do. They have been especially good during the special investigation by the State of Vermont. I felt the employees were being abused by two of the investigators but managed to put a stop to it by talking to Bill Rockford about it. He told me that if it continued after that day to contact him and he would handle it personally. When I returned to the bank, the investigators were having a "Cookie Party" with the help — but I wasn't offered any!

In regard to Bill Rockford and Dan Way, I have high respect for both of them. We had a lot of conversations over different issues and Mr. Way came several times to my office spending many hours on different issues. One that comes to mind is Mardon Industries. I went through the matter with him from A to Z and told him that maybe I should have handled it differently because of the pressure from the press and from the State. Mr. Way looked me in the eye and said "You handled it exactly the right way." If we had done differently, we would have run into trouble with his department. Mr. Way came to see me after the Kelton Compound auction, the auction the court appointed me to have, and after learning that the expense and proceeds were all for the Bank of Boston and not for Lyndonville Bank, he gave me a clean bill of health. Again, when I bought the Kelton real estate a year later from the Bank of Boston through their broker, Mr. Way came again to see me regarding the status of the situation. When I informed him, he said that everything was professional and legally done. He was very happy about it, patted me on the back and said "That's what I expected". I have not had as good luck with the "new Commissioner". I don't know her race, color, creed, where she was born or how she got to be where she is — but she sure knows all about me!

As most of you know, I was not happy with the Vermont Cease and Desist order and I never voted on it. I was upset with the way it was handled and with the smear tactics used by the Commissioner against us even after accepting their bribe and paying their price for settlement and cost of attorneys. We have nothing to hide and should have gone to trial. Our own attorney said we were clean and the people of Vermont would have then known the truth.

LSB 2:40

To: The Board of Directors   - 5 -   February 24, 1993

Special attention should be given to some of the loans -

One is the Shatney loan in Greensboro. We were slack on this as we thought the Land Trust was going to buy him out. They have not.

I have tried several times to contact Doug Jolly regarding the Jolly/Skeet loan but have been unable to reach him. When I was in Florida I called Skeet who told me Jolly was supposed to bring the note current. Something is beginning to smell about this loan and I feel special attention needs to be given to it.

Ryan's Roundhouse. I have been to Burlington three times to see J & B International Trucking, Inc. They are interested in purchasing the Roundhouse but there is more negotiating to be done. I believe they are qualified buyers. As for Kelton's bankruptcy, that should be settled soon and there should be quite a bit of recovery for L.S.B.

I was informed last weekend by Attorney Field that the Independent Bank Group is trying to foreclose on Greg Lussier's interest in the Florida property and the Wolcott property. I don't understand this as I believe the payments are all current with us. I did inspect the farm and cattle while I was in Florida and everything was in top shape. I guess there is some claim that Independent Bank Group is trying to call it a fraudulent transaction. I don't see that this can legally hurt us as we did demand the money from Noel and Doug Gilmour. They sold to Gregory Lussier and we financed him. I believe this was entirely legal but should have close attention. I'm beginning to believe this country is run on power rather than justice.

There are several other loans that also need attention and I'll be around if you need me. There should be a lot of recovery next year from the charge-off loans as we have been very heavy on them recently.

Mr. Murphy is still interested in Vinton Motors for $900,000. I believe a settlement is getting closer as he had a meeting with the telephone company on February 18th which he said was on the positive side. This has been dragging on for a year because of the E.P.A. inspection of the gas tanks. This was a costly item for the bank but I guess it is beginning to clear up. The telephone company is acting very cautiously. Mr. Murphy is also interested in the Subaru building and there are several other issues that will come up. I will always be willing to help in any way if you would like me to.

I thought I should set some of this down in writing as we have had several threatening calls at my home and office. I feel their bark is worse than their bite but you never know.

To: The Board of Directors — 6 — February 24, 1993

I hope the new President will work as closely with you Directors as I have and will keep you well posted. You can only work as a team if everyone communicates as a team.

I wish you all the best of luck in the days ahead.

Roger Lumm

CONVERSATIONS WITH CHARLES HOWE, CHAIRMAN OF THE BOARD OF LYNDONVILLE SAVINGS BANK & TRUST COMPANY

Wednesday, August 30, 1995

Charlie Howe called tonight after we were in bed. He said he had just heard today that I would be going to prison soon. He was very upset and kept saying "It isn't right. You have done nothing wrong." He kept repeating it. He said he was very sorry and if there was anything he could do to let him know. Just before he hung up he asked me if I had signed the Jasmin releases. I told him I would like to talk to him as I didn't like what the lawyers did. I didn't think it was right, after all that work and expense that we shouldn't have won. We had a winning case. Charlie said he would be up at his camp at Willoughby Lake on Sunday and would like to talk to me.

Sunday, September 2, 1995

I drove up to Charlie Howe's camp at Willoughby Lake in midday. I had a long talk with Charlie and showed him the papers on Jasmin that the lawyers wanted me to sign. I told him that I absolutely didn't approve of it and didn't think that the bank should lose any money on Jasmin. He said "Roger, go ahead and sign it. That's one case we will get rid of." And by doing so they would get along better with the F.D.I.C. I told him I didn't want to sign it unless the bank would give me a full release from it as I had reason to believe that Hale and Dorr were out to get me one way or another and thought that Hale & Dorr would insist on the bank suing me. Charlie said "Roger, the bank is not going to sue you." He said "He owns a lot of stock and all the directors are for you. We all know you have done nothing wrong. They just want to get rid of the suit as it has dragged on and the F.D.I.C. wants some of these cases settled." I told him "Look at these papers" and he admitted it was too broad. I told him I would sign one of the papers to help them out but would not sign the others and he said "Well, that will help us."

Thursday, September 28, 1995

After reading in the morning Free Press about Lyndonville Bank suing me, I called Attorney Gravel and told him about the suit in the Burlington Free Press. He said he tried to get me the night before but couldn't. He wanted to tell me before I read it in the paper but couldn't as it had to be filed in court first and the Free Press picked it right up. I said "Mr. Gravel, what's going on?" I said "You told me that you and Hale & Dorr wouldn't sue me unless you were forced to by the F.D.I.C. He said "Roger, I'm sorry but that's the way thing go. We just had to do it." I asked him "Why?" and "What for?" He said he wasn't at liberty to talk to me – shouldn't talk to me about it but as I was still pro se I could call some of the directors and get some information about it. At 6 p.m. that night I called Charlie Howe, Chairman of the Board, and asked him "What is going on?" I said "I have been cooperating fully on all these lawsuits for the bank at my own expense and gave you guys all kinds of information on these suits but wouldn't have if I had known you were going to sue me." He said the whole board had unanimously voted to sue me. I said "Charlie, just the other day you told me they wouldn't sue me." He said, "I know, but we were pushed into it and the whole board approved it – but I'm sorry." I said "Charlie, you know you're not only hurting me but also the bank and the stockholders for the suits are all frivolous." He said "You may be right, but I hope not." I hung up.

Field & Field, P.C.

Attorneys at Law

59 No. Main Street
P.O. Box 488
Barre, Vermont 05641

Sarah L. Field

Andrew R. Field
of Counsel

Phone (802) 476-8838
Fax (802) 476-4804

April 4, 1995

John C. Gravel, Esq.
Bauer, Anderson, Gravel & Abare
P. O. Box 123
Colchester, Vermont 05446

      Re: LSB - Hammang
           (Mardon Industries, Inc.)

Dear John:

Pursuant to your letter of February 17, 1995, I enclose certain
documents and writings taken from my file, which appear to address
matters sought by you, as well as other matters and news articles
that you might find helpful.

The enclosed covers the GE negotiations and closing, the "Boylan"
aborted transaction, the "Manosh" aborted transaction, and the
"Koster" sale. Joe Palmissano was responsible for having found
Koster and was largely instrumental along with Roger Lussier in
negotiating what was believed to be a most attractive sale price
for the machinery and equipment under the circumstances.

I participated with Charlie Shea in the GE negotiations; however,
Roger Lussier was responsible for effecting the favorable sale
price and terms over a great deal of resistance and pressure put
up by GE and its negotiators. I must say that Roger Lussier's
approach and ability to squeeze out the last dime in a liquidation
of security favored not only the bank, but Mardon Industries as
well, considering that the normal and usual bank and FDIC approach would have been merely to call the default, accellerate
maturity, foreclose the real property and promptly seek possession
and auction liquidation of the personalty. I doubt that other
banks (based upon my experience) would have advanced funds, <u>after
default</u>, to meet payroll, keep the operation going in order to
convert raw material on hand into finished goods and sale at high
prices against existing orders, while negotiating for private
sale of the personalty and realty at the same time. I know,
that as to Koster's purchase of the machinery and equipment, his
and his staff's inspection and observation of all the equipment in

John C. Gravel, Esq.
Re: LSB-Mammang
April 4, 1995   Page 2.

operation producing goods went a long way in effecting the best
possible price for the equipment.

The problem with Jerry Hammang at the time of the takeover and
apparently for some time prior thereto, he simply was not working
nor paying attention to the operation. When the bank agreeably
obtained possession under the UCC, we discovered mail piled up that
had not been opened for weeks. Further, Jerry did not appear to
help or give any input or assistance in effecting the continued
day-to-day operations and subsequent liquidation.

I did not observe any help of any nature being offered by Mrs.
Hammang, even to the extent of helping in simple office services,
although it may be that she could offer nothing. Quite frankly,
both Jerry and his wife seemed to simply disappear (except on
one or two occasions) during operations and negotiations with GE
and others. If Jerry had any expertise in the matter, his input
might have made it easier; fortunately, the "Mardon" supervisors
and foremen appeared to be very helpful and informative as to the
operation, so that negotiations could be conducted based upon a
fair knowledge and understanding.

                          Very truly yours,

                          _Andrew R. Field

ARF:JF
Enc..

P.S.   Please note in your records that I will be absent from
       the State from April 11, 1995 until May 15, 1995.

                          A. Field

Lyndonville
Savings Bank & Trust Co.

98 Broad Street, Lyndonville, Vermont 05851   (802) 626-1111

January 11, 1995

Federal Deposit Insurance Corporation
200 Lowder Brook Drive
Westwood, MA 02090

Attn: Paul H. Wiechman, Regional Director

Dear Mr. Wiechman:

We met with Patricia Cashman and John Lane today at the Vermont Department of Banking and Insurance office to discuss our progress toward resolution of the problems outlined in the recent Report of Examination. During the course of the meeting we raised the point that we are having a very difficult time living within the parameters of Section 337.6(b)(2)(i) of the FDIC Rules and Regulations as to the manner in which we are to determine local market yield for deposit products. During the Examination, it was established that the proper procedure for establishing local market yield was to survey only banks in our CRA area with state charters and to average our results on a product-by-product basis. We find that this methodology has been unduly restrictive in that it does not afford us the flexibility to be competitive and protect our liquidity position. The following are representative of the situations which have contributed to the loss in deposits resulting from our inability to compete effectively:

- o   National banks which are operating in our market are offering money market rates up to 110 basis points above the average of the state chartered banks. As a result, we have lost 16% of our money market deposits in a single month. These deposits belong primarily to our most desirable commercial accounts and are "local".

- o   Banks with state and national charters from beyond our designated CRA area advertise for deposit products in local newspapers. In many cases, they offer products with yields significantly above the average of the local state chartered banks.

- o   We are unable to establish a "market" average for Jumbo CD's. Our competition does not publish or quote rates to other banks. We are therefore effectively excluded from offering this product to attract local deposits.

Lyndonville
Savings Bank & Trust Co.

98 Broad Street, Lyndonville, Vermont 05851   (802) 626-1111

January 26, 1995

Vermont Department of Banking and Insurance
Drawer 20
Montpelier, VT 05620

Attn: Elizabeth Costle. Commissioner

Dear Ms. Costle:

As a follow-up to my letter of January 11 to Paul Wiechman, I have enclosed a copy of a flyer received in the mail by residents throughout our market area. The best rate that we are able to offer for a one year certificate of deposit using the average of state-chartered banks with offices in our market is 6.40 % APY. Our rate includes the 75 basis point margin allowed by the FDIC.

At our meeting on January 11, I mentioned that Community National Bank is paying rates on their money market accounts based upon the 13 week T - Bill rate plus .125%. The current rate being offered is therefore 5.9% on balances in excess of $10,000. The best rate we are able to offer staying within the parameters established by the FDIC is 4.81% APY. Community National is our biggest competitor in the Newport-Derby market.

I am concerned that we are continuing to lose local deposits solely on the basis of rate. The state chartered banks which we are allowed to use in our survey are experiencing soft loan demand and a low loan-to-deposit ratio. They simply do not have the liquidity concerns facing this Bank and therefore do not need to be aggressive in their deposit-gathering effort.

We continue to maintain a strong net interest margin and can justify being more competitive in this market. The FDIC's position on this matter is making it difficult to retain local deposits and has forced us to curtail lending.

We have as yet had no response to our January 11 letter. Any assistance or guidance you can provide in this matter will be appreciated.

Thank you.

Very truly yours,

Charles W. Bucknam, Jr.
President

MEMORANDUM

To: Board of Directors   August 15, 1994

Re: Management Exit Meeting

From· C. W. Bucknam

The management exit meeting for the current examination was held on August 11. Management was represented by C. Bucknam, W. Davenport, and E. Smith. Dave Stahler and Dean Parker each participated in part of the meeting. The FDIC was represented by Pat Cashman, Matt Sosik, and Jeff Salinetti. The Vermont Department of Banking and Insurance was represented by Dick Pettengill.

The following are some of the highlights of the meeting:

Loan Classifications:

Overall loan classifications have been reduced by about $1mm since the last examination. While this trend is positive, the situation remains very serious especially in light of the amount of charge-offs that have been absorbed during the past year. Approximately $1.3mm has been classified "loss" including about $500m attributed to Marcel Roberts, and $526m attributed to Beck and Beck. The Beck and Beck charge offs were taken prior to June 30 and we have been given time to correct weaknesses in the Roberts credit which may reduce or eliminate the amount of loss we have to take on that account.

The comment was made that our lending officers are not identifying weaknesses in their respective portfolios early enough. Island Farm, Inc. was cited as an example. Cash flow for this farm has been negative for two years, yet we have carried it as a "pass" loan.

Underwriting remains a primary concern. The Harold Castine loan with a current balance of $348m was not supported with any financial information, appraisal, or title work.

OREO:

We are being required to write down $623m in OREO. Of this amount, $190m was written down prior to June 30 on the Roundhouse. Also included is $232m attributed to the North Country Motors Building. Market value was established at the July 15 bid opening.

Reserve for Loan Losses:

Examiners concluded that our methodology for determining the ALLL was appropriate; but, we need to beef up the loan review process. Our failure to identify emerging problems in the portfolio causes us to underestimate reserve requirements.

Because of the losses we are being asked to take on OREO and in our loan portfolio, we may be required to amend our June 30 Call Report.

Violations:

Brokered Deposits

We are being cited for numerous violations relating to brokered deposits. Examiners have concluded that as of May 31 we were in violation of the requirement that we not offer deposit rates greater than 75 bp over the average being offered by institutions in our market with "like charters". We have interpreted this broadly to include all banks. The examiners claim that we must interpret the regulation more narrowly so that we include only state chartered banks in our survey. This means, for example, that we should not include Community National Bank rates in our calculations.

Any deposit which we accept that falls outside these parameters will be considered "brokered". This obviously has implications for the special rates that have been offered to some of our larger depositors. In order to protect the Bank from further criticism, we should offer only posted rates to customers.

Appraisals

We have numerous appraisal violations. In some cases, the lack of any appraisal was cited. In other cases, it is simply that the appraisal we procured does not meet USPAP requirements. Examiners recommend that we strengthen our appraisal review process. They also cited a few instances where we did not get the appraisal before funds were advanced. Chaput and Nash were examples.

Criminal Referrals

We were cited for failing to file a referral in the Royal Harrison matter in August, 1993 when we received Harrison's countersuit. Those referrals were filed during this examination.

Title Opinions

We were cited for violating state regulations by not procuring up-dated title opinions. Examiners acknowledged that this situation was corrected early in 1994.

FEB-23-94 WED 14:28   P. 01

FDIC

Federal Deposit Insurance Corporation
Westwood Executive Center, 200 Lowder Brook Drive
Westwood, Massachusetts 02090   • Tel. (617) 320-1600 • FAX (617) 320-1692   Legal Division
                                                                          Boston Regional Office

February 23, 1994

Wendy Davenport
Secretary to the Board of Directors
Lyndonville Savings Bank and Trust Company
98 Broad Street, Box 125
Lyndonville, VT 05851

Dear Ms. Davenport:

This is in response to your telephone request this morning
asking whether it would be a violation of Section 19 of the
Federal Deposit Insurance Act, 12 U.S.C. § 1829, for Roger
Lussier, the convicted former president and chairman of the board
of directors, to attend the annual shareholders meeting which is
due to commence today at 5:00 p.m..

Though there is nothing in Section 19 which on the face of
it would appear to prohibit Mr. Lussier's presence at the annual
meeting, that statute is very clear that the convicted person may
not participate directly or indirectly in the conduct of the
affairs of the bank.

Accordingly, we have no objection to Mr. Lussier's presence
at the annual shareholders meeting, subject to the Section 19
prohibition stated above. Attempting to influence bank policy or
the selection of directors would, in our opinion, constitute
participation in the conduct of the affairs of the bank.

You asked further whether Section 19 would prohibit Mr.
Lussier from selling his stock. Section 19 would not prohibit
such a sale.

If you have any further questions please feel free to
contact me.

Sincerely,

Paul D. Snyder
Senior Regional Attorney

SHEEHEY BRUE GRAY & FURLONG
ATTORNEYS AT LAW

RICHARD W. AFFOLTER
DAVID T. AUSTIN
R. JEFFREY BEHM
NORDAHL L. BRUE
MICHAEL G. FURLONG
WILLIAM B. GRAY
DONALD J. RENDALL, JR.
PAUL D. SHEEHEY
PETER H. ZAMORE

POST OFFICE BOX 66
BURLINGTON, VERMONT 05402
119 SOUTH WINOOSKI AVENUE
(802) 864-9891

BY FACSIMILE
October 10, 1991

Jeffrey B. Rudman, Esq.
Hale and Dorr
60 State Street
Boston, MA 02109

RE: Independent Bank Group; Douglas Gilmour

Dear Jeffrey:

This letter will follow up our telephone conversation on October 8, 1991. I would appreciate your making available to me at your earliest convenience complete copies of all liability insurance policies insuring directors of Independent Bank Group, Inc. and/or First National Bank of Vermont during the period 1976 through 1991, including declaration pages.

In connection with our discussion of Mr. Gilmour's status, I would also appreciate your making available to me any draft complaint or other documents which specify the claims you contemplate asserting against Mr. Gilmour and the factual basis therefor. When we have had the opportunity to review these materials or otherwise hear from you the specific claims you intend to assert against Mr. Gilmour, we will be happy to respond directly to your settlement solicitation.

I look forward to hearing from you.

Very truly yours,

SHEEHEY BRUE GRAY & FURLONG

Donald J. Rendall, Jr.

DJR/slm

cc: Mr. Douglas Gilmour

HALE AND DORR

COUNSELLORS AT LAW

A PARTNERSHIP INCLUDING PROFESSIONAL CORPORATIONS

60 STATE STREET

BOSTON, MASSACHUSETTS 02109

(617) 742-9100

(TELECOPIER)

(617) 367-6333   (617) 742-9308

TELEX 94-0472

MANCHESTER OFFICE
THE NUMERICA BUILDING
3155 ELM STREET
MANCHESTER, NH 03101
(603) 627-7600

WASHINGTON OFFICE
THE WILLARD OFFICE BUILDING
1455 PENNSYLVANIA AVE., N.W.
WASHINGTON, D.C. 20004
(202) 393-0800

October 14, 1991

BY FACSIMILE AND REGULAR MAIL

Donald J. Rendall, Jr., Esq.
Sheehey, Brue, Gray & Furlong
Post Office Box 66
119 South Winooski Avenue
Burlington, Vermont   05402

Re: Independent Bank Group

Dear Mr. Rendall:

This will acknowledge receipt of your facsimile letter dated October 10. That letter is not, in my view, consistent with our October 8 conversation. My belief is that you were to propose to me suggested ground rules for your client's cooperation with IBG and the individual banks in forthcoming litigation in exchange for not being named as a defendant in that litigation. Instead, you have asked me for certain documentary matter, including insurance policies.

Your request for those documents is hereby declined, although I will consider making available for your inspection relevant directors' and officers' insurance policies. Those policies will, I believe, persuade you that your client will be entirely without coverage in any litigation brought against him by IBG and/or its subsidiary banks.

To the extent that your client has in his custody, possession or control any documents reflecting any transaction between him and any of IBG's subsidiary banks or the Lyndonville Savings Bank, I hope and expect he will preserve those documents, as well as any documents describing any transaction involving him and Messrs. Lussier (Noel and Roger), Kelton, Gallerani, Platka and/or Gray.

Donald J. Rendall, Jr., Esq.
October 14, 1991
Page 2

    To the extent that any documents reflecting transactions with the above-named persons or entities are lost or destroyed after your receipt of this letter, we will ask that any tribunal reviewing these transactions draw inferences adverse to your client.

Very truly yours,

Jeffrey B. Rudman

JBR:mbm

Off. & Dir Leaving Bank:

Directors:

Fay Young	12/1/93	Resigned
A Elliott	10/6/93	Resigned
J Campbell	11/15/95	Fired
F Oeschger	9/21/94	Resigned
W Bartley		Resigned
B Beausoleil	1/12/94	Resigned
J Poulin	11/15/95	Resigned (then went back on)
J McClaughry	7/19/00	Fired

Officers:

A Jewell	Mar 93	Resigned
C Barrows	Oct 93	Resigned
R Hartley	Jan 94	Fired
W Rockford	Jan 94	Resigned
L Cleveland	Aug 95	Forced Resignation
J Kennison	Aug 95	Fired
M Bailey	Aug 95	Fired
W Davenport	Aug 95	Forced Resignation
D Turner	Dec 95	Fired
D Yates	99 or 2000	Resigned
C Willis	2000	Resigned(Mgr Newport Office)
S Gates	2000 0r 01	Resigned
Mike Claflin	"	Resigned
Charlotte Simpson	2001	Forced Resignation
Nancy Cass		Resignation
Sue Roberts		Resignation

To: Board of Directors   November 29, 1995

Re: David Turner

From: C. W. Bucknam

The Board of Directors voted to bring suit against Roger Lussier in September. A complaint was filed with the U. S. District Court in late September. On September 27, I notified our entire staff that we had taken this action and advised that the matter should not be discussed while in litigation "either inside or outside the Bank". This point was again emphasized at our monthly officers' meeting in October. On November 13, David Turner signed an affidavit in support of Roger Lussier which was filed with the court on November 20.

His action amounts to a wanton disregard for my instructions. Further, it places the Bank in an untenable position. We cannot have a member of our own officer staff working to undermine our efforts in a case as critical as this one is to this Bank.

I recommend that Turner be terminated immediately.

FDIC

Federal Deposit Insurance Corporation
Vestwood Executive Center
100 Lowder Brook Drive, Westwood, Massachusetts 02090   (617) 320-1600   Boston Regional Office

November 22, 1994

Board of Directors
Lyndonville Savings Bank and Trust Company
98 Broad Street
Lyndonville, Vermont   05851

Dear Board Members:

Enclosed for your confidential use is the Joint Report of
Examination, prepared by FDIC Examiner Patricia I. Cashman and State
of Vermont Examiner Richard L. Pettengill as of the close of business
June 6, 1994. Please note pages 1 through 8 constitute the core
section of the Report and the supplemental pages which follow are
provided as additional information in selected areas. We have also
enclosed the June 28, 1994, Electronic Data Processing Examination
prepared by FDIC Examiner Franklin Gray, III. It is requested that
these reports be reviewed and signed by each director and at your next
Board meeting a record of the action taken thereon be entered upon the
minutes. You are reminded that the report, composite rating and the
contents of this transmittal letter are subject to the confidentiality
restrictions embodied in Part 309 of the FDIC rules and regulations.

Report of Examination findings (Report), outlined in summary
comments on pages 1.1 through 1.10, discloses a continuation of an
unacceptable financial profile. The bank has not fostered meaningful
remedial action to eliminate unsafe and unsound practices identified
in previous Reports and addressed in five Cease and Desist Orders
(Orders).

Asset quality deterioration continues unabated as the Board and
management have been unable to resolve problem loans and identify
emerging credit weaknesses. Unacceptable underwriting and monitoring
practices have resulted in classified loan levels which exceed 20% of
the portfolio. Additionally, $2.6 million in Special Mention loans
contain lending weaknesses that should be remedied in a timely manner
to reduce the bank's exposure. Despite repeated criticisms,
inadequate loan files prevent realistic financial analysis and risk
assessments which are the foundation of loan analysis and the loan
valuation reserve methodology. Accordingly your staff's inability to
properly analyze and grade problem loans rendered the reserve
inadequate by $1.4 million. Operating losses have resulted from
excessive nonperforming asset levels, a low yielding investment
portfolio, other real estate writedowns and holding costs, credit
losses, and a high cost of funds. Future profitability appears remote
considering the level of balance sheet risk. Underestimated loan loss
provision expenses invalidated your profit plan which should be
revised to reflect realistic financial projections.

Board of Directors   -2-   November 22, 1994

Regulatory capital ratios have been maintained through asset shrinkage; however, the lack of positive earnings, poor asset quality, and the excessive volume of pending litigation impairs capital adequacy.

Excessive reliance on volatile out-of-territory deposits as funding sources and a decline in liquid assets has strain liquidity. Steps must be taken to reduce the bank's dependence on high cost funding, increase the level of liquid assets, and develop a crisis liquidity plan.

The Report details numerous weaknesses in the development and adherence to approved policies, internal controls deficiencies, and apparent violations of laws and regulations. Policy criticisms and apparent violations are repetitive in nature. The Board is reminded that violations of banking law and noncompliance with the Orders could result in the assessment of civil monetary penalties up to $1 million per day.

Examination findings note continued substantial noncompliance with three of the five Orders. In view of your failure to remedy identified unsafe and unsound banking practices and the bank's severely depressed financial condition, continuation of the Orders is warranted. In future written quarterly progress reports under the Orders, you should respond as though all references are to the June 6, 1994, Report of Examination. Specifically, classified asset action plans should be revised to incorporate classified assets listed in the examination report and the examiners' criticisms regarding the quality of workout strategies.

We have reviewed your request to execute a cross-collateralization agreement with Mr. Marcel Roberts in exchange for a six month foreclosure moratorium. Based on submitted materials and conversations with President Bucknam, this office interposes "no objection" to this workout strategy provided the forbearance period is limited to four months.

The findings of the concurrent Electronic Data Processing Report of Examination are also of serious concern. Some of the policies and procedures required by three specific provisions of the February 12, 1992, and February 25, 1993, CEASE AND DESIST ORDERS have not been met. Inadequate segregation of duties, an inactive steering committee, and no formal strategic plan are a portion of the deficient administration of your data processing department. These and the other exceptions are detailed in the report of examination. Failure to correct these areas not only reflects unfavorably on the directorate and management, but could effect the integrity of the data processed, the uninterrupted operation of the data processing department, and potentially the bank's capital.

In accordance with FDIC policy instituted on January 1, 1978, this letter will provide you with notice that the bank is again being formally designated a PROBLEM BANK due to its condition as reflected in the examination report. This notification is designed to enhance bank director's awareness of, and involvement in, the FDIC's supervisory efforts and to increase the effectiveness in such efforts.

Board of Directors   -3-   November 22, 1994

The Board is reminded that because the bank is in a "troubled condition" as defined under Section 303.14 of the Corporation's Rules and Regulations, the FDIC and the Commissioner of Banks (Commissioner) must be given thirty (30) days prior written notification of any addition or replacement of a member of the Board or the employment or change in responsibilities of any individual to a position as "senior executive officer." Also, since the bank is identified as being in a "troubled condition," the Board must recognize that the Federal Deposit Insurance Corporation has the authority to prohibit or limit certain forms of benefits to institution affiliated parties (golden parachute agreements) under Section 18(k) of the Federal Deposit Insurance Act. Furthermore, the bank is designated as an "adequately capitalized insured depository institution" under Section 337.6 of the FDIC's Rules and Regulations, effective June 16, 1992. Therefore, the bank may not accept, renew, or rollover any brokered deposits without the prior written permission of the FDIC. Additionally, the bank may not provide "pass-through" deposit insurance coverage to participants in or beneficiaries of certain employee benefit plan deposits unless the bank has provided proper notification in writing to participants or beneficiaries.

We request that the consideration of the contents of this letter be appropriately noted in the minutes of your next regularly scheduled Board meeting or a special Board meeting held to discuss the enclosed Report of Examination. Please submit a written response to all issues raised in this letter and the Report of Examination by January 16, 1995, indicating all corrective actions taken or planned. We are particularly interested in the steps taken to correct the deficiencies in the bank's lending polices and collection practices and steps taken to strengthen staffing. We would also appreciate President Bucknam keeping us informed as to the pending litigation. A copy of your response should be sent to the Commissioner of Banking, Insurance, & Securities Elizabeth R. Costle. Please address any questions or comments you may have to either Assistant Regional Director John V. Lane or Review Examiner Roger L. Bennett.

Sincerely,

Paul H. Wiechman
Regional Director

Enclosure

cc: Honorable Elizabeth R. Costle
      Commissioner of Banking,
        Insurance, & Securities
      State of Vermont

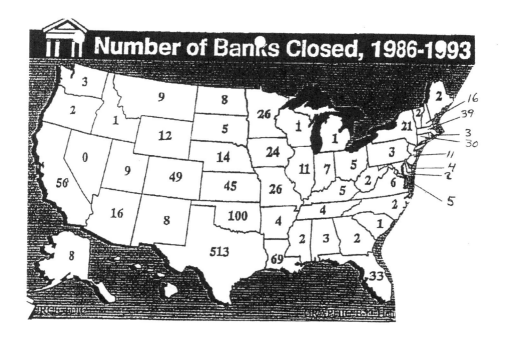

Number of Banks Closed, 1986-1993

Reprinted from the Wall Street Journal, November 29, 1993

Review & Outlook
A Banking Story

Treasury Secretary Lloyd Bentsen talks about dropping barriers to interstate banking, and that has some people worried that the days of the small town banker are numbered. But we suspect somebody will always be able to make money lending on a handshake and local knowledge, provided of course that Washington doesn't smother them in regulatory folderol. Consider the troubling case of Roger Lussier and Vermont's Lyndonville Savings Bank.

There's no doubt that Mr. Lussier wore a lot of hats. Besides being the bank's chairman, he invested in real estate deals and sold off foreclosed properties through his own auctioneering service. Mr. Lussier grew up on a nearby dairy farm and never got past the eighth grade. Even so, when he retired in February after 27 years, he left behind one of the best capitalized and most consistently profitable small banks in the country.

In September, the U.S. attorney in Vermont charged Mr. Lussier with 20 counts of bank fraud. If convicted, the charges carry $5 million in fines and 120 years in jail.

John McClaughry, a state senator who joined Lyndonville's board of directors after the events in question, attributes the charges to a clash of cultures. He cheerfully describes Lyndonville as a "junk bank," making risky loans at high interest rates to farmers in Vermont's hardscrabble Northeast Kingdom. "Roger doesn't fit the FDIC profile of a banker with a Wharton degree and a three-button vest," he tells us.

Vermont is a "strict foreclosure" state, meaning a bank selling foreclosed collateral not only can recoup its loan and expenses but legally keep any additional profit. Mr. Lussier, in our reading of the indictment, comes across as somebody who tried to liquidate bad debts on better terms that these for his borrowers.

The indictment accuses him of "secret self-dealing" and depriving the bank of "honest services" in his treatment of dairy farmer Maurice Provost. What happened was that the bank foreclosed on Mr. Provost's $1 million mortgage and then turned around and sold some of the property to a partnership involving Mr. Lussier, his brother, Mr. Provost and Mr. Provost's father. Later the partners resold the property for a $300,000 profit.

It's worth noting that Mr. Provost's problems began when the Agriculture Department withheld payments that were due under its herd buyout program, and Mr. Lussier helped save his business. "The bank got paid in full," Mr. Provost tells us. "My gripe is with the government. They want to indict Roger Lussier and make him look as bad as they can. But he went out on a limb to help people, more that other banks would."

Also figuring prominently in the indictment are the troubles of farm-equipment dealers Hollis and Maurice Rowell. The Chittenden Bank was about to foreclose on their $350,000 mortgage, and Mr. Lussier agreed to pay off the debt and oversee and orderly sale of their land, eventually bringing in $2 million. For their troubles, Mr. Lussier and his brother pocketed $200,000 in commissions.

Columnist Sam Hemingway of the Burlington Free Press uses words like "appalling" and "infamous" to describe Mr. Lussier's business dealings. He says the banker "orchestrated the squeeze play" against the Rowells.

That's not how the victims see it. "We were in a dire situation and Roger Lussier did exactly what he said he would do," Hollis Rowell tells us. "I've always been satisfied in any dealing I've undertaken with him."

Mr. Lussier is accused of aiding and abetting the misdeeds of Charlie Kelton, Vermont's biggest auto dealer until he went spectacularly bust. But the U.S. attorney offers no theory for how it would have benefited Mr. Lussier to let Mr. Kelton get away with kiting checks at Lyndonville. All the other cases show Lyndonville profiting from Mr. Lussier's dealings, which isn't surprising since he's one of the biggest shareholders.

Maybe something truly scurrilous is lurking in the closet, but right now Mr. Lussier's main offense appears to have been a failure to observe Washington's rococo conflict-of-interest fetishes. At the time the government was developing the case against him, New England still languished under the heel of the FDIC's Jimmy Loyless. Mr. Lussier's bank made money because he could sniff out reliable characters among potential borrowers. But in the FDIC's myopia, loans should be made the big-bank way, with your nose buried in the rule book. There ought to be a role in here somewhere, on all sides, for judgment.

There's no doubt that Vermont's banking establishment views Mr. Lussier as an unfortunate throwback to the days when cattle dealers ran the state's rural banks. "The regulatory mood in Washington changed, but he didn't change with the times," says one. Of course it's exactly this new regulatory mood that threatens to run small-town banking off a cliff.

In the wake of an S&L fiasco, the compliance headaches imposed by Washington now up 28% of overhead for a Lyndonville-size bank, compared with 9% for Citicorp or Chase Manhattan. Vermont's chief banking regulator, Elizabeth Costle, while no fan of Mr. Lussiers, complains that Congress has inflicted "a maze of paperwork and regulation."

We'd like to think the private sector could still make a living financing entrepreneurs instead of socking deposits into T-bills. But first Washington will have to get over its S&L neurosis and give bankers permission to act like bankers again.

DIRECTORS MEETING

September 12, 1995

A special meeting of the Directors of Lyndonville Savings Bank and Trust Company was held in the Derby Office of the Corporation in Newport/Derby, Vermont, on Tuesday, September 12, 1995 at 1:30 p.m.

The following Directors were present:

Charles Howe, Jeff Poulin, David Stahler, Winston Bartley, Dean Parker, John Campbell and John McClaughry.

Charles Bucknam and Daniel Yates were present during all of the meeting.

Also present for the entire meeting was Richard Johnston, Esq. of the law firm, Hale & Dorr

This special Board meeting was called for the purpose of meeting with Attorney Johnston to discuss the strategy to be employed to secure payment of the $426,000 from Roger Lussier as required under his criminal conviction; and whether to bring suit against Lussier for other losses attributable to him. The recent denial of Roger Lussier's appeal, the recent settlement of the Jasmin litigation, the status of other Lussier-related cases currently being defended by the Bank, and statute of limitations concerns suggested that timing was appropriate for decisions to be made on these issues.

Following discussion about strategy, scope, and ramifications of such action, Jeffrey Poulin moved that the Bank, through Hale & Dorr, working with Bauer, Anderson & Gravel, bring suit against Roger Lussier for all losses incurred by this Bank that are attributable to his wrongful actions while President and Chairman of Lyndonville Savings Bank. The motion was seconded by David Stahler and all members of the Board voted in favor of the motion, with the exception of John Campbell who voted against the motion.

The Board next considered a request by CNA Insurance, the Directors and Officers Liability carrier from 1988-1992, to hold them harmless for any further delay in acting to rescind those policies. CNA has claimed that the denial of the Lussier appeal strengthens CNA's position that CNA is entitled to rescind the policies. CNA has indicated a willingness to defer rescission and participate in settlements of existing lawsuits providing that the Bank agrees not to take advantage of future delays in rescission. CNA, as part of the agreement, will agree not to take rescission action at this time. This proposal by CNA is a tolling agreement that benefits the Bank in that it will preclude having to incur costs of litigating rescission at this time, and will provide the bank and CNA with the opportunity to investigate settlement options in the cases at hand. In addition, the Bank will retain the right to argue, in the case of rescission, that it was already too late as of the date of the tolling agreement to rescind the policy.

Upon a motion duly made and seconded, it was unanimously

VOTED: To authorize Richard Johnston, Esq. to enter into such an agreement with CNA on the Bank's behalf.

Mr. Johnston advised the Board that the completion of the settlement of the Jasmin case has been delayed because of Roger Lussier's decision not to sign a release for the Jasmins. The Jasmins have now insisted that the bank provide them with an indemnification agreement to protect them should they be sued at a later date by Lussier. The directors discussed the advisability of settling the Jasmins' claims even if such an indemnification agreement is necessary.

Upon a motion duly made and seconded, it was unanimously

VOTED: To enter an indemnification agreement with Jasmins holding them harmless in any action brought against them by Roger Lussier relating to the case being settled.

There being no further business, and upon a motion duly made and seconded, the meeting was adjourned at 4:55 p.m.

--------------------------------- ---------------------------------
Chairman   Secretary

Bank Growth

Year	Assets	Net Pretax	Tax pd	Div pd	Inc in Cap	Capital	LL Res	Cap&LLR	RRL Income
1964	6,334,260	32,499	0	14,250	18,249	585,550	111,380	696,940	
1965	6,817,877	40,839	1,967	15,000	23,873	609,433	121,784	731,217	875
1966	7,265,039	32,340	19,207	18,000	-4,868	604,565	109,414	713,979	1,250
1967	8,139,069	67,891	4,869	18,000	45,022	649,587	114,491	764,078	1,350
1968	9,442,445	133,605	6,546	25,500	101,559	751,146	115,989	867,135	1,725
1969	9,952,951	32,031	9,073	25,500	-2,542	748,604	147,175	895,779	2,025
1970	10,617,016	128,092	41,936	25,500	60,656	809,260	146,444	955,704	1,755
1971	11,847,570	174,706	46,242	25,500	102,964	912,224	145,429	1,057,653	2,120
1972	13,241,487	169,648	71,565	30,000	68,083	980,307	145,790	1,126,097	2,550
1973	14,457,792	124,528	22,853	30,000	71,674	1,051,982	139,161	1,191,143	2,600
1974	15,030,874	249,363	41,474	54,000	130,465	1,182,447	151,804	1,334,251	2,550
1975	16,939,332	118,691	14,702	45,000	106,779	1,289,226	152,744	1,441,970	2,400
1976	19,059,505	251,503	38,000	8,525	191,270	1,480,496	158,740	1,639,236	2,980
1977	22,438,397	274,721	41,715	50,490	101,771	1,582,267	140,392	1,722,659	3,120
1978	25,767,897	337,490	32,930	77,070	179,571	1,761,838	152,364	1,914,202	3,690
1979	27,902,750	548,720	153,844	112,750	370,638	2,132,476	165,376	2,297,852	3,900
1980	30,704,926	628,655	196,754	154,000	357,628	2,490,104	198,142	2,688,246	4,700
1981	36,705,473	749,304	203,118	176,000	242,985	2,733,089	246,675	2,979,764	6,325
1982	41,620,167	1,060,429	349,750	163,350	469,944	3,203,033	249,357	3,452,390	6,500
1983	50,611,646	685,321	94,528	148,500	587,525	3,790,558	249,357	4,039,915	7,300
1984	59,280,303	1,430,732	451,227	178,200	797,807	4,588,365	286,023	4,874,388	12,100
1985	73,902,062	1,525,824	403,948	65,340	1,070,237	5,658,602	338,500	5,997,102	33,000
1986	86,381,400	1,839,778	514,345	163,350	1,162,083	6,820,685	398,000	7,218,685	36,300
1987	97,061,356	2,381,538	548,842	196,020	1,370,365	8,191,050	445,100	8,636,150	60,350
1988	104,778,216	3,303,662	926,057	228,690	2,149,133	10,340,183	445,100	10,785,283	60,000
1989	127,122,036	4,005,908	1,091,101	228,690	2,510,548	12,850,731	445,100	13,295,831	60,000
1990	131,283,105	1,784,573	570,645	228,690	493,568	13,344,299	1,000,000	14,344,299	60,000
1991	138,994,540	-3,558,185	476,386	228,690	-4,341,017	9,003,282	6,558,259	15,561,541	100,000
1992	125,508,842	1,581,165	-518,180	228,690	2,371,666	11,374,948	3,876,314	15,251,262	
1993	120,853,314	1,462,227	178,691	0	1,287,109	12,662,057	3,487,750	16,140,807	
1994	99,670,775	-2,823,540	-1,044,915	0	-2,053,331	10,626,726	3,608,629	14,235,355	
1995	104,200,996	-358,605	34,835	0	-11,855	10,614,871	3,572,307	14,187,178	
1996	104,579,312	-283,633	149,912	0	207,024	10,821,895	3,093,227	13,915,122	
1997	108,284,926	777,795	-148,639	163,350	788,690	11,610,585	2,885,296	14,495,881	
1998	118,465,394	625,254	-535,646	151,331	293,532	11,904,117	2,470,352	14,374,469	
1999	121,024,483	1,242,707	292,624	230,023	665,868	12,569,985	2,188,444	14,758,455	
2000	127,057,000	1,124,000	195,000	347,000	866,015	13,436,000	1,814,000	15,250,000	

Hamel Land Transfers:

Irasburg & Coventry:

Hamel Sold:

Date	Acres	Purchaser	Sale Price	Per acre
1/28/93	40.3	Laurent Lussier	37,000.00	918.00 (no road front)
11/24/93	46.49	John Bruneau	41,841.00	900.00 " " "
9/24/93	10.4	MacLeod	10,000.00	1,000.00
7/29/95	10.3	MacLeod	10,000.00	1,000.00

Hamel deeded to LSB:

Date	Acres	Purchaser	Sale Price	
6/29/95	21.5	LSB	n/a	
"	20.5	"	"	(deed corrected on 9/8/95)
"	140.5	"	"	
"	65.2	"	"	
"	39.48	"	"	
"	M/H	"	"	
"	14.62	"	"	

Lyndonville Sold:

Date	Acres	Purchaser	Sale Price	Per acre
9/11/95	20.5	Fay Young	9,300.00	453.65
11/10/95	39.48	Charles Rockwell	18,100.00	458.46
6/7/96	140.5	Bob Lawson	65,000.00	462.63
6/7/96	65.2	Bob Lawson	15,000.00	230.06
6/7/96	14.62	Bob Lawson	10,000.00	684.00
11/7/96	21.5	Brent Rhodes	5,250.00	244.18
			Average per acre:	**407.20**

Lawson Sold: *LAWSON ʁ ʌ ʁ   408.50*

Date	Acres	Purchaser	Sale Price	Per acre
7/26/96	M/H (10a)	N.E. Vet Service	29,500.00	
6/22/99	11	Stacey	16,000.00	1,454.00
		Lawson's cost per acre after sale:		**248.00**

Fay Young Sold:

Date	Acres	Purchaser	Sale Price	Per acre
12/14/99	20.5	Darlings	28,000.00	1,365.85

Oeschger-Depo

4/3/96
By McConnel

Page 8:

Q Did Mr. Campbell approach you with anybody else?

A. No, he did not

Q After meeting with JC where he raised the possibility about you becoming a director, did you speak with anyone else about that possibility?

A No, I didn't

Page 12 thru 15:

Q Okay, what were the circumstances under which you left the bank as a director?

A We had a lot of OREO property that we were trying to sell and one of the pieces of property that we had was a No Country Motors building up in Derby, and we talked about disposing of some property, and that was one of the properties we talked of disposing. When we talked about it, I made it known that I was interested in being a purchaser at an auction or however they were going to get rid of the property, and I said very blankly that it that was going to be done, I wanted to be sure there was no appearance of anything with all the problems the Bank had, and we as directors voted to sell the building by sealed bid, a date was set and everything else, everybody was aware that I was going to be a bidder and one of the contentions of the FDIC was I had inside info about the bidding, and that's true. I knew that the minimum bid that the directors would take was $350,000. I approached a friend of mine and we put a bid in on the building of $408,000, the next closest bid was United Christian Academy in Newport. There was a group of ministers and friends trying to set up a school and they thought the No Country building would work. They put in a bid of around $400,000, but I don't believe they could have backed the bid up. They didn't have any money. The closest bid was around $400,000, but I don't believe it would have gone. But anyways, I had the highest bid. And I brought a sealed bid that night to the No Country building, there was approx seven people there, Bucknam, Stan McKenny from the Advisory Board, Dave Turner, Mt Barrup and Rev Genco from the academy. There was 5 or 6 people there. I handed the bid right there, they opened the bid, everything was fine. I called my partner, I told him we had the building, and for whatever reason, Bucknam called the FDIC and they said that I wouldn't be able to purchase the building. So the Directors had a meeting that I couldn't be a part of, and they went against what they had originally voted and said I wouldn't be able to buy the building. And I felt that I didn't like the appearance of it, I didn't like the situation it put me in, I didn't like going to my partner and saying, well, I didn't know what to say. I mostly told people, to try to keep the bank clear and to keep myself clear what I told people on the street was that because of the problems the bank couldn't clear the title and the sale couldn't go through. That's what I said and that's the way I left it. But after that I – I wrote a letter to the board stating that I didn't – I wasn't going to be on the Board anymore so –

Page 22 thru 25:

Q Was it your sense that management was looking after the related interests issue and would remind the board periodically that this had to be done?

A. Well, I always hoped that they would tell us those things because we – myself as a director I wouldn't have know it.

Q Was there ever a time that you recall that the other directors indicated that they had a personal interest in a loan that was being considered?

A Yes

Q   And do you recall circumstances in which the individuals who disclosed those related interests would not participate in the discussions in the approval of those loans?

A   Yes. Sometimes they may participate in the discussion because they might know more about the loan than somebody else, but when it came to the voting, they were not part of that

Q   In the event they didn't disclose it, would you consider that a breach of their obligation to you as a fellow board member?

A   I guess it would surprise me. You know, I thought somebody – I mean being that the discussion would be there on the loan and certainly if I was going to be a part of the loan I would certainly disclose it.

Q   And you'd expect your colleagues to disclose it as well?

A   I would because I think there would be open information,

Page 26

Q   But as a director if, for example, one of the related interests listed on RRL's sheet was going to be a beneficiary of a loan, you would expect that RRL to make that known to the Board before the loan was approved?

A   I would.

Q   You would also expect he would abstain from discussions of the loan – strike that -. He would abstain from voting on the loan?

A   Abstain from voting, yes.

Q   He might participate in discussion to the extent that Board members had questions?

A   Yes

Page 40:

Q   How much time do you think he (RRL) was putting in on behalf of the bank on a weekly basis?

A   I think he lived and breathed the Bank. I mean, I think he worked for the Bank all the time.

I didn't think anything – he didn't too much with me because I wasn't – it just wasn't that way, but I know, you know, a director would tell me that RRL would think nothing of calling him up 11:00 at night or 4:00 in the morning, or say meet some place at 3:00 in the morning or bring them back at 1:00 in the morning, and that's the part of RRL that I saw, you know, I saw him work very hard for the bank, which I guess I looked at it with the amount of stock and everything he had in the bank it was probably one of his biggest interests so it didn't surprise me, but he did put in a lot of time. When it was talked about him getting more money, I certainly didn't have a problem with it.

Page 42 & 43:

Q   Were you ever at a meeting where RRL would offer his opinion as to what collateral was worth based on his review of it?

A   We would all do that.

Q   And he did as well?

A   Yeah.

Q   Okay. Was he also active in negotiating the terms of the loan?

A   I guess we all had a part of that ---

Q   Do you recall any circumstances in which RRL would bring a potential loan to the board for

approval in which he had negotiated the terms himself?

A   If he would bring a loan to the board which any one of us might do that, he would probably

say, this is the loan and this is the – you know, the terms are laid out, but we would discuss

Page 47:
Q From your perspective as a director who did you feel had ultimate responsibility for operations of the Bank?
A Tom

Page 48:
Q Do you know if RRL was involved in operational issues of the bank at all?
A I don't know about that. I know that – I just know he didn't work in the bank. I thought as I say, Ashley Jewell was pretty much taking care of things and then we had D Turner, up in Derby, and you had the people – you had people inside the bank I thought running the bank, you know.
Q I guess my question was more did you have a sense that as part of his job description he would have ultimate authority for any operational issues?
A I didn't get that sense because I felt that again, Ashley Jewell was the one that was dealing with the inside operations of the bank, and I would even hear Roger ask him questions at meetings so, you know, I didn't feel Roger had much to do with what was going on inside the bank.

Page 50:
Q Do you know if any individual officers of the bank had lending authority that equaled or surpassed RRL's?
A Each officer had a lending authority because I know we would talk about that. I thought RRL's was like $50,000 and I thought D Turner had authority somewhere close to that and Lee Cleveland, but exactly what anybody had – but most – any loans I ever saw of any significance still always came before the board

Page 53 & 54:.
Q You were aware of circumstances where the board would ratify the action of RRL in the granting of loans?
Q I don't know if – I'm trying to think back. It seemed like once I remember where something had to be ratified because it had already been done, but that was, and I can't tell you when that was, but it was an exception. Most every time I remember the loan would be brought before the board and it might have been -- I think any time that a loan – not a anew loan, but if somebody was having a financial problem, let's say, and they had to be re – resituated or whatever, and be a case of possibly where RRL talked to them, and then he would come to Board and say, okay, I've met with them and this is the way we can redo this, that type of thing there. I don't ever remember a loan coming to the board and saying okay, this loan's a done deal and you've got to ratify this loan. That – I don't remember anything like that

Page 65 & 66:
Q Do you recall any circumstances when RRL believed – strike that. Do you recall any circumstances where RRL instructed Wendy to take out certain details of the discussion that were memorialized in the minutes?
A No, I don't remember any of that.
Q Okay, You never observed RRL at a meeting instruct her to take certain things out of the minutes.
A No
Q ---concerning the discussions of the loan?
A No

Page 89:
Q Did you ever observe RRL instruct bank employees to destroy bank records?
A No, I did not.

HAS ASSOCIATES, INC.

P.O. Box 84
Boston, MA 02171
(617) 472-5086
FAX (617) 472-6903

Northbridge Business Center
76 Northeastern Blvd., Suite 34
Nashua, NH 03062
(603) 880-4529
FAX (603) 880-4351

April 11, 1992

Board of Directors
Lyndonville Savings Bank & Trust Company
98 Broad Street
Lyndonville, VT   05851

Re: Management Plan (draft)

Directors:

We have prepared at your request a Management Plan for Lyndonville Savings Bank. The Management Plan was developed as a requirement of the Bank's Regulatory Order as agreed to between the Federal Deposit Insurance Corporation and the Bank's Board of Directors. The Regulatory Order requires the Board of Directors to develop and implement a Management Plan to satisfy the requirements of the Regulatory Order and to execute the Bank's Capital and Profit Plans.

Specifically, the Board of Directors was charged with the development, assessment and recommendations in the following areas:

a.   Identification of both the type and number of officer positions needed to manage and supervise properly the affairs of the Bank.

b.   Identification and establishment of such Bank committees as are needed to provide guidance and oversight to active management.

c.   Evaluation of each Bank officer and staff member to determine whether these individuals possess the ability, experience and other qualifications required to perform present and anticipated duties including adherence to the Bank's established policies and practices and maintenance of the Bank in a safe and

HAS ASSOCIATES, INC

          sound condition.

     d.   A plan of action to recruit and hire any additional or
          replacement personnel with the requisite ability,
          experience and other qualifications which the Board of
          Directors determine are necessary to fill Bank officer
          or staff member positions consistent with the Board's
          analysis, evaluation and assessment of the Bank's
          management needs.

     HAS Associates, Inc. has had discussions and meetings with
the Board members and Bank staff to develop appropriate
procedures for the development of the Management Plan. Their
input was considered throughout the entire process, however our
assessments and recommendations were made as an independent
consultant to the Bank.

     HAS Associates, Inc. reviewed the following documents to
assist in developing the Management Plan:

                    Bank's Cease and Desist Order
                    Current Organization
                    Bank's written operational policies
                     and procedures

     HAS Associates, Inc. also conducted comprehensive interviews
with the following:

                    Board of Directors
                    Chairman/President
                    Executive Vice President/Chief
                     Executive Officer
                    Treasurer/Chief Operations Officer
                    Vice President/Senior Lending Officer
                    Vice President/Loan Officer
                    Assistant Vice President/Compliance Officer
                    Assistant Treasurer/Personnel
                     and Marketing Officer

     The purpose of these interviews was to determine the
capability of each individual officer and to ascertain that
his/her job responsibilities were being properly carried out and
fulfilled in an effective manner. Based on our activities and
research, certain recommendations and findings are reported in
the attached Management Plan (draft).

     It is our opinion that the management of the Loan Department

HAS ASSOCIATES, INC.

and the activities related to classified loans, loan workout and OREO properties warrant special attention at this time. Lyndonville Savings Bank's problem loans may continue to increase over the near term. Appropriate management and loan workout skills are critical to both servicing the performing loan portfolio and the problem loans.

The level of management skills within the Loan Department is not adequate to deal with the current problems facing the Bank. The Senior Lender is functioning as a collector and the full Board of Directors is doing the loan workouts. In addition, the Loan Department lacks expertise in secondary market mortgage and other guaranteed (SBA) loan products and loan review procedures. Loan review is particularly important to maintaining quality within the loan portfolio. Proper grading of loans and early warning of potential problems can reduce the number of loans which eventually become serious problem loans.

We recommend that the Board consider hiring (full-time or consultant) an experienced Loan Administrator who has loan management, underwriting, review and workout experience to assist the Board and the Loan Department through this difficult period. We believe that the Bank would benefit significantly and think the FDIC would perceive the Loan Administrator as a positive addition to the Bank's staff.

After you have had an opportunity to review the draft of the Management Plan and the above comments, we can proceed with finalizing the Management Plan.

Sincerely,

Thomas F. Collins
Associate

TFC:ca

V.   MANAGEMENT ASSESSMENT

Roger R. Lussier, Chairman of the Board and President

Mr. Lussier has been a Director of the Bank since 1966 and has served as Chairman of the Board and President for the past twelve years.

Mr. Lussier has extensive executive level experience in all operating and administrative areas of the Bank. He is knowledgeable in areas of banking regulations and laws. He also has an in depth knowledge of the Bank's market area and customers.

Mr. Lussier has been in the Auction Business (real estate and farms) since the 1960's. He has expert skills and knowledge of the business, financial and credit issues related to residential and commercial real estate, commercial businesses, and the business of agriculture.

Mr. Lussier has overseen the growth of Lyndonville Savings Bank to its current position of being a significant provider of banking services to the Lyndonville area. He has been the singular person responsible for the profitable growth and efficient operations of the Bank.

Mr. Lussier has the full respect of the Bank's staff and the full support of the Board of Directors. With the support of the Board of Directors and the senior officers of the Bank, Mr. Lussier is willing and capable of leading Lyndonville

8

Savings Bank during this difficult economic period. His term of Director and President will end upon his retirement and the election of a new President at the end of this year.

DIRECTORS MEETING

June 15, 1992

A special meeting of the Directors of Lyndonville Savings Bank and Trust Company was held at the Main Office of the Corporation in Lyndonville, Vermont, on Monday, June 15, 1992.

The following Directors were present:

Roger Lussier, Charles Howe, John Campbell, Arthur Elliott, Robert Beausoleil, Fay Young and Fredric Oeschger.

Ashley W. Jewell, Andrew Field, Esq., and Peter Langrock, Esq. were present for part or all of the meeting.

Upon a motion duly made and seconded, it was unanimously

VOTED: To approve a loan to Richard Rooney for $150,000 for 15 years, 9.5%, 1-1/2 points up front; secured by apartment buildings and trailer park.

Upon a motion duly made and seconded, it was unanimously

VOTED: To approve rewriting Richard Rooney's existing loan on his trailer park to 3 over Prime, with 1-1/2 points for the rewrite.

Upon a motion duly made and seconded, it was unanimously

VOTED: To approve an additional $10,000 line of credit to Island Farms, Inc. for replanting corn, and the purchase of a tractor; secured by existing collateral.

Upon a motion duly made and seconded, it was unanimously

VOTED: To table, for more information, a request from Ralph Wright to release proceeds on a lot he has sold.

Upon a motion duly made and seconded, it was unanimously

VOTED: To approve a loan to Gary's Fuels, Inc. for $85,000 for payment on annual insurance premiums. This note will be paid back to us in 10 equal payments, and will be charged our standard rate.

RESOLUTION
OF
BOARD OF DIRECTORS

At a meeting of the Board of Directors of Lyndonville Savings Bank and Trust Company (Bank) held on June 15, 1992 at the Bank's main office in Lyndonville, Vermont, at which meeting all of the board of directors were present, the following resolution upon motion made and seconded was unanimously adopted, to wit:

RESOLVED, That,

WHEREAS, the Bank President, Roger R. Lussier, notified the Board 'hat he has received a notice in the form of a Stipulation from the FDIC ;eking his voluntary removal as President and member of the board of directors, a copy of which notice was read to the board; and

WHEREAS, as a result of the notice, Roger R. Lussier tendered his resignation for acceptance by the board if the board felt that it would be in the best interests of the Bank, the depositors and shareholders;

NOW, THEREFORE, inconsideration of the foregoing and after extensive discussion concerning the manner in which Roger Lussier has over the years to date, fulfilled his office and duties, his loyalty, sincerity, good faith and honesty in all dealings in promoting the best interests of the Bank, often at personal sacrifice, and not being unmindful of charges levied against him personally by the regulatory authorities, which charges the board, based upon its collective personal knowledge and upon its own review, believes to be unfounded, indiscriminate and without any material basis therefor, and as to the FDIC allegation of personal dishonesty, the same is contemptible and an affront to the integrity of the board; accordingly, be it resolved that Mr. Lussier's tendered resignation be and is hereby refused as not being in the best interests of the Bank. Further, the board hereby reconfirms its present employment contract with Mr. Lussier for the ensuing year.

FURTHER, BE IT RESOLVED, that the board of directors convey to the appropriate regulatory authorities, on behalf of the Bank, its grave cern and conviction that their past and any continued publication and w releases to the press of unjustifiaable adverse comments and allegations concerning the Bank (before being put to the test to prove the same) not only impairs the Bank's operations but serves to irreparably damage its reputation with the public and in the banking industry, for which there must ultimately be accountability.

Prior to the board discussions concerning the foregoing resolution and its adoption, board member Roger Lussier was excused from the meeting and did not participate in the discussion nor the vote in adopting the foregoing resolution.

The following board members were in attendance and participated in the discussion and adoption of the resolution:

Robert J. Beausoleil   Fay A. Young
Arthur B. Elliott   Charles C. Howe
John M. Campbell   Fredric Oeschger

Upon a motion duly made and seconded, it was unanimously

VOTED: To approving paying a retainer of $20,000 to Peter Langrock, who is representing the President and Chairman of the Board in relation to certain actions being taken by the FDIC.

No further business appearing, it was moved to adjourn.

_____   _____
Roger R. Lussier   Executive Vice President

TO: Lyndonville Savings Bank & Trust Co..

1033 Broad St. Lyndonville, Vt. 05851   Copy to

Vt. Banking Dept. 89 Main St. Drawer 20 Montpelier, Vt. 05620-3101

Re:Shareholders Request to inspect Records of Lyndonville Savings Bank.

The undersigned have been shareholders of common stock for a number of years and have always supported and been concerned with the Banks best interest.

In 1995 the bank sued in the U.S. District Court it's former President and Chairman of the Board Roger Lussier claiming that he was responsible for losses the Bank suffered on a number of mortgage loans which the Bank claimed were improperly or negligently underwritten and that Mr Lussier breached his Fiduciary duty to the Bank. This case has been widely publicized in the media. Recently the U.S. Appeals Court vacated and dismissed the case after finding that it had been misrepresented by the bank.

It has been indicated that Attorneys fees and costs paid by the Bank in this case and ;others has been very high. At several annual stockholder meetings of the Bank, Bank Directors and management when asked by the stockholders have refused to disclose how much has been paid out.

The foregoing seems to raise a question as to the propriety of the Board's conduct in the matters and a suspicion of misconduct, not in the Banks best interests nor that of it's depositors or shareholders : therefore, the undersigned would like to ascertain the propriety of the foregoing matters by examing accounting and other appropriate records of the Bank to discover what in fact was paid by the bank as its costs and legal fees etc.

Please answer with in ten days of the receipt of this letter, as to the date, place, time that will be convenient for the Bank to furnish appropriate records for examination.

Notice of the place, date and time to examine the above records can be mailed to: Fay Young Box 588 Lyndonville, Vt. 05851

Shareholder _____ Shareholder _____
Shareholder _____ Shareholder _____
Shareholder _____ Shareholder _____
Shareholder _____ Shareholder _____
Shareholder _____ Shareholder _____
Shareholder _____ Shareholder _____
Shareholder _____ Shareholder _____
Shareholder _____ Shareholder _____
Shareholder _____ Shareholder _____
Shareholder _____ Shareholder _____

OFFICE OF THE COMMISSIONER

STATE OF VERMONT
DEPARTMENT OF BANKING, INSURANCE AND SECURITIES

June 10, 1994

Hon. Franklin S. Billings, Jr.
United States District Court
District of Vermont
Rutland, Vermont

RE: Sentencing of Roger Lussier, Docket No. 93cr-50-1

Dear Judge Billings:

The Vermont Department of Banking, Insurance and Securities considers the crimes of Mr. Roger Lussier very serious, and asks this Court to adopt the sentencing recommendation of the United States Attorney.

It is my understanding that Mr. Lussier took the positions at trial that he was a simple country banker victimized by government intervention, and that his dealings caused no harm. I expect that he will continue to take these positions at sentencing. As Commissioner of Vermont's Department of Banking, Insurance and Securities, I would like to address Mr. Lussier's arguments in these areas. I have been with this Department since January of 1988, and became Commissioner in August of 1992. My work at the Department has afforded me personal familiarity with the manner in which banks are regulated in the State of Vermont, as well as the manner in which Vermont banks and bankers respond to regulation. I am also personally familiar with the manner in which the Lyndonville Savings Bank has been regulated, the manner in which Mr. Lussier, as bank president, chairman of the board of directors and major shareholder, has been dealt with by regulators, and the manner in which he has responded to regulation. I ask the Court to consider the reasons for bank regulation, and, further, to consider the real effects of Mr. Lussier's crimes.

As a result of a pattern of unsound banking practices discovered during examinations conducted in 1988, 1989, 1990, and 1991, this Department issued an Order to Cease and Desist against Lyndonville Savings Bank in December of 1991. The Department took action specifically because Mr. Lussier, as president, chairman of the board of directors and agent for the bank, participated on numerous occasions in Bank loans that provided Mr. Lussier, his business associates, friends and family members financial benefit. In some cases these loans were funnelled to borrowers through nominees. In one case, Mr. Lussier personally did the appraisal for property offered as collateral for a loan, the proceeds of which were used to pay a debt to Mr. Lussier.

Mr. Lussier's dealings with Charlie Kelton consisted of allowing Kelton to engage in a massive check kiting scheme, failing to report the check kiting in violation of federal regulations, and lying to bank examiners when questioned about the check kiting; of funneling loans to Kelton and his businesses through nominee borrowers; and of making direct loans to Kelton and his businesses despite knowledge of their financial distress. The transactions resulted in loans made by the Lyndonville Savings Bank to Kelton which far exceeded the institution's statutory lending limit, as well as Kelton's ability to repay, thus jeopardizing the institution's financial soundness.

One of the counts on which Mr. Lussier was convicted involved the Kelton check kiting and the fact that he allowed the scheme after it was brought to his attention by Lyndonville Savings Bank personnel. Check kiting defrauds all institutions used in the scheme, and inevitably results in an actual loss to at least one of the institutions used in the scheme. The Kelton check kiting scheme defrauded not only the Lyndonville Savings Bank, its depositors and shareholders, but First Vermont Bank & Trust Co., its depositors and shareholders, Bank of Vermont, its depositors and shareholders, and the former City Bank and Trust Co., of Claremont, New Hampshire, its depositors and shareholders. Mr. Lussier was a party to this massive fraud. Finally, and only because federal and state regulators discovered the check kiting, Mr. Lussier stopped honoring the Kelton checks. The inevitable multimillion dollar losses resulted. The extent to which each of the Vermont banks used in the scheme will bear the losses is currently the subject of litigation.

The purpose of bank regulation in Vermont is to "promote and maintain the solvency and liquidity of [banks] . . . to encourage competition among them, and to protect the public against unfair and unconscionable lending . . ." 8 V.S.A. § 1. The people of Vermont, through the Legislature, have established clear standards to promote these purposes. By and large, Vermont banks and bankers accept these standards and conduct their business according to the law. By and large, the Department has cooperative relationships with Vermont banks and bankers through which these standards are maintained. Mr. Lussier, on the other hand, chose to ignore these standards, chose to lie to regulators and generally refused to cooperate. His conduct resulted in violations of Vermont banking law on a scale that this Department has never before seen.

Mr. Lussier was no victim in these matters. Despite his lack of much formal education and claims that he was a simple country banker, he was very shrewd in his business dealings and in dealing with regulators. As a regulator, it was clear to me that Mr. Lussier controlled the bank and the board of directors, and that he knew and understood everything that went on in the bank. Mr. Lussier's crimes caused harm to Vermonters and to Vermont institutions.

Thank you for your consideration.

Sincerely,

Elizabeth R. Costle
Commissioner
Department of Banking,
    Insurance and Securities

DIRECTORS MEETING

December 27, 1989

A special meeting of the Board of Directors of Lyndonville Savings Bank and Trust Company was held at the principal office of the Corporation in Lyndonville, Vermont, on Wednesday December 27, 1989. Following the regular meeting.

The following Directors were present:

Robert Beausoleil, John Campbell, Arthur Elliott, George Hopkins, Charles Howe, Roger Lussier and Fay Young. Pearl Baird (Director Emeritus) was not present.

The following persons were also present for part or all of the meeting:

Du Bois S Thompson Jr., David Turner, and Marguerite Beane.

Upon motion duly made and seconded, it was unanimously

VOTED: That any employee who has worked for the bank one year or more should receive at least $6. per hour.

Upon motion duly made and seconded, it was unanimously

VOTED: To adjust the hourly rates and salaries of the following employees to become effective as of January 1, 1990:

Main Office	From	To
Bookkeeping:		
Wanda Wilkie, Supervisor	7.25	7.70
Monique Bailey Asst Supervisor	6.00	6.35
Charlotte Downes	6.40	6.75
Marcia Jenkins	5.50	6.10
Debbie Murray	5.25	6.00
Charlotte Simpson	5.75	6.25
EDP		
Sharon Baillargeon	6.00	6.50
Rodney Davis	6.00	6.40
Kim Willey	5.75	6.10
Customer Service		
Cathee Beveridge, Supervisor	6.00	
Dawn Leroux	5.00	6.00
Amy Taylor	5.25	5.50
Loans		
Sherrie Bull Supervisor	7.75	8.25
Judy Cushman, Asst. Supervisor	7.75	8.25
Jane Maxwell	6 00	6.35
Janet Smith	5.75	
Tammi Stahler	5.75	
Elaine Smith	7.50	7.75

736

Tellers		
Claire Brosseau, Supervisor	7.75	8.25
Sue Taylor Asst. Supervisor	7.00	7.40
Kim Drew	5.85	6.00
Stacy Olcott	5.00	5.50
Sharon Peters	6.60	7.00
Beverly Ruggles	5.50	6.00

Secretary		
Wendy Tucker	7.00	7.45

Accounting/EDP		
Lorraine Bickford	6.50	7.00

Part Time Employees		
Barbara Bailey	7.10	7.50
Amy Brill	5.00	5.60
Ruth Ingalls	5.00	6.00
Lucille Powers	5.90	6.25

MEMORIAL DRIVE		
Paule Gaskin, Manager	7.85	8.50
Lynn Masure, Asst. Mgr.	7.00	7.40
Kim Before	5.50	6.00
Annie Meyette	5.00	6.00
Linda Morel	5.50	6.00
Alice Sessions	5.25	6.00

DERBY OFFICE		
DeAnn Desrochers, Head Teller	7.75	8.15
Judy Kennison	5.50	6.00
Penny Johnson	5.50	6.00
Marlene Lancaster	5.85	6.00
Tammy Bapp, Customer Service	5.60	6.10
Anita Reed Loans & Bookkeeping	6.00	
Laurie Desmarais, Secretary	5.50	6.00
Debbie Lefebvre, Part time	5.00	5.50

OFFICERS		
Derby Office		
David Turner, Branch Mgr.	32,500.00	40,000.00
Rosemarie Hartley	19,000.00	20,500.00
Terrie Paul	16,640.00	19,000.00

Main Office		
Roger Lussier	60,000.00	
Du Bois S Thompson Jr.	46,000.00	
Marguerite M Beane	33,500.00	35,000.00
Ashley W. Jewell	37,000.00	40,000.00
M. Lee Cleveland	31,500.00	33,500.00
Charles Barrows	20,500.00	22,000.00
Jane Soulia	19,500.00	20,000.00
Eileen Beliveau	21,000.00	23,000.00
Bonnie Norway	18,500.00	20,000.00

No further business appearing, it was moved to adjourn.

JEFFREY L. AMESTOY
ATTORNEY GENERAL

BRIAN L. BURGESS
DEPUTY ATTORNEY GENERAL

WILLIAM E. GRIFFIN
CHIEF ASST. ATTORNEY GENERAL

STATE
OFFICE OF THE
109 S.
MONTPELIER
05609-1001

TEL: (802) 828-3171
FAX: (802) 828-2154

Post-It™ brand fax transmittal memo 7671 | # of pages ▸

To R. Gensburg	From Bill Griffin
Co.	Co.
Dept.	Phone #
Fax #	Fax #

October 27, 1992

Robert A. Gensburg, Esq.
P.O. Box 276
St. Johnsbury, Vermont   05819

   Re: Lyndonville Savings Bank and Trust Company
     Docket No. 91-103-B

Dear Bob:

  Your proposal makes no mention of the State's trial preparation expenses, which reminds me that I have not yet given you the numbers.

  The Banking Department's expenses to date are:

Bank Examiner	$24,723
General Counsel	6,000
Law Clerk	4,252
Hearing Officer	1,500
Depositions & transcripts	882
	$37,357

  In addition, I have spent about 200 hours on the case, at a (bargain basement) cost to the State in excess of $12,000. The State's total expenses exceed $50,000.

  Please let me know if the Bank proposes to pay these expenses as part of a settlement that would give the Bank cease and desist language that is more to its liking.

       Very truly yours,

       WILLIAM GRIFFIN
       Chief Assistant
       Attorney General

cc William Rockford

Legislators Meeting with LSB Directors and VDBI & FDIC: (12/31/91)

In Attendance:

Joseph Sherman, Senator

John McClaughry, Senator

Nancy Sheltra, Representative

Wallace Russell Jr, Representative

Robert Kinsey, Representative

Cola Hudson, Representative

Robert Starr, Representative

Jan Newpher, Caledonian Record

Jimmy Loyless, FDIC

Paul Snyder, FDIC

Ellen Kosmicki, FDIC

William Griffin, Asst AG

Jeffrey Johnson, Commissioner

Elizabeth Costle, VDBI

William Rockford, VDBI

Daniel Way, VDBI

Barbara Hann, VDBI

Excerpts:

Rockford: Can't have loans that are given without proper documentation. This is a new environment. That kind of banking just isn't allowed any more. There has to be an organized manner and documentation.

McClaughry: Is that a state or federal regulation?

Loyless: Not a regulation but prudent banking. Want to know if you are going to get paid back especially if you're an insured financial institution. Banks are lending depositors' money and board and management should know how they are going to be paid back so it doesn't become the government's obligation.

Starr: Good that it's done that way but from a business standpoint, knowing the way things have changed, it is somewhat ridiculous. If a person has been dealing with an institution for 25 years and in the past 3 or 4 years you go back to the bank, it takes 2 months to get through the paperwork –new changes may be protecting some banks, but against others. Makes it difficult for an honest person to do business.

Russell: Means that Lussier can't be involved as the bank president.

Loyless: We aren't saying that he can't be president any more.

Russell: Your main objective is to get rid or Lussier.

McClaughry: If half a dozen banks made the kind of loans that LSB is would not be nearly as complex. But on loans to farmers, loggers, LSB is the preeminent lender of that type. With others gone, it leaves LSB the prime place to turn. Other banks don't let you get in the door. I'm worried about keeping the blood flowing in the economy. If it becomes another Bank of Boston or Chittenden, it will become a deposit stop, it will dry up the credit in the state … this is about the credit crunch.

Kinsey: There's an attorney up there that needs to have his hands slapped. No member of the legislature is looking for a sweetheart deal for Roger. We want him to conform. Want to make sure you are not singling out Roger or any other director. As we move forward in this process, if Roger isn't being singled out, but if Roger tells you to go to hell that's Roger's problem …if practices are the same as the other banks, can support what you are doing.

Excerpts of Roger, Gravel and Johnston conversation 5/19/95:

Roger: Is it safe for me to work with you guys instead of against you guys? Now that guy Johnson scares the s--- out of me. All he wants to do is sue me. If I'm going to be sued – if you guys are setting me a trap to sue me, I don't feel right about it. I work my heart out. As far as I'm concerned I've done nothing wrong but he's trying to create some problems it looks like to me.

Lawyer: We don't want to sue you. That's the last thing we want to do but – let me finish with the insurance then we'll talk about that.

Roger: How legal is it to settle when you know you're being blackmailed and extorted?

Lawyer: Practically every lawsuit has some element of that.

Roger: What I'd like to ask you guys right now, are you guys trying to figure a way to sue me?

Lawyer: ? talked to you about it. We'd rather not have to sue you but ---

Roger: How long have you been talking about it?

Lawyer: John and Me?

Roger: I don't know whether to work with you guys or not. I'm willing to work but if you guys are just looking for a way to stab me in the back when I get done, I don't feel comfortable ---

Lawyer: From one of the first conversations we had we said "Look, we would like to have things work in a way that the bank and you are on the same side because in all these cases ---".

Roger: Well, I'd be an idiot if I didn't sue you for not putting on a good case. You know, you can go on and on with this. I don't want this stuff. I either want to work or not work but I gotta know ahead of time if you guys are planning on suing me. I mean, I've told you guys a lot of stuff and every time you came in here I opened everything up and gave you everything I had. I mean I'm not trying to take your place, I'm just defending my hide right now. The time's going to come when I have to charge instead of defend. I don't want to do that, I mean I didn't profit on any of the g—d--- deals they're suing me on an everything was done --- the whole board was at the closing. But then you've got a shadow of a doubt you might sue me anyway. I'd like to know if the board's ? if I've got immunity, I'll work but ----. Right now what I probably should do, I don't know, is probably, in defense of myself is counterclaim you guys if I lose. I was working full time for the bank. I was working for the bank when that happened. I don't want to put no smear on the bank. I want to get along.

Lawyer: And by the same token there are a lot of people, including the FDIC, who have said to us --- I have been asked, I don't know how many times by the FDIC "Why the hell haven't you got counterclaims in there against Roger? Or cross claims against Roger?" And I have said "Because we think these cases are defensible. We thing the best thing going is that Roger and the bank will try to operate to get these cases won." Then he said "Well, what about situations where you lose?" and I said "You know, we're prepared to have discussions with Roger about what we do in those instances." And that's one reason why we want to have this conversation today because we're sort of at a point where some of the cases are about to be ready ? settlement. Some of the cases are about to go to trial. We've got the FDIC still making these noises "What are you going to do about Roger?" And we haven't done anything about Roger because you have been cooperative and John ---.

Lussier: They've got ten times more power than you have. Why do they want you to do the dirty work?

Lawyer: Because they don't ? claim as much as the bank does. The bank is the one getting sued not the FDIC. The FDIC for some months has been saying "What have you been doing with Roger?" We said "We're working with him. We're going to try to beat these cases." The FDIC has said "Well, how are you going to win those cases? You know, how are you going to win those cases with Roger as the key witness?"

Lawyer: ? I'll bet you after what you've said about Kilmartin you know damn well he's going to pull out every trick he can. If that involves fabricating conversations that didn't take place, he may do that. So the point is, as I've said to FDIC, I think it would be helpful to have cooperation. I think it would be helpful to have him represented so that somebody can help him make judgments about ---

Lawyer: Well, a lot of these cases seem to fall sort of between the cracks of things you would ordinarily get insurance for and, by the way, some of them have been raised by Kilmartin and others ? because they allege things like fraud and racketeering that no insurance policy ever covers. Well anyway, the FDIC has said "Look, we're going to be in there in the next month or two doing our audit thing and we need to know what the story is with insurance. We need to know what the story is with Roger and what, if anything, you guys are going to do with him." We told them "We're working our butts off trying to get insurance and we've been cooperating with Roger so far ---"

Roger: Well, I've been cooperating with you guys. Every time you call – I really want to help all I can but boy, if you're going to get in with the FDIC and sue me afterwards, I'm a little nervous about that. You guys suing is just like me cutting another tree down.

Lawyer: Well, I guess what we're saying is that we could pacify all the extraneous forces – the FDIC, the shareholders – maybe later on. We could say to them, "Look we don't want to sue Roger. We want to still be friends and work together because it's in the best interest for both of us to do that ---"

Roger: But we reserve the right to change our mind.

Lawyer: ? that's right and that's fair.

Roger: That ain't fair. It might be right but it ain't fair.

Lawyer: It's fair for you to call a spade a spade." I don't know if you can figure out any other way ? We know it's going to be question number one on the FDIC's plate when they go in there and audit, and I don't think we can stall them another time. The last time ---

HALE AND DORR
COUNSELLORS AT LAW

60 STATE STREET, BOSTON, MASSACHUSETTS 02109
617-526-6000 • FAX 617-526-5000

RICHARD A. JOHNSTON
617-526-6282

August 2, 1995

BY TELECOPIER

(312) 565-0832
Christopher J. Graham, Esq.
Peterson & Ross
200 East Randolph Drive
Suite No. 7300.
Chicago, IL 60601-6969

Re: Lyndonville Savings Bank and Trust Company
    Various Matters
    Case Names: Jasmin, Beauregard, Guilmette

Dear Mr. Graham:

I am in receipt of your two letters dated July 28, 1995. I will attempt here to address the principal issues which you have raised in those two letters, as well as your letter of July 26.

1.   Arguments About Rescission

Having reviewed the details you have outlined purporting to support the insurer's right to rescind the policies, Lyndonville and I continue to disagree with your conclusion.

The fact that your client has waited until 1995 to consider rescinding the applicable policies on the basis of alleged misrepresentations is nothing short of outrageous. The facts demonstrate that Jasmin brought his suit in December 1989 and asserted third party claims against Mr. Lussier in July 1991. Your client was placed on notice of this third party claim at that time. Moreover, Mr. Lussier was removed from the bank by early 1993. The fact that your client has willingly accepted premiums from Lyndonville and issued policies during these developments without raising the spectre of rescission until the eleventh hour

Christopher J. Graham, Esq.
August 3, 1995
Page 2

of a potential judgment implicating its policies will be the basis of our estoppel and laches arguments to any trier of fact over coverage.

With respect to the law on rescission, I believe that your client will be unable to satisfy that burden under 8 V.S.A. §4205. Lyndonville and I take issue with arguments that the applications contained statements intending to deceive the insurer. I have attached a comprehensive refutation of the detailed statements which you provided on July 28 as to alleged deceit. Should your client seek to rescind the policies on something less than proof of false statements made with the intent to deceive, you must still demonstrate that misrepresentations were made. As our attachment demonstrates, your recitation of allegations pertaining to the Kelton check kite is not only inaccurate but fails to show how any officer or director had knowledge of an act, error or omission which might give rise to a "claim under the policy" (the language in the application).

We take issue with your constant effort to equate the knowledge of a Kelton overdraft with knowledge of a Kelton "check kite." The two issues are very different, and we believe that you will have substantial difficulty marshalling proof of the latter. Furthermore, your use of a retrospective analysis of who allegedly knew what when conveniently ignores the fact that by the time Lyndonville applied for this policy, Bank of Vermont had already been made whole in August 1988 for its alleged loses from the Kelton kite. There was no suggestion that the Bank of Vermont or anyone else would raise any claims regarding the alleged check kite. Indeed, neither Mr. Kelton nor banks other than Bank of Vermont allegedly involved in the check kite ever filed claims against Lyndonville, and Bank of Vermont did not sue Lyndonville until late 1993. There was no indication that the Jasmins, who were very close to Charlie Kelton and were seeking to assist him in obtaining financing through the Bank, later would sue the Bank. Based upon the best information available at the time, it did not appear that any consequences from the Kelton check kite would "give rise to a claim under the policy."

We disagree that <u>First National Bank Holding Company v. Fidelity and Deposit Company of Maryland</u>, is dispositive. The law in Vermont differs in material ways from Florida law. The third prong of the Florida statute appears to make it considerably easier for an insurer to rescind a policy than the comparable

AUG 05 '95 09:08AM HALE AND DORR

Christopher J. Graham, Esq.,
August 3, 1995
Page 3

Vermont law. Additionally, in Lyndonville's case, unlike in First National Bank, Mr. Lussier did not plead guilty, and his conviction on a general verdict[*] is on appeal. Thus, there is no final adjudication of the dishonesty issue at this time.

   2.   The Proposed Settlements

        a.   Indemnification of Mr. Lussier and Mr. Elliott

Assuming that the policies are not rescinded, Lyndonville and the directors believe that your client has an obligation to participate in the settlement of the Jasmin, Beauregard and Guilmette cases.[1] Your suggestion that there is no obligation to reimburse Lyndonville for settlements involving Roger Lussier and Arthur Elliott is misplaced. As I have advised your firm, to date FDIC has indicated to me that Lyndonville should not pay for the ongoing legal costs of Mr. Lussier and Mr. Elliott. I do not believe that there is an express FDIC prohibition at this point against indemnification of Mr. Lussier or Mr. Elliott as part of a settlement of litigation, particularly where:

· settlements may be necessary to help preserve the financial integrity of the Bank;

· Vermont state law provides directors with certain indemnification rights; and

· an agreement to indemnify Mr. Lussier and/or Mr. Elliott by the Bank would be subject to reimbursement by an insurer.

Rather, I expect the FDIC to look at prospective settlements on a case by case basis.

---

[*]   A more detailed discussion of problems with relying on the general verdict against Mr. Lussier appears below.

[1]   Lyndonville and the directors also assert that your client has obligations with respect to other cases. However, our focus for now is on Jasmin, Beauregard and Guilmette for the reasons stated in my letter of July 25.

Christopher J. Graham, Esq.
August 3, 1995
Page 4

        To my knowledge, Mr. Lussier has not waived claims for
indemnification against the Bank. Your suggestion that Mr.
Lussier's criminal convictions will bar him from seeking
indemnification ignores several pivotal issues. First, his
convictions are still on appeal and is subject to possible
reversal.

        Second, even if affirmed, Mr. Lussier's conviction does not
necessarily link him with dishonest conduct as contemplated under
exclusion (a)(5) of the policy issued by your client. Count 15 of
the Government's superseding indictment against Mr. Lussier
charged him with a scheme or artifice to defraud Lyndonville,
First Vermont Bank and Trust ("First Vermont") and the Bank of
Vermont through the Kelton check kite and loans associated with
that check kite. In support of this count, the Government alleged
that Mr. Lussier did one or more of the following things against
Lyndonville, First Vermont or Bank of Vermont:

        • he approved the use of the Kelton account to
          further the check kite (Indictment, p. 24, ¶ 7);

        • he arranged for Lyndonville to charge Mr. Kelton
          for the use of Lyndonville to further the check
          kite (Indictment, p. 24, ¶ 8);

        • he concealed the check kite (Indictment,
          p.24, ¶ 9);

        • he arranged for the kite to end and had losses
          resulting from the kite covered principally by
          Lyndonville loans made indirectly to Mr. Kelton
          (Indictment, p. 24, ¶ 10);

        • he misled an officer of First Vermont about his
          knowledge of the Kelton kite (Indictment,
          p. 25, ¶ 11); and

        • he concealed from FDIC examiners knowledge about
          the Kelton kite from August 1988 to October 1988
          (Indictment, p. 25, ¶ 12);

        Because the jury returned a general verdict on this count, it
is impossible to know upon which of these allegations the jury
relied or, more significantly, against which banks these acts
allegedly were committed.

Christopher J. Graham, Esq.
August 3, 1995
Page 5

Given these facts, we believe that your client will have substantial difficulty relying now upon Mr. Lussier's criminal conviction as a basis for applying exclusion (a)(5), which requires a final adjudication of active and deliberate dishonesty committed with actual dishonest purpose and intent which brought about or contributed to the loss claimed.

      b.   Proposed Writeoff of Debt

You have suggested that the proposed writeoff of debt by the Bank cannot constitute a liability subject to reimbursement out of the directors and officers policy. I disagree. There is no limitation in the definition of "loss" in the policy which supports your position. Just because Lyndonville may off-set its obligation to pay against a pre-existing debt does not make the value transferred fall outside of the definition of "loss". See e.g. UNR Industries, Inc. v. Continental Casualty Co., 942 F.2d 1101 (7th Cir. 1991)(bankruptcy reorganization plan requiring the transfer of company's stock to trust fund for benefit of asbestos victims constituted "loss" under applicable umbrella policy and triggered obligation of insurer to pay the cash value of the stock transferred).

Your views about the debtors' obligations to the Bank are misplaced. It is not necessarily true, as a matter of law, that the debtors can only recover against the director defendants if they also void the loans in the first place. Furthermore, because the loans in some instances are secured, bankruptcy filings by some debtors of the Bank would not necessarily render the debts uncollectible.

You should note that I did not indicate or imply that Lyndonville was looking to structure settlements in the ways I proposed solely to implicate the insurance policies. Rather, I have proposed, subject to insurer approval, that as part of an overall settlement of each of various claims, release of the debtors' obligations could be part of the package. While it is true that I do not represent the director-defendants, it is my understanding, based on discussions with Joe Bauer and John Gravel, that the director-defendants favor settlements along the lines proposed in my letter of July 25. In each case the debtors are looking for cash settlements from the Bank and director-defendants, in addition to writeoffs of the existing debts. We thought that it would be preferable to begin the settlement process by proposing writeoffs of debts to the Bank rather than

Christopher J. Graham, Esq.
August 3, 1995
Page 6

cash payments by the defendants. We also felt that the writeoff approach would make for simpler accounting. Indeed, I fully disclosed the proposal to you without mentioning it to any of the debtors -- evidence that the Bank is not trying to do anything inappropriate vis-a-vis the insurer. Frankly, we thought that you and your client would prefer such an approach as well. Since you are now suggesting that such an approach is improper, we can switch to proposals which include cash payments to the debtors, with the understanding that they still will be responsible for repaying their debts. Under such an approach, payments on behalf of the directors would be "liabilit(ies) incurred" by the directors.

Although the insurer has a right under the policy not to consent to settlement proposals, consent may not be unreasonably withheld. If your client declines to consent to settlements which are in the best interests of the Bank and other defendants, the Bank and/or the directors may settle without such consent and then seek to impose liability on the insurer. Having failed to participate in the settlement, the insurer would have only minimal rights to challenge the reasonability of the settlement.

3.   Bank Counsel Fees

For purposes of consistency, efficiency and effectiveness, Lyndonville has been largely responsible for defending the claims at issue in these cases. Because of the Bank's efforts, the individual director and officer defendants have benefited immeasurably from this consolidated defense and Lyndonville has been able to minimize the total litigation expenses that would be incurred if the legal work were scattered among the various defendants. Because this strategy has provided real value to the individual defendants, the Bank believes that your client should share in the payment of its counsel fees. In the Bank of Vermont case, your partner, Don Leventhal, encouraged the Bank to pursue such a strategy with respect to counsel: i.e. to have the Bank's counsel assume responsibility for key briefs without additional substantive briefs by directors' counsel. As I recall, Mr. Leventhal agreed that at the conclusion of the case, reimbursement of a part of the Bank's counsel fees -- representing the "joint defense" -- would be appropriate. I am disappointed that your client is attempting to back away from assuming its fair share of the responsibility for defending the directors' interests.

Christopher J. Graham, Esq.
August 3, 1995
Page 7

4.   Retentions

We understand that the Bank's self insured retention limit
for the three applicable policies are $50,000, $75,000 and
$125,000 respectively.   If your information differs on this point,
please inform me immediately.

5.   The Bank's Exposure

While the Bank may have some exposure in these cases, the
claims against the Bank will rise or fall with the specific
conduct of the individual defendant-directors.   Accordingly,
coverage under your policy above the applicable retentions is
directly implicated.   In formulating our settlement proposals to
contain contributions by both the Bank and the insurer, we have
discounted appropriately for the Bank's potential exposure and
believe that your client should pay the percentages detailed in my
previous letter.

6.   Concluding Comments

I have provided copies of your letters to counsel for the
directors and to Mr. Lussier.   Mr. Bauer and I intend to cooperate
with these parties in an effort to try to settle the Jasmin case
next week and the other cases thereafter.   We hope to have your
client's active involvement in the settlement process.   However,
if the insurer declines to participate -- either through
rescission, denial of coverage or unreasonable refusal to consent
to a proposed settlement -- the Bank intends to act in its best
interest and allow the consequences of the insurer's refusal to
fall, appropriately, upon the insurer.

Based on our telephone discussions on Monday, I understand
that you will be present at the Jasmin mediation on August 8.   I
request that you let me know your position on rescission of the
policy and the Jasmin settlement proposal by the end of this week.
As I have stressed on several occasion, there is only short period
of opportunity to settle the Jasmin case before trial starts on
August 14.   Because of the potential implications for all
defendants of a trial in which Mr. Lussier likely will invoke the
Fifth Amendment, it is imperative that we attempt to settle
Jasmin.   The same considerations apply to Beauregard and
Guilmette.

AUG 05 '95 09:11AM HALE AND DORR
Christopher J. Graham, Esq.
August 3, 1995
Page 8

I look forward to hearing from you.

Sincerely,

Richard A. Johnston

Richard A. Johnston   ᴍᴐ s

RAJ:meh
cc: Donald B. Leventhal, Esq.
    Mr. Charles Bucknam
    Joseph P. Bauer, Esq.
    John C. Gravel, Esq.
    W. Scott O'Connell, Esq.

RESPONSE TO STATEMENT OF FACTS RELATING TO
THE CHECK KITE AND NOMINEE LOANS TO KELTON
AS PREPARED BY PETERSON & ROSS

Jasmin and Bank of Vermont

    1.   Background

        (a) Lyndonville Savings Bank Loans to Mr. Kelton

LSB does not deny that there was a significant lending relationship with Mr. Kelton between 1985 and 1989. LSB does, however, take exception to your frequent use of the government's characterization that Mr. Lussier "arranged" these loans. For example, it is clear that Paul Gallerani and not Mr. Lussier arranged the so-called "four friends" loan. (See R. Jasmin Depo. of 4/27/95 at pp. 60-65; C. Kelton Depo. of 8/5/94 in LSB v. Jasmin at pp. 38-39.)

Additionally, all of Mr. Kelton loans were processed by LSB in the normal course of banking events, with the sole exception of the 3 million dollar loan requested by Mr. Kelton at the evening meeting of July 27, 1988. However, even this loan was ratified by the entire Board at its next regularly scheduled meeting. It is important to point out that all of loans were requested of the Bank by Mr. Kelton for what appeared to be legitimate business needs. Additionally, there is nothing in Volume 6 of Mr. Kelton's testimony in the criminal trial which in any way indicates that the "indirect loans" were not for legitimate Mr. Kelton family business needs. (See Cr. Tr. C. Kelton V.6 p. 11, et seq.; C. Kelton Depo. of 8/4/94 in BOV v. LSB at pp 31, 51.)

(b) <u>Kelton Kite</u>

Nowhere in any of the depositions or trial transcripts is there any statement by anyone that Mr. Lussier approved the use of Mr. Kelton's account to further the check kite. Firstly, the only two people who have absolute knowledge of these events are Mr. Kelton and Mr. Lussier. Kelton has testified consistently that the kite was of his own doing and that it was operated solely by himself. (See C. Kelton Depo. of 8/4/94 in BOV v. LSB at pp. 12, 22, 23, 24, 56, 81.) He has testified that no one at LSB assisted him in the operation of the kite. (See C. Kelton Depo. of 8/4/94 in BOV v. LSB at pp. 20, 26, 39, 79, 80, 108, 109; C. Kelton Depo. of 8/9/94 in LSB v. Jasmin at pp. 8, 12, 64-68.) He has testified that he and Mr. Lussier never discussed a check kite, but that during one conversation, Mr. Lussier did express concern to him over the balance of uncollected funds in his account and that interest would have to be charged in any future uncollected balances. (See C. Kelton Depo. of 8/4/94 in BOV v. LSB at pp. 13, 15, 81.) He has testified that he never told Mr. Lussier of his operation of a check kite and he does not know if Mr. Lussier knew that there was a kite in existence. (See C. Kelton Depo. of 8/4/94 in BOV v. LSB at pp. 12, 79, 80; C. Kelton Depo. of 8/4/94 in LSB v. Jasmin at pp. 68, 69.)

As to representations made to other banks, no bank was certain of the kite except for CitiBank, (See C. Kelton Depo. of 8/4/94 in BOV v. LSB at pp. 24, 51, 81, 86; C. Kelton Depo. of 8/4/94 in LSB

2

v. Jasmin at pp. 31, 32.) and all banks involved were monitoring the activity of Mr. Kelton's accounts. To state that Mr. Lussier knew of the kite and mislead others presumes his knowledge was proved in the criminal trial, instead of merely being alleged. There is no testimony in that trial, or in any of the other depositions, which proves that Mr. Lussier knew of the existence of the kite. Further, the other bank directors confirm that while they had concern over the activity in the account, as did all of the banks involved, they were not at all sure of the existence of a kite. (See Doug Nelson Depo. of 9/12/91 in LSB v. Jasmin at pp. 20, 48; Arthur Elliot Depo. of 9/12/91 in LSB v. Jasmin at p. 11; George Hopkins Depo. of 7/8/91 in LSB v. Jasmin at pp. 10, 12 40; Robert Beausoleil Depo. of 9/13/91 in LSB v. Jasmin at pp. 9, 15, 19, 36, 37.)

Lastly, it is important to note that even the Bank of Vermont in the litigation it brought against Mr. Kelton and his various businesses did not allege in its pleadings that Mr. Kelton had structured a check kite. That litigation referred to overdrafts and to various bank loans which were delinquent. Thus, there was no way for Mr. Lussier or any other Board Members to infer from the pleadings that Mr. Kelton had been operating a check kite. The only information they had from the pleadings was that there was an obligation due from Mr. Kelton to the bank which included overdrafts and certain delinquent loans. An overdraft certainly does not equate to a check kite. The burden of proof to show a

3

check kite is certainly much greater than merely alleging overdrafts were present. Certainly we feel that the state of the evidence would point to overdrafts, but would not amount to proof of knowledge of a check kite.

(c) Kelton's Proposed Bank of Boston Loan

There is near unanimity among the directors present at the July 27, 1988 meeting that it was represented by Mr. Kelton that he had a loan commitment from the Bank of Boston and that the financing he was requesting of the Lyndonville Savings Bank would merely be a stop-gap measure until the Bank of Boston funding was achieved. (See Doug Nelson Depo. of 9/12/91 in LSB v. Jasmin at pp. 37, 53; George Hopkins Depo. of 7/8/91 in LSB v. Jasmin at p. 8; John Campbell Depo. of 9/13/91 in LSB v. Jasmin at pp. 15, 44; C. Kelton Depo. of 8/4/94 in BOV v. LSB at pp. 41, 67.) The commitment which Mr. Kelton had from the Bank of Boston as a result of its letter to him dated March 9, 1981, was a three phased commitment. The first phase called for a refinancing of the existing Lyndonville Savings Bank obligations at a level of $4,280,000.00. The second phase envisioned a 5 million dollar working capitol line of credit, and the final phase envisioned a 3 million dollar floor plan line of credit. Thus, the total commitment was a credit line approaching 13 million dollars.

(d) Termination of the Kite

The kite ended as a result of Mr. Kelton having insufficient funds to cover deposits in his accounts at the Bank of Vermont. The

4

testimony does not show that Mr. Lussier arranged to stop the kite. The testimony does show that the Bank made a reasonable assessment of the situation and returned Mr. Kelton's checks drawn on uncollected funds in mid July of 1988. (See C. Kelton Depo. of 8/4/94 in LSB v. Jasmin at pp. 13, 14; C. Kelton Depo. of 8/4/95 in BOV v. LSB at p. 87.)

While the effect of this was to end the kite, it does not follow from the testimony that the Bank's intention was anything other than prudent banking practice. The testimony, taken as a whole, clearly reflects that the Bank had given Mr. Kelton several opportunities to resolve his checking account problems and that the Bank had indeed properly notified Mr. Kelton of their concerns.

(e) Bank of Vermont Sues and Attaches Kelton Assets

Mr. Lussier has testified that Mr. Kelton called him and told him of the Bank of Vermont's suit on July 27, 1988 and that Mr. Kelton had asked for help from the Bank. Mr. Lussier, as a result of this request, called an emergency meeting of the Board of Directors. The testimony of Mr. Kelton has never been clear as to whether or not he initially mentioned the overdraft portion of the Bank of Vermont lawsuit when he requested that Mr. Lussier call a meeting of the Board. (See C. Kelton Depo. of 8/4/94 in LSB v. Jasmin at pp. 14-17.) Again, we point out that the Bank of Vermont pleadings do not refer in any way to a check kite. They merely refer to overdrafts and certain delinquent loans. Certainly the Bank of Vermont had as much information concerning Mr. Kelton's

5

checking account activity as did the Lyndonville Savings Bank. Presumably, if they had had sufficient information of a check kite, they would have set forth that information in their pleadings. However, they chose to make reference only to the overdrafts.

(f) The Bank Board's "Midnight Meeting" with Kelton

The facts set forth in this section, although accurate, are somewhat skewed. What the Bank knew at the meeting of July 27, 1988 was that one of its better customers had an immediate financial need. They were aware of the threat to put Mr. Kelton out of business by the Bank of Vermont and that the suit involved overdrafts (not a check kite) and certain Bank of Vermont loans which were overdue. (See C. Kelton Depo. of 8/4/94 in BOV v. LSB at p. 47; Doug Nelson Depo. of 9/12/91 in LSB v. Jasmin at p. 33; Arthur Elliot Depo. of 9/12/91 in LSB v. Jasmin at pp. 21, 23; John Campbell Depo. of 9/13/91 in LSB v. Jasmin at pp. 15, 44, 50; Robert Beausoleil Depo. of 9/13/91 in LSB v. Jasmin at pp. 28,33.) They were also aware of a Bank of Boston loan commitment that Mr. Kelton (not Mr. Lussier) represented to be the ultimate source of funding to relieve his cash flow problems. (See Doug Nelson Depo. of 9/12/91 in LSB v. Jasmin at pp. 37, 53; George Hopkins Depo. of 7/8/91 in LSB v. Jasmin at p. 8; John Campbell Depo. of 9/13/91 in LSB v. Jasmin at pp. 15, 44.) The actions taken by Mr. Lussier and the Board at that meeting are no more than a reasonable response to an urgent request by a small, rural bank board. They wished to give their customer all the assistance they possibly could,

6

especially since it appeared that this assistance would be on a short-term basis in view of Mr. Kelton's representations that the Bank of Boston, through its commitment letter of March 9, 1988, was willing to extend credit to the Keltons to pay off the Lyndonville Savings Bank obligations and to provide a total credit line to Mr. Kelton of $12,980,000.00. As to the statement rendered by Mr. Kelton at his criminal trial that "maybe a crime had been committed and this would cover a crime", he clearly contradicts that testimony in his deposition of August 4, 1994 in BOV v. LSB at p. 53. Mr. Kelton's deposition testimony is a better representation of Mr. Kelton's uncertainty as to the facts and even the statement made in the criminal trial was a mere recollection that something like that might have been said.

        (e)   <u>The Jasmin and Alfred and Carol Kelton Nominee Loans</u>
                <u>to Pay Charlie Kelton's Bank of Vermont Overdraft</u>

It is clear from the testimony of all concerned that the Bank would not provide a 3 million dollar loan to Mr. Kelton and so informed him at the meeting of July 27, 1988. They did indicate that they would provide financing at the 1.5 million level, but that Mr. Kelton would have to find another qualified borrower for the remaining 1.5 million. (See Doug Nelson Depo. of 9/12/91 in LSB v. Jasmin at pp. 32, 52; Arthur Elliot Depo. of 9/12/91 in LSB v. Jasmin at pp. 29, 34, 37; George Hopkins Depo. of 7/8/91 in LSB v. Jasmin at p. 18; John Campbell Depo. of 9/13/91 in LSB v. Jasmin at pp. 17, 50; Robert Beausoleil Depo. of 9/13/91 in LSB v. Jasmin

7

at pp. 33-35.) It is also clear from the testimony that the Jasmins received no representations whatsoever from Lyndonville Savings Bank concerning this loan and that there were no conversations between the Bank and the Jasmins prior to the closing. (See R. Jasmin Depo. of 5/23/90 in LSB v. Jasmin at p. 62.) It is also clear that the Jasmins had a very close social and business relationship with the Keltons and that, in fact, the Jasmins had previously lent more than 1 million dollars to the Keltons over the years. (See R. Jasmin Depo. of 5/23/90 in LSB v. Jasmin at pp. 12, 17; C. Kelton Depo. of 8/4/94 in LSB v. Jasmin at pp. 35, 42; R. Jasmin Depo. of 2/20/90 in LSB v. Jasmin at pp. 11, 24; R. Jasmin Depo. of 1/4/90 in LSB v. Jasmin at pp. 20, 29; R. Jasmin Depo. of 4/27/95 in LSB v. Jasmin at pp. 64, 68.) The testimony of Mr. Kelton, Leslie Wells and Vernon Kelton was that the Jasmins clearly know of the financial problems of the Kelton businesses prior to taking out this loan. The proceeds from this loan were used to pay the obligations of Kelton owed to the Bank of Vermont.

(f) Concealment of the Kite

This section presumes actual knowledge of a check kite on behalf of Mr. Lussier. Once again, there is reliance upon the allegations set forth in the criminal complaint, but not upon the actual testimony of those concerned. For example, there is no mention of Mr. Kelton's statements that he never told Mr. Lussier about the check kite and that he did not know if Mr. Kelton knew of

8

the check kite. (See C. Kelton Depo. of 8/4/94 in BOV v. LSB at pp. 12, 22, 23, 24, 56, 81.) There is reliance upon a bank examiner's and FBI agent's review of the situation with an eye towards proving a criminal complaint. In other words, hind sight with a purpose. Clearly, the Federal Bank Examiners and the FBI had far superior resources and far superior investigative skills than did the Lyndonville Savings Bank. These investigative experts poured over the Bank records and took several statements in depositions and worked for months prior to handing down an indictment against Mr. Lussier. We believe it illogical to assume that a small rural bank in the Northeast Kingdom of Vermont could compete with the investigative skills of the FBI and the FDIC and produce a similar result in a sorter period of time.

The only indication that there may have been knowledge on the part of Mr. Lussier of Mr. Kelton's check kite came from former bank officer, Dubois Thompson. Even Mr. Thompson's statements do not confirm that a check kite existed or that ultimate knowledge of a kite was transmitted to Mr. Lussier. The testimony merely indicates that Mr. Thompson thought there might be a kite. We find it interesting that Mr. Lussier was the only one that Mr. Thompson told of this belief and that, while he attended every single Board meeting, he never raised this issue with any other Directors.

It is fairly clear from the testimony of the other Directors, including Pearl Baird, that Mr. Thompson never stated any belief that there was a check kite being operated by Mr. Kelton to the

9

Board of Directors. They all testified that there was concern in July about the amount of funds passing through Mr. Kelton's account. It is also clear that they were not sure that it was a kite and that they were not desirous of accusing Mr. Kelton of a crime if there was no crime being committed.

Much is also made of Pearl Baird's position on this matter. However, we feel that the testimony is clear that Ms. Baird never mentioned that she felt this was a check kite to any other Board members or to Mr. Lussier. She had concerns about the activity in Mr. Kelton's account. She was indeed worried about the activity in that account. That concern in no way imputes knowledge of a kite to any of the other Directors or to Mr. Lussier.

Lastly, Mr. Lussier has denied knowledge of a kite from the very beginning and in all of his various depositions has continued to deny he had any knowledge of the kite or assisted in any way with the continuation of the kite. Under the state of the evidence, it is just as likely that Mr. Lussier's version of the facts is accurate and not that version propounded by the government.

10

Field & Field, P.C.

Attorneys at Law

59 No. Main Street
P.C. Box 488
Barre, Vermont 05641

Sarah L. Field

Andrew R. Field
of Counsel

Phone (802) 476-8338
Fax (802) 476-4504

November 7, 1995

John C. Gravel, Esq.
Bauer, Anderson & Gravel
P. O. Box 607
Burlington, VT 05402-0607

      Re: Beauregard v. Lussier, et al

Dear John:

I have just returned to my office after being away for over a
month, and have noted your letter of October 12, 1995, requesting comments on the action brought by the bank against Roger
Lussier and his wife, Evelyn.

My comments as to the aforementioned action are as follows:

1.   It appears to me that some of the counts are knowingly
     unsupportable by existing undisputed evidence, which is
     or should be so known to bank's counsel.

2.   To the extent that Roger Lussier's conduct can be visited
     upon the bank, either to the bank's advantage or disadvantage,
     as the case may be, and his importance as a witness in pending
     cases for and on behalf of the bank as well as himself person-
     ally, I am rather surprised over the vicious and vindictive
     nature of the complaint in singling out Roger Lussier for all
     of the bank's loan portfolio problems.

3.   I am somewhat concerned over (i) prior legal advice given to
     Roger Lussier by your firm in pending loan litigation where
     he has elected to appear pro se, which involves some of the
     counts (as he has so indicted to me) and (ii) discussions be-
     tween our respective law firms representing co-defendants
     in the Beauregard case (your firm, the bank and mine, Roger
     Lussier and others), as to evidentiary matters and Roger
     Lussier's position concerning facts preparatory to litigation,
     all undertaken in confidence and trust.

                       Very truly yours,

                       Andrew R. Field

ARF:JF
Blind Copy to Roger Lussier

STATE OF VERMONT
CALEDONIA COUNTY, SS

CALEDONIA SUPERIOR COURT
Docket No. 155-6-00CACV

LYNDONVILLE SAVINGS BANK)
AND TRUST COMPANY,)
    Plaintiff,)
)
)
ROGER LUSSIER,)
    Defendant,)
)
    and)
)
APPLIED RESEARCH AND)
DEVELOPMENT, INC.,)
    Defendant.)

DEFENDANT'S MOTION TO DISMISS AND FOR SUMMARY JUDGMENT AS A MATTER OF LAW PURSUANT TO RULES 12(b),(h)(3) and 56(c)

TABLE OF CONTENTS

TABLE OF AUTHORITIES: CASES

TABLE OF AUTHORITIES: STATUTES and RULES

	PAGE
12 V.S.A. § 511	9,32
12 V.S.A. § 558	2,9,10,28,36
V.R.Civ.P 12(b),(h)	2
V.R.Civ.P 56(c)	2
12 U.S.C. § 248	20
12 U.S.C. § 281	20
12 U.S.C. § 287	20
12 U.S.C. § 323	21
12 U.S.C. § 324	21
12 U.S.C. § 325	21
12 U.S.C. § 329	21
12 U.S.C. § 503	3,16-19
18 U.S.C. § 2	5
18 U.S.C. § 215	5,6,15-18
18 U.S.C. § 982	5
18 U.S.C. § 1001	5
18 U.S.C. § 1005	5,6,15-18
18 U.S.C. § 1344	5
18 U.S.C. § 1957	5
F.R.Crim.P. 33	6
The Federal Reserve System: Purposes & Functions (1974)	20,21

TABLE OF CONTENTS FOR APPENDIX

<u>**TABLE OF CONTENTS FOR APPENDIX**</u>
(continued)

COMES NOW, the Defendants Roger Lussier and Applied Research and Development, Incorporated,[1] by and through, Roger Lussier, <u>pro se</u>,[2] and pursuant to Vermont Rules of Civil Procedure 12(b),(h) and 56(c),[3] and respectfully requests this Honorable Court to find that Lussier is entitled to Summary Judgment and Dismissal as a matter of law.[4]

I. INTRODUCTION

The Bank relies on 12 VSA § 558 as its sole basis for jurisdiction. As a general rule, this equitable statute permits a plaintiff to bring a new action when its original, timely-filed action was dismissed for lack of subject matter jurisdiction.

However, there are exceptions to this general rule. For instance, upon a finding of gross negligence or fraud, and particularly when a plaintiff engages in improper

---

[1] Defendants are hereinafter expediently referred to for purposes only of this motion as "Lussier". The Plaintiff is hereinafter referred to as "the Bank".

[2] <u>Pro se</u> pleadings are to be liberally construed. <u>Bingham v. Tenney</u>, 154 Vt. 96 (1990).

[3] Summary judgment pursuant to V.R.Civ.P. 56 may be granted to a moving party where the opposing party asserts a claim which is barred by the statute of limitations. <u>Tierney v. Tierney</u>, 131 Vt. 48 (1973).

[4] Lussier has entered a Limited Notice of Appearance for the sole purpose of filing the instant motion, and any reply to the Bank's answer, with this Court. Otherwise, Lussier generally reserves all of his rights and specifically reserves the option of retaining experienced counsel to argue in support of the instant motion at any hearing.

jurisdiction manipulation in its original action, as the Bank did here, the equitable benefits of statutes like 12 VSA § 558 are not available.

To begin with, the Bank, which was represented at all times relevant by its well educated and sophisticated fiduciary agents, President Charles Bucknam, John Gravel, Esq. and Richard Johnston, Esq., is chargeable with gross negligence and reckless disregard for the truth of a material jurisdictional fact.

However, as the original action wore on through appeal, it became plain that the Bank, through reliance on cunning litigators, finesse, and material omission, ultimately perpetrated a fraud on the United States District Court for the District of Vermont, that for a time resulted in an $8.7 million verdict being entered against Lussier.

The verified complaint filed at the outset of the original action, over the signatures of all three fiduciaries, falsely alleged in at least four instances, that the Bank was a member of the Federal Reserve System, entitled to recover against Lussier pursuant to the Federal Reserve Act, 12 U.S.C. § 503.

However, the Bank never was a member of the Federal

Reserve System and this simple, stark reality, compelled a
unanimous panel of the United States Court of Appeals for
the Second Circuit to mandate that a multi-million dollar
judgment against Lussier be vacated and that the original
action be dismissed for lack of subject matter
jurisdiction.

The cold, tawdry record in this case as revealed by
the Bank's own affidavits, makes plain that it selfishly
guarded its pre-trial knowledge that it was not a member of
the Federal Reserve System until after judgment was entered
in its favor.

Significantly, this revelation was not made as a
result of the Bank wrestling with its conscience and
deciding to come clean. Rather, the truth had to be
extracted, post-judgment, by Lussier's aggressive appellate
counsel, with all the leverage one might reserve for an
impacted wisdom tooth.

Now, some five long years after thumbing its nose at
this, the only court that was ever arguably available to
it, in favor of a Federal forum where the Bank would have
the strategic advantage of pressing what it believed to be
a prima facie case against Lussier (in light of the short
shrift paid by the Federal Reserve Act to convicted former
officers and directors of banks that actually are members

of the Federal Reserve System) the Bank insults the integrity of this Court with tacit prayers that it should be extricated from the mess created first by its repeated material misstatements of jurisdictional facts and apparent reckless disregard for the truth, and second by a jurisdictional shell-game built on the back of material omission, obfuscation, and other remarkable examples of gamesmanship.

The detailed facts and law to follow will clearly demonstrate that this is a classic case of a plaintiff not wanting to sleep in the bed it made for itself.

Accordingly, it is respectfully submitted, that this Court must find that Lussier is entitled to Summary Judgment as a matter of law, and that the case at bar must be dismissed.

II. BACKGROUND

Defendant Applied Research and Development, Inc. is a Vermont Corporation owned by Lussier. Defendant Lussier is the Bank's former President.

Following his resignation on February 24, 1993, Lussier was indicted in the United States District Court for the District of Vermont pursuant to 18 U.S.C. §§ 2, 215, 982, 1001, 1005, 1344, 1957. Letter of Resignation,

Ex. A; Indictment, Ex. B.

Committed to proving his innocence, Lussier took his case to a jury, which on December 22, 1993, convicted him on several counts, including the § 215 and § 1005 charges. United States v. Lussier, 71 F.3rd 456 (2nd Cir. 1995).[5]

Lussier was sentenced on June 21, 1994. The elements of his sentence included a 46 month term of imprisonment, a 24 month term of supervised release[6], a $100,000 fine, a $105,252 criminal forfeiture and restitution in the amount of $426,204.67. Judgment & Commitment Order, Ex. C.[7]

Lussier was allowed to remain at liberty pending appeal of his conviction and sentence. His conviction was affirmed by the United States Court of Appeals for the Second Circuit, Lussier, supra, and as ordered, on February 28, 1996, he self-surrendered to Allenwood Federal Prison Camp in Pennsylvania. Lussier remained in the custody of the Federal Bureau of Prisons until his release on July 1, 1999.

Shortly before the Circuit issued its October 17, 1995

---

[5] At this writing, Lussier's criminal case is again pending before the United States Court of Appeals for the Second Circuit pursuant to F.R.Crim.P. 33. United States v. Lussier, No. 98-1392.

[6] Lussier is presently in the midst of completing his term of supervised release, which will terminate in approximately one year.

[7] At all times relevant, the restitution order suffered from the simple fatal flaw of having been imposed in connection with a transaction for which Lussier was never even charged, much less convicted. Order of March 11, 1998 Eliminating Restitution, Ex. D; also, United States v. Lussier, 104 F.3d 32 (2d Cir. 1997), for procedural history.

opinion affirming Lussier's conviction, the Bank filed the
original action against Lussier and Lussier's wife Evelyn
Lussier, in the United States District Court for the
District of Vermont. <u>Original Complaint, Ex. E.</u>

The Bank also moved quickly to secure Writs of
Attachment on personal property. <u>Order of Approving Writ
Application, Ex. F.</u> Thereafter, Evelyn was dismissed from
the original action. <u>Order of Dimissal, Ex. G.</u>

After enduring the blandishments and rigorous economic
demands attendant to defending oneself in a Federal
criminal prosecution, in which, high profile counsel was
retained at great personal expense,[8] so overburdened was
Lussier by the time the Bank's original action was filed,
that at the aforementioned attachment hearing, with
everything on the line, Lussier argued in court <u>pro se</u>.

Not surprisingly, the Bank prevailed on all arguments
at the 1995 attachment hearing. Shortly thereafter Lussier
was off to the Poconos to commence his term of
imprisonment.

At the civil trial, which the Federal Bureau of
Prisons would not permit Lussier to attend, the Bank
"agreed to permit", Lussier's longtime friend and

---

[8] During his criminal proceeding, Lussier was represented by Peter Langrock, Esq., trial counsel
and by F. Lee Bailey, Esq., appellate counsel.

colleague, Attorney Andrew Field of Montpelier, appear as Lussier's counsel. <u>Affidavit of Attorney Richard Johnston, Ex. H.</u>

In contrast, the Bank leveraged its superior economic power over Lussier and was represented at all times in the original action by Richard Johnston, a senior partner of the legendary Boston firm, Hale & Dorr, as well as local Vermont counsel, Attorney John Gravel.[9]

Over the course of several years, the original action proceeded through discovery, a bench trial and ultimately on December 17, 1997, a verdict in the amount of $8,769,740 was entered against Lussier. <u>See, Memorandum of Decision, Ex. I.</u>

As is his practice, Lussier backed a different horse on appeal; this time retaining St. Johnsbury's David Williams as his counsel.

On appeal, the United States Court of Appeals for the Second Circuit, in a published opinion, unanimously ruled that the verdict against Lussier in the Bank's original action must be vacated and that the case should be dismissed for lack of subject matter jurisdiction. <u>Lyndonville Savings Bank & Trust Co. v. Lussier</u>, No. 98-

---

[9] The impressive bios of the Bank's lawyers, are published at http://www.haledorr.com and at http://www.vtlawoffices.com/bios/gravel/, respectively. Lussier notes that Attorney Gravel

7079 (2d Cir. 05/03/2000), Ex. J.

The Bank elected not to file a Motion for Rehearing En Banc or a Petition for a Writ of Certiorari to the United States Supreme Court. Accordingly, mandate issued in the original action on May 3, 2000.

Shortly after time expired for the Bank to pursue any further Federal appellate remedies, it brought a new action in this Court pursuant to 12 V.S.A. § 558.

However, based on the following relevant facts and applicable law, the Bank may not avail itself of § 558's equitable benefits.

Accordingly, since the Bank alleges no additional or alternative jurisdictional ground(s) upon which it might continue to proceed in this Court, this case must be dismissed with prejudice. [10]

III. RELEVANT FACTS

To keep this as simple and straightforward as possible, Lussier begins by asking this Court to take judicial notice that the law of the case in the original action, as made by the United States Court of Appeals for the Second Circuit is as follows:

---

continues as counsel for the Bank in the original action, and upon information and belief, Hale & Dorr is available to Attorney Gravel and the Bank, as a "resource" behind the scenes.

1.   The only Federal question in the original action was whether the Bank was entitled to a civil judgment requiring Lussier to pay the full amount of a Federal criminal restitution order that could not sustain an award.

2.   The invalid Federal restitution order did not underlie any of the state claims.

3.   The Bank's remaining claims against Lussier arose under state law and the district court's award of more than $8 million was based solely on these claims.

4.   The judgment was vacated and the case was dismissed for want of subject matter jurisdiction. Lyndonville, supra.

Given the law of Lyndonville, the only issue presented on the instant motion is whether under the totality of circumstances and facts of this particular case, the Bank is entitled to receive the equitable benefits of 12 V.S.A. § 558, in light of the choices it made before, during and after it proceeded in the original action, on state claims in the wrong forum.

At the outset, tedious though it may be, it is extremely relevant for this Court to be aware of the background and experience of the three fiduciaries who were

---

[10] Allegations contained in the new action are up to 12 years of age, well beyond the confines of 12 V.S.A. § 511. The Bank's new action dangles by the thread of its § 558 jurisdictional claim.

the primary actors on the Bank's behalf throughout all
critical stages of the original action.

(a) Lyndonville President Charles Bucknam

At all times relevant to the motion at Bar, Lussier's
successor, Mr. Charles Bucknam, was the Bank's President.
Mr. Bucknam has earned his living in the banking business
for over a quarter of a century.

Mr. Bucknam graduated from Cornell in 1966 with a
Bachelor of Arts degree in economics. He obtained his
Masters of Business Administration degree from the
University of Vermont with a concentration in finance in
1978. In 1989, after a course that spanned approximately
three years, he graduated and received his diploma from the
prestigious Stonier Graduate School of Banking.

Mr. Bucknam's list of professional affiliations is
impressive, too. Such affiliations include membership in
Robert Morris Associates, an educational organization
concentrating in commercial lending, the Independent
Bankers Association of America, the Vermont Bankers
Association and the American Bankers Association.

He also served on the Commercial Lending Committee of
the Vermont Bankers Association and the Government
Relations Committee of the Vermont Bankers Association.

Significantly, and of particular relevance to the question at bar, are the facts that during his career as a professional banker Mr. Bucknam worked for a number of banks that are members of the Federal Reserve System. In Massachusetts, he worked at BayBank and managed an office in Cambridge. After moving to Vermont in 1972, Mr. Bucknam worked at Howard Bank where he became a regional manager. In 1986 he joined the Caledonia National Bank and became bank president of that bank in June 1991. Deposition of Charles Bucknam, Generally, Ex. K; Trial Testimony of Charles Bucknam, Ex. L, pp. 34-38.

(b) Lead Counsel, Attorney Richard Johnston

In light of the bio of Attorney Richard Johnston, published to the Internet by Hale & Dorr, Note 6, supra, Lussier notes as a matter of public record that "Rich" as his personal web page indicates he apparently likes to be called, is a Senior Partner in the Litigation and Environmental Departments at Hale and Dorr LLP.

Attorney Johnston's professional affiliations include the Boston, Massachusetts, American and International Bar Associations.

Attorney Johnston graduated cum laude from Harvard Law School in 1976, and magna cum laude from Cornell University in 1972, where he was elected to Phi Beta Kappa.

Attorney Johnston's practice concentrates on domestic and international business litigation, environmental litigation and health law litigation. He has also represented numerous clients involved in business litigation in state and federal courts throughout the United States, including high technology companies, manufacturers, and banks.

He has tried cases in Massachusetts and over a half-dozen other states. His litigation practice has had a substantial international component. He has represented foreign governments, banks and companies in litigation in the United States. He has been involved in international arbitrations in Europe and Asia. He has participated as a speaker on international arbitration at American Bar Association and Boston Bar Association programs, and he has spoken at international legal conferences in Israel and South America.

Attorney Johnston has been involved in numerous environmental Superfund cases, including the Industriplex site in Woburn, Massachusetts, the Nyanza Site in Ashland, Massachusetts, the National Fireworks Site in Hanover, Massachusetts, the Helen Kramer Landfill in New Jersey, and the Davis Landfill Site in Rhode Island.

He has tried environmental cases in state and federal courts. Mr. Johnston has published Environmental Planning Catch 22: Kleppe v. Sierra Club, Harvard Environmental Law Review (1976), analyzing the concept of comprehensive environmental impact statements for the synergistic effect of multiple projects. He is co-author of Phase-Out of Ozone-Depleting Substances: The Montreal Protocol and beyond, and author of a paper on alternative dispute resolution in environmental cases.

Attorney Johnston, also has spoken at seminars on environmental insurance matters, liability issues facing corporate environmental managers, and Brownsfield legislation. He is currently head of Hale & Dorr's environmental litigation group.

Attorney Johnston has represented hospitals, nursing homes, prescription benefits management companies, national pharmacy chains, individual pharmacies, clinical laboratories, physicians, medical practice groups, medical management companies and other medical providers in litigation, regulatory matters, reimbursement issues and Medicare/Medicaid audits and investigations.

(c) Attorney John Gravel

Similarly, in light of biographical information

available on Attorney Gravel's individual web page, the
following is a matter of public record.

Attorney Gravel is described as "one of the firm's
most active courtroom lawyers." Attorney Gravel lists
banking, bankruptcy, business/corporate, civil litigation,
probate and estate planning within his areas of practice.

Attorney Gravel received his J.D. from Boston College
in 1972. Thereafter, he was chair of the VBA Committee on
Specialization in 1981-82; chair of the VBA Business Law
Committee 1989-90; member of the VBA Committee that drafted
New For-Profit Corporation law with responsibility for
drafting new section on close corporations; member of the
committee that drafted new non-profit corporation law. Both
have been enacted by the Vermont legislature. Attorney
Gravel is also a member of the Vermont Statutory Revision
Commission as well as being the individual responsible for
sponsoring Attorney Johnston's pro hac vice plea, to appear
in the Federal District Court as lead counsel for the
Bank.

(d) The Creation of a "Prima Facie" Case

As this Court continues to review and consider the
facts relevant to the instant motion, it is important to
keep in mind that Lussier was convicted pursuant to 18

U.S.C. §§ 215, 1005.

During the preparation and filing of the original action, these counts of conviction loomed large in the Bank's mind, as was revealed by Attorney Johnston at the outset of the 1995 attachment hearing. At this first-ever hearing conducted in the original action, Attorney Johnston had this to say:

> "…[A]s to the second principle count, which is violation of the Federal Reserve bank conduct statutes, we have cited in the complaint two separate statutes, 18 U.S.C. § 215 and 18 U.S.C. § 1005 of which Mr. Lussier was convicted in his criminal trial. 12 USC sec 503 says that if someone knowingly violates those statutes, the victim, in this case the bank, is entitled to recover against the person for his conduct. Whereas here, Mr. Lussier was convicted, the bank has **prima facie** proof that he knowingly committed violations of those statutes, and as such, the bank is entitled to recovery." Transcript of Attachment Hearing, p.11, Ex. M (emphasis added)

Not that he would disagree, but Lussier would really be stunned were the Bank to argue here that this Court was not available to it when it filed the original action in 1995.

That said, Lussier once again asks the Court to take judicial notice that had the Bank timely-filed its original action in state court, it would not have been able to proceed via the unmerciful Federal Reserve Act, which as Attorney Johnston noted, is effectively so beneficial to any member bank seeking to recover from a defrocked former officer, that the question is not <u>whether</u> such a bank will receive judgment, but <u>when</u>.

Further, as a matter of law, had the Bank timely-filed their state claims in state court, it would not be strictly limited, as it is now, to alleging only § 558 jurisdiction.

(e) The Fatally False Verified Complaint

At the 1995 attachment hearing, Attorney Johnston stood before a Federal judge, and when he looked across the aisle what he saw for an opponent was a disgraced, destitute, convicted, hapless, pro se, former bank president, mere days away from leaving the state to serve a 46 month term of imprisonment. This is also precisely what the Federal judge saw.

So by simply arguing that the Bank was a member of the Federal Reserve System, Attorney Johnston handily convinced the Federal court that it actually had a <u>prima facie</u> case, and that accordingly, Lussier had no chance of prevailing in the original action, as a matter of law.

Understandably, the Court had no difficulty finding "sufficient facts to show that it is reasonably likely that the Plaintiff will succeed in its claims against the Defendants pursuant to 12 U.S.C. § 503" and the Order approving the application for a writ of attachment was issued. Ex. F.

The Court relied on the verified complaint submitted over the signatures of Mr. Bucknam and Attorneys Johnson and Gravel, wherein the Bank repeatedly asserted that it was a member of the Federal Reserve System entitled to relief under the Federal Reserve Act.

Also, in the Memorandum of Law provided to the Court by the Bank in support of the writ application, the Bank again unambiguously stated, that it "is a member of the Federal Reserve System". Memorandum of Law, Ex. N.

And as noted, Attorney Johnson stared down a Federal judge and orally republished these written allegations, with the primary objective of taking Lussier completely out of commerce.

Quoting now from the Verified Complaint, Ex. E, the Bank alleged the following in four instances:

> "This court has subject matter jurisdiction pursuant to…12 U.S.C. § 503 (liability of bank directors and officers)." ¶5.
>
> ***
>
> "Lyndonville is a member of the Federal Reserve Bank system." ¶59.
>
> ***
>
> "Roger Lussier is liable to the bank pursuant to 12 U.S.C. § 503 because as a director and officer

of a bank in the Federal Reserve Bank System he knowingly violated 18 U.S.C. § 215 and 18 U.S.C. § 1005." ¶61.

* * *

"Lyndonville is entitled to recover damages from Roger Lussier pursuant to 12 U.S.C. § 503." ¶62.

Lussier once again asks the Court to take judicial notice that the Bank carefully published, in these four discrete instances, essentially the same false allegation and orally argued in support of them because it needed a Federal judge to believe that it truly was a member of the Federal Reserve System before it could take control of Lussier.

If the Bank didn't want Chief Judge Murtha to believe it was a member of the Federal Reserve System, presumably it would not have alleged membership in a Verified Complaint, submitted over the signatures of the three above named fiduciaries acting on the Bank's behalf.

Unfortunately, for the Bank, in light of the detailed published opinion issued by the United States Court of Appeals for the Second Circuit, it is now law "that Lyndonville had never been a member of the Federal Reserve system. Hence, the only federal question remaining in Lyndonville's civil suit was its restitution claim." Lyndonville, supra.

Absent the critical lynchpin of Federal Reserve Membership, the Bank's legal status was that of a Vermont citizen suing another Vermont citizen on nothing but state claims in Federal court.

(f) The Bank's Pre-trial Knowledge

Count II in the original action, is the count that provides the Federal Reserve connection, or stated differently, the Bank's *prima facie* case.

According to Attorney Johnston, the Bank included the allegation of Federal Reserve System membership in the Verified Complaint as the "predicate **factual allegation** for the Section 503 claim pleaded in Count II." Johnston to Williams, p.2, Ex. O. (emphasis added).

Post-judgment, the Bank finally admitted that Mr. Bucknam and Attorneys Johnston and Gravel, had actual pre-trial knowledge that the Bank was not a member of the Federal Reserve System. Post-Judgment Affidavit of Charles Bucknam, Ex. P; Post-Judgment Affidavit of Richard Johnston, Ex. H.

Whether the Bank actually knew it was not a member of the Federal Reserve System on the day the Verified Complaint was filed in the Federal court is a question this Court ought to consider based on the totality of circumstances and these additional facts.

Prior to being President of the non-member bank at bar, Mr. Bucknam was President of the Caledonia National Bank, a bank that was a member of the Federal Reserve System at all times relevant to Mr. Bucknam's then-presidency.

As members of the Federal Reserve System, these banks own shares in the Federal Reserve Bank, receive dividends on their shares, and are subjected to reserve and capital requirements and periodic examinations by Federal Reserve Examiners. 12 U.S.C. §§ 248, 281, 287.

These Banks also have to comply with laws and regulations regarding mergers with other banking institutions, establishment of branches, relations with bank holding companies, interlocking directorates, and loan and investment limitations. The Federal Reserve System: Purposes and Function (1974) 20.

In February 1991 the Federal Reserve Bank issued a Cease and Desist Order against Caledonia National Bank after Federal Reserve examiners examined the Caledonia National Bank. Deposition of Charles Bucknam, Ex. K, pp. 63-64.

In his deposition, President Bucknam explained that the Federal Reserve regulates bank holding companies, while the FDIC does not. Id., Note 1.

Between 1992 and early 1993, Mr. Bucknam was also the President of the Independent Bank Group, a bank holding company that operated three national banks. Id., pp. 160-161.

In late 1993, Mr. Bucknam applied for a job at the Lyndonville Savings Bank, a state chartered, non-member bank. Before taking the job, Mr. Bucknam reviewed a number of FDIC Cease and Desist Orders all of which were captioned as follows:

> "In the Matter of
> LYNDONVILLE SAVINGS BANK AND TRUST COMPANY
> LYNDONVILLE, VERMONT
> INSURED STATE **NONMEMBER** BANK" (emphasis added)

State chartered banks must apply for membership in the Federal Reserve System. 12 U.S.C. §§ 321 et seq.

Upon becoming a member of the Federal Reserve System, State chartered banks are required to buy stock and comply with the reserve and capital requirements of the Federal Reserve Banking law. 12 U.S.C. §§ 323-324,329.

As a condition of membership, state-chartered member banks are subject to Federal Reserve Bank supervision and examination. 12 U.S.C. §§ 325; The Federal Reserve System; Purposes and Functions (1974) 20.

Federal Reserve Regulation H defines the requirements

for State bank membership in the Federal Reserve System and establishes minimum levels for the ratio of capital to assets to be maintained by state member banks.

In January 1994, Mr. Bucknam became acting president of the Lyndonville Savings Bank. Trial Testimony of Charles Bucknam, p.77, Ex. L.

In the complaint verified by Mr. Bucknam on September 29, 1995, the Bank's attorneys, repeatedly refer to FDIC Cease & Desist Orders all of which trumpet the Bank's non-member status on their face. Ex. E.

In light of the foregoing and in light of Mr. Bucknam's impressive list of credentials, accrued over the course of a professional banking career that has spanned nearly a quarter century, it certainly seems unlikely that Mr. Bucknam didn't know of the Bank's non-member status prior to the filing of the original action. [11]

(g) The Simultaneously Filed Two Inconsistent Motions

On, or about, July 25, 1997, the Bank did two things simultaneously. First, in one pleading styled, Joint Motion

---

[11] Lussier will be the first to recognize that it might be unseemly for him, of all people, to pound his chest too hard, in the absence of direct evidence that the Bank knew *from the day of filing* that its pleadings and arguments, repeatedly and materially, falsely alleged a critical jurisdictional fact. But to be sure, in the original action, President Bucknam filed no less than five affidavits. Each was submitted pursuant to the pains and penalties of perjury. In contrast, Lussier asks this Court to take judicial notice that in the instant case, President Bucknam's affidavit is not submitted pursuant to the pains and penalties of perjury. Cf. Affidavits in Original Action with Affidavit in

for Separate Trials, it sought the dismissal of Count II. In a separate document styled as Motion to Further Amend Complaint, it republished Count II. Both of these motions were consented to by defense counsel.

In the Joint Motion for Separate Trials, the Bank explained that it "did not intend to pursue Count II, and the same may be dismissed by the Court with prejudice". Ex. R, p.2.[12]

In the cover letter the Bank submitted to the Court along with these motions, the Bank emphasized to Judge Murtha that the "two consented-to Motions are intended to clarify and simplify the pleadings and trial of this case." Johnston to Judge Murtha, Ex. S.[13]

Knowing that Federal subject matter jurisdiction hung in the balance, the Bank certainly did not want to file anything, such as, for example, a Motion to Dismiss Count II, since such an overt act might focus more attention to the fatally false verified complaint than was minimally

---

New Action, Exs. Q1-Q6.

[12] The Court will note that Count II is the Federal Reserve Act count that was pleaded in support of the Bank's false averments that it had a prima facie Federal cause of action against Lussier on what the Second Circuit held in Lyndonville were, at all times relevant, state claims. Ex. E. Lussier can also just see the Bank answering that the republication of the false allegations was also nothing more than just another honest mistake. Lussier notes that each time the Bank argues it made a mistake of this nature, it admits gross negligence, reckless disregard for the truth, or both, which is all this Court needs to find that, once again, jurisdiction is wanting.

necessary.

The Bank avoided filing a <u>Motion to Dismiss Count II</u>, by burying the dismissal of Count II in the fine print of motion papers that on their caption omitted any mention of Count II's dismissal and simultaneously incorporating the dismissed material in a separate document.

This made the blithe, express reference to Count II appear as something of an afterthought that would have little, if any, impact on the case at bar.[14]

Indeed, the vista painted by the Bank was that of a conscientious, considerate, cooperative plaintiff simply trying to clarify and simplify life for a busy court.

This approach apparently had some appeal to the Court as the consented to motions were granted.[15]

So clever was the Bank, that the extensive record in this case reveals not one instance where the Bank's

---

[13] Try as he might, Lussier does not understand how the simultaneous dismissal and re-filing of Count II simplified and clarified anything. It is respectfully suggested, however, that, given the legal tightrope the Bank was walking, it surely had its reasons to act out is desperation.
[14] Lussier would be surprised to see the Bank expressly argue the Count II was ever dismissed. Under attack from appellate counsel, Attorney Johnston on three occasions in his letter responding, was willing to go only so far as to explain that this last minute flurry of activity "<u>effectively</u> dismissed Count II." <u>Ex. H</u>. (emphasis added)

[15] The Bank may argue in its answer that had its jurisdictional theory been so outrageous, the Federal court would have dismissed the original action <u>sua sponte</u>. In anticipation of this argument, Lussier observes that a court would have to be mighty jaded to suspect that the senior partner of a Boston mega-firm would stand before it and repeatedly and falsely argue in support of the lone factual predicate allegation that authorized his client to press its state claims in Federal court. The fact is, the leveling of this patently false jurisdictional theory was <u>so</u> outrageous that no reasonable person could ever anticipate that any bank would be so stupid as to allow it to be filed in the first place.

decision to dismiss Count II raised a flag either with defense counsel or the Court.[16]

It is significant and relevant to the proper resolution of this motion, that even though the Bank admits it had actual knowledge, pre-trial, of its non-membership status, it did not promptly seek to prosecute its state claims in this Court.

Rather, the Bank would have us believe that, without ever saying so, it stealthily pressed forward on some foolish theory that since Lussier was once ordered to make restitution to it in a Federal criminal case, that this permitted the Bank to sue him in Federal court on the other counts. This is not the "Federal Reserve" theory relied upon by the Bank, or the Court, with regard to the attachment that took Lussier out of the running in the original action.[17]

---

[16] Far from raising a flag, defense counsel, on the one hand, and at the Bank's behest, readily stipulated to the dismissal of Count II, but then on the other hand, also at the Bank's behest, freely stipulated that subject matter jurisdiction survived the dismissal of Count II. Lussier's elderly friend and trial counsel, also apparently never noticed, that even after the Bank dismissed Count II, that just three days later, it cleverly and surreptitiously "refiled" the entirety of Count II, by republication in its Second Amendment to Verified Complaint. Ex. T, p.1, ¶ 67. Thus, with the benefit of hindsight, the entire history of Count II is that on various pre-trial occasions, the count was filed, dismissed and re-filed. This reality prompted Lussier's aggressive appellate counsel to expressly conclude the following in a letter to Attorney Johnson and otherwise in Lussier's appellate reply: "It appears, therefore, that as of July 1997, the Bank was still falsely claiming membership in the Federal Reserve System in documents filed in the United States District Court, District of Vermont." Lussier's Appellate Reply Brief, Ex. U, Williams to Johnston, Ex. V.

[17] The sheer folly of the Bank's baseless fallback theory of jurisdiction was fully exposed when at oral argument, and obviously exasperated by having to "repeat the same question" to the Bank's counsel over and over again, Judge Sotomeyer of the United States Court of Appeals for the Second Circuit, unloaded on Attorney Johnston:

Once again, Lussier asks the Court to take judicial notice that under Lyndonville, it is the law of this case that jurisdiction was defeated because Lussier successfully demonstrated on appeal that all of the Bank's contrived, jurisdictional fall-back positions were "insubstantial, implausible, or completely devoid of merit."

VII. A STUNNING POST-TRIAL DISCOVERY

The Bank's dismissal of Count II definitely caught the eye of newly retained appellate counsel, who was not one to be cajoled by the Bank's assembly of cunning litigators.

Between trial and appeal, Attorney Williams pressed the question of non-membership with the Bank. Attorney Williams sought a second deposition of Mr. Bucknam. But Attorney Johnston would have none of that.

The best Williams was able to get from the Bank was Mr. Bucknam's sworn affidavit that since the Bank relied on the Federal Reserve for several services such as, for example, "coins and food stamps" he "believed that

---

Judge Sotomeyer: What you're basically saying to me is that congress intended to create a similar cause of action like the one that you dismissed because you weren't a member of the federal reserve bank, and let you bring all your state law claims of fraud and breach of fiduciary duty into federal court merely because a restitution order was issued. We have now created an independent, Congress intended an independent basis for you to do that.
Johnston: Not merely because the restitution order existed.
Judge Sotomeyer: *There is no other basis for federal jurisdiction.*
Attorney Johnston: *Understood....* Transcript of Oral Argument. Ex. W. last page (italics added)

Lyndonville was a member of the Federal Reserve System."
Ex. P.(emphasis added)

The Bank essentially wanted Attorney Williams to
believe that under all the circumstances, what he
complained of amounted to nothing more than an excusable
mistake.

VIII. THE BANK'S POST-TRIAL CONDUCT

The Bank's stated position with regard to the above,
is basically that it wouldn't change a thing. It has
expressly, and without apology, aggressively defended its
actions and inactions as having "appropriately corrected"
its original position that Lyndonville was a member of the
Federal Reserve System. Johnston to Williams, Ex. X.

On appeal, Lussier's counsel characterized the Bank's
post-trial conduct as "brazen", Ex. U, and noted that even
after Count II was dismissed, the Bank continued to falsely
claim membership in the Federal Reserve System.

Amazingly, the Bank revealed its belief that a state
court proceeding would result in "an almost certain
judgment against Lussier[.]" Bank's Appellate Answer, Ex.
Y, p.33.(emphasis added)

By contrast, a Federal forum, pursuant to the Federal
Reserve Act, promised certain judgment to the Bank, in view

of the finality of Lussier's conviction resulting from his failure to prevail on appeal of his § 215 and § 1005 convictions.

The Bank's most recent surprising post-trial act, comes with the filing of the instant complaint and no doubt, the hope, that the stench of its disingenuous posturing in the original action would not be brought to this Court's attention.

This Court must not stand by and permit the Bank to pursue Lussier afresh pursuant to 12 V.S.A. § 558.

Accordingly, it is respectfully submitted, based on the foregoing facts and the legal argument to follow, that this Court must dismiss the instant case and enter an order for summary judgment in favor of Lussier.

IV. ARGUMENT

AS A RESULT OF ITS GROSS NEGLIGENCE AND/OR FRAUD ON THE FEDERAL COURT, THE BANK IS NOT ENTITLED TO THE EQUITABLE BENEFITS OF THE VERMONT RENEWAL STATUTE, 12 V.S.A. § 558

At the outset, Lussier acknowledges pursuant to Leno v. Meunier, 125 Vt. 30 (1965), that § 558 means what it says, that limitations statutes are to be liberally construed, that, as a general rule, a plaintiff is permitted to bring a new action in state court, even when the original dismissed action was originally brought in

Federal court, and interestingly, that under <u>Leno</u>, not every instance of so-called "jurisdiction manipulation" (such as changing primary residence) bars a <u>worthy</u> plaintiff from obtaining the renewal benefits of § 558.

But in distinguishing <u>Leno</u> from garden variety fraud on the court cases, the Leno Court took the time to explain that "[g]enerally speaking, a fraud on the court must be such a course of intentional and successful deception and conduct by a person in respect to a matter in court which result in a perversion and obstruction of justice." <u>Id</u>. at 32.

Not surprisingly, the respect for the integrity of judicial process, that resounds in <u>Leno</u>, can be found in nearly every case wherein equities are balanced in assessing the applicability or non-applicability of renewal statutes similar to the one invoked by the Bank in the case at bar.

In fact, the United States Supreme Court wrote, in a Leno-like vein, well over a century ago, that:

> "Cases might be supposed, perhaps, where the want of jurisdiction in the court was so clear that the bringing of a suit thereon would show such gross negligence and indifference as to cut the party off from the benefit of the saving statute." <u>Smith v. McNeal</u>, 109 U.S. 986 (1883).

The libraries of cases appear to contain nothing but bad news for the Bank; that is unless this Court is of a mind to believe the laugher it will hear from the Bank, that the reason it now comes into Court foisted on its own petard is a simple matter of innocent mistake.

If it is a mistake, it is unreasonable and inexcusable.

Even if for some reason that Lussier cannot imagine, this Court does not smell something overtly fishy, the Court in White v. Tucker, 369 N.E.2nd 90, 94 (5th Appellate District Ill. 1977), notes that in several jurisdictions where the original action was dismissed for lack of jurisdiction, "great negligence" or a lack of "good faith" is sufficient to bar the application of a renewal statute.

This reality renders any defense of "innocent mistake" unavailable to the Bank, where as here, the lawyers, before filing the Verified Complaint, and relying on it to essentially take economic control of Lussier, had a solemn duty to investigate the truthfulness of their pleadings prior to filing.

As Attorney Johnston wrote in one letter to Lussier's counsel, in 1998, well after judgment had been entered in favor of the Bank, membership status was pled as a "predicate factual allegation."

Accordingly, this case is completely distinguishable from the body of cases on the panel's mind in Gaines v. New York City, 109 N.E. 594, 596 (N.Y. Court of Appeals 1915), where it was observed that jurisdictional questions "are often obscure and intricate."

This issue here is simple.

A person cannot have a good faith belief that it is a member of the Federal Reserve System. This is particularly true, where, as here, the individual good-faith claimant has prior first-hand knowledge that such membership implicates far more than the occasional ordering of coins and food stamps.

There can be no doubt, that what the Court has before it is a case of material misrepresentation and ommission, not mistake.

Were this fiasco a mistake, all questions of the availability of Federal subject matter jurisdiction could have been settled by simply picking up the phone and accessing readily available public records, just as Lussier's appellate counsel did between judgment and appeal.

In Lussier's opinion, a tough case for the Bank to contend with is Hardin v. Cass County, 42 F. 652 (1890).

In Hardin, the plaintiff brought an action in the

federal court and pleaded falsely, merely for the purpose of giving the court jurisdiction of the amount.

It was held that the equitable construction given the statute allowing a new action cannot be invoked by one who knowingly practices a fraud on the jurisdiction of the court and that, accordingly, the benefit of the statute should be denied when it is manifest that the plaintiff counted on a false statement in order to give his cause a colorable standing in court, as he preferred a judgment on his genuine claim from the Federal rather than the state court.

The Hardin Court sat slack-jawed, just as Lussier imagines the Bank has rendered this Court, when it noted that "there was not only an inherent want of jurisdiction in the court in which [the original action] was brought, but the plaintiff knew it[.]" Hardin, supra at 656.

In the instant case, it is inescapable, that the Bank, with full knowledge both of its rights and the falsity of its claim, chose to waive claim to any rights it may have had under 12 V.S.A. § 511.[18]

Remarkably, the Bank now is in the position of having

---

[18] Solely for the purpose of this motion, Lussier does not argue that 12 V.S.A. § 511 was not available to the Bank when it filed its state claims in Federal court in 1995. See, Warner v. Citizens National Bank, 267 F. 661 (6th cir. 1920), construing a renewal statute and noting that when a suit is brought after the time fixed by statute, the burden is on the plaintiff to plead and prove that it would be inequitable to apply the immediate application of the doctrine of laches.

to beg this Court to completely ignore the spirit of "equitable construction" as a condition precedent to releasing it from the trap it sprung on itself. Obviously, this the Court cannot do.

Unfortunately for the Bank, Lussier has a few more arrows remaining in his quiver. See, Gaines, supra (renewal statutes exist to "save the rights of the honest rather than fraudulent suiter."); Vason v. Nickey, 293 F.Supp 1405, 1406 (W.d. Tenn. 1968) ("When the plaintiff has been grossly negligent or was not acting in good faith when he erroneously pursued an action in a court which did not have jurisdiction, the saving statute is not available to him."); Phillips v. Whittom, 192 S.W.2nd 856 (S.Ct.Mo. 1946) ("The defendant in the litigation also has some rights, and is entitled to complain of an unreasonable and unjust abuse of the process of the courts….[T]he negligent bringing of a void action will not toll the statute of limitations if the plaintiff's negligence be great enough."); Krueger v. Walters, 179 S.W.2nd 615 (Kansas City, MO Court of Appeals, 1944).

It is inescapable that these three fiduciaries knew of the Bank's non-membership before trial and that only under post-judgment badgering from appellate counsel did the house of cards upon which judgment was obtained, come tumbling down.

The totality of circumstances also suggest that for a short time, the Bank's attorneys probably raised a glass and toasted the fraudulently obtained $8.7 million verdict.

Neither Lussier, nor this Court, need devote much further effort to this matter. The facts are simple and straightforward. Indeed, most of the operative facts are law.

In its answer to this motion, the Bank will argue, as it must, that it made a mistake and that the mistake is reasonable and excusable. It will righteously puff out its chest and tell the Court how magnanimous and forthcoming it was in ensuring Count II was dismissed before trial.

It will speak of a good-faith belief in its utterly meritless, fallback theory of jurisdiction, on which it claims to have proceeded through trial, and argue that it had this alternative theory in mind from day one, notwithstanding Judge Sotomeyer's incredulity when she spanked the Bank.

Finally, the Bank will hope that this Court ignores the undeniable reality, that even as it actively participated in the dismissal of Count II, it coyly ensured that defense counsel was on paper with a stipulation that Federal subject matter jurisdiction existed in the wake of the dismissed count.

It is law that the bank filed a false complaint.

It is law that it secured an attachment of property pursuant to that false claim.

It is fact, that it failed to disclose its pre-trial knowledge of the falsity of its claim until after the trial was over and judgment was entered in its favor.

It is likewise inescapable, that had the Bank not been cornered by the dogged determination of appellate counsel, it would have booked the $8.7 million judgment as a contingent asset, the attached shares of stock would be sitting in the Bank's vault and Lussier's land would be up for auction.

And then, like the cat that swallowed the canary, the Bank would have chuckled to itself, taking great satisfaction in its ability to outfox an elderly country lawyer and finesse a busy Federal judge to such an extent that for a time, it actually got away with knowingly litigating its state claims in Federal court and securing a judgment thereon.

V. SUMMARY

The best that can be said about this case was that the Bank's attorneys were grossly negligent when they secured a writ of attachment based on a pleading that they knew, or should have known to be materially false. This alone, drastically tilted the scales of justice in favor of the Bank at trial.

Had the Bank been a member of the Federal Reserve System, the Bank would not now be before this Court.

The worst that can be said about this case is that the Bank knowingly perpetrated a fraud on the Federal court. The Bank would like this Court to believe that President Bucknam made an honest mistake that was both reasonable and inexcusable and that the attorneys are not in any way accountable for the filing of their fatally flawed pleadings. This is an absurd expectation.

The Bank proceeded in the Federal court for its prima facie value. It did so recklessly and negligently. It should not now be rewarded for its "mistakes."

VI. CONCLUSION

WHEREAS, it is settled law as to what this Court must do under the circumstances of this particular case.

Accordingly, Lussier prays that this Court will find that in light of the Bank's negligence, lack of good faith, reckless disregard for the truth and/or fraudulent misconduct in the original action, the Bank is not entitled to the equitable benefits of the Vermont renewal statute, 12 V.S.A. § 558.

Further, Lussier respectfully asks this Court to dismiss the above captioned matter, enter summary judgment in his favor, and provide such further relief as to the Court may seem just and proper.

Respectfully submitted,

[signature]

ROGER LUSSIER
Pro se
Post Office Box 192
Lyndonville, Vermont 05852
802.626.5448

CERTIFICATE OF SERVICE

I, Roger Lussier, do hereby certify that a copy of the foregoing Motion to Dismiss has this day been forwarded to John Gravel, Esq., attorney for the Bank.

Date___6-13-04___   *[signature]*
                                     ROGER LUSSIER, pro se

UNITED STATES DISTRICT COURT
DISTRICT OF VERMONT

Lyndonville Savings Bank and Trust Company, Plaintiff,	)))))	
v.	))	Civil Dkt. No. 95-CV-287
Roger Lussier and Evelyn Lussier, Defendants.	))	

AFFIDAVIT OF WENDY J. DAVENPORT

The undersigned, WENDY J. DAVENPORT, hereby states the following to be true and correct based upon my actual knowledge and belief as to events occurring at the Lyndonville Savings Bank and Trust Company ("the Bank") during the time material to the case at bar.

1. I was employed at the Bank from approximately April 1988 until August 1995.

2. I was employed as an executive secretary to the Chief Executive Officer and the Executive Vice President of the Bank. Thereafter, I was promoted to the position of Corporate Secretary and Executive Assistant.

3. One of my duties as an employee of the Bank was to prepare the agenda and packets for the meetings of the Board of Directors ("the Board"). I also attended regularly scheduled Board meetings and recorded the minutes of Board meetings from, on or about October 1988, until on or about August 1995.

4. I also assisted the Bank's retained counsel in compiling information they needed to adequately defend the Bank against the claims incorporated into the Complaint.

5. I have reviewed the Complaint filed in the above-captioned matter, together with the Affidavit of Charles Bucknam.

6. When I attended regularly scheduled Board meetings, I typically witnessed a Board that was animated and actively engaged in free and open discussion regarding any and all issues that would come before it.

7. I personally know each and every one of the Board members and I do not perceive any one of them as being pushovers, patsies, or mindless parrots standing in wait to blindly rubber stamp any of the loan proposals placed before them.

8. It was certainly not unusual for individual Board members to dissent or disagree among themselves.

9. Roger Lussier was not in charge of negotiating or purchasing insurance and insurance-related coverage for the bank. Another Board member, George Hopkins was the Bank's insurance agent. Then-Chief Executive Officer and Executive Vice President Dubois Thompson was in charge of securing appropriate insurance coverage for the Bank and it's officers. The entire Board regularly voted on the amount of coverage deemed appropriate.

10. Thereafter, appropriate insurance applications were presented to Roger Lussier for his signature as the Bank's President and Chairman of the Board.

11. What the Complaint characterizes as a "$45,000" fine, in reality simply constitutes reimbursement to the State of Vermont Department of

Banking and Insurance, for costs incurred by that agency in connection with auditing and investigating the bank; i.e., the "Special Exam".

12. I also acted as the Stock Transfer Agent for the Bank. With specific reference to the stock transactions incorporated in the Complaint, I am able to inform the Court that I personally coordinated such transfers.

13. I personally presented the stock certificates to Charles Bucknam for his signature as the Bank's President. To the best of my knowledge, in the course of coordinating the above noted stock transfers, I placed a call either to the Federal Deposit Insurance Corporation and/or to the United States Attorney for the District of Vermont for purposes of securing permission to transfer the stock. I distinctly remember being concerned that Roger Lussier might not be allowed to transfer his stock in light of his situation with the Federal government.

14. To the best of my knowledge the only individuals who have actual knowledge as to the circumstances surrounding the Board's approval of the transactions at issue (since they were the only persons regularly present in the Board room) are: Arthur Elliott, Douglas Nelson, John Campbell, Pearl Baird, George Hopkins, Robert Beausoleil, Charles Howe, Fay Young, Frederic Oeschger, Dubois Thompson, Roger Lussier and myself.

15. Finally, the Court should be aware that it was the Board's practice that Chairman Lussier would not vote except for purposes of breaking a tie.

16. Executed under the pains and penalties of perjury pursuant to 28 U.S.C. § 1746 this _13th_ November, 1995.

Wendy J. Davenport
WENDY J. DAVENPORT

I, Wendy Davenport, state the following upon the pains and penalties of perjury, and on my own personal knowledge.

1. In 1994 I got a phone call from Roger Lussier that he was transferring some of his stock to Evelyn Lussier or to the two of them jointly. Charles Bucknam, bank president, signed the new stock certificates.

2. At some point in time Charles Bucknam asked me to throw away the files relating to whether the bank would apply to become a national bank rather than staying a state bank, saying that they were no longer needed or words to that effect; so I did throw those files away.

3. I worked with Hale & Dorr to locate insurance coverage information. I located a policy number for a policy, but I could not find the policy itself. I continued to look for the policy off and on for some time, until Charles Bucknam told me to stop looking because it was a waste of time, or words to that effect.

Wendy Davenport
Wendy Davenport

STATE OF VERMONT
COUNTY OF CALEDONIA

On this 3rd day of November, 2000, Wendy Davenport personally appeared before me and swore to the truth of the foregoing upon the pains and penalties of perjury, and that the signing hereof was her free act and deed.

Lisa Choate
Notary Public
My commission expires 2/10/03.

UNITED STATES DISTRICT COURT
DISTRICT OF VERMONT

Lyndonville Savings Bank and Trust Company., Plaintiff,)))))	
v.)	Civil Dkt. No. 95-CV-287
Roger Lussier and Evelyn Lussier, Defendants.)))	

AFFIDAVIT OF DOUGLAS NELSON

The undersigned, DOUG NELSON, hereby states the following to be true based on my actual knowledge of the circumstances surrounding the activities of the Board of Directors at Lyndonville Savings Bank and Trust Company during the time relevant to the above captioned matter.

1.   I was on the Board of Directors ("The Board") of the Lyndonville Savings Bank and Trust Company "(The Bank") when it acted on the Jasmin, Guilmette, Beauregard, Bank of Vermont, Jolly, Hammang, Gray, Wright, and Palmisano transactions.

2.   In this capacity I was duty bound to attend Board meetings and to participate in the free and open discussions that would regularly occur when The Board was presented with a loan request.

3.   I have reviewed with care the Complaint filed by The Bank against Roger and Evelyn Lussier together with the Affidavit of Charles Bucknam.

4.   Mr. Bucknam was not employed by The Bank during the time material to the Complaint, and, accordingly, he was not present when The Board made most of the decisions material to the Complaint.

5.   If asked, I would testify that Roger Lussier did not ever dominate or control, or attempt to dominate or control The Board; and,

6.   Roger Lussier never carried out an official act on behalf of The Bank without appropriate Board approval, and, *To The best of my knowledge*

7.   The Board was, at all material times, comprised of independent, successful, strong-willed businessmen; and,

8.   The Bank's allegations as set forth in the Complaint and Affidavit are completely inconsistent with my belief and understanding that Roger Lussier never engaged in any improper or illegal conduct in connection with the allegations which give rise to the filing of The Bank's Complaint.

9.   In fact, to the best of my knowledge, Roger Lussier and the entire Board endeavored, at all material times, to act conscientiously and in the best interest of The Bank and its stockholders.

Executed under the pains and penalties of perjury pursuant to 28 U.S.C. § 1746(1) this __*10*__ November, 1995.

DOUGLAS NELSON

UNITED STATES DISTRICT COURT
DISTRICT OF VERMONT

Lyndonville Savings Bank and Trust Company., Plaintiff,)))))	
v.))	Civil Dkt. No. 95-CV-287
Roger Lussier and Evelyn Lussier, Defendants.)))	

AFFIDAVIT OF FRED OESCHGER

The undersigned, FRED OESCHGER, hereby states the following to be true based on my actual knowledge of the circumstances surrounding the activities of the Board of Directors at Lyndonville Savings Bank and Trust Company during the time relevant to the above captioned matter.

1.   I was on the Board of Directors ("The Board") of the Lyndonville Savings Bank and Trust Company "(The Bank") when it acted on the Guilmette, Beauregard, Jolly, Hammang, and Gray transactions.

2.   In this capacity I was duty bound to attend Board meetings and to participate in the free and open discussions that would regularly occur when The Board was presented with a loan request.

3.   I have reviewed with care the Complaint filed by The Bank against Roger and Evelyn Lussier together with the Affidavit of Charles Bucknam.

4.   Mr. Bucknam was not employed by The Bank during the time material to the Complaint, and, accordingly, he was not present when The Board made most of the decisions material to the Complaint.

5.   If asked, I would testify that Roger Lussier did not ever dominate or control, or attempt to dominate or control The Board; and,

6.   Roger Lussier never carried out an official act on behalf of The Bank without appropriate Board approval; and, *, TO THE BEST OF MY KNOWLEDGE F.O.*

7.   The Board was, at all material times, comprised of independent, successful, strong-willed businessmen; and,

8.   The Bank's allegations as set forth in the Complaint and Affidavit are completely inconsistent with my belief and understanding that Roger Lussier never engaged in any improper or illegal conduct in connection with the allegations which give rise to the filing of The Bank's Complaint.

9.   In fact, to the best of my knowledge, Roger Lussier and the entire Board endeavored, at all material times, to act conscientiously and in the best interest of The Bank and its stockholders.

Executed under the pains and penalties of perjury pursuant to 28 U.S.C. § 1746(1) this _10_ November, 1995.

FRED OESCHGER

UNITED STATES DISTRICT COURT
DISTRICT OF VERMONT

Lyndonville Savings Bank and Trust Company., Plaintiff,))))	
v.)	Civil Dkt. No. 95-CV-287
)	
Roger Lussier and Evelyn Lussier,) Defendants.)	

AFFIDAVIT OF FAY YOUNG

The undersigned, FAY YOUNG, hereby states the following to be true based on my actual knowledge of the circumstances surrounding the activities of the Board of Directors at Lyndonville Savings Bank and Trust Company during the time relevant to the above captioned matter.

1. I was on the Board of Directors ("The Board") of the Lyndonville Savings Bank and Trust Company "(The Bank") when it acted on the Jasmin, Guilmette, Beauregard, Harrison, Bank of Vermont, Jolly, Hammang, Gray, Beck & Beck, Wright, and Palmisano transactions.

2. In this capacity I was duty bound to attend Board meetings and to participate in the free and open discussions that would regularly occur when The Board was presented with a loan request.

3. I have reviewed with care the Complaint filed by The Bank against Roger and Evelyn Lussier together with the Affidavit of Charles Bucknam, which is a matter of public record.

4. Mr. Bucknam was not employed by The Bank during the time material to the Complaint, and, accordingly, he was not present when The Board made most of the decisions material to the Complaint.

5. If asked, I would testify that Roger Lussier did not ever dominate or control, or attempt to dominate or control The Board; and,

6. Roger Lussier never carried out an official act on behalf of The Bank without appropriate Board approval; and,

7. The Board was, at all material times, comprised of independent, successful, strong-willed businessmen; and,

8. The Bank's allegations as set forth in the Complaint and Affidavit are completely inconsistent with my belief and understanding that Roger Lussier never engaged in any improper or illegal conduct in connection with the allegations which give rise to the filing of The Bank's Complaint.

9. In fact, to the best of my knowledge, Roger Lussier and the entire Board endeavored, at all material times, to act conscientiously and in the best interest of The Bank and its stockholders.

Executed under the pains and penalties of perjury pursuant to 28 U.S.C. § 1746(1) this _10th_ November, 1995.

Fay Young
FAY YOUNG

UNITED STATES DISTRICT COURT
DISTRICT OF VERMONT

Lyndonville Savings Bank)
    and Trust Company.,)
        Plaintiff,)
)
      v.)   Civil Dkt. No. 95-CV-287
)
Roger Lussier and Evelyn Lussier,)
        Defendants.)

AFFIDAVIT OF MARILYN HUGHES

The undersigned, MARILYN HUGHES, hereby states the following to be true based on my actual knowledge and belief.

1. I was employed by the Lyndonville Savings Bank and Trust Company from approximately 1960 until approximately 1984.

2. During this period of time I was employed as a bookkeeper, a loan processor, a customer service representative and as a executive secretary.

3. I was present in the Board room during meetings that were presided over by then-Bank President and Chairman of the Board Roger Lussier for the purpose of recording the minutes of such meetings.

4. On these occasions I had the opportunity to witness firsthand the manner in which Roger Lussier conducted himself as the Bank's President and Board Chairman.

5. I regularly witnessed free and open discussion with regard to any and all matters that would come before the Board.

6. I am not aware of any occasion wherein Roger Lussier unduly influenced the Board or any one of its members.

7. I am not aware of any occasion wherein Roger Lussier unilaterally arranged loans.

8. The Board, under Roger's leadership, in my opinion, at all times acted conscientiously and in the best interest of the Bank and its stockholders.

Executed under the pains and penalties of perjury pursuant to 28 U.S.C. § 1746(1) this _____ November, 1995.

Marilyn Hughes
MARILYN HUGHES

UNITED STATES DISTRICT COURT
DISTRICT OF VERMONT

Lyndonville Savings Bank and Trust Company, Plaintiff,	))))	
v.	))	Civil Dkt. No. 95-CV-287
Roger Lussier and Evelyn Lussier, Defendants.	))	

AFFIDAVIT OF MERRILL CLEVELAND

The undersigned, MERRILL CLEVELAND, hereby states the following to be true and correct based on my actual knowledge of the circumstances surrounding the activities of the Lyndonville Savings Bank and Trust Company ("the Bank") during the time relevant to the above captioned matter.

1. I was an employee of the Bank from approximately January 1972 until approximately August 1995.

2. At the outset I was employed as a loan officer. I also spent a significant amount of time as the Bank's most senior loan officer.

3. I was responsible for originally introducing Ralph Wright as a potential Bank customer to the Board and serviced his various needs to the Board in many instances after the initial loan.

4. Royal Harrison was brought in by several directors. I became the contact person at the Bank for any further services Mr. Harrison required and I was responsible for conveying such needs to the full Board.

5. On various occasions when I was required to attend Board meetings, I observed independent members of the Board who did not appear to hesitate to speak their mind.

6. Roger Lussier was not involved with the day to day operations of the Bank. Roger Lussier did not function as the Bank's principal lending officer. If I was asked to testify as to who was the Bank's principle lending officer I would testify that it was the full Board.

7. I was the person whom the Bank entrusted with the responsibility of loan documentation and other activities ancillary to ensuring that loans were closed consistent with the Bank's then-practices.

Executed under the pains and penalties of perjury pursuant to 28 U.S.C. § 1746 this ___ November, 1995.

MERRILL CLEVELAND

UNITED STATES DISTRICT COURT
DISTRICT OF VERMONT

Lyndonville Savings Bank and Trust Company., Plaintiff,)))))	
v.)))	Civil Dkt. No. 95-CV-287
Roger Lussier and Evelyn Lussier, Defendants.))	

AFFIDAVIT OF ARTHUR ELLIOTT

The undersigned, ARTHUR ELLIOTT, hereby states the following to be true based on my actual knowledge of the circumstances surrounding the activities of the Board of Directors at Lyndonville Savings Bank and Trust Company during the time relevant to the above captioned matter.

1. I was on the Board of Directors ("The Board") of the Lyndonville Savings Bank and Trust Company "(The Bank") when it acted on the Jasmin, Guilmette, Beauregard, Harrison, Bank of Vermont, Jolly, Hammang, Gray, Beck & Beck, Wright, and Palmisano transactions.

2. In this capacity I was duty bound to attend Board meetings and to participate in the free and open discussions that would regularly occur when The Board was presented with a loan request.

3. I have reviewed with care the Complaint filed by The Bank against Roger and Evelyn Lussier together with the Affidavit of Charles Bucknam.

4.   Mr. Bucknam was not employed by The Bank during the time material to the Complaint, and, accordingly, he was not present when The Board made most of the decisions material to the Complaint.

5.   If asked, I would testify that Roger Lussier did not ever dominate or control, or attempt to dominate or control The Board; and,

6.   Roger Lussier never ^TO MY KNOWLEDGE HE carried out an official act on behalf of The Bank without appropriate Board approval; and,

7.   The Board was, at all material times, comprised of independent, successful, strong-willed businessmen; and,

8.   The Bank's allegations as set forth in the Complaint and Affidavit are completely inconsistent with my belief and understanding that Roger Lussier never engaged in any improper or illegal conduct in connection with the allegations which give rise to the filing of The Bank's Complaint.

9.   In fact, to the best of my knowledge, Roger Lussier and the entire Board endeavored, at all material times, to act conscientiously and in the best interest of The Bank and its stockholders.

Executed under the pains and penalties of perjury pursuant to 28 U.S.C. § 1746(1) this _10th_ November, 1995.

ARTHUR ELLIOTT

STATE OF VERMONT   )
)
COUNTY OF *CALEDONIA*   ) ss.

AFFIDAVIT OF ARTHUR ELLIOTT

NOW COMES Arthur Elliott, and being duly sworn and under oath states the following based upon his personal knowledge:

1. I was a member of the board of directors of the Lyndonville Savings Bank and Trust Company (the "Bank") from 1985 to 1993, during which period of time Roger Lussier was President and Chairman of the Board.

2. Since about 1987, I have known that Roger Lussier was an owner of a corporation known as ARDI.

3. I was in attendance at the Bank board of directors meetings in September 1988 when a loan was approved in the amount of $1,950,000 to Herbert Gray, and I knew at the time that Roger Lussier and Herbert Gray jointly had a New York real estate investment.

4. As a board member, it was always the board procedure that if a member had an interest that should be disclosed, he was expected to indicate that he had an involvement in the matter and to disqualify himself from voting. The member was not expected to go into any details as to his involvement.

5. It was not an uncommon practice for three or four members to approve a proposed loan by a personal or telephone meeting, and to thereafter have the loan approved or ratified at a formal board meeting, and I have been personally involved in such personal or telephone meetings.

6. I was in attendance at the board meeting on May 2, 1990, when the board approved a $700,000 dairy farm loan to Hamel, at which meeting the board had complete financial information as to the farm assets, value and income and expense projections to support the loan, which I recall because Director Fay Young and myself presented all such information to the board based upon our personal inspections, appraisals and financial analysis

Further, before the above board meeting, I was in attendance at times when Roger Lussier disclosed to directors Campbell, Young and Beausoleil that he had been helping Hamel manage his dairy operation finances, that he and his wife had loaned money to Hamel, and had a mortgage on their farm, all of which directors were also in attendance at the meeting when the loan was approved.

7. It was a board practice during my tenure over the years to never record or reference discussions in board minutes concerning loan transactions.

8. I was in attendance at the board meeting on September 14, 1988, when the Gray loan was approved for $1,950,000, and

I recall that the board was furnished financial information and recall going over a whole bunch of figures, including an appraisal.

9. I wrote all the checks drawn on Yankee Development bank accounts and I recall the corporation borrowing $500,000 from the Bradford Bank, all of which proceeds were used only for the corporation's obligations. Further, I know that no money was transferred to Herbert Gray or used for payments on any debt owed by Gray to LSB.

10. I was in attendance at a board meeting on October 26, 1988 when a $700,000 loan was approved to McCormick, at which meeting the board had for review extensive financial information on McCormick and his corporation, income tax returns and confirmations from brokers as to the value of the corporate stock pledged to secure the loan.

11. On April 2, 1996, I was deposed by attorneys for the Bank in an action by the Bank against Roger Lussier in the Vermont Federal District Court. Attached hereto as Ehxibit A is a transcript of pages 32., 35., 51., 64., 65., 66., 68., 69., 70., 71., 72., 77., 78., 83., 84., 85., 87., 90., 91., 92., and 93. of my testimony, portions of which are highlighted to support the foregoing statements.

12. I have never observed nor knew Roger Lussier to dominate, control or attempt to dominate or control members of the Bank board.

13. During the period of time that I served on the Bank board, the members thereof appeared and were known to me to be independent, successful and strong-willed business people.

14. I was in attendance on December 24, 1991, at a board meeting when the board considered and approved taking deeds-in-lieu of foreclosure from Herbert Gray and his wife on the two (2) St. Johnsbury automobile dealership financed by the Bank, and I know it was clearly discussed prior to the vote of approval that the Bank was to take the deeds as payment in full of the total secured debt owed by the Grays to the Bank and the discharge thereof. Further, the board considered the then value of the properties to be equal to or greater than the unpaid Gray debt being discharged.

15. I was in attendance on June 19, 1991 at a board meeting when the board considered and approved taking a reassignment to it by Ryan of the Railway Roundhouse lease that was security for the Bank loan to Ryan, and it was agreed by the board at that meeting that in return for the voluntary reassingment of the Bank's security to it that the reassignment to it was to represent payment of over $1,500,000 of the Ryan's outstanding debt to the Bank.

Dated this _6th_ day of _September_ 1997.

_____
ARTHUR ELLIOTT

Sworn to and subscribed in my presence by Arthur Elliott this the _6th_ day of _September_, 1997.

Before me,
_____

Directors Voting Against RRL and winning: (displayed by year)

Year Reported Director	86	87	88	89	90	91	92	Total
Beausoleil	6	10	6	1	3	2	1	29
Campbell	6	11	7	1	2	2	1	29
Elliott	6	10	5	1	3	2	1	28
Hopkins	6	9	7	1	2			25
Nelson	5	10	6					21
Baird	5	10	6					21
Oeschger						1	1	2
Young				1	2	1	1	5
Howe				1	3	2		6
Bovee	4							4

Source:
These numbers are taken from the minutes and records of the Corporation, as recorded in the Official Minutes of the Lyndonville Savings Bank and Trust Company.

STATE OF VERMONT
DEPARTMENT OF BANKING, INSURANCE AND SECURITIES
Montpelier, Vermont 05602

IN RE:)
)
LYNDONVILLE SAVINGS BANK   )   Docket No. 91-103-B
AND TRUST COMPANY   )

<u>BANK'S PRE-HEARING REQUESTS FOR FINDINGS OF FACT</u>

1.   Prior to granting a loan to Aristede Hamel and Debra
Hamel on May 4, 1990 the respondent Bank reviewed and considered
the following matters presented to its board:

    a.   the assets, liabilities and the income and expenses
        related to their dairy farming operation;

    b.   the value of the Hamels' farm, machinery, equipment
        and cattle as appraised and determined by board
        members Arthur Elliott and Fay Young; and

    c.   the disclosure by Roger Lussier to the board of
        previous loans Roger Lussier and his wife made to the
        Hamels, which were to be repaid out of the Bank's loan
        proceeds.

2.   Roger Lussier left the board meeting after
presentation of the Hamels' loan transaction and was not
thereafter present for the vote on the subject loan.

3.   The real property appraisal of the Hamel property made
by Fay Young, Arthur B. Elliott and Roger Lussier assigned a
value of $665,000.00 to the real property.

4.   In November of 1991 John W. Stevens, a licensed
Vermont real estate appraiser, appraised the Hamel real property
and assigned a value of $728,500.00 thereto.

5.   Prior to granting a loan to Herbert C. Gray and
Rebecca Gray on September 23, 1988, to finance the Grays'
purchase of two automobile dealership properties in St.
Johnsbury, Vermont (the Vinton Motors and Gagnon Motors
properties) from Carl Kelton, Sr. and his wife Shirley Kelton
and from two separate corporations owned by Mr. and Mrs. Kelton
the respondent Bank reviewed and considered the following
matters presented to its board:

1

a.   Mr. and Mrs. Grays' personal assets, liabilities and income;

b.   financial statements of income and expenses of the two Kelton corporations realized in operating their respective St. Johnsbury dealerships;

c.   the appraised value of the dealership properties as determined by members of the Bank's board;

d.   the disclosure by Roger Lussier that he and Herbert Gray held a joint interest in a parcel of non-income producing real estate in New York; and

e.   the fact that no automobile inventory was a part of the asset purchase by Mr. and Mrs. Gray.

6.   On December 13, 1986 Bruce A. Taylor, MIA, a Vermont real estate appraiser, assigned a fair market value of $950,000.00 to the Vinton Motors Property, and on July 7, 1987 Bruce A. Taylor assigned a fair market value of $1,000,000.00 to the Gagnon Motors Property.

7.   On January 30, 1991 the Bank made an $85,000 loan to Anthony J. Aiossa.

8.   This Aiossa loan was originally proposed to the Bank as an assignment by Noel Lussier of a promissory note Mr. Aiossa made to Noel Lussier, and to be an unsecured loan. Roger Lussier opposed granting the loan on this basis, and recommended a 20% or $17,000 reserve against the loan. The board approved the loan with this condition, one member opposed. Noel Lussier did not have personal liability for the repayment of the note when the loan was closed, and subsequent to the closing he guaranteed the note and so became personally obligated as he previously agreed.

9.   All loans made by the Bank to Noel Lussier, and all dealer retail contracts purchased by the Bank from Noel Lussier were based upon consideration of

a.   Noel Lussier's relatively current financial statements showing current assets, liabilities and income;

b.   a substantial cash reserve account on deposit at the Bank as security for all loans, direct and indirect, of Noel Lussier; and

c.   the security given under each dealer retail contract and the liability of consumer purchasers under the retail contracts.

10. Prior to granting certain loans characterized by the Department as the "Four Friends Loan" respondent Bank reviewed and considered the following presented to its board:

a. relatively current financial statements showing reported assets, liabilities, income and expenses of:

i.   Noel Lussier and his wife Barbara Lussier;

ii. Paul Gallerani and his wife Roberta Gallerani;

iii. Herbert Gray and his wife Rebecca Gray;

iv. Raymond Jasmin and his wife Janice Jasmin;

v.   Carl Kelton, Sr. and his wife Shirley Kelton; and

vi. Kelton Motors, Inc.

b. the value of improved real estate to be given by Carl Kelton, Sr., Shirley Kelton and Kelton Motors, Inc. under a first mortgage to the Bank as appraised and determined by members of the Bank's board;

c. $100,000 was to be deposited with the Bank as additional security for the $800,000 loan made jointly to Paul Gallerani and Roberta Gallerani, and Herbert Gray and Rebecca Gray;

d. $100,000 was to be deposited with the Bank as additional security for the $800,000 loan made to Raymond Jasmin and Janice Jasmin and guaranteed by Noel Lussier and Barbara Lussier;

e. After the Four Friends loan was consummated Paul Gallerani, Roberta Gallerani, Herbert Gray and Rebecca Gray were each personally obligated to repay $800,000 to the bank and jointly had the capacity to do so.

f. After the Four Friends loan was consummated Raymond Jasmin and Janice Jasmin were each personally obligated to repay $800,000 to the bank, and Noel Lussier and Barbara Lussier were each personally obligated to do so if Raymond Jasmin and Janice Jasmin did not. The Lussiers and the Jasmins jointly had the capacity to repay this debt.

11. On July 23, 1986 the Bank, the Bradford National Bank and the Bank of Vermont jointly loaned three million dollars to

3

Kelton Motors, Inc. and related interests which paid in full and satisfied the Four Friends Loan.

12.   Upon payment in full of the aforementioned $800,000 loans, the $100,000 security deposits made under each loan and held by the Bank was released and returned to the depositors.

13.   Jean Campbell has spent over 30 years actively engaged as a real estate agent and broker in Vermont, and has extensively bought and sold dairy farms, dairy cattle and related farm machinery and equipment;

14.   Roger Lussier has spent over 30 years actively engaged as an auctioneer, and in owning, buying and selling real estate dairy farms, dairy cattle and related farm machinery and equipment, and operating the same;

15.   Fay Young has spent over 30 years as a real estate broker in Vermont, has been retained to appraise real estate of every kind, has owned and operated dairy farms;

16.   Arthur Elliott has extensive experience in appraising real estate as a Vermont town lister, and from owning and operating motel properties and woodlands, including sugarbush operations and sales

17.   Philip Bovee is a former owner and operator of automobile dealerships.

18.   Prior to granting a loan to David Guilmette and JoAnn Guilmette and Auto Miser, Inc., jointly ("Giulmette"), as concerned a Barre automobile dealership formerly owned by Kelton, the respondent Bank reviewed and considered the following matters presented to its board:

a.   financial statements of "Guilmette".

b.   relatively current income and expense statements of "Kelton" as pertains to the Barre dealership operation.

c.   appraisals as to value of the Barre dealership property and machinery and equipment; and

d.   appraisals as to the value of "Guilmette's" home and camp properties.

19.   Prior to granting a loan to Jack Ryan and Margaret Ryan ("Ryan") to finance their purchase of Railroad Roundhouse property from Charlie Kelton's of White River Junction, Inc., respondent Bank reviewed and considered the following members presented to its board;

4

a. financial statements of the "Ryans" and income expense statements of their Rutland trucking operation and balance sheets.

b. income and expense statements concerning the former owner's operation of the Railroad Roundhouse property.

c. appraisals as to value of the Roundhouse property, machinery, equipment and inventory.

20. on infrequent occasions and from time to time either Roger Lussier or Reginald Lussier, Vermont licensed auctioneers, conducted public auctions of respondent Bank's foreclosed property or security on a fee basis substantially below regular fees charged by auctioneers. On occasion they did so without fees charged to the Bank.

21. A $1,000,000 loan made by respondent Bank evidenced by a note dated 11/12/87 was based upon:

a. secured unconditional repayment obligations of Kelton Motors, Inc., Kelton's, Inc., Carl E. Kelton, Sr., Shirley Kelton (owners of said corporations), Vernon C. Kelton and Doreen Kelton (officers and employees of Kelton Motors, Inc.) and Timothy Wells (attorney for Keltons and their corporations) and Leslie Wells (officer and employee of Kelton Motors, Inc.);

b. mortgages on real estate owned by all of above personal obligors and Kelton's, Inc.;

c. security agreements as to machinery, equipment of Kelton Motors, Inc.;

d. appraised values of aforementioned property;

e. financial statements of all obligors;

f. review and approval of the foregoing by the board of the respondent Bank.

22. A $1,000,000 loan made by respondent Bank evidenced by a note dated 5/2/88 was based primarily on:

a. secured unconditional obligation to repay of Charlie Kelton's Chevrolet Oldsmobile, Inc. (the principal beneficiary of the proceeds), Kelton Motors, Inc., Carl Kelton and Shirley Kelton (owners of said corporations) based upon unconditional guarantees of the note;

b.   Carl E. Kelton, Jr. and Kimberly Kelton were makers of the note at the request of Carl E. Kelton, Sr. upon which makers the Bank did not rely for payment;

c.   first mortgage on "Chevrolet-Oldsmobile" St. Johnsbury automobile dealership property and equipment;

d.   amendment of all mortgages previously given under a prior 11/12/87 loan as additional security;

e.   appraised value of St. Johnsbury dealership real estate;

f.   income and expense statements as to operation of St. Johnsbury dealership;

g.   current financial statements of Kelton Motors, Inc. and "Keltons".

h.   Review and approval of foregoing by board of respondent Bank.

23.   A $1,200,000 loan made by respondent Bank evidenced by a note dated 5/2/88 was based primarily on:

a.   secured unconditional obligations to repay of Charlie Kelton's of White River Junction, Inc., Kelton Motors, Inc., Carl E. Kelton, Sr., Shirley Kelton, Vernon Kelton and Doreen Kelton;

b.   first leasehold mortgage on Railroad Roundhouse and first security interest in all machinery and equipment owned by Charlie Kelton's of White River Junction, Inc.;

c.   pledge of shares of stock of Randolph National Bank;

d.   amendment of all prior mortgages as additional security;

e.   appraised value of Roundhouse leasehold, machinery and equipment and pledged stock;

f.   financial statements of Charlie Kelton's of White River Junction, Inc. and Kelton Motors, Inc.

g.   review and approval of foregoing by board of respondent Bank;

h.   note was signed by Vernon Kelton and Doreen Kelton at request of Carl E. Kelton, Sr.

6

24. A $1,500,000 loan was made by respondent Bank evidenced by a note dated 7/29/88 and was based primarily on the following matters reviewed and approved by the said Bank's board:

    a. Unconditional guarantee of repayment by nine (9) separate corporations owned by "Keltons", seven (7) of which conducted separate and independent automobile dealership operations each in various Vermont towns, under separate franchises and day to day management, and by Carl Kelton, Sr. and Shirley Kelton.

    b. financial income and expense statements on the separate and independent operation of each of the aforementioned corporations;

    c. financial statements and income tax returns over a period of years of Carl and Shirley Kelton;

    d. appraised values of "Keltons" personal assets, and substantial antiques;

    e. appraised values of each of the aforementioned dealership properties;

    f. mortgages on all dealership properties, machinery, and equipment;

    g. first security interest in all "Kelton" antiques;

    h. amendment of all prior "Kelton" and "Wells" mortgages;

    i. note assigned by Alfred M. Kelton and Carol Kelton at the request of Carl Kelton, Sr., upon which makers respondent Bank did not rely for payment thereof;

    j. loan proceeds were agreeably disbursed to Kelton Motors, Inc.

25. On 7/29/88 respondent Bank loaned $1,500,000 to Raymond Jasmin, his wife Janice Jasmin, and Peter Jasmin, with the knowledge that said Jasmins by their agreement with Carl E. Kelton, Sr., would reloan the loan proceeds to Kelton Motors, Inc. The subject loan was based primarily on the following matters reviewed and approved by the Bank's board:

    a. financial statements as to balance sheet and income expenses of the Jasmins and their business operations;

    b. first mortgage on "Jasmins'" business real estate and property in White River Junction;

7

c.   appraised value of "Jasmins'" real estate;

d.   income tax returns of Jasmins' for a period of years.

26.   Richard Lussier, at all times material to this proceeding, was anadult children of Roger Lussier who did not live in Roger Lussier's household.

27.   At all times material to this action, Noel Lussier was Roger Lussier's adult brother. Noel Lussier did not live in Roger Lussier's household.

28.   At all times material to this action, Jonathan Lussier was Roger Lussier's adult nephew and the son of Noel Lussier. Jonathan Lussier did not live in Roger Lussier's household.

29.   Prior to making loans to Vernon Kelton and Doreen Kelton, Alfred Kelton and Carol Kelton, Raymond Jasmin and Janice Jasmin, Peter Jasmin and Timothy Wells and Leslie Wells beginning on May 2, 1988, the Bank sought and obtained an opinion from its counsel that the loans did not exceed the limitations on loans provided for in 8 V.S.A. §1203. The Bank, and its directors, reasonably relied on that opinion as a part of the loan underwriting process.

30.   Neither respondent Bank nor its president Roger Lussier nor any other officer or director of the Bank have violated any regulations duly promulgated by the Vermont Department of Banking, Insurance and Securities.

31.   Neither respondent Bank nor its president Roger Lussier nor any other office or director of the Bank have violated any Vermont statute governing Vermont banking institutions.

Dated at St. Johnsbury, Vermont this 22nd day of September, 1992.

Robert A. Gensburg, Esq.
Attorney for Defendant

STATE OF VERMONT

Senator John McClaughry
Caledonia-Orange District
Concord, VT 05824
(802) 695-2555

Senate Chambers
Montpelier, VT 05602
1-800-322-5616
(802) 828-2228

December 24, 1993

Dear Roger and Evelyn,

The verdict by the jury was utterly unconscionable. I was absolutely shocked that 12 men and women could listen to all that and conclude that you acted with criminal intent. This is a tragic miscarriage of justice.

Roger, I have absolute confidence in your honesty and integrity. I would gladly trust you with all the money I have. You have done a great deal for the people of the Northeast Kingdom. I admire your tremendous courage in the face of this shockingly wrong verdict.

Frankly, I think Langrock made a mistake in trying to get that jury to believe that your were a poorly educated woodchuck who just happened to make hundreds of thousands of dollars in business deals. It obviously wasn't true, and his attempt to make them believe it may have damaged the credibility of your case. A well known trial attorney friend of mine had the same opinion.

I would be eager to go to a sentencing hearing to speak my piece for you, or help in any other way I can. Don't hesitate to ask.

God bless you for all you've done for so many people.

Sincerely,

John McClaughry

2/16/96

Roger — I was shocked and disappointed to read that the Appeals Court rejected your appeal on the "may acquit" issue.

If you have to go to prison, you at least can go with a clean conscience. I dont know how in hell Van De Graf can look himself in the mirror.

I will drop by next week sometime.

John

Not Printed at Taxpayer's Expense

West Burke, Vt. 05871
Jan. 17, 1983

Dear Roger:

/Even though I have written a card of thanks to the
full Board of Directors I want to thank you especially.

I know that you had a great deal to do with my party
and I shall be forever grateful. It was so much more than I ever
expected.

The money was more than I could have ever hoped for and
the silver plate with all of the names of the Directors was a great
idea.

It seems that no matter how busy you are, you find time
to listen and for the many, many times you have listened to me –
Thank You.

Because of the personal interest you have in the employees
and because of the devotion you have for LSB, it has really grown. I
hope that you will be there for many years to come.

Sincerely,

Pearl

──────── *Established 1837* ────────

THE
ALEDONIAN-R

Serving Northeastern Vermont and the North Country of New F

St. Johnsbury, Vermont • Saturday, September 21, 1996

Northeast Kingdom

Lussier Supporters Protest
Conviction With A Petition

By DANA GRAY

The criminal charges currently keeping Roger Lussier in a Pennsylvania federal prison should be dropped according to a group of people numbering 1,600 and counting.

One of Lussier's sons, Reginald Lussier, figures he has sent about 2,000 petitions out to people.

"Lots of these people who are signing (the petition) are customers of (the Lyndonville Savings Bank) or were at one time," said the younger Lussier.

His father is currently serving a 46-month prison sentence at the Allenwood Penitentiary in Montgomery, Pa., for convictions on 17 charges, including bank fraud and money laundering.

Prior to the criminal allegations, the elder Lussier had been president of Lyndonville Savings Bank since 1977 and one of the bank's directors for 27 years.

In May 1994, he was sentenced for his criminal activity and appealed his conviction and sentence. Every appeal failed, including the latest one, which didn't make it to its intended destination, the U.S. Supreme Court.

Since Feb. 28, Lussier has been serving his federal prison sentence.

Although Lussier is no longer free to fight his convictions, he has realized through his son's petition forms that there are people willing to fight for him.

"It makes him feel good inside to know that there are still people here who believe in him," said Reginald Lussier.

The younger Lussier has put his name and his auctioneering business logo atop a letter accompanying a petition form.

The letter addresses "Dear Friend or Associate." Within the body of the letter, Reginald Lussier states, "I am seeking your support through petition against this miscarriage of justice for a pardon, or at least a new trial, so the truth can come out ... If you have any doubt as to his guilt, would you please sign the petition."

On a second piece of paper are the words "We, the undersigned, petition the Federal Government against the conviction of Roger Lussier and ask that all charges be dropped and he be released." Below the statement is space for 20 names.

Reginald Lussier said most of the petition forms have been mailed out but some businesses have displayed them. Regarding the expense in shipping the forms by mail, the younger Lussier said, "If we get anything out of it, it's well worth it."

He admitted he doesn't know how many names would matter, or if the names will matter at all, but he's hoping to get his father a second chance.

"It's just a statement saying that things should be looked at again," he said. "It may not do any good but it won't do any harm."

"There's still a gray area whether anybody did anything wrong."

Reg Lussier said at the very least he'd like to see the petition aid in getting his father released from prison sooner.

"(The Allenwood Penitentiary) is not the country club people think it is," he said.

At this point, with names still coming in, the younger Lussier said he's unsure how many names he will try to accumulate or even to whom he intends to send the letter. He knows the names are going somewhere and he welcomes even more.

"Even if I sent them in today, I'd still take more," said Reg Lussier.

To the Editor:

I thought it interesting that the article in Wednesday's Burlington Free Press titled, "Court Overturns Ex-Banker's Conviction," appeared on the last page of the last section that had any news on it. I could not find any mention of this news in several newspapers that had devoted much space to this trial and its original outcome, which most of the time had appeared on the front pages.

The article in the Free Press stated that Judge Franklin S. Billings Jr. erred when instructing the jury about the law covering conspiracy. I would call this very serious, as it seriously affected the lives of two men and their families. Perhaps if Judge Billings had not been so anxious to convict and sentence everybody in the bank scandal, and had been more interested in the true facts on both sides, he wouldn't have made this serious and expensive mistake.

I wonder if Judge Billings will be asked to pay for his mistake, as he has made others do for theirs. Will he pay a fine, will he receive probation time, will he have to do community service, and will he have to pay restitution for all the thousands of dollars that his mistake has cost the taxpayers and the defendants in this case, and for the cost of another trial, if there is one. Or will Judge Billings walk away free and continue to receive his big, fat paycheck from the government and the taxpayers, while others pay dearly for their mistakes and his.

Bill Hill
Hardwick

10-26-95

John L. Pacht

Hoff, Curtis, Pacht, Cassidy & Frame   January 18th, 1997
Box 1124
Burlington, Vermont, 05408-1124   . .. ... ED

                                                   JAN 2 8 1997
Dear Counselor:

There are several items I wish to write you about and I request
your response to them as soon as possible. Now that another
year has begun here it is time for me to get as clear as possible
a view of the road ahead. It seems that all I have sone since
1992 is get ready or respond to some legal matter, and then another.

1). What do you see as the realistic outcome from the current
cases we are involved with? I feel that with the settlement of
Beauregard and Guilmette at no loss to the bank that the record
is also running against most of the current claims against me.
What is your view regarding the present results?

2). The bank case continues to be my biggest disappointment.
As I see it from here, we have spent all of that money and I have
yet to see the evidence we called for, I have yet to see any
theory of defense in the pending case, that the information sought
from Bucknam seems to be willingly stalled. I had been assured that
his deposition would cover about 55 pages of questions. All I have
seen is the partial day and one-half of his comments to simple
questions, and then silence. I have not seen a list of witnesses,
or any evidence that the bank has complied with the requests of
myself, or the court as to materials and discover. And, I must
say John, I have not seen more than the one letter telling them that
actions will delay the trial; actually more an action of their
contempt of process and court. But, they have received everything
they wanted from me, and have given nothing. Remember, they are
the plaintif!

And when we talk about this case it is always about more money,
that I might just as well give it to you as to them! Now why is
that? If they are entitled to it than better them, if they are not
entitled to it, why should I be at risk for their loss and then
also pay the fees for legal services as well? As I have said,this
case is my disappointment. And I don't see what sending more money
after it is going to do for us: after all of this time and money
we have not even been able to complete Bucknam's interview! Why?

3). You mentioned at one time that the insurance company had
offered to assist in your fees. I have not heard anymore regarding
that. As you may recall, I asked to see their proposal and
communications related to their offer. I have seen nothing.

4). The Assistant U.S. Attorney in his several letters over the
last six months keeping asking for conversations regarding ARDI,
and seems to be making some suggestions regarding an offer. But I
have nothing here that reflects any proposals or understandinngs.
What is your understanding regarding ARDI, and the status of
any other conversations with them?

page two, Pacht

I received a letter from you, from them last week asking about
my intentions regarding the property I had put up. I have replied
to them from here that I had paid the taxes again, would offer to pay
interest to date and asked for additonal time to sell the property.
I believe I can sell it for a better price that going to foreclosure.
But I also told the government that I had spent the money given to
you for my defense and that any funds available would be used for
my bank case and that I would deal directly with them regarding
their concerns. It is just not reasonable value to spend the little
I have now for things I can do pro se. In my letter I informed them
that you would not be asked to continue that representation and
to write me directly in response to my offers.

5). I thought your reply to the banks reply for partial judgement
that you had filed was very good. It seems so clear to my in your
brief that I can't see what can be reasonably expected except
that the court agree with you. What do you expect to happen in
that particular motion? Can't that motion and the issues about
limitations having run past six years be settled in advance of
any trial? I would think you could hold out for a decision on this
before going forward to the unrealistic schedule of April 1st, for
trial.

I believe the bank is attempting to run the clock on the schedule
to trial; wanting a trial of "their" facts with us still blind.
I wish to be clear that if it is possible to get a decision from
the court before continuing with case issues that we should do so!
It will help reduce the burden of defense, and also give us a
realistic case to try...much later. I do not believe that Johnson
is keeping good faith with this process, and I shall be keeping
all of my communications ready to present to the court in a
motion to delay until they have complied with the court order.
I think a motion to summary judgement for failure to disclose
discovery is overdue. Also contempt?

6). As to money, I am out! With everything seized, attached, and
my stock taken with compensation, I can do very little. I would
assume that the court will regard my putting up the amount I did
as a more than reasonable retainer and that the court will not
dismiss your firm upon a request alone.

7). And as to my 2255; I have filed my motions with the District
Court. Among my claims is new law from the Supreme Court that shall
bring issues into court that had been avoided previously. I assume
that a successful 2255 would change much of our current legal
matters. But I have no idea of the schedule.

Let me have your responses as soon as possible.

                                        Sincerely,

                                        Roger Lussier

I shall attempt to call you early next week. But I wanted this
to get started towards you even if we speak before then.
I need the written responses to our conversations because of my
need to study them, and the time between events.
                                        Roger

REXFORD & KILMARTIN

A PROFESSIONAL CORPORATION

ATTORNEYS AT LAW

22 THIRD STREET

NEWPORT, VERMONT 05855

802-334-7386

NCAN FREY KILMARTIN

PAUL R. REXFORD
(1911-1991)

LANGROCK SPERRY
AUG 2 5 1993
& WOOL

24 August, 1993

Peter F. Langrock, Esq.
Langrock Sperry & Wool
PO Box 351
Middlebury, VT 05753

Re: Guilmette, et al vs. Elliot and Lussier

Dear Peter:

This is to acknowledge and confirm formally in writing your phone call to me of August 18th.

Because of the nature of the accusation which you have made against me, as Lussier and Elliot's attorney, that I am unable to exercise my professional judgment for the Guilmettes due to of my personal feelings and beliefs about Roger Lussier and the fact that you have made this a formal Motion of Disqualification before the Court, I believe it important to memorialize in writing, both the fact of the conversation and its contents.

My understanding is that you wanted the phone call to be on a "personal" basis and that it should not be considered in the context of our respective professional representation of our clients.

I consider your call unethical, overreaching and an attempt to injure and destroy my relationship not only with the Guilmettes, but also with other clients who have claims and actions against Roger Lussier and Lyndonville Savings Bank.

As a knowledgeable and competent attorney, you knew and intended that I report the contents of our conversation to my clients, because I am required to do that by the Code.

You have fabricated, along with your client, the meritless and frivolous accusation that my unknown, personal and subjective feelings about Roger Lussier, Arthur Elliot and the Lyndonville Savings Bank prevent me from exercising professional judgment for the Guilmettes, knowing that I have a duty of full disclosure to my clients under DR 5-101 relative to any such accusation.

Peter F. Langrock, Esq.
08/24/93
Page - 2

Thus, the obvious and undeniable intention of you and your clients, (who must have authorized you to call me on a "personal" basis) in you placing a "personal" phone call to me, was to further fabricate a conflict, and require me to report it to my clients, so that they could feel further vulnerability and insecurity about the ethics, competency, quality and legality, of my continued representation.

Obviously you had to have Roger Lussier's consent to calling me on a "personal" basis, or you would run afoul of DR 5-101 by not fully disclosing to your client your "personal interest" as a "colleague of mine" and talking to me independent of your professional representation of your client. EC 5-1

Probably you will argue that your "personal" interest in calling me as an "old colleague" and suggesting that I "abandon" the Guilmettes and their claims, was consistent and congruent with the interests of your clients to disqualify me, even though it was based upon your personal and subjective feelings, and was not done in the sole exercise of professional judgment for your client.

Possibly you will argue that you were really doing it for the Guilmettes out of a sense of paternalism and your personal, non-professional desire for them to achieve all of their legal objective against your clients and others. However, that would put you in direct violation of the Code in regard to Roger Lussier. DR 5-101, 105(A).

Possibly you will argue that you were simply communicating with me, as the Guilmettes' attorney, or as a witness. The problem is that the Motion to Disqualify is an independent proceeding before the Court, and you have made me a party to that proceeding. Thus, your communication to me could be only to advise me to get an attorney and not discuss, in any manner whatsoever, your substantive claims or give me advice. DR 7-104(A)(2)

If I view your phone call as a continuation of your clients' patterns of threats, intimidation and other illegal conduct, to prevent me from representing people in actions against Roger Lussier or the Lyndonville Savings Bank, or tortious interference with protected relationships, I am certainly on sound footing. DR 7-102 (A) (1) (2) (3) (6) (7) (8).

It appears that you have had a very serious lapse of professional judgment in calling me and suggesting I remove myself as Guilmettes' attorney, and you need to report it both to your client [DR 5-101(A)] and the Professional Conduct Board. DR 1-103(A)

Assuming you are still going to remain the attorney for Roger Lussier and Arthur Elliot in the Guilmette litigation, I am writing you under separate cover relative to our demand for settlement against Roger, Arthur and the Lyndonville Savings Bank. I will be sending that letter to the office of the Richard E. Davis, so that office can forward it to the LSB for consideration.

Peter F. Langrock, Esq.
08/24/93
Page - 3

I certainly do not want to be discourteous and cause you any unnecessary embarrassment or humiliation by calling further attention to your lapse of professional judgment for your clients, Elliot and Lussier, by raising this issue in a settlement letter.

Possibly I've made some egregious mistake in my analysis or understanding of your phone call. If so, you can enlighten me in writing.

Sincerely,

Duncan Frey Kilmartin

DFK/cjc

cc: Mr. and Mrs. David Guilmette

guilmett\93-6g.ltr

REXFORD & KILMARTIN
A PROFESSIONAL CORPORATION
ATTORNEYS AT LAW
22 THIRD STREET
NEWPORT, VERMONT 05855
802-334-7386

DUNCAN FREY KILMARTIN

PAUL R. REXFORD
(1911-1990)

8 September, 1993

Peter F. Langrock, Esq.
Langrock Sperry & Wool
PO Box 351
Middlebury, VT 05753

Re: Guilmette, et al v. Elliot and Lussier

Dear Peter:

I have your letter of August 27, 1993, and I must have misunderstood either or both our phone call and your letter.

I assume when you spoke of "an appearance of impartiality" in your letter, you meant "an appearance of impropriety". However I don't recall you mentioning your professional concern over an appearance of impropriety.

What you referred to in our phone conversation was whether there was a real conflict or "an appearance" of a conflict. I do recall pointing out to you in regard to "appearances" that you were currently representing Roger Lussier in regard to potential criminal charges on the federal level, while at the same time representing him in civil matters, and that your efforts in one arena or the other might give rise to an "appearance" that you were using your position in one arena to better your position in the other.

However, assuming you are correct, and your focus in the phone call was an "appearance of impropriety" on my part, your focus would fall under Canon 9 and Disciplinary Rule DR 9-101. I read the Disciplinary Rule after receiving your letter and nothing that you have alleged in your Motion to Disqualify remotely relates to DR 9-101 or the phone call.

Peter F. Langrock, Esq.
09/08/93
Page - 2

Ironically, it is Mr. Lussier who has publicly claimed on several occasions that I have the ability to influence improperly various persons and entities. I've never said anything about that.

Turning to the Ethical Considerations, especially 9.2, I find them very comforting, in view of the accusations made in the Motion to Disqualify. I think I am known to never subordinate my duty to clients or to the public, because the full discharge of my obligations may be misunderstood (by my adversary?) or may tend to subject me or the legal profession to criticism (by my adversary?).

Quite frankly, I consider this a case in point. Roger makes accusations that my positions are being misunderstood by him, so that he can get me to subordinate my professional duties to my clients and abandon them.

What is readily apparent is that Roger Lussier and you are not concerned with diminishing **public confidence** in the legal system or in the legal profession, but only whether Roger, as a defendant, perceives my public, personal and professional conduct as "ethical" to him or to "his" bank.

Your letter is enlightening for several reasons.

You acknowledge that I, as the subject of the Motion to Disqualify, might have a legal defense. Does this mean you might have no legal basis for your Motion?

You wish to see whether I, as a party unrepresented by counsel, might withdraw without court intervention. If I have a legal defense (your Motion is without basis). Why would I withdraw without court intervention? Are you or Mr. Lussier concerned about Court intervention.

Were you giving me advice by raising the "law" of what you call "an appearance of impartiality (sic impropriety) which would be inappropriate".

I am sure you did not intend to use the word "partiality" in favor of my clients, since that would be most appropriate. That is consistent with inspiring the confidence, respect and trust of my clients, the Guilmettes.

Although I am not the judge, I hope that my conduct as a member of the profession inspires the confidence, respect and trust of the public. The fact remains, that Roger Lussier and the Lyndonville Savings Bank are not the public. They are my clients' adversaries.

Your letter continues what I have referred to as "paternalism" for the Guilmettes. You seemingly remain fixated as to whether I have a conflict (congruence) of

Peter F. Langrock, Esq.
09/08/93
Page - 3

interest with the Guilmettes, or the appearance of a conflict with the interests of the Guilmettes, neither of which would be inappropriate after full disclosure and consent. You also know under DR 5-101(a) it is none of your business or Roger Lussier's business. That is solely the Guilmettes' business with their attorney.

Wouldn't it make more sense, Peter, to admit your mistake and withdraw your Motion to Disqualify?

Sincerely,

Duncan Frey Kilmartin

DFK/cjc

cc: Mr. and Mrs. David Guilmette

guilmett\93-6m.ltr

STATE OF VERMONT

Senator John McClaughry
Caledonia-Orange District
Concord, VT 05824
(802) 695-2555

Senate Chambers
Montpelier, VT 05602
1-800-322-5616
(802) 828-2228

June 3, 1992

Chairman
Federal Deposit Insurance Corporation
550 17th St NW
Washington DC 20429

Dear Sir:

I call your attention to the enclosed story in the Rutland VT Herald of May 27, 1992.

Your assistant regional dirctor, James Loyless, is quoted as saying "It's not unreasonable to think that, based on what's happened over the (last) year, " that a Vermont bank director might be removed by the FDIC.

In the next sentence Mr. Loyless adds "If it's being contemplated, I couldn't comment on it."

Nice try, but a little late.

    t Mr. Loyless has done byy running his mouth is to supply just enough speculation to support a headline saying "Bank Officers Face Possible Removal", accompanied by a photo of the bank officer in question, Roger Lussier, of the Lyndonville Savings Bank & Trust Company, a bank in my Senatorial district.

I trust you will agree with me that Mr. Loyless' remarks, if quoted correctly, have gone past the border of ethical procedure by an FDIC officer. Clearly the news story has damaged the reputation of Mr. Lussier and possibly threatened the financial status of his bank.

If the FDIC decides to announce an action against a bank officer or a bank, that is one thing. It is quite another for the FDIC to fuel speculation about its possible actions, to the detriment of the named individuals and institutions.

In my opinion, the FDIC owes Mr. Lussier an apology, and Mr. Loyless a reprimand.

I should add that I have no connection with the Lyndonville Bank. Mr. Lussier is a friend of mine of long standing, but I have not discussed this matter with him or any other person at the Bank.

Yours truly,

John McClaughry

Not Printed at Taxpayer's Expense

FEDERAL DEPOSIT INSURANCE CORPORATION, WA ⏤ฺ, DC 20429

OFFICE OF THE CHAIRMAN

July 6, 1992

Honorable John McClaughry
State of Vermont
Caledonia-Orange District
Concord, Vermont 05824

Dear Senator McClaughry:

This is in response to your June 3, 1992 letter regarding an article about the Lyndonville Savings Bank and Trust Company in the Rutland Herald on May 27, 1992. We have read the article and share the concerns voiced in your letter that the comments attributable to the FDIC could possibly have led to speculation and concern within the banking community and the local market place. In this regard, please be assured that we are sensitive to the possible ramifications of news articles and we have a policy that employees are not to publicly discuss information related to specific institutions or potential lawsuits.

Relating to the article in the Rutland Herald, it was apparent that the reporter had specific information on the May 20, 1992 meeting prior to contacting our office. While we have long-standing instructions to our senior regional office personnel to refrain from discussing any open operating insured institutions on a name basis, this particular instance alerted us to the need to reissue those instructions. More recently assigned senior personnel, such as Mr. Loyless, will be reminded of our policy.

We appreciate your interest in the matter. If you have any questions, please do not hesitate to contact me.

Sincerely,

William Taylor

STATE OF VERMONT
SENATE CHAMBER
MONTPELIER
05602

January 7, 1992

Jeffrey Johnson, Commissioner
Department of Banking and Insurance
Montpelier, VT 05620-3101

Dear Jeff:

Re: Lyndonville Savings Bank

The Burlington Free Press on December 24 carried a story which was later rewritten by the Associated Press that attributed statements to Sen. John McClaughry and I which were not accurate.

I understand that Senator McClaughry spoke about this erroneous story when you met several days later at your office in Montpelier with representatives of the Northeast Kingdom legislative delegation and of the FDIC.

The enclosed article by Senator McClaughry, which appeared in the Caledonian Record on December 31, 1991, is a good representation of my views on this issue.

While I cannot defend any of the loans or lending practices of the Lyndonville Savings Bank because I and the other members of the Northeast Kingdom legislative delegation do not have the necessary facts, I can tell you that the Lyndonville Savings Bank does play an important role in the economy of the Northeast Kingdom. Unlike other banks which choose to make loans to Brazil, Argentina and other foreign governments, and unlike many banks right here in Vermont who consider certain loans high risk and therefore will not make them, the Lyndonville Savings Bank has continued to do business with dairy farmers, loggers and small businesses that are the economic backbone of the Northeast Kingdom.

I also understand that you did not make a statement that was attributed to you, criticizing Roger Lussier for lacking a high school diploma. We both know how the press is sometimes sloppy, in your case suggesting that you made the remark and in the case of Senator McClaughry and I suggesting that we were "defending" the Lyndonville Savings Bank.

Jeffrey Johnson, Commissioner   January 7, 1992
                                                           Page 2

All I ask is that you treat the Lyndonville Savings Bank as you would any
other bank in Vermont.

Thank you.

Sincerely,

Senator Vincent Illuzzi
Assistant Republican Leader

VI:mlc
Enclosure
66641.5   .

cc: Sen. John McClaughry

John McClaughry

Concord, Vermont 05824

June 1, 1994

Hon. Franklin Billings
Federal District Court
U.S. Court House
Rutland VT 05701

Re: US v. Roger Lussier

Dear Bill:

When you sentenced Paul Gallerani and Herbert Gray, you stated that the issue was "greed and power", and emphasized the victims of the acts of which these two men were convicted.

If one looks at the Roger Lussier case dispassionately, I do not think one can ascribe the defendant's actions to the drive for "greed and power". Nor do I think you can identify any victims of the defendant's acts; in fact, the supposed "victims" testified in Lussier's favor.

I have known Roger Lussier for twenty two years. "Greed" is about the last thing I would ascribe to Roger. Many times over the years he has made a risky character loan, out of his own pocket, to make a business deal work. Often times he has taken a loss, and laughed it off. This man lives modestly and has been a real friend to his community.

"Power"? I have had occasion in my life to interact with lots of men who wanted power, including men in the U.S. Senate and the White House. I know what the drive for power looks like. There is not a bit of it in Roger Lussier. He didn't want to order people around; he just wanted to make deals work, and if they paid off, put the money back to work in the depressed Northeast Kingdom to make more deals work.

If you look at the Lussier record, I think you will find that the man made mistakes — not a few of them technical. But if a trip to jail requires a showing of the defendant's drive for "greed" and "power", and the existence of "victims" of wrongdoing, then I suggest that Roger Lussier does not deserve to go to jail. Fines, probation, exclusion from serving the Bank he built up for 27 years, community service – but not prison.

If the sentencing guidelines do not allow you to avoid requiring prison time, I respectfully request that you consider suspending that part of the sentence. Otherwise, a real injustice will be done.

I do not owe Roger Lussier anything. I am writing this letter entirely on my own initiative as a matter of justice to a man who I firmly believe never had any shred of criminal intent about him, who was prevented by an inept counsel from taking the stand in his own defense, and who has done a lot of good for a lot of people and his community.

Yours truly,

John McClaughry

(No acknowledgement necessary)

THE WEEKLY JOURNAL OF ORLEANS COUNTY, VERMONT

VOLUME 15. NUMBER 40

OCTOBER 5, 1988

Foreclosure challenged

by Paul Lefebvre

NEWPORT — A dispute over property values is casting a cloud over the disposition of a five-farm foreclosure that occurred in August between the Lyndonville Savings Bank and Trust Company and Maurice and Marylee Provost of Derby.

A creditor in the proceedings, Agway Inc., has raised questions about the bank's sale of the five farms to the defendants' parents, Richard and Regina Provost of Derby, shortly after the foreclosure went into effect.

A hearing in Orleans County Superior Court has been scheduled for Thursday to determine if the sale was based on fair market value.

Attorneys for Agway asked for the hearing last month after learning that the senior Provosts had signed a seller's agreement five days before they acquired the property to sell two of the farms for sums Agway claims represent "enormous profits."

According to Agway's claim, the two farms sold respectively for 98 per cent and 40 per cent over an appraised market value that was set just two days before the seller's agreement was signed.

In its motion this week, Agway is expected to ask the court for an independent appraisal of the property, to settle what it calls the "enormous discrepancy" between the appraised value submitted by the bank and the present price listed in the seller's agreement.

Agway's interest in the hearing stems from roughly a $102,000 debt that is owed to it by Provost Farms. As one of the junior creditors in the proceedings, however, its chances for collecting that debt hinge on the court's ruling Thursday on another motion from the bank.

Lyndonville Savings Bank has asked the court for a deficiency judgement — a judgement granted when the sale price of a foreclosed property is less than the amount owed. If the court rules in the bank's favor, Agway won't collect a dime.

Thursday's hearing is the latest chapter in an unfolding story of a roughly $1-million foreclosure that began about a year ago on five farms in Derby, Holland, and Morgan. The focus of the story has switched back and forth — from allegations that Maurice Provost violated the terms of his participation in the whole herd buy out to a sharp contest among creditors vying to establish priority for receiving payment.

But the most startling charge to arise so far is Agway's present allegation that there "is substantial doubt about the credibility" of the bank's appraisal and its sale of the property to other members of the Provost family.

"This doubt is enhanced by the fact that the Plaintiff's sale of the subject property to Richard and Regina Provost on August 18, 1988, appears to have been something less than an arm's length away," say the Agway memorandum that's dated September 7.

On Tuesday the bank's attorney, Andrew Field, characterized Agway's charge as vindictive.

"They're just a bunch of disgruntled creditors," he said. "They got nothing out of it."

As the plaintiff in the case, Lyndonville Savings Bank initiated foreclosure proceedings against Maurice and Marylee Provost last September for falling behind on a promissory note of $1.6-million.

According to the bank's claim, Provost Farms defaulted on a principal of $958,097 and interest in the amount of $101,851 on four notes, with the earliest going back to 1978.

As collateral for the loans, the bank held mortgages on the old Hayward Farm and the Dumas Farm in Morgan and Derby; the LeBlanc Farm and the Provost Home Farm, both in Derby; and the former Page Farm in Holland.

Twenty-four additional creditors were named in the suit as co-defendants, including Richard and Regina Provost because of an interest they held in the mortgaged properties.

Taken altogether, according to figures listed in the bank's claim, the Provost Farms owed these creditors over $600,000.

Court records indicate that all creditors had sought judicial relief for their debts, and some had placed attachments of one sort or another against the five farms. The debts ranged from a high of $116,118 from Nutrite Inc. to $287 from C.H. Dana, Inc. of Hyde Park, as the result of a small claims judgement.

Both the Internal Revenue Service and Vermont's tax department had placed liens against the property before the foreclosure started, according to court records

In its claim filed on September 2, the Lyndonville Savings bank also asked the court to shorten the time of redemption — the period of time granted defendants to buy the property for the amount owed.

That request was immediately challenged by some of the major creditors, including the federal government. After asserting the priority of its lien over all other attachments, the government stipulated that under the federal tax lien a "decree of foreclosure must provide for an additional redemption period of six months from the date of the sale."

The government brief further stipulated the property must be sold at a judicial sale, "free and clear" except for the "rights of redemption invested in the United States by statute."

At the same time the federal government was

articulating its preeminent legal standing in the case, Agway started to assert its claim over the other creditors.

Included among the creditors from this area were the Chittenden Trust Company, $61,252; W. S. Mitchell, $31,621; Howard Bank, $4,568; Community National Bank, $61,956; and DeLaBruere's Auto Sales, $1,770.

By the end of the year, Agway had filed a memorandum arguing that the other creditors had failed to preserve the priority of their attachments because of filing and recording errors.

Meanwhile, in a memorandum of its own, the bank was trying to prove that Richard and Regina Provost had given up their claims to the property when they twice approved loans between their son and the Savings Bank.

To that end, Mr. Field furnished the court with copies of two subordination agreements in which the couple agreed to "subordinate in favor of the Lyndonville Savings Bank and Trust Company mortgages for themselves, their heirs or assigns."

A month later, Mr. Field was back in court, asking for a "default/summary judgement" in favor of the bank. In his memorandum, dated January 29, he argued that there was "no genuine issue to any material fact" in the case, and that Mr. Provost had retracted allegations that he made in his initial response to the foreclosure.

At the outset of the proceedings, Mr. Provost sought to shift responsibility for the default onto the bank. He contended the bank had failed to challenge the federal government's decision to terminate his payments for participation in the whole herd buy out program.

Mr. Provost was accepted into the program in August of 1986, and according to a brief prepared by his lawyer, M. Jerome Diamond of Montpelier, the defendant entered into a "trust agreement" with the bank.

Under the terms of the agreement, according to the brief again, the bank would "receive and disburse to itself and others the payments due to Maurice Provost under the Dairy Termination Program."

As a result of his participation in the program, the brief continues, the bank "received and accepted" buy out payments of roughly $725,000, with the understanding it would receive an additional sum of $78,073. for each of the four years remaining in the program.

On August 7, 1987, a year later, Mr. Provost received written notification that his annual buy out payment had been denied.

Feds have no comment

(Continued from page thirty-six.)

"No basis or reason for the denial was provided," says the brief.

A federal official for the Agricultural Stabilization and Conservation Services (ASCS), the agency that administers the program, declined this week to discuss the case.

But on Tuesday Mr. Diamond said that both the 1987 and the 1988 payments had been withheld, a total of roughly $156,000.

Mr. Diamond said the charges against Mr. Provost were "grossly unfair," and he was still waiting for the results on an appeal to the ASCS board.

"In the meantime," he added, "a man's life has been destroyed."

Mr. Provost repeatedly has denied allegations that he violated any terms of the program, which forbids participants from producing milk or keeping dairy cows in their barns. And through his lawyer in the foreclosure proceedings, he has accused the bank for failing to go after the payments as his trustee.

"Not only is there no default," said Mr. Diamond in his brief, "but the plaintiff is obligated to pursue the payments due it under the program, including appropriate appeals from decisions denying payments, prior to being allowed to invoke rights of foreclosure."

By February, both Agway and Nutrite had joined the fight to prevent a summary judgement for foreclosure.

In a memorandum opposing the bank's request for a quick settlement, Nutrite argued that the issue of priority among creditors still had to be determined. As a result of the federal tax lien against the property, the company argued, the court must adjudicate all claims before establishing a redemption schedule or going ahead with a foreclosure order.

By this time, however, Agway was pushing ahead with its own claim that prior attachments imposed by other creditors were no longer binding. And in April, a hearing was held before Judge Alan Cheever to hear both Agway's claim and the bank's motion for a default-summary judgement against Mr. Provost.

Although the judge turned down the bank's request, Agway prevailed with its claim and moved to the head of the line among private creditors.

In June Mr. Field notified the court that an agreement had been struck between the Lyndonville Savings Bank and Provost Farms.

According to the terms of the agreement, Mr. Provost would have three days to redeem his property after the judgement became final. Also included in the agreement was that the foreclosure would carry a strict time limit on redemption.

Accompanying the notice of agreement was a proposed redemption schedule, which listed the priority other creditors would have to follow to redeem the property before it was sold outright by the bank.

On July 5 Judge Alan Cheever accepted the agreement and confirmed the default in the amount of $1,144,147 plus interest. The last date for redemption was set for August 10.

As the result of a mortgage they held on the property, Richard and Regina Provost were given the maximum time allowed by the redemption schedule to buy the property back for the price of the default.

The court also, however, accepted a request from Agway and agreed to retain jurisdiction in the matter until after the land was sold.

On August 18, after the redemption deadline had passed, the bank sold all the property to Richard and Regina Provost for $994,619. And on August 24 Mr. Field filed a motion for a deficiency judgment on grounds the sale did not satisfy the judgment, leaving a deficiency of $188,300.

By way of supporting the sale price of the farms, Mr. Field attached a copy of a property appraisal conducted for the bank by Franklin Temple of St. Johnsbury.

In his letter to the bank, dated August 20, Mr. Temple stipulated that he has been appraising farms and rural land for 32 years for the Federal Land Bank in Springfield and the Farmers Production Credit Association of St. Johnsbury.

After noting the restrictions placed on the farms for their involvement in the whole herd buy out and "the problems and delays of subdividing in Vermont," he set a market value of $973,000 on August 11.

The pressing issue facing the court this week, said Mr. Field Tuesday, is whether the bank sold the farms at fair market value.

If the court rules the bank's sale was based on a fair market value, Mr. Field believes the judge will grant his motion for a deficiency judgement.

Agway is contending the selling price was too low, and in its motion before the court asking for an independent appraisal, the creditor also has raised "serious questions" over the circumstances of the sale.

"Defendant is informed and believes, as partial consideration for this sale, Richard and Regina Provost executed a promissory note to the Plaintiff, which was guaranteed by Noel Lussier, the brother of the president of the Lyndonville Savings Bank."

Agway also contends that Mr. Lussier is further acting as a broker for the couple in their attempt to sell the property to third parties.

On August 13, the memorandum continues, five days before the bank's sale, Mr. and Mrs. Provost entered into an agreement to sell two of the five farms.

Under the terms of the agreement, the memorandum states, the Provosts are to receive $160,000 for the 140-acre LeBlanc Farm and $260,000 for the 200-acre Hayward Farm.

But the bank's appraiser, the memorandum notes, set a fair market value just a few days earlier of $81,000 on the LeBlanc Farm and a $160,000 value on the Hayward Farm.

Mr. Field said Tuesday there was nothing improper about the bank's sale, and the transaction allowed Richard Provost to recover some of the debt incurred by his son.

"If I was his daddy, I'd buy it too," he said of the property.

But if the court rules in Agway's favor and orders an independent appraisal for the farms, the company will still have a chance to recover its debt.

In its memorandum Agway noted that the Lyndonville Savings Bank still holds an assignment from Maurice Provost on the remaining buy out payments of roughly $320,000.

Secondly, the memorandum continues, the bank also holds a mortgage on farmland the defendant owns in Quebec.

And if the court should determine that the fair market value of the farms exceeded the Provost Farms' debt on the day the bank acquired the property, says the memorandum in its final thrust, "then the collateral security which the Bank possesses would be released and would become available to the Provosts' other creditors."

The attorney for Agway was unavailable for comment Tuesday, but Mr. Diamond said he was puzzled by the company's action.

"Agway had the opportunity to redeem it if they thought the property was worth more," he said.

MANPOWER,
RESERVE AFFAIRS
AND LOGISTICS

GILBERT M. TURNER
NATIONAL CHAIRMAN

THOMAS J. RILEY
STATE CHAIRMAN

OFFICE OF THE ASSISTANT SECRETARY OF DEFENSE
VERMONT COMMITTEE FOR EMPLOYER SUPPORT
OF THE GUARD AND RESERVE
152 BANK STREET
BURLINGTON, VERMONT 05401
(802) 864-4744

October 12, 1983

Mr. Roger Lussier
21 Park Avenue
Lyndonville, Vermont 05851

Dear Mr. Lussier:

As Chairman of the Vermont Committee for Employer Support of
the Guard & Reserve I am delighted to inform you, Mr. Lussier,
that you have been nominated for, and selected by our State
Committee to be awarded this organization's highest award
for recognition of your unselfish and patriotic support of
this country's National Guard and Reserve Forces.

You have been nominated by Mr. Jacque Chayer, and in the
evaluation by the Vermont Committee, your support of and
contributions to this nation's defense effort far exceed
those normally expected.

For your outstanding support to the National Guard, the
members of this Committee have elected to award you the
highest award which can be given, the "PRO PATRIA" award.
In fact only one Pro Patria award may be made annually by
each state committee.

We should like to present this award to you at the luncheon
of the Annual Meeting of the Vermont State Chamber of Commerce
on Friday, October 28, 1983.

May I also suggest that you invite Mr. Jacque Chayer to join
you. Cost of the luncheon is only $7.00 and it is requested
you confirm your reservations by return mail in the enclosed
envelope.

I look forward to meeting you at the awards luncheon.

Sincerely,

Thomas J. Riley, Chairman
Vermont Committee
Employer Support of the Guard & Reserve

U.S. Department of Justice

Federal Bureau of Prisons

Federal Prison Camp

Allenwood, Montgomery, PA 17752-9718

July 15, 1998

Roger Lussier
Register Number: 03541-082
Allenwood Federal Prison
Montgomery, PA 17752

Dear Mr. Lussier:

This is in response to your request for Compassionate Release from federal custody dated July 1, 1998. You have requested a Compassionate Release consideration because your wife's depression has grown worse and this is causing a significant burden on your entire family in many ways as outlined in your letter.

Many offenders experience difficult burdens during their period of incarceration and, unfortunately, this often negatively impacts their families as well. While the reasons outlined in your letter are somewhat compelling in nature, they are relatively common difficulties that offenders experience. A review of your status indicates that you are serving a forty-six month term for Bank Fraud, False Entries, Commissions for Procuring Loans, and Monetary Transactions. Your projected release date is June 29, 1999, via Good Conduct Time release. According to your unit team, you have made a very good adjustment to confinement, completed several programs, and received outstanding work reports.

Due to the serious nature of your offense, your presence in the community could cause undue public attention and could minimize the intent of the law. Also, you are eligible for placement in a community corrections center in early 1999. Your unit team is recommending a five month referral for halfway house placement based upon your adjustment to confinement and significant release needs.

Therefore, I am not recommending a Compassionate Release in your case. Should you have further concerns, you should contact a member of your unit team.

Sincerely,

Bobby P. Shearin
Warden

Roger Lussier B-2
Box 1000
Montgomery, PA 17752

August 5, 1998

Joseph R. Biden, Jr.
Judiciary Committee
3021 Federal Building
844 King Street
Wilmington, DE 19801

Dear Senator Biden:

Thank you for any consideration you have given us in our request for
Compassionate Release from Allenwood. The Warden turned the request
down and I have submitted to the Office of General Counsel for their
consideration on appeal.

At this time I would like to provide you with some materials and a
letter that I sent to the Attorney General. My case was a clear and
frightning example of how a prosecutor can lie to a court, create,
withhold, manipulate, evidence, and buy testimony from witnesses by
granting them immunity, light sentences, and financial incentives
to testify "properly" and convict an innocent party.

I would like some good to come out of this injustice to my family.
In my quest to clear my name, I volunteer to provide your office
or the Department of Justice with full cooperation and materials
to demonstrate a need for checks and balances in the administration
of justice.

We are still hoping that the Bureau of Prisons will rule favorably
on the request for release to be able to help my wife. In the meantime, I hope that my case could serve as an example of a need to
revamp some of the practices of the department to insure a fair
trial for those that may follow. Criminals should not convict innocent
people for the rewards they can earn.

Sincerely,

Roger Lussier

Letter to the editor ____ _1- 26 - 94_

Roger Lussier, "an honorable man who keeps his word"

Dear Whomever,

I was pleased to read bank board member John McClaughry's commonsense thoughts in the article regarding the Roger Lussier case. I'm with him on the "Who is the government trying to protect?" I'm also in agreement with Roger's conclusion that "The government desires to get rid of all small banks." I'd also add, "And all small businesses."

Strange, we have a Federal Reserve system which is neither Federal, nor Reserve. It is nothing but a few international bankers who our government granted the authority to print FUNNY money (with nothing to back it) and charge interest on it. Our Constitution doesn't grant authority to private bankers to print our money. It grants this authority to our Congress, who obviously couldn't handle this responsibility. Why, Attorney Downs, question the integrity of LSB, a small town bank which makes loans to farmers, loggers, and small business in the area, and makes money doing it, when you could be studying this unconstitutional Federal Reserve system. A system which incidentally is long, long overdue for an impartial audit.

As for U.S. Attorney Van de Graaf, instead of wasting hard-earned tax dollars on a case such as this, when you should have been out in Arkansas checking into the bank which has cost we taxpayers $60-million. Yes this probably would have upset President Hillary and her husband, but who knows, you might just have saved them from losing money doing business in Whitewater with their slippery friend McDougal.

So, where am I coming from?? I love my country, but I greatly fear my totally out-of-control, felonious government. Attorney Van de Graaf's boss, Janet Reno, and her allowing the incineration of the innocent children at Waco, and before her time, the murder of Randy Weaver's wife and son. I have known Roger Lussier, the banker and auctioneer for years. I have always found him to be an honorable man who keeps his word. So, if he made a few bucks for himself while making a few deals possible for LSB, who cares?? I wouldn't swap a handshake from Roger for a signature from Van de Graaf, his boss Janet Reno, or her boss Bill Clinton.

Sincerely,
Francis B. Holt
Fort Myers, Florida